Praise for *The Gothic Wanderer*

"This book makes me realize we are all Gothic wanderers. We look for meaning and ethics in life as we plod our way through a fantastic landscape peopled by strangers and strange things. As Tyler Tichelaar shows us, when we mature, we move from fearing the outcasts among us to recognizing ourselves in them. *The Gothic Wanderer* shows us the importance of its title figure in helping us to see our own imperfections and our own sometimes contradictory yearnings to be both unique and yet a part of a society. The reader is in for an insightful treat."
— Diana DeLuca, Ph.D. and author of *Extraordinary Things*

"Make no mistake about it, *The Gothic Wanderer* is an important, well researched and comprehensive treatise on some of the world's finest literature. This book is never dull and always enlightening. It is recommended as a useful addition to the library of those studying the nature and mystery of man."
— Michael Willey, author of *Ojisan Zanoni*

"I have long been fascinated with vampires, what has attracted people to long-held beliefs in them, and what led to so many manuscripts about the vampire and other 'monsters' written by such nineteenth century authors as Mary Shelley, Bram Stoker, and their ilk. *The Gothic Wanderer* offers much food for thought in its discussion on how *Dracula* became the 'ultimate revision' of the old Gothic wanderer as depicted in nineteenth century literature. I was amazed that Stoker had such a long tradition to draw upon, including nineteenth century novelists who covertly created a dialogue about their own political, religious, and social concerns over the French Revolution. I feel this addition to Gothic studies was highly energetic in content and exceeded my expectations."
— Lorelei Bell, author of *Vampire Ascending* and *Vampire's Trill*

The Gothic Wanderer:
From Transgression to Redemption

Gothic Literature from 1794—present

Tyler R. Tichelaar, Ph.D.

Foreword by Marie Mulvey-Roberts, Ph.D.

The Gothic Wanderer: From Transgression to Redemption; Gothic Literature from 1794 - present
Copyright © 2012 by Tyler R. Tichelaar. All rights reserved.

1st Printing - October 2012

> Library of Congress Cataloging-in-Publication Data
>
> Tichelaar, Tyler R.
>   The Gothic wanderer : from transgression to redemption : Gothic literature from 1794 - present / Tyler R. Tichelaar.
>   p. cm.
>   Includes bibliographical references and index.
>   ISBN 978-1-61599-138-9 (pbk. : alk. paper) -- ISBN 978-1-61599-139-6 (hardcover : alk. paper) -- ISBN 978-1-61599-140-2 (ebook)
>   1. English fiction--19th century--History and criticism. 2. Vampires in literature. 3. Gothic revival (Literature)--Great Britain. 4. Horror tales, English--History and criticism. 5. Horror tales, American--History and criticism. I. Title.
>   PR868.T3T53 2012
>   823'.0872909--dc23
>   2011047323

No part of this book may be used or reproduced by any means, graphic, electronic, or mechanical, including photocopying, recording, taping or by any information storage retrieval system without the written permission of the publisher except in the case of brief quotations embodied in critical articles and reviews. Inquiries should be addressed to:

Modern History Press, an imprint of Loving Healing Press
5145 Pontiac Trail
Ann Arbor, MI 48105

www.ModernHistoryPress.com
info@ModernHistoryPress.com
Tollfree (USA/CAN): 888-761-6268
London, England: 44-20-331-81304

Distributed by Ingram Book Group (USA/CAN), Bertram's Books (UK), Hachette Livre (FR), Agapea (SP).

eBook editions available for Amazon Kindle, B&N Nook, Kobo reader and other platforms.

To all those in this modern age who wander, feeling lost:

My fellow wanderers,

May you find your reward and your rest.

Also by Tyler R. Tichelaar

The Marquette Trilogy
Iron Pioneers
The Queen City
Superior Heritage

More Historical Fiction
Narrow Lives
The Only Thing That Lasts

Gothic Fiction
Spirit of the North

Nonfiction
My Marquette: Explore the Queen City of the North
King Arthur's Children: A Study in Fiction and Tradition
Authors Access: 30 Success Secrets for Authors and Publishers
   with Victor R. Volkman and Irene Watson

Contents

Acknowledgments	v
Foreword by Marie Mulvey-Roberts	vii
Introduction	ix
Our Long Love Affair with the Gothic	ix
PART I - *Creating the Gothic Wanderer*	1
Chapter I – The Gothic Wanderer's Origins in the French Revolution	1
The Optimism of Romantic Poets	1
Family as a Metaphor for Political Order	3
Conspiracy Theories in Gothic Literature	8
Rise of the Gothic Wanderer	10
Chapter II – *Paradise Lost* and the Legitimacy of Transgression	13
Primogeniture and Transgressions Against the Family	17
Feminine Gothic Revisions of *Paradise Lost*	21
The Mysteries of Udolpho: Eve's Vindication	23
Masculine Gothic Revisions of *Paradise Lost*	29
The Monk: Condemning the Transgressor	34
Melmoth the Wanderer: A Sympathetic Transgressor	37
Conclusion	40
Chapter III – The Wandering Jew	43
The Monk: Creation of the Gothic Wandering Jew	46
"The Rime of the Ancient Mariner": Adapting the Wandering Jew	48
St. Leon: A Wandering Jew with Rosicrucian Secrets	50
Melmoth the Wanderer and Anti-Semitism	53
Chapter IV – The Rosicrucian Gothic Wanderer	59
The Rosicrucians' Origins	59
St. Leon: Rosicrucianism and the Evolution of Reason	63
St. Irvyne: Rosicrucianism and the Rejection of Atheism	75
Melmoth the Wanderer: The Sympathetic Rosicrucian	77
Conclusion	79

Chapter V – Gambling as Gothic Transgression — 81
The Mysteries of Udolpho: Gambling as a Threat to Love — 85
St. Leon: Gambling Destroys the Family — 88
The Vampyre: Money Circulating Like Blood — 92
Ernestus Berchtold: Gambling and Incest — 94
Conclusion — 97

PART II - *Subversive Gothic Wanderers* — 99

Chapter VI – "A Wandering Jewess": Fanny Burney's *The Wanderer* as Gothic Novel — 101
The Wanderer as a Revision of *Evelina* — 102
Juliet as Female Gothic Wanderer — 105
Female Identity — 108
Women's Employment as Gothic Horror — 112
Juliet's Metamorphoses and Immortality — 113
Gothic Forest Scenes and Anti-Romanticism — 116
Stonehenge: Symbol of the Immortal Soul — 123

Chapter VII – The Existential Gothic Wanderer: Mary Shelley's *Frankenstein* and *The Last Man* — 129
Frankenstein: Critical History and Position in the Gothic Wanderer Tradition — 129
Rosicrucian Elements in *Frankenstein* — 131
Frankenstein as Existential Revision of *Paradise Lost* — 134
The French Revolution, Illegitimacy, and the Family in *Frankenstein* — 144
Frankenstein's Existential Ending — 147
The Last Man: The Rejection of Romanticism — 149
The Sibyl: Immortality and Prophecy — 150
Lionel Verney as Gothic Wanderer — 151
The Existential Plague — 153
The Gamble with Death — 156
The End of Human History: Deconstructing Lionel's Manuscript and Shelley's Novel — 158
Conclusion — 162

PART III - *From Transgression to Redemption* — 163

Chapter VIII – Teufelsdrockh as Gothic Wanderer and Everyman: Carlyle's *Sartor Resartus* — 165
Teufelsdrockh's Christian Origins — 166
Carlyle's Theory of Symbols — 168
Teufelsdrockh as Gothic Wanderer — 169
Teufelsdrockh's Despair — 172
The Metamorphosis from Wandering Jew to Everyman — 174
Natural Supernaturalism: Reinventing the Gothic — 176
Gothic Structure and Narrative Strategy — 177

Chapter IX – The Gothic Wanderer Redeemed: Edward Bulwer-
Lytton's *Zanoni* and Charles Dickens' *A Tale of Two Cities*   183
   Zanoni: Redemption of the Rosicrucian   184
   Dickens' Carlylean Gothic   192
   A Tale of Two Cities: Rosicrucian Immortality and Christian
   Redemption   195

Chapter X – The Gothic Wanderer at Rest: *Dracula* and the
Vampiric Tradition   209
   Origins and Early Literary Uses of the Vampire Legend   210
   Glenarvon and the Byronic Vampire   213
   The Vampyre: Establishing Fictional Vampire Elements   220
   Varney the (Sympathetic) Vampyre   223
   Dracula's Historical Origins   227
   Dracula: The New Wandering Jew and Anti-Semitism   229
   Dracula as Antichrist: The Gothic Redemption of Catholicism   234
   The Redemption of Dracula   238

Chapter XI - Modern Interpretations: from Wanderer
to Superhero   245
   The End of Fear: The Gothic Wanderer's Evolution
      to Superhero   245
   Evolution and the Gothic   245
   The Imperial Gothic   247
   Tarzan: The Gothic Wanderer Turned Superhero   249
   Tarzan's Superhero Literary Descendants   252
   The Modern Heroic Vampire   254
   Conclusion   258

Bibliography   261
   Primary Works   261
   Films   266
   Secondary Works   266

Index   281

About the Author   290

Acknowledgments

This book began as my dissertation at Western Michigan University, so first I would like to thank my dissertation committee, Scott Dykstra, Jil Larson, and Dale Porter, for all the hours spent reading and commenting upon this work.

Next, I thank my publisher Victor Volkman of Modern History Press for suggesting the expansion of this study to the modern day treatments of the Gothic.

Thank you to Susan Siferd for all her moral support during the writing of the dissertation, and for the memories of a wonderful trip to England to present at the Edward Bulwer-Lytton conference and to lay flowers on Fanny Burney's grave.

I thank Irene Watson for helping me to reconsider this book as more than an academic, scholarly work, but one which can resonate with why the Gothic matters to us today.

Thank you to Diana Deluca for her many suggestions to make the argument more attractive to readers.

Thank you to Larry Alexander for suggestions of modern "Gothic" novels I might otherwise not have considered.

To my parents and brother, who did not understand but permitted my early desire to have a dusty bedroom so it would feel like a haunted house, my wearing plastic vampire teeth, or my constantly quoting lines from my record *A Story of Dracula, The Wolfman, and Frankenstein*.

Finally, to my literary ancestors, the great writers of the Gothic, especially:

Mrs. Radcliffe, Fanny Burney, Jane Austen, Charles Dickens, and Bram Stoker

My early and best teachers of what makes good writing.

Foreword

The classic Gothic novel is stocked with villains, swooning heroines, rescuing heroes and banditti, but there is no character quite as compelling as that of the eternal wanderer. The idea of an individual outliving generations and witnessing important events throughout history has always been intriguing. Ranging even further than Woody Allen's Zelig, who keeps popping up at key historical moments during the twentieth century, he can boast with the best and the worst of them: "I was there." Just like the wanderer, this book takes a chronological path to span centuries, step by step, chapter by chapter. Having entered Gothic literature in the form of the Wandering Jew in Matthew Lewis's *The Monk*, this figure, as Tyler R. Tichelaar shows, continues to wander into other novels in various guises from the Rosicrucian sage, through the Female Everywoman, to those of Bram Stoker and Stephenie Meyers' vampires.

As a not-so-distant relative of Dr. Faustus, these Gothic characters invariably choose to become monsters by consenting to the gift of bodily eternal life, though some have immortality thrust upon them. The Romantics cast their wanderers as relatively benign figures, but here we see the way in which they wander out of the trammels of Romantic convention into Gothic spaces. In common with the captain of the ghost ship, *The Flying Dutchman*, another famous wanderer whose voyages circumnavigate the globe, the entire earth becomes the terrain of such wanderings, as well as the stage for an eternity of suffering, a microcosm of the human condition.

The Gothic wanderer occupies a perplexing domain in space and time. As a being outside nature whose protracted existence is an aberration, his timelessness seems to cut him off from history, in the sense that he remains always outside it. Marked out in some way, he has become the ultimate embodiment of the other, whose destiny is to walk alone. His very monstrosity is a symptom of his rejection. This state of exile means that the wanderer is always on the edge and at the edge, a monster of the in-between and as such, the supreme outsider. Indeed, he reflects back to the Gothic, its own fascination with borders and transgression.

This book delves into the subjectivity of the Gothic wanderer in flight from self, on an endless trajectory of looking towards the end, even though his unnatural existence is validated by those, including the reader, who must look backwards into his past. Part of the mortal immortal's teleological quest lies in mending the fractured self. Within this refreshing study, Tichelaar adroitly plots the rocky road from transgression to transcendence, rocky as when, for example, the redemptive treatment characterizing versions of the legend meted out by Victorian novelists meets resistance at the fin de siècle.

The wanderer is a repository of history, a storehouse of memory for the human race, and yet, he carries the burden of being blasted by the divine. The punishment for transgression is to be denied what Derrida calls, the gift of death. But as *The Gothic Wanderer* reveals, not all peripatetic immortals regard eternal life as a curse. By tracing the footprints of the Gothic wanderer, from those of the transgressor to the coveted moments of redemption and beyond to the more modern status of super-hero, Tichelaar demonstrates the power of the Gothic wanderer as an allegorical figure, with whom everyone can identify. This perennial and uncanny Everyman undoubtedly deserves the time and space which this invaluable book-length study has accorded him.

Marie Mulvey-Roberts, Ph.D.
University of the West of England, Bristol, UK
Author of *Gothic Immortals*

Introduction

Our Long Love Affair with the Gothic

> While yet a boy I sought for ghosts, and sped
> Through many a listening chamber, cave and ruin,
> And starlight wood, with fearful steps pursuing
> Hopes of high talk with the departed dead.
> I called on poisonous names with which our youth is fed;
> I was not heard—I saw them not—
> When musing deeply on the lot
> Of life, at that sweet time when winds are wooing
> All vital things that wake to bring
> News of birds and blossoming,—
> Sudden, thy shadow fell on me;
> I shrieked, and clasped my hands in ecstasy!
> — Percy Bysshe Shelley, "Hymn to Intellectual Beauty"

I love the Gothic. Most of us do, even if we don't know exactly what the term "Gothic" means. It may mean different things to all of us, yet those things are closely related. Some of us might think of the Goth look where teenagers wear all black. Others might think of Gothic cathedrals. And a smaller percentage of us might think about classic Gothic literature—the great eighteenth and nineteenth century novels of Mrs. Radcliffe, Mary Shelley, Bram Stoker, and several others.

We love the Gothic partly because we have a fascination with being scared. I love to be scared—I don't go for the gory horror films of today, but I love suspense and the greatest Gothic literature builds up such suspense. But more importantly, Gothic literature reveals much about who we are, what we fear, and to what we aspire.

I was always fascinated with the Gothic—commonly called horror, or simply, when I was growing up in the 1970s and 1980s, what was "scary." I didn't know the term Gothic and wouldn't know it until well into high school, but I knew the Munsters, the Addams Family, Casper the Friendly Ghost, Broom-Hilda the Witch, and countless other characters in popular culture from that time who were often watered down children's versions of the Gothic.

I remember the "Creature Feature" film being shown Saturday afternoons on TV50 from Detroit, and I loved *Love at First Bite* (1979) starring George Hamilton as Dracula—when it was broadcast on TV for the first time, my brother and I had a big fight over the TV (we only had one in the house in those days) because it was aired opposite *Yogi's First Christmas*, which he wanted to watch.

I was the proud owner of the Weebles Haunted House complete with Weebles that "wobble but they don't fall down"—including the witch with a removable pointy hat, a glow-in-the dark ghost, two Weeble children to be scared, secret panels, trapped doors, and a treasure chest with bats inside. All of it scary but wonderful!

In fourth grade, I was Dracula for Halloween—I remember still the thrill of running so my cape would flap in the wind, and I can still taste the plastic vampire teeth. Nor did I ever miss going through a Haunted House at the fair, and my friends and I commonly played haunted house, turning our bedrooms or the family room into a mansion of monsters and ghosts. Again, I was always Dracula.

And perhaps best of all, I owned the wonderfully dramatic record *The Story of Dracula, the Wolfman and Frankenstein* from Power Records. This fabulous $33\text{-}^{1/3}$ record came with a read along book in graphic novel form (we called them comic books back then) and it combined into one dramatic tale the stories of its title characters. I played this record over and over again and still have my copy today. I constantly quoted it to others, including the pivotal scene when the werewolf (oddly not the Wolfman but Vincent von Frankenstein's girlfriend Erika—Wolfwoman, I guess) attacks the Count, causing him to become enraged and reveal himself by declaring, "You dare!! You dare lay your paws on me! On me?! Low beast, you'll die for this, die at the hands of the Prince of Darkness...FOR I AM DRACULA!" Recently, when I was working on this introduction, I dug out the record to engage in nostalgia and left it on my coffee table. My brother came over to visit and saw the record there and rolled his eyes. When I asked whether he wanted to listen to it, he said, "No, I never want to have to listen to that record again." Apparently, I played it one—or maybe fifty—too many times.

But all these details could be dismissed as children's games and just good fun (despite the fanatics who would ban *The Wizard of Oz*, or more recently, the *Harry Potter* books and films because they contain depictions of witchcraft). Only, I think on some innocent level that I could not have articulated when I was ten years old, I was even then searching for meaning—to understand the mystery of life, even if it were only the simplified notion of good and evil. I was a very religious child who had read the entire Bible by fifth grade, loved to play at being various characters from the Bible—mostly Moses or Jacob—and wanted to grow up to be a priest. So if I were such a "religious nut"—as one friend called me—how do I explain my fascination with horror and the supernatural?

And how explain my curiosity over an activity that countless children have attempted over the years? Yes, I am one of those many children who locked himself in the bathroom in the dark, stared into the bathroom mirror, and then tried to find out whether it was true that if I could say, "Bloody Murder!" one hundred times without blinking, the devil would appear in the mirror. But I was never able not to blink before I could say it one hundred times, or I would inevitably lose count.

Still, the quest for forbidden knowledge was strong in me at an early age. The fascination with Good and Evil thrilled me like it does many children, but I wanted proof that the supernatural forces of Good and Evil truly existed. Years later, when I discovered Percy Shelley's lines quoted above, I was stunned by how perfectly he captured what I felt, his experiences matching mine of nearly two centuries later. And like Shelley, I eventually grew to love Intellectual Beauty.

As I reached my teen years, I discovered literature, having always loved to read, and soon novels like *Jane Eyre* and *Wuthering Heights* and the works of Charles Dickens and Jane Austen became my primary fascination. It would be Jane Austen who really converted me into being a disciple of the Gothic. When I was about sixteen, I listened to an audio book version of *Northanger Abbey* with an introduction that explained the novel's purpose as a satire of the Gothic novels, particularly of Mrs. Radcliffe's *The Mysteries of Udolpho* (1794). Of course, I had to read Mrs. Radcliffe. Her novel had to be special ordered from the bookstore and although it was well over 600 pages, I devoured it in a week, reading it every free minute before and after school. The prose was beautiful, the suspense fabulous, the Gothic world frighteningly fascinating. I went on to read the rest of Radcliffe's novels while I was still a teenager as well as reading other Gothic classics like Horace Walpole's *The Castle of Otranto* (1764) and William Beckford's *Vathek* (1786). *Dracula* (1897) and *Frankenstein* (1818) followed, and in college when I discovered the Romantic poets, I could put all these books into context.

What was it about these books that thrilled me so much? Why did *The Mysteries of Udolpho* seem like such a wonderfully pleasant book to read, as well as a suspenseful page-turner? What about *Dracula* made me afraid to go to sleep, yet want to read it again—and enjoy the original novel so much more than the film versions of it—save for Coppola's fabulous *Bram Stoker's Dracula* (1992)? I don't know that I asked myself that question until the late 1990s when my fascination with literature and my desire to be a novelist led me to being a Ph.D. candidate in the literature program at Western Michigan University. The result would be my writing a dissertation titled *The Gothic Wanderer: From Transgression to Redemption*, which has now been expanded into this book. And I wasn't the only enthusiastic student of the Gothic—at least two of my fellow doctoral candidates at the time also wrote about the Gothic in their dissertations.

Of all the subjects a person could write a dissertation on, why did I choose nineteenth century Gothic novels? I also loved Dickens, the Arthurian legend, Anthony Trollope, eighteenth century epistolary novels—why choose the Gothic over one of these topics? The reason was because I could relate to the Gothic; it resonated with me in ways those other great literary works did not at that time in my life. And I wanted to write about why it resonated with me, why I thought the Gothic mattered so much to people—I wanted to write what was called a "reader-response" dissertation, but I was dissuaded from it by my professors—told it would not be good for my academic career.

Now that I have long since left academia behind, I can straightforwardly say that academics too often forget that while they are the keepers of the culture, in order to pass that culture on, they have to show people why that culture matters—how it still relates to them. While at Western Michigan University, I had the opportunity to co-teach a class on the British Survey of Literature with Dr. Stephanie Gauper. During that class, she commented to me about my teaching, "The students like you because you make them understand how the literature is relevant to their lives. Most teachers don't do that." I always felt that was one of the greatest compliments I ever received. And while, in my dissertation, I made the mistake not to explain why the Gothic mattered and was still relevant to our lives, in this book, written for a wider audience, I wish to remedy that by stating that the Gothic is very relevant to our lives, that it speaks to us today, two hundred years after the great Gothic novels were written because what the people in the decades following the French Revolution and during the Victorian period dreamt, feared, longed for, and sought, is still what we dream, fear, long for, and seek today. The Gothic is perhaps the most relevant piece of literature for the twenty-first century, and its continuation in the novels of Stephen King and Anne Rice, the popular books and films of the *Twilight* series, and the countless vampire books, films, and television series being produced each year, testify to this fact.

But how does it speak to us? Why is it still relevant to us? Let me give one more example from my own history to make my point.

In the fall of 1995, I moved to Kalamazoo, Michigan, in the same state as my hometown of Marquette, but nearly five hundred miles from home—in fact on a different peninsula—I might as well have been in another state, in some ways, in another country. I had culture shock in Kalamazoo—it was the big city compared to what I was used to—I didn't know the people, the city streets, the weather, the mindset of those people. I was isolated, lonely, and downright miserable in Kalamazoo, wondering why I had ever made the decision to leave my hometown, but realizing the job market in Upper Michigan offered nothing for me, so I would have to go on to finish my degree, to become an English professor, and to take a job wherever one might exist—meaning I would never get to return home.

The Gothic Wanderer: From Transgression to Redemption   *xiii*

I felt even more depressed and despairing when I looked at the future. If not for good friends and family and a telephone to talk to them on, I never would have gotten through those years. I would have defined these feelings as homesickness if I had not discovered a better word for it. That word I learned that first semester at Western Michigan University while taking a course on the Brontë sisters.

    I decided in that class to write my final paper on the theme of colonialism in the Brontës' novels. In my research, I came across the term "displacement" to describe the African character in one of the Brontës' juvenilia. Instantly, I understood that word as perfectly describing my own feelings and experience. I was displaced. I was convinced that while I loved teaching and studying literature, I would never get to go home—I felt depressed when not terrorized by the thought. The job market in academia was such that it was unlikely I would ever find a tenure-track job at Northern Michigan University in Marquette. I foresaw myself moving from one university to another, always separated from my family and friends.

    I stuck it out to finish my Ph.D. but my feelings of displacement did not get better. The job market—academia itself—was largely a nightmare—the MLA convention like a massive haunted house of pale young men in black suits, looking like blood-drained humans, fearful of interviewers yet hoping to be hired for tenure-track jobs. When I did find a job, it was a lowly one-year instructor position at Clemson University where I was given the equally "blood-draining" task of teaching up to 107 students per semester in a variety of composition and British literature survey courses (one literature and three composition sections). I had, consequently, upwards of five hundred papers per semester to grade and was paid $24,000 a year. And I had to do it in a hellishly hot climate I hated, while again feeling displaced. I have no doubt many people love Kalamazoo and South Carolina and I do not wish to disparage those places—my point is that I was unhappy and felt like a Gothic wanderer in them. Equally, we are all shaped by our individual preferences, likes and dislikes, and we all have different levels of tolerance. Here in Marquette, Michigan, I'm sure many people find our long winters and 200+ inches of snow per winter equally hellish, as roads between six foot snowbanks become like Gothic labyrinths, and bone-chilling temperatures seem like undeserving torture. Any place can be interpreted as "Gothic" if we so choose because Hell is in the mind—and the Gothic is nothing if not an exploration of human psychology and what we fear, as well as how we choose to let guilt and fear color our perspectives—one man's transgression may be another man's freedom.

    And while my personal example may not seem nightmarish to most, it was like torture to me at the time, and it was in the midst of that nightmare that I began my doctoral dissertation. I chose to write about the Gothic wanderer because I felt myself to be like a Gothic wanderer, displaced and wandering through the mysterious maze of academia and the academic job market. In the chapters that follow, while I will discuss the Gothic novels themselves without commentary on how their themes relate to our lives today—something I don't doubt my readers can figure out for themselves, let me here briefly list a few examples of how these Gothic wanderer figures speak to who we—men and women, young and old, rich and poor, from all races and religions—are today, and who we have always been.

The Gothic's popularity arose at the time of the French Revolution as people questioned the legitimacy of their government—the monarchy—as well as the governments that replaced it, and the entire social order and its institutions, especially organized religion. Paranoia and conspiracy theories were common—our political concerns have not changed much today and continue to be reflected in our fiction. Just as the early Gothic novels theorized that certain secret societies were manipulating the French Revolution, today, we are no less fascinated by conspiracy theories—whether it be Dan Brown's *The Da Vinci Code* with its alleged revelation of the Catholic Church's cover-up of the lost bloodline of Christ's children via Mary Magdalene (the Gothic has always loved to pick on the Catholic Church), or beliefs that the government is withholding information from us about everything from terrorists to UFOs. In the twenty-first century, the U.S. Government has even been accused by some of staging the 9/11 terrorist attacks as an excuse to invade Iraq.

Concerns about the patriarchal system, legitimate children, and the sanctity of the family were common in early Gothic novels—how much more today when divorce is prevalent and children are frequently born outside of marriage, mothers take men to court and have DNA paternity tests given to verify who a child's father may be, while in politics we hear about the need to return to "family values."

The Wandering Jew is one of the key figures in the Gothic, and although we may not be cursed to wander like him, our jobs and the economy often force us to move to unfamiliar places, to find employment in sectors we feel uncomfortable with, to experience displacement. At the same time, the Wandering Jew is a metaphor for the plight of the Jewish people. The effects of the Holocaust—a horror the nineteenth century Gothic novelists never could have imagined—still haunt us, and the Jewish people still struggle with prejudice and violence directed against them, even after having a homeland established in Israel.

The Rosicrucian Gothic wanderer is obsessed with finding the secret to eternal life. Are we any less obsessed with it today when we value youthfulness, and when studies predict that half of Americans born in the late twentieth century will live to see age one hundred? The Gothic fascination with life-extension continues for us today.

The Gothic concern with gambling is no less relevant today. Gambling in Gothic literature is viewed as a transgression, a way to achieve wealth to advance oneself in society, and consequently, it usually results in destruction for the gambler and his family. Today, gambling is an even bigger problem than it was two centuries ago. We constantly hear tales of lottery winners who waste their millions, only to become bankrupts. We know of people who invest in the stock market, or worse, get taken advantage of in Ponzi schemes, only to lose everything. We continually worry about the economy, and most of us continue to have financial difficulties or an unhealthy relationship with money, while longing for wealth that we falsely believe will solve all our problems.

Working conditions became a Gothic concern with the rise of the Industrial Revolution. In Dickens' day, horrendous working conditions were being fought against. In the early twentieth century, the rise of unions helped to solve many of those problems, establishing an eight-hour work day and the weekend. But how many of us today find ourselves working long hours? What industry did to the Victorians, modern technology has done to us, making us connected 24/7 and perhaps improving communication but also resulting in expectations to work constantly.

Perhaps no novelist in all of literature has been more visionary or speaks more to our time than the Gothic novelist Mary Shelley. The issues in *Frankenstein* are the very issues of stem cell research, cloning, and the other quandaries of science we continue to argue over today. The need for responsible science is now more important than ever. In *The Last Man*, Shelley introduced the fear of a worldwide plague which today remains a terrifying possibility. Shelley's vision of the future is frighteningly accurate in many ways. In recent decades, the scare of AIDS and the bird and swine flu have made people fear worldwide human extinction as a possibility. The possibility of nuclear war and biological warfare has made it possible that man could someday be responsible for his own extinction, unintentionally, or intentionally. The recent film *Contagion* (2011) is just one of many works that speak to these fears.

In the Victorian period, a religious crisis arose with the introduction of theories of evolution. Organized religion began slowly to lose its hold over people. Those shifts have only continued to the present day. The understanding that we are spiritual beings having a human experience has become a mantra in recent decades. More and more people have quit subscribing to organized religion but come to describe themselves as spiritual, and this desire to connect with our spiritual (supernatural) selves has led many down less traditional Western paths, including to eastern religions, beliefs in reincarnation, listening to entities who channel their messages through humans, an emphasis upon "the Goddess," and the creation of new religions such as Scientology. In many cases, a general move away from institutional Christianity has not led to atheism but what might be termed a spiritual reawakening that allows humanity, if not the autonomy from God that Milton's Satan sought, then at least the "faith, hope, and self-esteem" that Percy Shelley dreamt of for humanity.

The vampire is the nineteenth century Gothic wanderer figure who has remained most popular in the twenty-first century and continues to be reinvented. Despite his "evil" nature, he has become glamorous and attractive; the lines between good and evil have been blurred; we now have dark heroes and sympathetic villains. The continuing popularity of the vampire two centuries after he was first introduced to English readers speaks to how much the Gothic still influences our lives today.

While the bulk of this study will cover nineteenth century British Gothic fiction, I will offer in the epilogue some insight into how the themes of that period's Gothic literature have continued and been transformed in twentieth and twenty-first century literature, some still noticeably Gothic, such as Stephenie Meyer's *Twilight* series and Anne Rice's vampire novels, while other influences are hard-pressed to be termed "Gothic" but still have Gothic elements or owe a debt to the Gothic, including such popular figures as Tarzan and Batman.

The Gothic wanderer is still with us today; he has lost a lot of his angst over the centuries, but the figure still fascinates us. This study will hopefully help to explain a little of why we love the Gothic—because we discover in the Gothic wanderer our very selves.

Tyler R. Tichelaar, Ph.D. and Gothic Wanderer
October 31, 2011
Marquette, Michigan

PART I -
Creating the Gothic Wanderer

Chapter I – The Gothic Wanderer's Origins in the French Revolution

While a great deal of criticism has been written about wanderers in Romantic poetry, the Gothic wanderer's distinct significance has been largely ignored. The Gothic wanderer, a contemporary figure to the Romantic wanderer, offers an equally important commentary upon the nineteenth century's political and social concerns. Like the Romantic poets, the Gothic novelists adapted the figure of the wandering outcast from Milton's *Paradise Lost* to comment upon the French Revolution and its implications for social struggle and political debate in Britain. The Gothic novels of the 1790s were metaphorical discussions of the French Revolution's legitimacy and whether the Revolution would benefit humanity or result in complete disaster. The Gothic wanderer figure reflected a fear that the Revolution would cause the breakdown of social order and the family's dissolution, thus resulting in individual alienation. While Romantic wanderers were primarily depicted as heroic rebels, by contrast, the Gothic wanderer suffers pangs of guilt and is often eternally damned for transgressing against authority. A brief discussion of the French Revolution's influence on the Gothic wanderer's creation will provide a background for understanding the figure's evolution over the course of the nineteenth century from a symbol of transgression into a Christian symbol of redemption.

The Optimism of Romantic Poets

The French Revolution evoked numerous reactions in England, varying from praise and hope to trepidation and fear. Several people, particularly radicals and intellectuals, hoped that the French Revolution would be as successful in casting off the yoke of tyranny as had been the American one. While many feared that the Revolution foreshadowed the coming Apocalypse, the Romantic poets hoped the Revolution was the beginning of a new age that would evolve into an age of peace on earth and humanity's regeneration. Numerous Romantic poems express this millennial view in the decades following the French Revolution including William Blake's *The French Revolution*, "Song of Liberty," "America," and "Europe," Robert Southey's "Joan of Arc," Samuel Taylor Coleridge's "Destiny of Nations" and "Religious Musings," the conclusion of William Wordsworth's "Descriptive Sketches" and portions of the *Prelude*, and Percy Shelley's "Queen Mab." M.H. Abrams remarks that all these works depict a:

> ...panoramic view of history in a cosmic setting, in which the agents are in part historical and in part allegorical or mythological and the overall design is apocalyptic; they envision a dark past, a violent present, and an immediately impending future which will justify the history of suffering man by its culmination in an absolute good; and they represent the French Revolution (or else a coming revolution which will improve upon the French model) as the critical event which signals the emergence of a regenerate man who will inhabit a new world uniting the features of a restored paradise and a recovered Golden Age. (332)

The Romantic poets' optimism is reflected in their personal remembrances of the French Revolution, long after it failed to succeed as had been hoped. Wordsworth would declare in the *Prelude*, "Bliss was it in that dawn to be alive, / But to be young was very Heaven!" (*Prelude* (1850) XI, 108-9). Similarly, Robert Southey felt that "few persons but those who have lived" during the French Revolution "can conceive or comprehend... what a visionary world seemed to open upon those who were just entering it. Old things seemed passing away and nothing was dreamt of but the regeneration of the human race" (Abrams 330).

This optimistic spirit sorely diminished as the Revolution progressed, culminating in the royal family's executions and the Reign of Terror. The Romantic poets lost their faith that the Revolution foreshadowed humanity's return to an edenic state. And during the Reign of Terror, the Gothic novelists began to express their own skepticism about the Revolution's results, questioning its purpose and legitimacy. Most importantly, the Gothic debated how the social order could be maintained in a world that lacked the traditional forms of government. Because the monarchy had been a central focus of government, people feared that its destruction would result in the dissolution of all units of society, including the family. The Gothic became greatly concerned with how the family could be preserved or reinvented to ensure its survival during this time of political chaos. Lynn Hunt's *The French Revolution as Family Romance* provides a useful analysis of how the French Revolution was interpreted by witnesses as a large scale version of a family crisis. While Hunt does not discuss the response of British literature to the French Revolution, the French people's concerns and the reflection of those concerns in French literature are parallel to the concerns the English expressed in their own writings. The British Gothic novel adapted this concern over the family's future by creating plots that centered on family secrets and inheritances.

These plots were attempts to reinvent the family in a new form so it could survive in the new post-revolutionary age.

Family as a Metaphor for Political Order

An increased emphasis upon the family was the natural result of how the political order was interpreted by eighteenth century Europeans. Hunt notes that prior to the French Revolution, most Europeans viewed a king as a father who ruled over his nation, which represented his children (xiv). The French royal family's execution resulted in the French people feeling they had become like orphans (2). While the monarchy's dissolution could be viewed as justifiable, it remained difficult to imagine a government not based upon a monarchy, thus providing a family model. French literature of the period reflects this difficulty by creating narratives or "family romances" (xv). Lynn Hunt uses the term "family romance" to refer to the "collective, unconscious images of the familial order that underlie revolutionary politics" (xiii). The family order was reinvented in literature to reflect the new order that rejected monarchy. Without a king as the nation's father, people feared disorder would result because the normal laws of social order and legitimacy no longer applied (Hunt 143). To prevent both future tyranny from another king and complete anarchy, the French people sought to be autonomous by creating a democratic brotherhood, as reflected in the Revolution's emphasis upon "fraternity" (Hunt xiv). French literature reflected the discourse on how such a fraternity could be formed to provide liberty and equality for all, yet still retain authority to ensure its citizens' loyalty and obedience (Hunt 3).

The new political order in France passed legislation that would restructure the family to reflect the current political changes, including the monarchy's abolishment. This legislation was heavily influenced by theories that arose from the Enlightenment. During the eighteenth century, philosophers believed that humanity had finally evolved into its maturity, and therefore, people should be autonomous rather than subservient to a ruler. At the same time, new emphasis was being placed upon the stage of childhood and how a person matured into an adult. Once mature, children were viewed as individuals and equals to their fathers, so while they should continue to respect their fathers, they were no longer bound to obey them (Hunt 17-8). With the monarchy's end, these theories of the Enlightenment influenced the creation of legislation that changed the family structure, predominantly by limiting a father's control over his children. After 1789, laws restricted paternal authority by establishing family councils to replace the father's unlimited control. By 1792, adults were declared not subject to paternal authority and the age of majority was lowered to twenty-one. While within marriage fathers retained predominant authority over children, new divorce laws provided that divorced parents had equal authority over their children. Simultaneously, divorce became more common because marriage was declared to be only a civil contract (Hunt 40-1). The regulation of inheritance laws prevented a father from controlling his children by threatening their inheritances. On November 2, 1793, laws were even passed that granted illegitimate children equal rights of inheritance with their legitimate siblings if paternity could be proven. This last law diminished traditional emphasis upon legitimacy by declaring that all siblings deserved equal treatment (Hunt 66).

While such changes provided increased equality and liberty for children, many feared that because these laws limited paternal power, the family unit would break down. To prevent such dissolution, the government promoted the family as an important element for the nation's well-being. Children became the shared responsibility of both parents and the government. Robespierre declared, "The country has the right to raise its children," and Danton similarly remarked, "Children belong to society before they belong to their family" (Hunt 67). Such statements reflect the Revolution's democratic and nationalistic goals where everyone owed allegiance to the national good rather than to one individual. The family's role in this new order was to educate children in the national ideals so they would become good citizens. In several ways, the government promoted this new role of the family. Robespierre established festivals focused upon the need to reinforce family values (Hunt 154) and a 1793 Proposed Constitution stated that "The fathers and mothers of the family are the true citizens" (Hunt 151). The family's role was no longer as a place of authority, but as a moral guide in the creation of autonomous individuals who could contribute to the new French government's democratic goals.

French literature reflected these attempts to restructure the family and its role. Novels prior to the Revolution tended to depict families in crises as the result of a father's actions, but by the end of the eighteenth century, emphasis was placed upon bastard or orphaned children who must make their ways in the world (Hunt 29, 34). The illegitimate child became a favorite character in literature because it reflected the confusion over the period's political environment. Hunt states that in a world without a father/king, the illegitimate and autonomous individual must search for a sense of place; therefore, literary characters sought knowledge of their pasts and births, while fearful of incest that resulted from ignorance over their family relationships. The illegitimate child was often depicted as seeking to gain an unwilling father's acknowledgement. Such plots reflected the unfairness of patriarchal authority and the Revolution's desire to overturn such tyranny (Hunt 40). Plots focusing on orphans removed fathers from significant roles, and when father figures were retained, the father was often rehabilitated by depicting him as a nurturer and guide to his children so they could become autonomous adults. Motherhood was also emphasized in literature to provide fathers with less prominent roles and less power over their children (Hunt 190). These examples demonstrate that French literature used the family as a metaphor to reflect the changing political climate of the French Revolution.

In England, concern over the Revolution was also discussed in terms of a family crisis. A pamphlet war occurred in which views upon the Revolution were debated. Among the most noted pamphlet writers at the time were Edmund Burke, William Godwin, and Mary Wollstonecraft. Each of these writers used the family metaphor in discussing the French Revolution, although Burke held opposite opinions about the consequences of the current political crisis from Godwin and Wollstonecraft. William Godwin would later turn to writing Gothic novels, of which *St. Leon* (1799) particularly, would emphasize how acts of transgression or rebellion cause family crises, but can ultimately result in a new and stronger family unit.

Edmund Burke's reaction to the French Revolution was one of fear and skepticism. He believed that the French monarchy's destruction would result in a decline of chivalry and manners and that man would cease to be noble or civilized. In Burke's view, overthrowing the French monarchy was a criminal act that destroyed the established institutions that had evolved from centuries of custom and thought. He feared the Revolution would establish governments without precedent, and therefore, without any reliable sources of authority. Burke's emphasis upon custom included the monarchy, which he felt was a figurehead around which centered the traditions that composed the social order. Burke believed that a form of filial devotion must be felt toward a monarch if the government is to retain the people's loyalty and obedience (Hunt 3). Even if a monarch were oppressive, Burke feared that the people who usurped the monarch's power would only become worse tyrants, a view which the Reign of Terror would later verify (Paulson, *Representations* 220). In *Reflections on the Revolution in France* (1790), Burke expressed his opposition to the Revolution by using the family metaphor to show the indignity of rebelling against the monarch. Burke praises the institution of monarchy when he refers to the English political structure as providing a "sort of family settlement" (40) that resulted from "profound reflection" (39). Burke believes England is a superior nation precisely because of its monarchy and its patriarchal laws of inheritance.

> ...it has been the uniform policy of our constitution to claim and assert our liberties, as an entailed inheritance derived to us from our forefathers, and to be transmitted to our posterity; as an estate specially belonging to the people of this kingdom without any reference whatever to any other more general or prior right....We have an inheritable crown; an inheritable peerage; and an house of commons and a people inheriting privileges, franchises, and liberties, from a long line of ancestors.

> This policy appears to me to be the result of profound reflection; or rather the happy effect of following nature, which is wisdom without reflection, and above it. A spirit of innovation is generally the result of a selfish temper and confined views. People will not look forward to posterity, who never look backward to their ancestors. Besides, the people of England well know, that the idea of inheritance furnishes a sure principle of conservation, and a sure principle of transmission, without at all excluding a principle of improvement. (39-40)

Burke's views suggest that the patriarchal laws of inheritance provide the best government because they provide stability. He then compares this political system to a family structure:

> ...in this choice of inheritance we have given to our frame of polity the image of a relation in blood; binding up the constitution of our country with our dearest domestic ties; adopting our fundamental laws into the bosom of our family affections. (40)

Against these laws of inheritance, governed by the established monarchy, the French people have rebelled "against a mild and lawful monarch" (40). Burke condemns the French people's "barbarous philosophy" (45) that the king is an equal to the common people because "On this scheme of things, a king is but a man; a queen is but a woman" (45). Burke declares his outrage over the viewpoint that:

> Regicide, and parricide, and sacrilege, are but fictions of superstition, corrupting jurisprudence by destroying its simplicity. The murder of a king, or a queen, or a bishop, or a father, are only common homicide; and if the people are by any chance, or in any way gainers by it, a sort of homicide much the most pardonable. (45)

Burke is outraged that the common people may be deemed more important than a monarch. The fall of the monarchy makes Burke morosely declare that "the age of chivalry is gone....the glory of Europe is extinguished forever" (44). Burke's use of the family metaphor suggests that with the monarchy's fall, traditions and customs will be destroyed, including parental authority, which will severely threaten the family unit.

In contrast, William Godwin and Mary Wollstonecraft used the family metaphor to argue for the rights of man and to support the French Revolution. In *Enquiry Concerning Political Justice, and its Influence on Morals and Happiness* (1793), Godwin refutes Burke's statements, but he uses the same family metaphor for his own purposes. Godwin supports the Revolution's reinterpretation of the family as not a place for patriarchal authority, but as an environment in which children mature into adults who will become capable citizens of a government that emphasizes democratic equality. Godwin declares that adults should not be subservient to parental authority, and by extension to a patriarchal monarch.

> The reverence which is due from a child to his parent, or rather to his senior in age and experience, falls under the same rules as have already been delivered. Wherever I have good reason to believe, that another person knows better than myself what is proper to be done, there I ought to conform to his direction. But the advantage which he possesses, must be obvious, otherwise I shall not be justified in my proceeding... The deference of a child becomes vicious, whenever he has reason to doubt that the parent possesses essential information, of which he is deprived. Nothing can be more necessary for the general benefit, than that we should divest ourselves, as soon as the proper period arrives, of the shackles of infancy; that human life should not be one eternal childhood; but that men should judge for themselves, unfettered by the prejudices of education, or the institutions of their country. (158)

Similarly, Mary Wollstonecraft argues in *A Vindication of the Rights of Woman* (1792) that "A slavish bondage to parents cramps every faculty of the mind." This bondage is especially true for the female sex because "girls, from various causes, are more kept down by their parents, in every sense of the word, than boys....and thus taught plausibly to submit to their parents, they are prepared for the slavery of marriage" (qtd. in Paulson, *Representations* 226-7). Wollstonecraft not only speaks out against monarchy, but all forms of patriarchal authority, by which men and especially women suffer. Both Godwin and Wollstonecraft reject that a father has any right to authority over his adult children. By extension, monarchs should have no right to tyrannize over a people who have become educated and mature enough to govern themselves.

British Gothic novels echoed similar concerns to those of the pamphlet writers; however, rather than discuss the Revolution directly, the Gothic novels of the 1790s created family plots and scenes of rebellion as metaphors for the French Revolution, a metaphor their readers understood (Paulson, "Gothic" 534). Gothic novels questioned whether transgressions would destroy the family, or whether the family could survive if recreated under a new social order. The Gothic emphasized the religious implications of such rebellions because governments were based in traditions believed ultimately to be sanctioned by God. The Gothic often equated rebellion, therefore, be it against a king or other form of authority, with a rebellion against God. Some Gothic novelists believed such rebellions would result in divine punishment, while others questioned whether these transgressions were acceptable if they would result in a greater good for humanity.

While the Gothic genre originated with Horace Walpole's *The Castle of Otranto* in 1764, only in the decades following the French Revolution did Gothic novels reach their height of popularity, largely because of their indirect political commentary upon the issue of revolution. During the 1790s, two-thirds of all novels published had a Gothic theme (Clery 70). Readers turned to Gothic novels because they responded to the concerns of the revolutionary period, offering a practice ground for how political issues might be dealt with in the real world (Punter, "Narrative" 11). The traditional Gothic trappings of gloomy, decaying castles and confinement in prisons or monasteries now resonated with memories of the Revolution's origins in the Bastille; hence, prisons became recurring images in the Gothic (Paulson 534). The mob that freed the Bastille prisoners would also inspire mob scenes in many novels, including Matthew Lewis' *The Monk* (1796) and William Godwin's *St. Leon* (1799).

The Gothic's use of the supernatural added to its attraction for readers of the period. The disorder caused by the French Revolution resulted in great anxiety and fear among people. Gothic novels attempted to interpret the causes of such fear and to depict human fears in supernatural form. Prior to the French Revolution, eighteenth century literature had frowned upon an interest in the supernatural because of the dominant belief in rationality that grew out of the Enlightenment. The Marquis de Sade, in his critical essay "Idée sur les romans" (1800), justified the supernatural's popularity in the Gothic novel as the result of the French Revolution. Ronald Paulson summarizes the marquis' argument: "the bloody upheavals of the French Revolution had rendered everyday reality so horrific that contemporary writers necessarily had to invoke the supernatural and demonic realms for material which could still shock or startle their readers" ("Gothic" 536). These horrors also provided a cathartic release for readers from their fears about the French Revolution (Paulson, "Gothic" 536).

Conspiracy Theories in Gothic Literature

One manner by which the Gothic provided comfort was the creation of fabulous explanations for the French Revolution's causes. In *Mythology of the Secret Societies,* J. M. Roberts discusses how conspiracy theories were popular at the time because they attempted "to impose some sort of order on the bewildering changes which suddenly showered upon Europe with the Revolution and its aftermath" (qtd. in Paulson, *Representations* 223). Roberts argues that Christians particularly found such theories comforting.

> Educated and conservative men raised in the tradition of Christianity, with its stress on individual responsibility and the independence of the will, found conspiracy theories plausible as

an explanation of such changes: it must have come about, they thought, because somebody planned it so. (qtd. in Paulson, *Representations* 223)

The most popular conspiracy theories were linked to such secret societies as the Freemasons, Illuminati, and Rosicrucians. Both the Illuminati and the Rosicrucians were sworn to work for the increase of human knowledge and the betterment of humanity (Paulson, *Representations* 24). Beliefs arose that these groups had secretly organized the French Revolution, and they were controlling its events. Such theories were believed to have support in symbols of the French Revolution. For example, evidence that the Freemasons might have caused the Revolution existed in the fact that Dr. Guillotine was himself a Freemason, and the triangular shape of the guillotine's blade was a Freemason symbol (Paulson, *Representations* 241).

While Gothic novels reflected these conspiracy theories, they condemned characters who acted as potential conspirators. Rosicrucians were frequently depicted in Gothic novels because the secrets they possessed—the philosopher's stone and the elixir of life—could threaten the social order. The elixir provided the Rosicrucian with longevity so he had more time to manipulate events toward his purpose, while the philosopher's stone, which turned lead into gold, allowed him to create great wealth, thereby granting him power over nations' economies. Another common Gothic feature was the swearing of secret oaths, which reflected the oaths of secret societies believed to have caused the French Revolution (Macdonald 192). D.L. Macdonald has traced such oaths in several Gothic novels where characters swear not to reveal some form of secret knowledge. In Ann Radcliffe's *The Mysteries of Udolpho* (1794), Emily St. Aubert swears to her father that she will destroy certain papers without reading them. Emily is unaware that these papers hold family secrets, the knowledge of which could only benefit her. In Polidori's *The Vampyre* (1819), a secret oath occurs when Aubrey swears to Lord Ruthven that he will not reveal for one year the crimes that Ruthven has committed. A similar oath occurs in Charles Maturin's *Melmoth the Wanderer* (1820) when Melmoth asks an English clergyman to conceal the fact of his death. In *Varney the Vampyre* (1847), a sexton swears not to reveal that Varney is a vampire, while Varney remarks that the sexton need make no oath for he will remain silent from fear for his life. In Bram Stoker's *Dracula* (1897), Lucy makes Mina promise not to tell her mother about her sleepwalking. Renfield is also sworn to secrecy so he cannot reveal Dracula's secrets to the male protagonists. Finally, Mina forces her friends to swear that they will not tell her their plans for Dracula's destruction so she cannot be forced to impart them to Dracula (Macdonald 191).

The Gothic frequently depicted conspiracies as resulting in disastrous events that the conspirators could no longer control. In *Frankenstein*

(1818), Victor believes his ability to restore life will make him a benefactor to humanity, but Victor is unable to control the Monster he brings to life. Paulson suggests that the Monster is representative of the Jacobins who grew out of control during the French Revolution (*Representations* 241). Similarly, Jane Blumberg remarks that the Monster is composed of various body parts that reflect the atrocities of the French Revolution, committed in an attempt to regenerate humanity (49). Blumberg concludes that the Frankenstein Monster is "the dark, destructive and unrestrained manifestation of the Revolution ("more or less than man"), which, had it not been abandoned by educators and guides, might have been the savior of mankind" (51)

Rise of the Gothic Wanderer

The need to find an explanation and source for the French Revolution's events reflected a Christian belief that history evolves according to God's divine plan. Interpretations of the French Revolution as a transgression against God caused both the Romantic poets and the Gothic novelists to turn to Milton's *Paradise Lost* to support their beliefs for or against the legitimacy of transgression. The Romantic poets would interpret *Paradise Lost* to justify rebellion against tyrannical forms of authority. The Gothic novelists, however, were divided upon transgression's legitimacy. These differing viewpoints resulted in two distinct forms of Gothic and the creation of the Gothic wanderer figure.

Eugenia DeLamotte has divided the Gothic into comic and tragic forms (54). Kate Ellis makes a similar division, but uses the respective terms of feminine and masculine Gothic (*Contested* xii-iii). Comic or feminine Gothic novels maintain the status quo and typically conclude with a marriage. In contrast, tragic or masculine Gothic novels take seriously the illicit and irrational by refusing to create happy endings. Masculine Gothics instead condemn the transgressive Gothic wanderer. Feminine Gothic tends to be written by female novelists and to contain female wanderer heroines. By contrast, the masculine Gothics are usually written by men and contain male main characters who fail as heroes. Finally, feminine Gothic is generally written in a third person point of view, while the masculine Gothic is written in first person. Few exceptions exist to these divisions, although *Frankenstein* is a notable exception because Mary Shelley is a female novelist who writes masculine Gothics with male characters and first person narration.

While these two Gothic forms both emphasize wandering characters, the tragic Gothic uses its very form to highlight wandering because it is typically composed of several narrative fragments that reflect the disorder a wanderer feels. These numerous fragmented narratives also provide a difficulty in determining the work's meaning in comparison to feminine Gothics where there is only one narrative voice that interprets everything. For example, *Frankenstein* is a masculine Gothic partly because it is composed of several first person narratives. The novel's outer frame is Walton's narrative, while inside this frame is Victor Frankenstein's narrative, which includes within it that of the Monster, who not only tells his story, but repeats the story of the DeLacey family. These multiple narratives provide a defiance of closure because the Monster can tell Walton he will destroy himself by burning on a bier, but Walton does not give an eye-witness account of this occurrence. Because the multiple narratives are all written in first person, there is no omniscient narrator to assure us that the Monster does carry out his own destruction. Instead, the reader is left with the uncomfortable fear that, even though the novel has ended, the Monster may still be wandering somewhere. The intentional difficulty of interpretation which such Gothic novels create is a reflection of the French Revolution's chaotic events and the Napoleonic wars, which people feared could not be easily resolved with any positive results.

The division of feminine and masculine Gothic equally reflects two separate views upon the legitimacy of the French Revolution. The feminine Gothic rewrites *Paradise Lost* to vindicate Eve, and by extension, all women from transgression. Feminine Gothic suggests that transgressions committed for benevolent reasons, such as the French Revolution, are permissible and can be beneficial. Female heroines become only temporary wanderers, whose search for knowledge results in their ability to return home with the wisdom needed to establish a domestic form of paradise. In contrast, the masculine Gothic condemns transgression as only resulting in tragic displacement and condemnation, just as people feared the French Revolution would bring about the fall of social order.

While the Gothic wanderer's creation was the result of this discourse upon the French Revolution, the figure would evolve over the course of the nineteenth century. Eventually the emphasis upon transgression would develop into a question of how transgression could be redeemed, and by the late Victorian period, the Gothic wanderer was allowed to repent for his transgressions and rest from his wanderings. And over the course of the twentieth century, his descendants would metamorphose from transgressors into superheroes.

The Gothic wanderer is a neglected, but important figure, who provides an enriched reading of not only Gothic, but Romantic and Victorian literature, and even twenty-first century literature. Many Gothic novels are significant artistic texts that deserve far more critical attention. Several of these works, including *The Wanderer* and *Ernestus Berchtold*, have only been republished in recent years after being out of print for nearly two centuries. Other Gothic novels have been dismissed as merely thrillers that are of little importance to the literary tradition. Even *Frankenstein* and *Dracula* have only received serious critical attention in the last few decades. In their depiction of Gothic wanderers, these novels reflect serious nineteenth century issues of politics, society, religion, and race. By studying the Gothic wanderer, a better understanding can be reached of nineteenth century and twentieth century literature and its cultural context.

Chapter II – *Paradise Lost* and the Legitimacy of Transgression

The French Revolution's concern with legitimate power and rebellion against tyranny resulted in new interpretations of Milton's *Paradise Lost*. From these interpretations and revisions of *Paradise Lost* were created both Romantic and Gothic wanderer figures who were based upon Milton's characters. Milton had depicted Satan, Adam, and Eve as suffering from guilty consciences and inner turmoils as a result of their transgressions against God. During the French Revolution, Milton's literary depiction of transgression was interpreted in relation to the French monarchy's overthrow. Writers questioned whether the actions of Milton's characters were truly definable as transgressions or whether they were rightful forms of rebellion against a tyrannical God as the French Revolution was widely interpreted as a rightful rebellion against the tyranny of monarchy. While Milton had intended for *Paradise Lost* to "justify the ways of God to men" (I, 26), the Romantic poets read a subversive thread into the poem, best exemplified by Blake's remark that Milton was "of the Devil's party without knowing it" (*Marriage* 70). The Romantic poets believed Satan's actions were justifiable and praiseworthy, and they used Satan as the basis for their own Romantic wanderer characters whose acts of rebellion were celebrated as displays of heroism. Consequently, the Romantic poets believed the French Revolution was not a transgression against a patriarchal monarchy, but an act of heroism to create liberty for the French people.

The Gothic novelists created a more complex view than the Romantic poets in their revisions of *Paradise Lost*. While Gothic novelists differed upon the extent to which the French Revolution could be interpreted as a negative event in human history, most Gothic writers treated the Revolution as an act of transgression. Gothic interpretations of *Paradise Lost*, therefore, were usually more traditional in their agreement that Satan, Adam, and Eve were transgressors deserving of punishment. While the Gothic frowned upon transgressions, it also attempted to define what acts really were transgressions, and the degree of seriousness attached to a certain transgression. While the Romantic poets focused upon Milton's Satan as the prototype for their rebellious yet heroic Romantic wanderers, Gothic novelists incorporated not only Satan, but also Adam and Eve as sources for their Gothic wanderer figures; each of Milton's characters transgresses for a different reason, so the Gothic felt each transgression could be explored individually for its motivations and consequences.

The Gothic debate upon transgression resulted in the creation of two Gothic subgenres, which Kate Ellis has termed the masculine and the feminine Gothic (*Contested* xii-iii). The masculine Gothic typically focuses upon a transgressive male character, based on Satan, who is condemned for his transgression. Feminine Gothic, however, questions the motivations behind an act of transgression. Focusing upon the desire for forbidden knowledge, the feminine Gothic rejects Milton's treatment of Eve as a transgressor simply because she sought to better herself and become Adam's equal. Feminine Gothic novelists revised *Paradise Lost* by creating female characters, based upon Eve, who commit subversive acts. Patriarchal society may view these subversive acts as transgressions, but they are ultimately beneficial and lead to the creation of a new form of Eden. An exploration of Milton's treatment of Satan, Adam, and Eve as wanderers provides a better appreciation of how Gothic novelists adapted the wanderer as a figure for social commentary upon the French Revolution's "transgressions."

Wandering is a major activity in *Paradise Lost*. Some form of the word "wander" appears in Milton's epic approximately thirty-four times, most frequently in relation to Satan, the other devils, and to Adam and Eve, although stars, rivers, and appetites are among other items mentioned in the context of wandering. Isabel MacCaffrey, having studied Milton's use of wandering in *Paradise Lost*, states that wandering almost always has a "pejorative" or "melancholy connotation" (188). Wandering is appropriate in this sense, for it is the activity engaged in by Satan and the other devils when they are cast from Heaven. They are placed outside the order created by God, and without God, their existences have no real structure or purpose. Similarly, Adam and Eve are described as wanderers when they are forced to leave Eden: "They hand in hand with wand'ring steps and slow, / Through Eden took thir solitary way" (XII 648-9). Wandering is here equated with being an outcast and separated from God.

Satan's role as wanderer is a continual attempt to escape and reject his wanderer status. After realizing he cannot return to Heaven, Satan decides he will become God's equal by setting up a rival kingdom in Hell, and by forcing humanity into sin as part of his continual war against God. Critics have often regarded Satan's journey to earth to accomplish humanity's fall as based upon quest literature. MacCaffrey argues that these scenes resemble medieval and Renaissance literary quests where the hero must face several obstacles prior to achieving his goal. Typically, these obstacles are allegorical in nature—in Spenser's *Faerie Queene*, the Redcrosse Knight must battle the dragon Error and numerous other allegorical villains. Milton similarly places typical obstacles along Satan's path from Hell to earth and in his journey through the Kingdom of Chaos (MacCaffrey 197). Satan sees himself in the role of hero for he is confident in his ability to lead the other devils in the reestablishment of their power. Milton combines these heroic aspects of Satan's character with more traditional depictions of Satan as a wanderer and outcast to make him a rounded and even sympathetic villain (MacCaffrey 192-3).

Satan's attempt to evolve from wanderer into hero is dependent upon his own perception of his identity. Satan realizes that to be truly godlike, he must reject his guilty feelings over his rebellion. His guilt stems from his need for God's approval, for without such approval, he is an outcast. Once Satan rejects the need for God's approval, he no longer needs to define himself as an outcast. Instead, he can become an autonomous individual who creates his own self-definition. Satan's strongest moment of character occurs when he determines he will no longer seek God's approval or feel guilty for his rebellion against God.

> So farewell Hope, and with Hope farewell Fear,
> Farewell Remorse: all Good to me is lost;
> Evil be thou my Good; by thee at least
> Divided Empire with Heav'n's King I hold
> By thee, and more than half perhaps will reign:
> As Man ere long, and this new World shall know. (IV, 108-13)

Satan's declaration exhibits his hunger for power, and his desire to create a rival kingdom of evil that will equal and hopefully surpass the good of Heaven. Rather than being a wandering outcast, he now perceives himself as having a purpose in his quest to rival God. His first action is to wage a war against humanity as a way to retaliate against the punishment God has inflicted upon him. Satan fails to be autonomous, however, for in trying to free himself from his wandering outcast status by reversing God's definitions of good and evil, he is still validating those definitions and showing that his concern with them controls him. Furthermore, Satan fails to achieve the role of hero because he is not perceived as such by the other characters. By manipulating Adam and Eve's fall into sin, Satan hopes to win the approval of his fellow devils. Instead, the devils are turned into snakes by his actions, and when he returns to Hell, Satan is greeted by their hissing. At the poem's conclusion, Satan retains his wanderer role, and Milton later states in *Paradise Regained* that Satan continues to wander in "eternal restless change" (MacCaffrey 202). Satan repeatedly acts to improve his situation, yet ironically, his actions always degrade him. This irony of attempts at self-betterment resulting in degradation would become a major attribute of the Gothic wanderer who searches for forbidden knowledge or autonomy and instead acquires the role of wandering outcast.

Milton's depictions of Adam and Eve are equally important sources for Gothic wanderer figures. Eve's desire to eat the apple of the Tree of Knowledge would become the source for many feminine Gothic novels. These works created plots that were revisions of *Paradise Lost* to vindicate women who act subversively against the patriarchy to improve their situations. While society may view women as transgressors for attempting to better themselves, women are only transgressing against a code created by the patriarchy to control women. In contrast, the masculine Gothic would treat Eve as similar to Satan in committing a sin of pride and desiring to be autonomous (Ellis, *Castle* 143). Adam would be adapted by Gothic novelists to create wanderers who are less often complete villains than sympathetic transgressors or the victims of transgression. Adam is the hero of *Paradise Lost* because he is capable of heroic deeds, such as transgressing out of love for Eve, and consequently, being able to endure suffering (Abrams, *Norton* 1435). Consequently, the male Gothic wanderers inspired by Adam's character are men who heroically endure their sufferings until the time when they may rest from their wanderings. Adam's transgression, however, remains a form of rebellion against God that is not completely excusable.

Central to *Paradise Lost*'s influence upon the character of the Gothic wanderer is that transgressions committed in Gothic novels are the result of a desire for forbidden knowledge. Even when Satan transgresses to gain autonomy and power, it is because he desires to know what it is like to be a god. Kate Ellis argues that for Adam and Eve, the desire is not merely to be godlike, but because God is their father, they desire the knowledge of their parent (*Castle* 156). The plots of Gothic novels focus upon a character's desire for knowledge of his or her parents' pasts and family histories. Often this knowledge is a family secret that has not been imparted to the child because the parent does not feel the child is mature enough to receive the knowledge (Ellis, *Castle* 156). Such forbidden knowledge exists in nearly all Gothic novels—whether the main character be Caleb Williams who wishes to discover the secrets in the trunk that belongs to his fatherly employer, Mr. Falkland, or Emily St. Aubert who seeks knowledge of her past after watching her father weep over the mysterious miniature portrait of a woman she does not recognize. Once the knowledge is attained, the type of knowledge and how it is used determines the character's future. Most Gothic novels use the revelation of knowledge as the impetus for the character's downfall or self-destruction, although some Gothic novels allow the knowledge to enrich or improve the character's situation. The acquisition of knowledge is usually linked to the family by the knowledge relating to a family secret. This knowledge may harm the family unit as in *Paradise Lost* when Adam and Eve sought their Father's knowledge, resulting in their fall, and by extension, that of the human family. Gothic novels use variations of this scenario to motivate plots that feature Gothic wanderer characters.

All Gothic wanderers long for knowledge despite the consequences that such knowledge may bring. Critics regard this longing as a metaphor for the desire to return to the Edenic state. The Gothic wanderer, not content to live in a fallen world, attempts to revoke the fall by committing a transgression that is involved with the quest of knowledge. The Gothic wanderer believes that such an act will return him to his former innocence (Ellis, *Castle* 166). He or she attempts to justify the act, although the act is never legitimate but rather takes the form of a transgression against the laws of patriarchy, God, or Nature. Gothic wanderers are willing to commit any type of transgression to achieve the desired return to an Edenic state. Transgressions can encompass anything from breaking religious or cultural taboos, engaging in black magic, or simply disobeying a parent. Whatever form the transgression takes, it is always a metaphor for the original transgression committed by Adam and Eve in the Garden of Eden (Ellis, *Castle* 38; Graham, Introduction xiii). The Gothic wanderer usually fails in recreating Eden by a transgression, resulting in a similar displacement to that of Adam and Eve when they were forced to wander from Eden into an unfriendly world (Roberts, *Gothic* 137). Adam and Eve's displacement from the Garden of Eden was horrific for them, not only for their physical displacement, but more specifically because they had transgressed against God, their Father. Similarly, Satan's rebellion had been a rebellion against the father figure. The Gothic views both acts of transgression as resulting in the destruction of familial ties. Building upon *Paradise Lost*, the Gothic interpreted the French Revolution as a family story in which the French people had transgressed against their father, the French king. Meanwhile, the French viewed themselves as rejecting their bad parents, in the form of their king and queen, to create a government not focused upon patriarchal authority, but upon an autonomous brotherhood, composed of the monarch's children which encompassed all the French people (Hunt xiv). Gothic novels used *Paradise Lost* to create commentary upon the French Revolution's shared concern over the legitimacy of rebellion against patriarchy, and to explore how the family unit could be reinvented to preserve the family under a new, non-patriarchal form of government.

Primogeniture and Transgressions Against the Family

Gothic novelists reflected their concern with the family's importance by interpreting Satan and Eve's transgressions as being motivated by the primogeniture system's discrimination against them. Because the Gothic typically elevated bourgeois values over aristocratic ones as its response to the French Revolution's legitimacy, the Gothic was critical of primogeniture practice and its concern with heredity and inheritance. The Gothic defined primogeniture, the inheritance by the eldest male child, in a broader sense to refer to the injustice experienced by second born, female, or illegitimate children who were denied the privileges of their older and legitimate male sibling. Gothic novelists depicted the primogeniture system as frequently responsible for destroying the family unit because it could result in siblings turning against each other. Ironically, in Britain, the primogeniture system had originally been established to preserve the family and its estate; if the eldest male child inherited the complete estate, the estate could be preserved in its entirety for generations rather than continually being divided by each generation according to the number of children born. Even the eldest child was less the inheritor than the warden over the estate; in England, entails were usually placed upon an estate to prevent it from ever being sold or bankrupted by its current owner so it would be preserved for future generations. Furthermore, younger children were generally recompensed for not inheriting the family estate by monetary inheritances, lesser estates, or positions found for them in the church or military. Nevertheless, Gothic novelists felt the tradition of primogeniture and the accompanying laws of inheritance, legitimacy, and heredity were unfair and destructive to the family unit. Gothic novelists criticized the patriarchal emphasis upon first born, legitimate male children by creating Gothic wanderers who were often illegitimate, female, or second born children. These characters become Gothic wanderers because they feel like outcasts or orphans for being discriminated against by the patriarchal system and its elevation of primogeniture.

Gothic novelists drew upon *Paradise Lost*'s treatment of the primogeniture theme to expose the injustice of the aristocratic laws of inheritance. Satan uses the unfairness of primogeniture as his reason for rebelling against God, feeling that as God's son, Christ is unfairly favored over him (Gilbert and Gubar 202). God, however, states that Christ's position is due to his personal merit and not by favor or birthright:

> [Christ]...hast been found
> By Merit more than Birthright Son of God,
> Found worthiest to be so by being Good
> Far more than Great or High.... (III, 308-11)

Because God judges by merit over birth, Satan is not discriminated against by a form of primogeniture, yet he uses primogeniture as an excuse for his rebellion. After he is cast from Heaven, Satan again uses the law of primogeniture as an excuse to cause Adam and Eve's fall. Because he was born before Adam and Eve and he is an angel rather than a human, Satan believes he should not be forced to live in Hell while humanity dwells in an earthly paradise (Hughes 240). Satan jealously believes God is denying him his birthright by favoring humanity: "All hope excluded thus, behold instead / Of us out-cast, exil'd, his new delight, / Mankind created, and for him this World" (IV, 105-7). By causing humanity's fall, Satan achieves his revenge for not receiving the rewards he believes he merits. Satan acts as a hypocrite because he complains about primogeniture when it discriminates against him, yet he approves of it when it may favor him. Eve also feels the injustice of the primogeniture system because it makes her Adam's inferior. Although Adam and Eve are both God's children, Adam is favored because he is first born and male. Eve's transgression of eating the apple, therefore, is motivated by her desire to be Adam's equal.

The theme of primogeniture, influenced by *Paradise Lost*, would be second in Gothic novels only to that of transgression for the motivation behind Gothic plots. Ellis argues that the Gothic villain is usually a second son, who advantageously uses the unfairness of the primogeniture tradition as an excuse to transgress against patriarchy as Satan and Eve do in *Paradise Lost* (*Castle* 43). Primogeniture is a primary element in Gothic revisions of *Paradise Lost* because it motivates the usurpations that threaten legitimate inheritance, which was socially perceived as the foundation for family security (Ellis, *Castle* 57). Primogeniture becomes the motivation for a second born son hating his older brother, a replay of the Cain and Abel story, where Abel is the favored son (Ellis, *Castle* 44). Furthermore, the law of primogeniture demands legitimate births; consequently, many children are born out of wedlock in Gothic novels, resulting in their being disinherited, which motivates their wandering. Finally, women often inherit property in Gothic novels, suggestive of their right to equality with men. Of course, such inheritances can only occur if there are no legitimate male heirs. Even when women legally inherit property, they may be perceived as a threat to the patriarchal system. Furthermore, when a woman married, her inherited property would become her husband's possession. These examples display the Gothic's concern with the injustice of the primogeniture system and its ability to destroy the very family unit it was intended to preserve.

The Gothic's focus upon the family is an attempt to explore how the family unit may still be preserved by creating new social structures that reflect bourgeois values and reject old aristocratic laws of inheritance. The Gothic was celebrating bourgeois values and creating a myth about the bourgeoisie's origins and its value system which had helped it to gain social and financial power (Punter, *Terror* 127). The bourgeois family was often depicted as overthrowing patriarchal institutions of the monarchy, nobility, and the Catholic Church, reflecting the Gothic's support of revolution against patriarchy and any system that opposed the creation of a middle class and a democratic system of equality (Williams 22). The Gothic is both radical in its rejection of aristocratic and patriarchal values, yet it remains conservative by valuing the (bourgeois) family. Aristocratic and bourgeois families are typically at the center of Gothic novels as topics of debate, thus illustrating Ann Williams' astute observation that "Gothic plots are family plots; Gothic romance is family" (22-3).

Because the family is the principal point of organization in a Gothic novel, to understand a Gothic plot, one needs to understand the familial connections between all the main characters (Williams 45). It is not a coincidence then that characters in Gothic novels discover themselves related to all the other characters. In *The Monk*, Ambrosio discovers he has a sister, Antonia. *Wuthering Heights* centers around the intermarriages of the Earnshaw, Linton, and Heathcliff families, while in *Jane Eyre*, the heroine coincidentally finds herself related to the Rivers so the novel can bring about Jane's sudden rise in class status through the inheritance of her deceased uncle's fortune. The Gothic novel thrives upon having the family at its core because this core provides for the disclosure of family secrets and the unexpected fabulous inheritances which accelerate and often resolve the plots by rewarding the good characters and punishing the evil ones.

Vital to this interest in the family is the Gothic house or castle, which serves as the family's central symbol. Williams argues that the "House" in a Gothic novel refers not merely to the building but to the family itself (45). One might think of "The Fall of the House of Usher" as an example, for at the story's conclusion, the family and the house are simultaneously destroyed. Similarly, Dickens' Bleak House can refer to both the actual house and the Jarndyce family who live there, for the family's prolonged legal case has destroyed many of the family's lives, making their existence bleak indeed.

The wedding scene is also central to the Gothic's concern with the family because marriage is the ritual that creates the family order, linking one family to another to make possible the Gothic novel's complex family relationships. Williams argues that the Gothic relies upon these complex family relationships to make a "thematic assertion that human experience creates a web of intricate connections, partly known, partly hidden (though no less powerful)" (171). Ann Tracy, in her study of Gothic motifs, has shown that the number of weddings in Gothic novels outnumbers even the more familiar elements such as storms, fainting females, corpses, and confinement (Williams 68). Marriages connect all the main characters to create one large extended family. For example, in *The Mysteries of Udolpho*, the family relationships are extremely complex and confusing, yet necessary to the plot's resolution. Emily St. Aubert is, through her paternal aunt's husband, the Marquis de Villeroi, a distant relative to Count de Villefort, Lady Blanche's father. By her mother, Emily is related to the Quesnels who are themselves distant cousins to the villainous Montoni, a cousin to Laurentini/Sister Agnes. Laurentini sought to marry the Marquis de Villeroi but was rejected by him, making her revenge herself by killing Emily's aunt, the Marchioness. Although Montoni is a relative by marriage on Emily's mother's side, Montoni marries Emily's paternal aunt, creating multiple connections between characters on both sides of the St. Aubert family. These complex relationships create an extended family among all the characters, but more importantly, the family ties allow for the discovery of past family secrets which affect the hero or heroine, usually in the form of inheritances or creating/preventing incestuous relationships.

Any act that destroys the family unit is treated as a transgression in the Gothic novel. The Gothic borrowed the theme of incest from *Paradise Lost* as a severe example of transgression against the family. Several critics have noted that the Gothic's use of incest plots is derived from *Paradise*

Lost in the famous scene where Satan finds Hell's gate guarded by Sin and Death (Gilbert and Gubar 207, Williams 142). Satan does not recognize Sin as his daughter or even realize he has a child by her. Sin explains to Satan that she is his daughter, while Death is their mutual child, born of incest by Satan's sinful rebellion against God (II, 746-815). Gothic novelists were fascinated by this passage and especially that Satan does not recognize his own daughter or his child by her. Rape would be a typical attempt by a male Gothic wanderer to feel powerful, but the realization of the rape being an act of incest would then destroy that feeling of power. Incest is a frequent Gothic motif because it poses a severe threat to the family by confusing and corrupting the lines of inheritance and the legitimacy of children born from it (William Day 120). In the Gothic, incest frequently occurs within aristocratic families, further reflecting the bourgeoisie's rejection of the aristocracy as corrupt.

Paradise Lost's concern with primogeniture and family dynamics, therefore, was applicable to the Gothic novel's concern with how rebellion would affect the family. The Gothic viewed any act that threatens the family as an act of transgression. While these acts of transgression would take various forms, the issue of primogeniture was often a key motivator behind the act of transgression. Masculine and feminine Gothic novels used the primogeniture theme, originally borrowed from *Paradise Lost*, to create their own commentaries upon the legitimacy of rebellion against patriarchy, and whether rebellion was a form of transgression. The feminine Gothic would question what constitutes transgression by creating situations that are revisions of Eve's act of transgression. In turn, the masculine Gothic would reject the feminine Gothic's revision of *Paradise Lost* by retelling *Paradise Lost* from a more conservative perspective.

Feminine Gothic Revisions of *Paradise Lost*

The feminine Gothic tradition was primarily a rejection of *Paradise Lost* because Milton placed Eve in an inferior role to Adam. Milton's poem not only justified the ways of God to man, but it also justified the ways of man toward woman by promoting the belief that women were created to be subordinate to men. Eve is depicted as inferior to Adam because she is created from part of him, while Adam was individually created. Consequently, Eve is a lesser part of Adam and should serve him as would his arm or leg. When Raphael visits the Garden of Eden, he treats Eve as inferior by speaking only to Adam; Adam must later teach Raphael's instructions to Eve. Likewise, Satan recognizes Eve as the weaker and hence inferior of the couple; he chooses to tempt Eve rather than Adam because he finds Adam's intellect and strength intimidating, while Eve is "Not terrible," and therefore, the easier target (IX, 480-93). After the fall, Eve remains inferior, being forced to sleep while Michael privileges Adam with an explanation of God's plan for humanity's eventual salvation. Adam remains Eve's superior because he is later to explain to her God's plan (XI, 367-9).

Sandra Gilbert and Susan Gubar argue that it is Eve's role as inferior and even the "other" that is responsible for her decision to rebel against God by eating the apple (191). Eve admits that her unhappiness with her inferior role motivates her decision. She debates whether she should eat the apple and become Adam's equal, or whether she should share the apple with Adam.

> But to Adam in what sort
> Shall I appear? shall I to him make known
> As yet my change, and give him to partake
> Full happiness with mee, or rather not,
> But keep the odds of Knowledge in my power
> Without Copartner? so to add what wants
> In Female Sex, the more to draw his Love,
> And render me more equal, and perhaps,
> A thing not undesirable, sometime
> Superior: for inferior who is free? (IX, 816-25)

Eve selfishly seeks to keep her transgression a secret so she may become Adam's equal, fearing that if he eats the fruit, he will remain her superior. Yet her love for Adam makes her jealous and fearful that if God destroys her for her sin, Adam may remarry. She decides she would prefer that Adam and she both be dead rather than separated. Her inferiority makes Eve act selfishly, and consequently, Adam appears all the more heroic by his self-sacrifice when he eats the apple so he may remain with her. Nevertheless, the possibility remains that had God created Eve to be Adam's equal, she would not have acted selfishly and humanity would not have fallen.

Not only does Milton make Eve inferior to Adam, but of her two fellow females in the poem, Eve is linked to Sin rather than to Urania. Eve's connection to Sin primarily revolves around their mutual ability to produce children and to experience the pains of childbirth (Gilbert and Gubar 198). Eve was able to bear children prior to the Fall, but only after she sinned did God decree that childbirth would be painful for her; similarly, Sin experiences pain when her own child, Death, rapes her, and she gives birth to the hellhounds.

> Ingend'ring with me, of that rape begot
> These yelling Monsters that with ceaseless cry
> Surround me, as thou saw'st, hourly conceiv'd
> And hourly born, with sorrow infinite
> To me, for when they list, into the womb
> That bred them they return, and howl and gnaw
> My Bowels, their repast; then bursting forth

>   Afresh with conscious terrors vex me round,
>   That rest or intermission none I find. (II, 794-802)

God decrees that Eve will also have a painful childbirth: "By thy Conception; Children thou shalt bring / In sorrow forth, and to thy Husband's will / Thine shall submit, hee over thee shall rule" (X, 194-6). Eve's transgression has brought her only sorrow, while she retains her inferior position. While Sin has given birth to Death, Eve's transgression results in Death, for the human race will now be mortal rather than immortal. Finally, both Eve and Sin are compared to serpents. Sin is described as a "Snaky Sorceress" (II, 724) and Eve's tempting of Adam links her to Satan's disguise as the serpent that tempted her. Gilbert and Gubar suggest that these parallels between Satan, Sin, and Eve are intended to form an "unholy trinity" in *Paradise Lost* to rival the holy one Milton creates of God, Christ, and Adam (199).

Female Gothic novelists rebelled against these numerous depictions in *Paradise Lost* of women as sinful and inferior. In their Gothic novels, women rejected Milton's misogynistic attitude toward Eve by liberating her from having committed a transgression in seeking knowledge to better herself. Women novelists created female heroines who had their origins in Eve, and then they created male characters to represent the patriarchal oppression Eve experiences because God made her inferior. One of the key components, therefore, in the feminine Gothic's revision of the Fall is the validation of a female's rebellion against the patriarchal father by making the rebellion have beneficial results (*Castle* 57). Eve had intended to bring about good for herself in eating the apple—in the feminine Gothic novel, good is finally allowed to result from female transgressions against patriarchy. Female Gothic novelists, therefore, used their medium to illustrate how women could reject the myth of *Paradise Lost* to bring about "Paradise Regained" (Williams 146). The most important of the early feminine Gothic novels to rewrite the myth of *Paradise Lost* by vindicating Eve from transgression was Ann Radcliffe's *The Mysteries of Udolpho*. Radcliffe's revision of *Paradise Lost* would influence not only future female Gothic novelists, but it would provide a tradition for the masculine Gothic to react against.

The Mysteries of Udolpho: Eve's Vindication

In *The Mysteries of Udolpho* (1794), Ann Radcliffe created the first female Gothic wanderer. Emily St. Aubert is a revision of Eve, who is not a transgressor, although at times she fears she is. Emily journeys from her happy home of La Vallée, through both the rugged terrain of mountainous lands and the conflicts of the human heart, and finally returns to her childhood home to achieve the restoration of an Edenic past, which all Gothic wanderers seek but rarely achieve. Emily's wandering results in her regaining what she lost when her father died: the security of her identity and legitimate birth, her happy home, and her fiancé, Valancourt. Like Eve, Emily acts to gain knowledge in a manner that patriarchy would view as a transgression. Her father has ordered her, upon his death, to burn several papers without reading them, but Emily's curiosity makes her glance at the papers. Radcliffe's purpose is to show that what Emily learns from the papers, while making her feel guilty for violating her father's prohibition, ultimately results in Emily's benefit so she can eventually return home. Emily, therefore, is a revision of Eve because she benefits from the forbidden knowledge she acquires.

Emily's wanderings begin when her father dies and she is forced to leave her childhood home, La Vallée. Her separation from her home parallels Adam and Eve's separation from God and Eden when they and their descendants are forced to wander the earth until God allows humanity to enter Heaven. La Vallée is reminiscent of the Happy Valley in Dr. Johnson's *Rasselas* (Williams 166), both places being types of Eden where everyone should be content. Rasselas and his companions, however, feel they must have knowledge of the world before they can truly know happiness, for their innocent lives in the Happy Valley only bore them. Like Rasselas, Emily must leave her Happy Valley to experience the world's trials if she is fully to appreciate her happiness. William Day agrees that La Vallée is an Edenic place, but primarily because Emily's parents are less distinctly masculine and feminine than Adam and Eve. St. Aubert is whole because he has both a fatherly, masculine side as well as an appreciation for the more feminine domestic pleasures. This mixture is far different from male Gothic villains, such as the novel's Montoni, who have no real use for women except as sources for money, pleasure, and power (*Circles* 105-6). The Gothic male villain always lacks the feminine element; consequently, his overly masculine characteristics cause his downfall. Emily's quest is partly to find a man who shares the same qualities as her father—Emily loves Valancourt, but before she will marry him, he must prove he has both manly virtue and the good feminine qualities of Emily's father (William Day 106). Radcliffe depicts Valancourt and the villainous Montoni as extreme versions of the father figure who compete to replace the deceased St. Aubert in their relationships with Emily. Radcliffe also plays with gender role reversal, making Emily dominant in her and Valancourt's relationship. When Emily hears rumors about Valancourt's poor reputation, Valancourt is placed in a position usually attributed to a romance novel's heroine, where the woman must prove her virtue before the man she loves will accept her (William Day 107). By the novel's conclusion, Emily is definitely the couple's dominant member. When Emily is imprisoned in Udolpho, she expects Valancourt will rescue her. Instead, she rescues herself by using her common sense to escape at the right moment when the castle doors are accidentally left open. Furthermore, Emily is wealthy and owns property while Valancourt is a poor second son. By her wealth and her ability to protect herself,

Emily proves herself the stronger member of the couple, thus affronting Milton's depiction of women as the weak and inferior sex.

Not only does Emily physically rescue herself, but she also frees herself from her own irrational fears and superstitions. Williams declares that Emily is on a quest for Reason (165), and in addition, she is also on a quest for knowledge and self-identity. Shortly before her father's death, Emily sees St. Aubert weeping over a woman's picture, a woman Emily does not recognize; as a result, Emily undergoes an identity crisis by questioning if this woman is her true mother. She desires knowledge regarding the truth about her birth, but she is only further perplexed when on his deathbed, her father orders her to destroy certain papers without her reading them. Emily obeys, but while destroying them, she accidentally reads part of one of the papers. Although Radcliffe does not reveal what Emily has read, the information is enough to make Emily further concerned about her true parentage. The scene is vital to an understanding of Emily's role as a revision of Eve. Emily feels she has transgressed by reading the paper, and her father, symbolic of patriarchy, acts as a censor upon her mind. This pivotal moment, as described below, begins as Emily is about to destroy the papers.

> The solitary life, which Emily had led of late, and the melancholy subjects, on which she had suffered her thoughts to dwell, had rendered her at times sensible to the 'thick-coming fancies', of a mind greatly enervated. It was lamentable, that her excellent understanding should have yielded, even for a moment, to the reveries of superstition, or rather to those starts of imagination, which deceive the senses into what can be called nothing less than momentary madness. Instances of this temporary failure of mind had more than once occurred since her return home; particularly when, wandering through this lonely mansion in the evening twilight, she had been alarmed by appearances, which would have been unseen in her more cheerful days. To this infirm state of her nerves may be attributed what she imagined, when, her eyes glancing a second time on the arm-chair, which stood in an obscure part of the closet, the countenance of her dead father appeared there. Emily stood fixed for a moment to the floor, after which she left the closet. Her spirits, however, soon returned; she reproached herself with the weakness of thus suffering interruption in an act of serious importance, and again opened the door. By the directions which St. Aubert had given her, she readily found the board he had described in an opposite corner of the closet, near the window; she distinguished also the line he had mentioned, and, pressing it as he had bade her, it slid down, and disclosed the bundle of papers, together with some scattered ones, and the purse of louis. With a trembling hand

she removed them, replaced the board, paused a moment, and was rising from the floor, when, on looking up, there appeared to her alarmed fancy the same countenance in the chair. The illusion, another instance of the unhappy effect which solitude and grief had gradually produced upon her mind, subdued her spirits; she rushed forward into the chamber, and sunk almost senseless into a chair. Returning reason soon overcame the dreadful, but pitiable attack of imagination, and she turned to the papers, though still with so little recollection, that her eyes involuntarily settled on the writing of some loose sheets, which lay open; and she was unconscious, that she was transgressing her father's strict injunction, till a sentence of dreadful import awakened her attention and her memory together. She hastily put the papers from her; but the words, which had roused equally her curiosity and terror, she could not dismiss from her thoughts. So powerfully had they affected her, that she even could not resolve to destroy the papers immediately; and the more she dwelt on the circumstance, the more it inflamed her imagination. Urged by the most forcible, and apparently the most necessary, curiosity to enquire farther, concerning the terrible and mysterious subject, to which she had seen an allusion, she began to lament her promise to destroy the papers. For a moment, she even doubted, whether it could justly be obeyed, in contradiction to such reasons as there appeared to be for further information. But the delusion was momentary.

'I have given a solemn promise,' said she, 'to observe a solemn injunction, and it is not my business to argue, but to obey. Let me hasten to remove the temptation, that would destroy my innocence, and embitter my life with the consciousness of irremediable guilt, while I have strength to reject it.'

Thus re-animated with a sense of her duty, she completed the triumph of integrity over temptation, more forcible than any she had ever known, and consigned the papers to the flames. Her eyes watched them as they slowly consumed, she shuddered at the recollection of the sentence she had just seen, and at the certainty, that the only opportunity of explaining it was then passing away for ever. (102-4)

This passage is highly significant because it shows how truly curious Emily is to read the papers despite the censorship of her father upon her mind. Even the narrator's claim that Emily involuntarily looks on the sheets without realizing what she is reading suggests that Emily is subconsciously attempting to transgress and gain forbidden knowledge, despite her more conscious wish to obey her father's commands. Furthermore, Emily's reason for transgressing is similar to Eve's argument for eating the apple. Eve had believed that eating the apple would make her godlike, or at least Adam's equal. Emily subconsciously feels it could be beneficial for her to share her father's knowledge, making her commit an "involuntary" transgression. Once she has slightly transgressed, she feels "Urged by the most forcible, and apparently the most necessary, curiosity to enquire farther" (103). While her curiosity may be "forcible," more importantly, Emily feels it is "necessary." Why Emily feels this necessity is unexplained, partly because the reader is to be left in suspense, but also because Emily's own reasoning is somewhat irrational and she claims necessity when she is merely curious. Because of the earlier scene of St. Aubert weeping over the miniature, the reader assumes that the papers contain information about Emily's family and possibly her birth. Although Emily decides to keep her solemn promise to her father, she realizes she has already transgressed simply by reading one sentence of the papers. Radcliffe later displays that Emily has not transgressed because if Emily is to be secure about her birthright and retain faith in her parents' love, she needs the knowledge forbidden by her father (Ellis, *Castle* 114). Had Emily burned the papers and not read any of them, she would have remained curious all her life about the identity of the woman in the miniature. Instead, Emily has stirred her curiosity, and she remains curious throughout the novel until the moment when her curiosity may be satisfied. While Eve was punished for her transgression of seeking forbidden knowledge, Emily is rewarded by her discovery of family secrets when she inherits the Castle of Udolpho and she returns to La Vallée, a wiser and happier woman.

As several critics have pointed out, Emily's transgressions are against the patriarchal order (Miles 141). It is Emily's father who forbids her to read the papers she destroys. At other times, she disobeys the evil patriarchal figure, Montoni, by exploring parts of Udolpho which he has forbidden her to enter. Each time Emily transgresses in the novel, she faints as in the passage above. Robert Miles argues that Emily faints at these moments because St. Aubert is a censor in her mind (141). As the novel's primary patriarchal figure, St. Aubert becomes Emily's conscience in the same way God is a censor and conscience for the Christian. Emily's fear of transgressing her father's orders results in self-punishment when she falls into unconsciousness, yet never in the novel does her curiosity truly harm her. Curiosity is less Emily's vice than her inability to think and act logically. Instead, she often gives into her irrational fears and indulges in feelings of guilt. Had Emily been rational, she would have realized her father was not forbidding her knowledge so much as protecting her from it. Before his death, St. Aubert had warned Emily against allowing her imagination to be over-active.

> 'Above all, my dear Emily,' said he, 'do not indulge in the pride of fine feeling, the romantic error of amiable minds. Those, who really possess sensibility, ought early to be taught,

> that it is a dangerous quality, which is continually extracting the excess of misery, or delight, from every surrounding circumstance. And, since, in our passage through this world, painful circumstances occur more frequently than pleasing ones, and since our sense of evil is, I fear, more acute than our sense of good, we become the victims of our feelings, unless we can in some degree command them. (80)

St. Aubert warns Emily against being excessively fearful of possible evil, yet these fears are what she continually indulges in throughout the novel, allowing her reason to be victimized by her over-active imagination. At times even the reader must wonder how Emily's sensibility can make her act so irrationally. For example, when Emily is in Udolpho, she has no evidence to support her conviction that Valancourt is a prisoner in the castle. Similarly, Emily suspects supernatural causes for the music in the woods surrounding the Chateau-le-Blanc when she should seek a rational explanation for it. Had Emily not been so quick to jump to such a shockingly unhappy conclusion as her father's infidelity in marriage, but based her conclusions upon the love and affection she had always witnessed between her parents, she would not have brought about her own identity crisis. Then Emily could reasonably have read the papers and dealt with the information they contained, information that affects Emily far less terribly than she imagines. When at the novel's conclusion, Emily has learned to think rationally and benefitted from knowing her family's past, which her father had forbidden, Radcliffe makes it clear that knowledge does not cause suffering, but rather, it will add to one's understanding and ability to function in the world.

The knowledge Emily gains by the novel's conclusion makes her a strong and independent woman, the equal of a man, just as Eve had dreamt of being Adam's equal. To an extent, Emily even becomes superior to her lover Valancourt. Valancourt is a second son, so unlike Emily, he does not have property of his own. Emily is the one who provides the home for them, subverting the traditional image of the male as the breadwinner and head of the household. Emily thus vindicates Milton's Eve, making woman no longer man's inferior, but his superior.

The final knowledge Emily must gain is about marriage. Throughout the novel, Emily learns about marriage's extremes; she witnesses her parents' happiness, and she contrasts this with the mistreatment of her aunt by Montoni, and the knowledge of her other aunt, the Marchioness de Villeroi, who was poisoned by her husband. Both of Emily's aunts were ultimately murdered by their husbands to gain their wives' property. Emily fears Valancourt similarly only seeks to marry her for her property. Valancourt's position as second son enhances this fear because second sons were commonly believed to be predatory males who only married for wealth. The primogeniture system, therefore, has resulted in Valancourt and other second sons becoming discriminated against. Emily's concern over Valancourt's intentions are increased when she hears rumors of his gambling, his time in prison, and his living with another woman. Because Montoni engaged in these same immoral activities, Emily fears Valancourt is a second Montoni (Miles 147). Finally, Emily learns the truth about Valancourt's vices, realizing they were not as severe as rumored, and she also learns of his generous deeds, making her willing to excuse his behavior and to marry him when she sees that "his look, his voice, his manner, all spoke the noble sincerity which had formerly distinguished him" (669).

The Mysteries of Udolpho, therefore, is a feminine Gothic revision of *Paradise Lost* by vindicating Eve from wrongdoing in her desire for knowledge. Mrs. Radcliffe declares that women cannot remain innocent; they must have knowledge if they are to survive amid the evils of the world (Ellis, *Castle* xii-iii). Emily is able to pass from a stage of innocence to experience where she gains knowledge that allows her to reclaim her home and to create a new version of Eden. Radcliffe rejects the notion that Emily has transgressed by seeking knowledge, and she suggests that women must commit acts that patriarchal society views as transgressions if they are to better themselves and gain security rather than being the victims of men. Emily's aunts were murdered for their naivety about their husbands' true intentions, but Emily's curiosity and quest to understand the true nature of marriage and that of her potential husband results in her being able to achieve an Edenic state of marital happiness. Emily is equal if not superior to Valancourt because of her knowledge and she brings wealth to the marriage, making her financially independent.

Masculine Gothic Revisions of *Paradise Lost*

Mrs. Radcliffe is often considered the mother of the feminine Gothic novel, but she is also a source for the masculine Gothic because male writers created Gothic novels that responded to her own. Male Gothic novelists sought to create male rather than female Gothic wanderers and to depict these male wanderers as sympathetic rather than simply as the villains they tend to be in the feminine Gothic. Kate Ellis argues that the difference between the two branches of Gothic is that feminine Gothic depicts the heroine reclaiming territory that has been usurped by the villain (as Emily reclaims La Vallée, her aunt's property, and even the Castle of Udolpho, all of which Montoni has attempted to steal); in contrast, masculine Gothic depicts the male protagonist in exile from the domestic space that has become woman's domain (*Castle* xii-iii).

Ellis argues that the differences of feminine and masculine Gothic arose because of a change in gender roles among the bourgeois class at the close of the eighteenth century. Because bourgeois and upper class women had servants, they spent their leisure time entertaining themselves by reading, which increased the number of women writers and the need for literature appropriate to a female audience (*Castle* 15). At the same time, men were involved in business and increasingly worked outside the home, resulting in a woman becoming, if not in name then in fact, the head of the household. In *The Contested Castle,* Ellis interprets the Gothic as a means for writers to discuss the desire of the male, who feels alienated and displaced in his own home, to regain control of that home from female family members (xiv-v). The feminine Gothic treats the male desire for control of the home as an attempt to usurp power from women and to steal their property, as Montoni does in *The Mysteries of Udolpho.* Because the feminine Gothic depicted men as predatory, in revising *Paradise Lost,* an important component was a female character's subversive rebellion against the father and all men who represented patriarchy, and the validation of that rebellion by the female character benefitting from it (*Castle* 57).

The masculine Gothic reacted against this feminine Gothic treatment of men as villains who victimized women. Masculine Gothic, instead, depicts its male protagonists as victims of transgression, although that transgression was often committed by them and brought about their own downfall (William Day 18). William Day clarifies, however, that no strict distinction exists between masculine and feminine forms of the Gothic because the Gothic creates gender role reversals for both male and female characters. In the masculine Gothic, while men are usually hungry for godlike power, they also endure the same victimization that women suffer—bondage and placement in sadomasochistic roles, which are traditionally feminine because they are positions of inferiority (76). The feminine Gothic reverses gender roles by allowing women to be dominant over men, as Emily St. Aubert is the dominant spouse when she marries Valancourt. William Day concludes that both male and female Gothic characters are subject to fears that "unman" a person, making him or her vulnerable and submissive (76).

The masculine Gothic reacts to the feminine Gothic by equally drawing upon *Paradise Lost* to create Gothic wanderer figures. Margaret Anne Doody makes a compelling argument that the Gothic novel was the genre where men were first depicted as rounded individuals and real human beings rather than stereotypical heroes or villains ("Deserts" 572). The Gothic novel's achievement of rounded male characters is largely owing to *Paradise Lost* where Satan can simultaneously be a hero and a villain. Rather than be purely evil, Satan wars with his conscience, feeling guilt, yet trying to justify his rebellion against God. Although Satan shares some of the same aspects as Gothic villains like Montoni or *The Monk*'s Ambrosio, his character also evokes sympathy, which makes him the source for the male Gothic wanderer who is less truly a villain than a confused human being, striving to do good but blind to his own selfishness and other character flaws that bring about his and his loved ones' downfall.

Doody argues that it is these sympathetic, Satan-based, Gothic male characters who provide the transition between stereotypically rational, and hence often annoying, male characters like Samuel Richardson's Sir Charles Grandison and the more complex Victorian and non-Gothic male characters of Henry Esmond, Arthur Clennam, Pip, Paul Emmanuel, Lydgate, and Clym Yeobright ("Deserts" 572). To illustrate this transition that the masculine Gothic provides, Doody uses a scene in Samuel Richardson's *Sir Charles Grandison* (1753-4) that shows the assumed rationality of men as opposed to the more emotional, and consequently, irrational behavior of women. In the passage, Sir Charles comments upon a dream Harriet Byron has had:

> My Harriet has been telling me how much she suffered lately from a dream, which she permitted to give strength and terror to her apprehensions from Mr. Greville. Guard, my dear Ladies, against these imbecillities of tender minds. In these instances, if no other, will you give a Superiority to our Sex. (qtd. in Doody, "Deserts" 529)

What a contrast between Sir Charles Grandison's implication that men do not have nightmares and the nightmarish visions Jonathan Harker experiences when he is imprisoned in Dracula's castle, visions which he can scarcely distinguish between being real or merely dreams!

Doody further argues that the Victorian novel is indebted to its Gothic predecessors because it allowed men to be depicted as "wanderers through a strange and puzzling world, men who feel guilt without being villainous, men who know weakness, self-division, terror and failure" ("Deserts" 572). Doody continues:

> Men could not be fully present in the novel until they could be shown as self-divided, wary, torn by their own unconscious and divided motives, even weak, erring and guilty—and shown thus without being exhibited as villains or failures. It was the Gothic novel, in all its implication, that saved men from being seen as the sex without a full consciousness. The Gothic novel gave them the freedom to have—and to live in—nightmares. ("Deserts" 572)

To Doody's list of fully rounded male Victorian characters, I would add more borderline Victorian Gothic characters, who are less villains than confused or haunted men for whom the reader feels sympathy and even an attraction toward. Such characters who owe a debt to their earlier Gothic predecessors include Diogenes Teufelsdrockh, Glyndon, Little Nell's grandfather, Dr. Manette, Sidney Carton, Rochester, Heathcliff, Jonathan Harker, and even Dracula. Several of these characters will be explored in later chapters on the Victorian treatment of the Gothic wanderer figure.

For these male Victorian Gothic characters, the nightmare they are locked inside is no longer a castle or prison, but it is a haunting from within (Ellis, *Castle* 166). Even a character like Dr. Manette is not merely haunted by his imprisonment in the Bastille, but his mind remains haunted for years after his body is freed. Similarly, although Jonathan Harker escapes from Dracula's castle, he remains mentally tormented by the experience. Other Victorian Gothic characters are never imprisoned yet still suffer. Little Nell's grandfather is pursued and haunted by Quilp, but his conscience is what truly torments him. Not surprisingly, it is always after the grandfather gambles that Quilp appears in the novel, acting as a symbolic censor upon his mind (Cordery 50). Like their earlier Gothic predecessors, these Victorian male Gothic wanderers equally owe a debt to Milton's Satan. Satan is the first wanderer for whom Hell is within him because of his tormented conscience. Milton describes Satan's internal conflict as:

> Horror and doubt distract
> His troubl'd thoughts, and from the bottom stir
> The Hell within him, for within him Hell
> He brings, and round about him, nor from Hell
> One step no more than from himself can fly
> By change of place: Now conscience wakes despair
> That slumber'd, wakes the bitter memory
> Of what he was, what is, and what must be
> Worse; of worse deeds worse sufferings must ensue. (IV, 18-26)

Satan is trapped within his evil nature; he regrets his past deeds, and he is torn by a desire to reform and the knowledge that instead he will continue to commit evil because his nature is continually descending into an internal and eternal Hell. Satan passes his tormented conscience onto his Gothic successors who in turn influence Victorian male characters, allowing them to be rounded and sympathetic characters because they have guilty consciences.

The masculine Gothic's reaction to the feminine Gothic also draws upon *Paradise Lost* in its treatment of women and the conflicting feelings men have toward them. A pure Gothic villain, a man without a conscience such as Montoni, has no concern for women save how he may use them to his advantage. A male Gothic wanderer, by contrast, has a conscience which makes him concerned about his treatment of women. The male Gothic wanderer attempts to reconcile his masculine desire for godlike power with his more feminine conscience. This internal conflict results in male Gothic wanderers desiring female companionship to soften their states as outcasts, yet they remain aloof from a desire to enter into marriage. Consequently, male Gothic wanderers are selfish in their treatment of women, yet their awareness of their selfishness causes them torment. This distinction between marriage and the male Gothic wanderer's desire for female companionship is best understood by the Gothic's adaptation of *Paradise Lost*.

Adam is crucial as a representative of the male desire for marriage as opposed to mere female companionship. When he is first created, Adam is lonely and longs for a companion, remarking, "In solitude? What happiness, who can enjoy alone, / Or all enjoying, what contentment find?" (VIII, 364-6). In response, God creates Eve to be Adam's wife. While sleeping, Adam first envisions what Eve will look like and he feels things "unfelt before, / And into all things from her Air inspir'd / The spirit of love and amorous delight" (VIII, 475-7); later when Adam first sees Eve, he knows she is informed "Of nuptial Sanctity and marriage Rites" (VIII, 487). From the beginning, therefore, Adam is interested in having a wife. His love for Eve is so great that he chooses to sin because he feels he could not bear their separation.

> How can I live without thee, how forgo
> Thy sweet Converse and Love so dearly join'd,
> To live again in these wild Woods forlorn?
> Should God create another Eve, and I
> Another Rib afford, yet loss of thee
> Would never from my heart; no no, I feel
> The Link of Nature draw me: Flesh of Flesh,
> Bone of my Bone thou art, and from thy State
> Mine never shall be parted, bliss or woe. (IX, 908-16)

The distinction between Adam's desire for marriage and a male desire for mere female companionship is quickly revealed after he eats the apple. Suddenly, Adam no longer speaks words of love and affection, but merely desires Eve to satisfy his lusts.

> Carnal desire inflaming, hee on Eve
> Began to cast lascivious Eyes, she him
> As wantonly repaid; in Lust they burn:
> Till Adam thus 'gan Eve to dalliance move. (IX, 1013-6)

Married bliss has been transformed into Lust. For the male Gothic wanderer, female companionship is desirable so he may satisfy his lusts without a commitment toward the woman's happiness. Male Gothic wanderers also seek female companionship out of loneliness because of their exiled state, rather than from a desire for marital love. Numerous masculine Gothic novels contain such relationships including Matthew Lewis' *The Monk* (1796), William Godwin's *St. Leon* (1799), Mary Shelley's *Frankenstein* (1818) and Charles Maturin's *Melmoth the Wanderer* (1820).

The masculine Gothic, therefore, serves as a response to the feminine Gothic and its depiction of male characters. Masculine Gothic equally is interested in the exploration of what is a transgression and what are the consequences of transgression. Unlike feminine Gothic, masculine Gothic treats the search for forbidden knowledge as transgressive and punishable, but while it punishes its transgressive characters, it sympathizes with their desire for forbidden knowledge. A brief exploration of *The Monk* and *Melmoth the Wanderer* will illustrate how the masculine Gothic differs in its treatment of transgression and how it draws upon *Paradise Lost* for its own creation of Gothic wanderer figures.

The Monk: Condemning the Transgressor

Matthew Lewis' *The Monk* (1796) was partially written as a response to Radcliffe's *The Mysteries of Udolpho*. Most critics emphasize that Lewis reacted to Radcliffe's explanation of the supernatural in a rational manner by causing the supernatural to be part of reality in *The Monk*. More importantly, Lewis engaged with Radcliffe in the debate over what was a transgression. *The Monk* creates in its main character, Ambrosio, a male Gothic wanderer who is punished for his transgressions. The novel also creates two female Gothic wanderers, the Bleeding Nun and Matilda, who are also punished for their transgressions. While these female characters commit much more serious transgressions—murder and necromancy—than Emily St. Aubert's desire for forbidden knowledge, nevertheless, they reflect Lewis' belief that transgression should be punished and that transgressing to gain forbidden knowledge cannot be justified. Before turning to Ambrosio as a reaction to the feminine Gothic's treatment of male characters, I will briefly explore Lewis' treatment of these female transgressors.

The Bleeding Nun is a threat to the patriarchal system, specifically the Catholic Church and the patriarchal family. Her transgression against the Catholic Church occurs when she breaks her religious vows to take a male lover (Williams 119). Later, she murders her lover's older brother, so he can inherit the family estate and title. Her lover is then so repulsed by her criminal behavior that he murders her. The Bleeding Nun's transgression against the patriarchal family, therefore, is twofold. First, she has threatened the lines of inheritance by murdering the rightful heir. Second, by taking a lover outside of marriage, she has presented the possibility of illegitimate children, which would corrupt the family's legitimate lines of inheritance. These forms of transgression are further intertwined because the Catholic Church is itself a type of patriarchal family; the clergy is organized along familial lines by containing fathers, mothers, sisters, and brothers, with the priests being the family's fatherly heads (Williams 46). The Bleeding Nun acquires Gothic wanderer status because her transgressions result in her spirit being unable to rest. For a hundred years, her ghost appears and haunts her family. When she haunts her relative, Raymond, he has an exorcism performed and he lays her bones to rest in the family vault, thus reconciling the Bleeding Nun with her patriarchal family (Williams 119). Lewis' other main female Gothic wanderer,

Matilda, engages in necromancy and fornication outside of marriage. Her transgressions are so great that at the novel's conclusion, she is revealed actually to be Satan. This link between Satan and a female Gothic wanderer enforces *Paradise Lost*'s link between Satan and Eve, thus retaining in *The Monk* the idea that women are sinful and transgressors.

Despite these negative portrayals of women as transgressors, Lewis also understands that patriarchal society is often responsible for women being forced to transgress. The Bleeding Nun was forced by her parents to enter the convent when "she was too young to regret the pleasures, of which her profession deprived her" (173). Consequently, she is restricted by her patriarchal society from making her own choices. A similar situation exists with Agnes and Raymond. Raymond encounters the Bleeding Nun when he is attempting to elope with Agnes, whose family will not allow her to marry him. The Bleeding Nun's situation, therefore, becomes a parallel to that of Agnes, especially since Agnes' attempt to elope with Raymond fails and she is forced into a convent. Raymond gains access to Agnes in the convent, resulting in Agnes becoming pregnant. Her child's death at birth may be interpreted as Agnes' punishment for transgressing. Yet, at the novel's end, Raymond and Agnes are able to marry, reflecting that Lewis did understand how women were mistreated by patriarchal society, although he is ambiguous about whether patriarchal oppression is an excuse for female transgression.

Ambrosio, the novel's main character, is the first male Gothic wanderer who is both a villain and yet retains some of the reader's sympathy. Like the novel's female characters, Ambrosio's transgressions arise from the restrictions imposed upon him by his patriarchal society. Lewis depicts Ambrosio as a victim of his environment, yet Ambrosio's ultimate punishment nevertheless reflects that people have free will and are responsible for their own transgressions. At the novel's opening, Ambrosio is a victim of the primogeniture system, although he is ignorant of his victimhood because he does not know the truth of his birth or family background. Ambrosio's mother, Elvira, was the daughter of a shoemaker, but she caught the eye of a young nobleman, who married her in secret. After she gave birth to Ambrosio, her father-in-law, a marquis, learned of the marriage and attempted to have Elvira sent away, but instead, she and her husband fled to the Indies. In their hurry to be gone, they left their son, Ambrosio, behind them. The marquis spread rumors that the child had died, then left Ambrosio on the steps of a convent where he was adopted and raised as a monk (Lewis 13). Although Ambrosio is a first born child and legitimate, because of the deemed importance of hereditary lines, his mother was considered unworthy to marry into a noble family and produce the family's heir; therefore, both she and Ambrosio are victims of (or transgressors against) the primogeniture system. Had it not been for the primogeniture system's snobbery, Ambrosio could have remained with his family, and consequently, he may not have gone astray as a result of being raised in the convent's unnatural setting. Lewis, therefore, acknowledges that society victimizes people, yet he is ambiguous about whether transgressions are permissible because of one's deprival by his or her social environment (Ellis, *Castle* 145). Ambrosio's transgressions are ultimately punished, so Lewis would seem to be advocating that despite one's situation, a person's free will makes one responsible for his or her choices between right and wrong. Because Ambrosio chooses to transgress, he is punished.

As a transgressor, Ambrosio encompasses all the masculine Gothic elements of the male Gothic wanderer. Ambrosio is not a physical wanderer, but his soul wanders from God, making him a literary descendant of Milton's Satan. Typical of male Gothic wanderers, Ambrosio overreaches in his desire for godlike power. Like Milton's Satan, Ambrosio's transgressions arise from his selfish individual will (Howard Anderson xvi). His sexual desires are not connected to a desire for marital love, but from a selfish lust that he satisfies with Matilda. Ambrosio desires power, and sex makes him feel powerful because he can dominate a woman. Ultimately, Ambrosio's desire for power is a desire for autonomy so he need no longer fear the consequences of sin, just as Satan wishes to be all powerful, first by being exalted over Christ in Heaven's hierarchy, and later by setting up a kingdom of Hell to rival Heaven. Ellis links *The Monk* to *Paradise Lost* because after Ambrosio's fall into sin, he wants "to eat again of the tree of knowledge to fall back into the state of innocence" (*Castle* 148), the innocence being his life before he met Matilda and indulged in lust. Ellis argues that it is not the fall itself which prevents Ambrosio from achieving paradise, but how he reacts after his fall (*Castle* 148). Rather than regretting his behavior and reconciling himself to God by rejecting further sin, Ambrosio continues to transgress, and then to commit one transgression to hide another, as when he murders Elvira so she cannot expose his sexual designs upon Antonia.

While Ambrosio's sexual relationship with Matilda is based on the typical desire by a male Gothic wanderer to satisfy his lusts in female companionship, Ambrosio's attraction to Antonia arises from a desire more closely aligned to the desire for marital love. Ambrosio feels Antonia will somehow complete him, making him experience again the wholeness of character he had known before he fell into sin. Ambrosio is unaware that the attraction he feels for Antonia originates from her being his sister. As his sister, Antonia is Ambrosio's double who will complement his overly masculine side with her femininity, thus achieving wholeness and stability for his character (William Day 122). Ambrosio has been formerly thwarted from achieving such wholeness because his religious vocation prevents him from marriage. He now attempts to achieve such wholeness by an aggressive rape of Antonia. Rape, ironically, is an over-extertion of masculinity, so it cannot make him whole by reconciling his masculinity with femininity. First, it makes him completely masculine during the act, but later results in his feminine side becoming dominant (William Day 123). Following the rape, Ambrosio realizes his failure to achieve wholeness:

> Scarcely had He succeeded in his design, than He shuddered at himself and the means by which it was effected. The very excess of his former eagerness to possess Antonia now contributed to inspire him with disgust; and a secret impulse made him feel, how base and unmanly was the crime which He had just committed. (384)

Ambrosio's transgression results in his degrading his masculinity to unmanliness, the same situation that occurs for Adam in *Paradise Lost*; God tells Adam that by obeying Eve in sinning, "Thou didst resign thy Manhood" (X, 148). Ambrosio soon feels even more unmanly and disgusted when he learns that he has raped his own sister and killed his mother. In disgust at his sins, Ambrosio believes God will never forgive him; his greatest sin becomes then, not rape or murder, but like Marlowe's Dr. Faustus, his unwillingness to believe in God's mercy and forgiveness. To protect himself from eternal damnation, Ambrosio commits another sin to cover the previous ones when he swears eternal allegiance to Satan, seeing this form of damnation as the only means to his salvation (William Day 124). Of course, Ambrosio is relying upon Satan's trustworthiness, which is never reliable, so ultimately, Ambrosio is destroyed and loses his soul.

The Monk responds, therefore, to *The Mysteries of Udolpho* by questioning what types of forbidden knowledge are permissible. Emily St. Aubert is benefitted by her curiosity to learn the truth about her family background. In contrast, Ambrosio's desire for carnal knowledge is based upon a selfishness that only inflicts pain upon himself and others. Ambrosio is potentially sympathetic because he is the victim of a transgression committed by a patriarchal society that denies him his birthright; nevertheless, Ambrosio is punished for committing transgressions by his own free will.

Melmoth the Wanderer: A Sympathetic Transgressor

Charles Maturin's *Melmoth the Wanderer* (1820) is a masculine Gothic novel that also relies upon *Paradise Lost* for the creation of its male Gothic wanderer. The novel's title character is also a transgressor, yet he becomes more sympathetic than *The Monk*'s Ambrosio. Melmoth declares his affinity to both Satan and Adam when he states "mine was the great angelic sin—pride and intellectual glorying! It was the first mortal sin—a boundless aspiration after forbidden knowledge" (499). Because of his sins, Melmoth has achieved a cursed prolonged lifespan, and he must wander the earth with a guilty conscience until he can find someone to take his place, or until an appointed day when God will send him to eternal damnation. Melmoth continually fails to find someone to take his place, and his loneliness only increases as a result. Melmoth then decides to find a female companion to ease his personal alienation; this desire results in his seduction of Immalee. Melmoth acts like Satan in trying to tempt Immalee into sin when he explains religion to her, just as Satan lied to Eve about God's reason for forbidding her to eat from the fruit of the Tree of Knowledge. Immalee is herself a type of Eve because she is completely innocent; she has grown up isolated upon an island, which has left her ignorant of humanity and its crimes. While Melmoth is a type of Satan, to Immalee he is more like Raphael because he explains God's ways to her. Immalee, therefore, is a privileged Eve because in *Paradise Lost*, Eve was not allowed to hear Raphael's words (Baldick, *Melmoth* xvi).

Melmoth's guilty conscience and his dual role as Raphael and Satan, which suggests the synthesis of good and evil in his nature, make him a sympathetic male Gothic wanderer. While Melmoth selfishly desires female companionship from Immalee, he feels the guilt of knowing their union would mean the loss of her soul. Finally, he is overcome by selfishness and agrees to marry her, although he also warns her of the risk she is taking. Melmoth is depicted as torn by his conscience when he agrees to marry her: "[Melmoth] cursed himself; and then, with the selfishness of hopeless misery, he felt that the curse might, by dividing it, be diminished" (353). Immalee urges Melmoth to marry her before her parents force her into another marriage. Melmoth finally agrees, but he demands that the ceremony be performed in secret. Melmoth then takes Immalee to a gloomy place of evil power, where Immalee "felt that the hand that united them, and clasped their palms within his own, was as cold as that of death" (394). Melmoth thought he could lessen his punishment if Immalee shared it with him, but he has only made his punishment worse because of the guilt he feels in causing her damnation. Because Melmoth insists that the marriage be kept secret, Immalee's parents still try to force her to marry another man. Melmoth attempts to rescue Immalee from this second marriage, but in the attempt, he slays Immalee's brother and is recognized by people as the legendary cursed Melmoth. He then flees, leaving Immalee to be taken prisoner by the Inquisition for her sinful marriage to Melmoth. While in prison, Immalee gives birth to a child, but both the child and Immalee then die. Melmoth's selfishness has only resulted in two deaths and the increase of his guilt and despair.

Maturin created Melmoth as an example of the punishment that results when people give into temptation. Melmoth's numerous transgressions are enacted because he fears isolation from humanity, but by transgressing, he only brings such a situation upon himself (Roberts, *Gothic* 144). Maturin believed no rational man would risk his soul by succumbing to such temptations, as he states in the novel's preface, where he quotes from one of his own sermons:

> 'At this moment is there one of us present, however we may have departed from the Lord, disobeyed his will, and disregarded his word—is there one of us who would, at this moment, accept all that man could bestow, or earth afford, to resign the hope of his salvation?—No, there is not one—not such a fool on earth, were the enemy of mankind to traverse it with the offer!' (5)

Maturin creates Melmoth the Wanderer as a warning against committing a transgression that could endanger one's soul. Maturin uses the novel to revise *Paradise Lost*, with Melmoth as a version of Satan, so a modern audience would view Christianity in a new context that would make its old truths striking and memorable.

Like Matthew Lewis, Maturin does not approve of transgressions, but he also understands how patriarchal institutions are themselves transgressive in their treatment of people and their destruction of the family. Ellis argues that Maturin blames institutions more than individuals because institutions fail to judge people individually or to make exceptions for moral gray areas (*Castle* 176). In agreement with Ellis, Baldick argues that *Melmoth the Wanderer* depicts how it is not the devil but man and his creations of poverty and inherited property that are people's worst enemies (*Melmoth* xviii). Maturin creates such social criticism in the novel's other male Gothic wanderer, Alonzo, whose story is similar to that of Lewis' Ambrosio. Alonzo is born illegitimate, so his parents consider him a child of sin. Although his parents marry after his birth, his illegitimacy results in his being disinherited in favor of his younger brother, Juan, who was born in wedlock. Alonzo's mother, a revision of Eve, seeks to return to the state of innocence she knew before engaging in pre-marital sex. She attempts to wash away her sins by dedicating Alonzo to God and placing him in the convent to be raised (*Castle* 174). The actions of Alonzo's mother show that she is a victim of the patriarchal Church which acts as a censor upon her mind. Alonzo, like Ambrosio, is raised in a monastery but rather than resort to criminal deeds, he becomes the victim of them.

After years of seclusion in the monastery, Alonzo meets his brother Juan and they form an instant friendship. Juan feels the primogeniture system has unfairly granted him the birthright that belongs to Alonzo. Learning of his brother's unhappiness in the convent, Juan attempts to help his brother escape, but the escape is foiled and Juan is murdered in the process. Primogeniture has thereby destroyed both the legitimate and illegitimate child. Later, when Alonzo does escape, he cannot go to his parents for help because the Church has turned them against him; instead, he must wander about as a fugitive. The Church has assisted the patriarchal system's demand for legitimate children by making Alonzo's mother feel guilt over her illegitimate son. Now the Church and the patriarchal system force Alonzo to become a physical wanderer. Alonzo is himself aware that the Church turns several of the other monks into spiritual wanderers. Alonzo refers to one monk as a "wandering angel" (108) when the monk is savagely whipped for showing kindness to a disfavored monk (108). The monks are themselves part of the Church's own family structure with its hierarchy that works against the familial love and unity it should instead promote. Fortunately, Alonzo escapes from the monastery and Spain, thus freeing him from his wandering state.

Melmoth the Wanderer, therefore, uses *Paradise Lost* to create a transgressive title character as an example of how transgressors are punished. Nevertheless, it furthers the depiction of Gothic wanderers as sympathetic by creating rounded male characters. The novel also recognizes that social institutions can be transgressors as well as individuals. Patriarchal institutions such as the patriarchal family and religion can destroy the family unit by emphasizing hereditary lines and inheritances when love and familial bonds should instead be elevated.

Conclusion

Paradise Lost served as the source for the Gothic wanderer's creation, although the feminine and masculine Gothic traditions used Milton's epic in different manners to discuss what is a transgression, to what degrees transgressions were permissible, and whether a distinction could be drawn between rebellions against patriarchal institutions as permissible and rebellions against God as deserving of punishment.

The feminine Gothic revises *Paradise Lost* by exonerating Eve from blame for seeking knowledge forbidden by a patriarchal figure and showing how knowledge can only benefit a person. The masculine Gothic, in contrast, supports the prohibition against seeking forbidden knowledge by creating male Gothic wanderers who suffer similar fates to Milton's Satan by becoming outcasts. Nevertheless, while these male Gothic wanderers are punished for their transgressions, they are depicted in a sympathetic manner, resulting in their becoming the first rounded male characters in fiction. The masculine Gothic criticizes transgression, yet it rejects the notion that rebellion is itself a form of transgression. Masculine Gothic criticizes social institutions as themselves transgressive; therefore, rebellion against these transgressive institutions is justified.

Despite their differences, the masculine and feminine Gothic both believe in the preservation of the family, which they interpret as the central unit of society, and necessary for social order. This conservative stance by the Gothic is commented upon by Stephen King in his treatise on horror fiction, *Danse Macabre*: "The writer of horror fiction is neither more nor less than an agent of the status quo" (qtd. in Williams 172). King explains that we are fascinated by horror because "it is a reaffirmation of the order that we all crave as human beings....It is not the physical or mental aberration in itself which horrifies us, but rather the lack of order which these abberations seem to imply" (qtd. in Williams

172). The early Gothic novels, based in a reaction to the French Revolution, attempted to imagine ways to maintain social stability while reforming the injustices committed by social institutions. Ultimately, the Gothic novel created Gothic wanderers to express the value of the family as society's most important unit. The worst transgressions are those committed against the family, including the greater human family whose father is God. Those who transgress (be it against the family, humanity, or God) become outcasts—the ultimate punishment for the Gothic wanderer. The Gothic equates the family with a form of Eden, so the isolated Gothic wanderer views a return to the family as a means of salvation. The early Gothic, however, denies the Gothic wanderer a return to the family by depicting him as an irredeemable transgressor. Only during the Victorian age, as will later be discussed, would the Gothic wanderer achieve redemption.

Chapter III – The Wandering Jew

While *Paradise Lost* was the primary source for Gothic novelists in their creation of Gothic wanderer figures, two legends, those of the Wandering Jew and the Rosicrucians, were also significant as influences. The Wandering Jew only appears in one Gothic novel, Matthew Lewis' *The Monk*, but this brief appearance inspired numerous Romantic poems and Gothic novels where characters were created who were based upon the Jew. While Milton's characters were significant in the Gothic wanderer's creation because they explored the themes of transgression and the sanctity of the family, the Wandering Jew is most important for creating the wandering status of these Gothic outcasts. The Wandering Jew was also important in exploring a specific outcome of transgression— rebellion against God which results in a curse of prolonged life. My purpose is not to discuss the Wandering Jew as a legend or the meaning of that legend, but to explore how the Wandering Jew was adapted by Gothic novelists to explore transgression against God. A brief survey of the legend's origins is, however, necessary to understand the Wandering Jew's characteristics and how the Gothic novelists adapted these characteristics for their own purposes.

The Wandering Jew was originally a symbol of the Jewish people who were themselves wanderers and outcasts among the world's settled nations. In 70 A.D., the Jews rebelled against Rome, only to have their rebellion defeated. The Romans punished the Jews by dispersing them from their homeland and selling thousands of them into slavery. This dispersion resulted in the Jewish people migrating all over the known world and becoming residents in every European country. Because Christians blamed the Jews for the crucifixion of Christ, wherever the Jewish people settled, they were mistreated and often forbidden to reside in certain countries. Consequently, even when they settled somewhere, prejudice against them would frequently result in their migration elsewhere after a short time; the Jewish people were continually forced to wander about Europe seeking a place where they could live unmolested. During the Middle Ages, one of the harshest penalties frequently imposed upon the Jewish people was a prohibition against their owning property, which added to their wandering status and inability to remain in one place for extended periods. Because they needed a source of income that they could not achieve by living off the land, many Jews took advantage of

Christianity's prohibition to its followers of being usurers. The Jewish people filled the needed position of moneylenders, and they frequently became wealthy as a result. Consequently, the Jewish people had two primary stereotypes attached to them: they were wanderers, and they were greedy people who were constantly grasping for money.

Europeans who were jealous of the Jews' wealth spread fabulous derogatory tales about them: Jews possessed hidden and heavily guarded treasures; Jews possessed the evil eye by which they could curse and destroy people; Jews had horns or tails, and they emitted foul odors of brimstone and sulphur which suggested their alliance with Satan because they were responsible for Christ's crucifixion. Jews were even accused of draining blood from Christians to use for sorcery practices (Zatlin 135n). Particularly in times of social upheaval or economic crisis, such stories were circulated to encourage anti-Semitism and to validate removal of Jews by forced emigration or even extermination.

From all this anti-Semitism arose the medieval legend of the Wandering Jew. In most versions of the legend, the Wandering Jew was a shoemaker named Ahasuerus who refused to allow Christ to rest on His way to the cross. Christ punished Ahasuerus by forcing him to wander the earth without death or any form of rest until Christ's return on the final Judgment Day. Usually, this cursed condition is interpreted to mean that Christ will eventually redeem Ahasuerus who will have atoned for his sins by his prolonged wandering (Hurwitz 222, Tennyson 201). As he wanders the globe, the Wandering Jew remarkably appears without explanation at the sites of great historical events such as the sack of Rome, the crusades, and decisive Napoleonic battles; these appearances at great events suggest that the Jew may have supernatural powers that allow him to appear wherever he chooses (Tennyson 212). The Jew's constant wandering is enhanced by his fear that Christians will learn his true identity, so he must continually move from place to place so he is not identified and thus mistreated.

Because Christ is usually depicted as loving and forgiving, it is odd that a story would have circulated of his uttering such a terrible curse against the Wandering Jew for such a minor unkindness. Isaac-Edersheim offers the explanation that the Wandering Jew should not be understood as merely an individual sinner, but as a force in opposition to Christ, a type of superhuman figure who must be defeated (190, 198). While numerous psychological and historical explanations have been offered for the Wandering Jew legend, the Gothic novelists chose to represent him as a transgressor, and therefore, a force in opposition to Christ. The Wandering Jew is appealing to readers because everyone has a bit of wanderlust in him or her, and the Jew represented the common human fear of becoming an outcast (Isaac-Edersheim 197).

The Gothic uses wandering as a metaphor for guilt and despair, and the Wandering Jew became the perfect vehicle for depicting such emotions. The Wandering Jew feels great guilt over his transgression, a guilt that becomes nearly unbearable because of his extended life. The Wandering Jew frequently yearns to escape from his punishment by committing suicide, yet he is unable to accomplish such a deed because he cannot die until Christ's return: if the Jew tries to drown himself, the water pulls away, refusing him entrance; if he tries to jump into a volcano, he is spit out alive, and in battle, no man is able to harm him, so his prolonged life becomes only prolonged misery. Isaac-Edersheim remarks that the Jew's prolonged life symbolizes the human repressed desire not to die (196), but ultimately, this desire is rejected when life-extension is fully considered. Marie Roberts observes that the legend becomes a lesson upon man's moral responsibility to reconcile himself to death, for not only is death inevitable, but the reverse would be far worse (*Gothic* 208).

The Wandering Jew was only a minor figure in British literature before his adaptation by Gothic novelists. The first recorded reference in England of the Wandering Jew was in 1228 in the chronicle of the monastery of St. Alban's, entitled *Flowers of History* by Roger of Wendover (Roberts, *Gothic* 74). Among the other medieval depictions of him, the most notable appears in Geoffrey Chaucer's "Pardoner's Tale" where an old man must wander the earth until he can find someone willing to exchange youth for his old age. The Wandering Jew's popularity in literature increased during the seventeenth century. He is given the name of Ahasuerus in an anonymous German pamphlet of 1602 entitled *Kurtze Beschreibung und Erzehlung von einem juden mit Namen Ahasverus* (Roberts, *Gothic* 75); Ahasuerus would become the favored name for the Jew, although Matthew Paris also wrote a story in the seventeenth century, naming the Jew Cartaphilus (Tennyson 202). During the seventeenth century, the Wandering Jew also becomes credited with healing powers attributed to the Rosicrucians, as stated in Peck's *History of Stamford* and Aubrey's *Miscellanies* (Roberts, *Gothic* 74). Later, the legend of the Wandering Jew and the Rosicrucians would become blended together in Gothic literature. Other notable treatments of the Wandering Jew prior to the Gothic novel occur in late eighteenth century German literature. Goethe wrote a fragmented tale either simultaneously with or directly after his famous *The Sorrows of Young Werther* (1774), but it was not published until 1836 (George Anderson 168-73). Christian Schubart also wrote a fragment published in 1783 called *Der Ewige Jude* (Roberts, *Gothic* 78). Finally, Reichard's *Der Ewige Jude* (1785) ambitiously chronicled the Jew's entire wanderings throughout history (Roberts, *Gothic* 75). None of these early treatments, however, popularized the Jew or were of significant influence to the Gothic tradition. Matthew Lewis' *The Monk* (1796) is primarily responsible for the Wandering Jew becoming an important Gothic figure.

The Monk: Creation of the Gothic Wandering Jew

Matthew Lewis was the first and only Gothic novelist to use the Wandering Jew as an actual character in a Gothic novel. Lewis' portrayal of the Wandering Jew was so popular that it resulted in numerous adaptations where Gothic novelists created characters based on the Wandering Jew, as well as the Romantic poets making the Wandering Jew a frequent character in their poetry. While Lewis' depiction of the Wandering Jew owes a debt to Schubart's depiction, it is primarily his own imaginative version (George Anderson 177). Lewis was responsible for first depicting the Wandering Jew with a burning cross upon his forehead, a characteristic that later became a standard feature of the Jew's appearance (Andrews 85). While the link between the Wandering Jew and the biblical Cain may have already existed, Matthew Lewis popularized it by using the burning cross to recall the mark placed on Cain after he murdered his brother. A tradition existed that Cain's mark was shaped like a cross, so Lewis similarly chose to make the Jew's mark exist in the form of a cross to symbolize the Jew's rejection of Christianity (George Anderson 179). The Jew's link to Cain was relevant because Cain was already understood to be a wandering outcast while Abel was commonly interpreted as a character similar to Christ; Cain's murder of Abel was compatible with that of the Wandering Jew as an example of how the Jewish people were blamed for murdering Christ. Like the Wandering Jew, Cain is also traditionally a wanderer. Following his murder of Abel, Cain is told by God: "You shall become a restless wanderer on the earth." Cain fears the hatred of other men, however, so God declares that no one is allowed to kill Cain, and to prevent against accidents, "the Lord put a mark on Cain, lest anyone should kill him at sight" (Genesis 4:12-15). Similarly, the mark on the Wandering Jew's forehead is what reveals his identity to others.

In *The Monk*, the Wandering Jew only makes a brief appearance, but it is a stunning one. The Jew appears to exorcise the Bleeding Nun so she will no longer haunt Raymond. Raymond describes the Jew's appearance:

> He was a Man of majestic presence: His countenance was strongly marked and his eyes were large, black, and sparkling: Yet there was a something in his look, which the moment that I saw him, inspired me with a secret awe, not to say horror. He was drest plainly, his hair was unpowdered, and a band of black velvet which encircled his fore-head, spread over his features an additional gloom. His countenance wore the marks of profound melancholy; his step was slow, and his manner grave, stately, and solemn. (168)

Raymond does not recognize the Wandering Jew until the Jew describes his situation:

> "....Fate obliges me to be constantly in movement: I am not permitted to pass more than a fortnight in the same place. I have no Friend in the world, and from the restlessness of my destiny I never can acquire one. Fain would I lay down my miserable life, for I envy those who enjoy the quiet of the Grave: But Death eludes me, and flies from my embrace. In vain do I throw myself in the way of danger. I plunge into the Ocean; The Waves throw me back with abhorrence upon the shore: I rush into fire; The flames recoil at my approach: I oppose myself to the fury of Banditti; Their swords become blunted, and break against my breast: The hungry Tiger shudders at my approach, and the Alligator flies from a Monster more horrible than itself. God has set his seal upon me, and all his Creatures respect this fatal mark!"
>
> He put his hand to the velvet, which was bound round his fore-head. There was in his eyes an expression of fury, despair, and malevolence, that struck horror to my very soul. An involuntary convulsion made me shudder. The Stranger perceived it.
>
> "Such is the curse imposed on me," he continued: "I am doomed to inspire all who look on me with terror and detestation. You already feel the influence of the charm, and with every succeeding moment will feel it more. I will not add to your sufferings by my presence...." (169-70)

The mark on the Wandering Jew's forehead is so frightening that he refuses to reveal it to Raymond. Later, however, the Wandering Jew demands of the Bleeding Nun how her soul may find peace. When she is reluctant to tell, he reveals to her the burning cross upon his forehead, which compels her to answer. During this scene, Raymond had been instructed not to look on the cross, but now he cannot resist:

> He [the Wandering Jew] spoke in a commanding tone, and drew the sable band from his fore-head. In spite of his injunctions to the contrary, Curiosity would not suffer me to keep my eyes off his face: I raised them, and beheld a burning Cross impressed upon his brow. For the horror with which this object inspired me I cannot account, but I never felt its equal! My senses left me for some moments; A mysterious dread overcame my courage, and had not the Exorciser caught my hand, I should have fallen out of the Circle.
>
> When I recovered myself, I perceived that the burning Cross had produced an effect no less violent upon the Spectre. Her countenance expressed reverence, and horror, and her visionary limbs were shaken by fear. (172)

The Bleeding Nun's fear forces her to reveal her history of murder and that she will not rest until her bones are reburied at her ancestral castle. She has haunted Raymond because he is a relative whose duty it is to provide her with a proper burial. While the Wandering Jew is heroic because he provides a way for the Bleeding Nun to rest, he remains unable to achieve a similar rest for himself. Upon bidding Raymond farewell, he remarks, "Youth, farewell! May the Ghost of your Relation enjoy that rest in the Tomb, which the Almighty's vengeance has denied to me for ever!" (176).

William Day remarks that this scene between the Wandering Jew and the Bleeding Nun is created merely for its sensational effect, rather than to show any serious encounter between the spiritual worlds of good and evil or those of the supernatural and the physical (38). Nevertheless, the enormous popularity of this scene influenced the creation of numerous Romantic poems that found an element of spiritual truth in Lewis' creation. The Wandering Jew's kindness, despite his cruel fate, evokes the reader's sympathy. While the Jew has committed a transgression, his centuries of eternal wandering seem an intense punishment for denying Christ rest, especially when compared to the Bleeding Nun's much shorter punishment for her more severe crime of murder. Yet the scene must be read metaphorically, with the understanding that the Jew's crime serves as a symbol for the entire Jewish race's rejection of Christ as Son of God, whereas the Bleeding Nun's crime is an individual murder of a sole human being. Christianity states that the only way to salvation is to believe that Christ is the Son of God, so while even murder can be forgiven, denial of Christ is an unpardonable sin. Lewis' depiction of the Wandering Jew, however, grants the Jew the reader's sympathy. The scene was so popular that it inspired numerous contemporary plays and ballets (George Anderson 180) as well as influencing Gothic novels and Romantic poetry. Lewis' successors would build upon the psychological implications of a character like the Wandering Jew who is a sympathetic transgressor and who feels remorse for his crime to create some of the greatest Gothic wanderers in literature.

"The Rime of the Ancient Mariner": Adapting the Wandering Jew

The first major literary work influenced by Lewis' depiction of the Wandering Jew was Samuel Taylor Coleridge's Ancient Mariner. Coleridge stated that he found himself offended by *The Monk* despite the "happy conception" of the burning cross on the Wandering Jew's forehead (Williams 115). Nevertheless, Coleridge considered writing a poem about the Wandering Jew, and in the end, borrowed from Lewis' Wandering Jew and the legend itself to create his own wanderer character in "The Rime of the Ancient Mariner" (1798) (George Anderson 181). Like the Wandering Jew, the Ancient Mariner is forced to wander the earth, unable to rest, except momentarily after he has told his horrible tale. Coleridge also elaborated upon Lewis' depiction of the Wandering Jew's eyes. Lewis had described the Jew's eyes as large, sparkling, and capable of creating both awe and horror in the one they gaze upon. The Ancient Mariner's eyes are hypnotic or mesmeric, controlling the Wedding Guest so he is unable to move away from the Mariner until he has heard his tale (Abrams, *Norton* 336). The Wedding Guest describes the Mariner's eyes as "glittering" (3, 13), and he is so frightened he asks the Mariner, "Why look'st thou so?" (80) and he admits to the Mariner, "I fear thee and thy glittering eye" (228).

Coleridge's depiction of glittering eyes would become a more popular element than the Wandering Jew's mark of the cross in the creation of future Gothic wanderers. Hypnotic eyes are attributed to such diverse characters as later depictions of the Wandering Jew, Melmoth the Wanderer, Dracula, Svengali, and Matthew Arnold's Scholar-Gipsy, all of whom have mesmeric powers. While the hypnotic eyes serve somewhat different purposes, they all allow for control over others, usually by forcing a hypnotized person to carry out the hypnotizer or mesmerist's demands. Continually, characters feel possessed or controlled by the mesmerist, as if they no longer possess their own bodies. In Edward Bulwer-Lytton's "The Haunted and the Haunters" (1857), a character with mesmeric powers hypnotizes the narrator and forces him to utter what was in his mind. Consequently, mesmerism may be equated with mind-reading and unlocking the secrets of the soul. In H. Rider Haggard's *Benita* (1906), the evil Jew, Jacob Meyer, wishes to mesmerize the title character. Benita, in response, fears that "If once I allowed his mind to master my mind, although I hate him so much, I might become his slave" (292). While mesmerism in such cases may allow control over the body, it also allows control over the soul and may result in that soul being lost or damned. The Ancient Mariner's eyes give him the power to change the Wedding Guest's soul by making him "A sadder and a wiser man" (624). Other Gothic wanderers use their hypnotic eyes for more evil purposes. A Gothic wanderer who has the power to make others lose their souls is symbolic of the wanderer's role as an outcast of God, and the fear that one can be damned by association with such an outcast.

While numerous Romantic poems depict the Wandering Jew or characters based upon him, "The Rime of the Ancient Mariner" was the only Romantic poem to make a significant addition to the Jew's depiction that would influence later creations of wanderer characters. George Anderson rightly remarks that references to the Wandering Jew in Romantic poetry are so common that it is pointless to collect them all because they only show the story's popularity while not always adding to or changing the Jew's characteristics (181). The Gothic novel made more significant innovations than Romantic poetry in creating Gothic wanderer figures based upon the Wandering Jew legend. Two of the best examples of characters based on the Wandering Jew in Gothic novels are William Godwin's *St. Leon* and Charles Maturin's *Melmoth the Wanderer*. An exploration of these two novels will provide a basis for understanding depictions of Wandering Jew based characters in later nineteenth century Gothic novels.

St. Leon: A Wandering Jew with Rosicrucian Secrets

William Godwin's *St. Leon* (1799) is the first novel to use elements of the Wandering Jew legend in the creation of a main character who is a Gothic wanderer. Prior to *St. Leon*, however, William Godwin had played with the possibility of the Wandering Jew theme in his first novel *Caleb Williams* (1794) to emphasize the title character's position as an outcast. Interestingly, this novel appeared before *The Monk*, showing the popularity of the legend in England even before Lewis elaborated upon it. In the novel, when Caleb is fleeing from his pious Christian employer, Mr. Falkland, he disguises himself by wearing a Jew's clothes and by studying Jewish mannerisms so his disguise will be convincing (Vol.3, Chapter 8). Caleb considers himself an outcast, declaring "I was a solitary being, cut off from the expectation of sympathy, kindness, and the good will of mankind" (287), and he questions whether he should allow his life to continue "Accursed world! dead to every manly sympathy; with eyes of horn and hearts of steel! Why do I consent to live any longer? Why do I seek to drag on an existence, which, if protracted, must be protracted amidst the lairs of these human tigers?" (292). Interestingly, when Caleb does disguise himself as a Jew, he does so partly to quit wandering and to settle in one place, a state opposite to that of the Wandering Jew. While disguised as a Jew, Caleb engages in literary work, an idea that may have influenced Maturin because one of the Jewish characters in *Melmoth the Wanderer* is a writer. His use of the Jewish disguise in *Caleb Williams* may have remained in Godwin's brain when five years later he wrote *St. Leon*.

William Godwin's second novel borrows from the Wandering Jew legend by depicting its main character as a wanderer. *St. Leon* is set in the sixteenth century to provide for such historical "horrors" as the Spanish Inquisition and the economic troubles and wars of sixteenth century Hungary. The title character is a Gothic wanderer primarily because he learns the Rosicrucian secrets of the philosopher's stone and the elixir of life. Because the philosopher's stone allows St. Leon to acquire tremendous wealth, people suspect him of engaging in sorcery and he is reported to the Catholic Church. Eventually, St. Leon is taken prisoner by the Spanish Inquisition for committing crimes against the natural order decreed by God. Although St. Leon escapes from the Inquisition, he must become a wanderer to avoid people who suspect him of possessing supernatural knowledge, or who may recognize him and again report him to the Inquisition. St. Leon finds partial protection in his travels because the elixir of life allows him to become youthful whenever he chooses, thus at times making him unrecognizable.

Although George Anderson is correct in stating that *St. Leon* is less influenced by the Wandering Jew legend than the Rosicrucian one (180-1), Godwin definitely had the Wandering Jew in mind while creating the story. The Rosicrucians, as a religious occult group, were not specifically associated with the state of wandering. Consequently, Godwin's use of Rosicrucianism would be responsible for the Rosicrucian and Wandering Jew legends becoming intertwined and often almost indiscernible in Gothic novels when depicting the Gothic wanderer. Godwin uses Rosicrucianism so St. Leon can achieve the supernaturally extended life of the Wandering Jew by finding the elixir of life. St. Leon's occult knowledge forces him to flee from Christians who consider him a sorcerer just as the Wandering Jew must flee from fear of mistreatment by Christians.

Even before St. Leon discovers the Rosicrucian secrets, he considers himself a wanderer. In his youth, he loses his parents, thereby becoming an orphan without any known relationship to the rest of humanity. After he marries and has children, St. Leon continues to feel disconnected from humanity. His sense of isolation increases when his gambling addiction separates him from his family. St. Leon feels that gambling made him "a solitary wanderer on the face of the earth" (68), and he even feels he is "destined by nature to wander" (80). He wishes his family would reproach him for his gambling that has impoverished them, and he comments of his wife, "It would have become her better, I thought, like me, to have cursed her fate, and the author of that fate" (82). St. Leon curses himself, feeling he deserves a fate of eternal wandering because he has destroyed his family. Later, after St. Leon learns the secrets of the philosopher's stone and the elixir of life, he compares himself to the biblical Melchizedek: "A man who, like Melchisedec, is 'without end of life,' may well consider himself as being also, like him, 'without father, without mother, and without descent.'" (165). St. Leon is referring to a passage in Hebrews 7:1-3 where St. Paul describes Melchizedek:

> This Melchizedek, king of Salem and priest of the Most High God, met Abraham returning from his defeat of the kings and blessed him. And Abraham apportioned to him one tenth of all his booty. His name means "king of justice"; he was also king of Salem, that is, "king of peace." Without father, mother or ancestry, without beginning of days or end of life, like the Son of God he remains a priest forever.

St. Leon feels a connection to Melchizedek because of his own life extension and lack of family, but he overlooks the connection St. Paul draws between Melchizedek and Christ, suggesting that St. Leon can learn from his situation and benefit others by his experiences. By the novel's end, however, he will make this realization and become a benefactor. The connection to Melchizedek also connects St. Leon to the Wandering Jew, for while Melchizedek was not himself a Jew, he became an important figure in Jewish tradition.

The most significant connection to the Wandering Jew in the novel is St. Leon's meeting with a Jew. The scene occurs when St. Leon escapes from the Spanish Inquisition and seeks shelter by bursting into a home and threatening the inhabitants if they do not hide him. The home belongs to a Jewish man, Mordecai, who agrees to hide St. Leon. St. Leon soon realizes how fortunate he is to have sought shelter with the old man, not only because Mordecai is frail and dares not disobey him, but because as a Jew, Mordecai sympathizes with St. Leon as a mutual victim of religious persecution. Mordecai and his people have been forced to convert half-heartedly to Christianity by the Spanish Inquisition (342). St. Leon explains to Mordecai that he is fleeing from the Inquisition, although he does not reveal that he possesses the Rosicrucian secrets lest Mordecai will frown upon him as a sorcerer. Mordecai willingly hides St. Leon, explaining to him:

> Stranger, you little know by how strong a motive you have now engaged me to your cause. We poor Jews, hunted on the face of the earth, the abhorrence and execration of mankind, have nothing but family affections to support us under our multiplied disgraces; and family affections are entwined with our existence, the fondest and best loved part of ourselves. (345)

This speech notes the similar outcast state of St. Leon and Mordecai, but it also marks a difference between them. The family Mordecai refers to is his young daughter who lives with him. Mordecai is not without family while St. Leon has now lost his wife and he has abandoned his children so they will not share in his persecution. Mordecai, although Jewish, is less a Wandering Jew figure than St. Leon because he has a family. The scene emphasizes, therefore, the Gothic concern with transgressions against the family. While the Catholic Church is persecuting the Jews, it has not succeeded in destroying their families. St. Leon's gambling, however, has isolated him from his wife and children. While this scene is relatively short, Godwin's depiction of a kind and loving Jewish family is surprisingly open-minded for his period when compared to other anti-Semitic depictions in the works of his contemporaries. The scene inspired a similar scene in *Melmoth the Wanderer* where a main character meets a Jew, but unfortunately, this scene is extremely anti-Semitic.

Melmoth the Wanderer and Anti-Semitism

Charles Maturin's *Melmoth the Wanderer* (1820) also draws upon the figure of the Wandering Jew to create its title Gothic wanderer character. Like Ahasuerus, Melmoth is cursed by God to wander the earth with a protracted lifespan. The novel takes place in the year 1816, but Melmoth has lived since before 1646, the year his portrait was painted (18). Melmoth will not have as prolonged a life as the Wandering Jew, however, because he has a specific time allotment in which to find someone who will take his place before his soul completely belongs to Satan. Nevertheless, the length of Melmoth's extended life is sufficient for him to regret his sin and feel the full effect of the curse. The reason for Melmoth's punishment is ambiguously stated by him as, "mine was the great angelic sin—pride and intellectual glorying! It was the first mortal sin—a boundless aspiration after forbidden knowledge" (499). Notably, pride was also the sin of Milton's Satan.

Melmoth is further linked to the Wandering Jew by having a powerful glance, as did Coleridge's Ancient Mariner. Melmoth's eyes are so frightening that when his relative, John Melmoth, looks at the family portrait of Melmoth the Wanderer, he thinks he sees the eyes of the portrait move (19). Another example of Melmoth's powerful gaze occurs when Melmoth haunts the character, Stanton, whom he warns "the glance of these eyes shall be reflected from every object, animate or inanimate, till you behold them again" (44). Stanton is so disturbed by the continual sight of Melmoth's eyes that he ends up in an insane asylum. Melmoth, therefore, can use his gaze to control a person's mind or even to destroy it. Stanton's fear of the eyes results in his insanity, just as the Wedding Guest fears the Mariner's eyes because they affect his emotions and his soul. Melmoth may have similar powers over people's souls as suggested by his Satanic nature, reflected in his eyes' "fiend-like brilliancy" (54).

At the novel's conclusion, Melmoth's prolonged life appears to end. No one witnesses Melmoth's death and there is no final body, suggestive that like the Wandering Jew who cannot die, Melmoth yet lives on. Melmoth's final fate is rather like that of Marlowe's Dr. Faustus because the demons come to him while he is alone in a room (George Anderson 189-90). While Faustus is carried off to Hell, however, the demons apparently take Melmoth from the room to toss him over a cliff. His garment is later found hanging off the cliff, but Melmoth's body is never found. This unknown fate reflects Melmoth's sources in the Wandering Jew legend since the Wandering Jew's existence is mysterious, although he is almost never allowed to rest from his wanderings. Melmoth may not have died, for Maturin intended a never written sequel in which Melmoth would return. Balzac did write a sequel, *Melmoth Reconciled* (1835), in which Melmoth is able to find someone to take his place and thereby rest from his wanderings. This short sequel is lacking in Gothic atmosphere and effectiveness, but Balzac does retain the concentration upon Melmoth's eyes which create a "piercing glance that read men's inmost thoughts" (283). The French work is also progressive compared to British Gothic in that it allows the Gothic wanderer to rest, which would be denied to Gothic wanderers in British fiction until the Victorian period.

Maturin's most interesting use of the Wandering Jew legend, however, may not be in the character of Melmoth but in Maturin's treatment of Jewish characters in a scene inspired by the encounter with Jewish characters in *St. Leon*. In *Melmoth the Wanderer*, Alonzo Moncada escapes from the Spanish Inquisition's prisons, where he was being punished for his refusal to obey his parents and become a monk. Like St. Leon, Alonzo breaks into the home of a Jew who has recently converted to Catholicism to prevent his execution by the Inquisition. When Alonzo first enters the house, he finds himself in an empty room. The first item he sees is a mysterious book whose writing he cannot understand. Alonzo first thinks it is a book of sorcery, but he later learns it is a Hebrew Bible. Alonzo then hides behind a curtain when an old man and his son enter the room. The father informs his son that although he has always pretended to be a Catholic, he is really a Jew. The time has come for the son to know his true heritage and decide whether like his father, he will secretly practice the Jewish religion, or he will betray his father to the Inquisition. Before the boy can answer, Alonzo takes advantage of the situation by rushing from behind the curtain and threatening to reveal the Jew's secret unless the Jew shelters him (248). In fear for his life, the Jew, named Solomon, willingly hides Alonzo in his home. While St. Leon and Mordecai had sympathized with each other because of their mutual position as outcasts persecuted by the Inquisition, Alonzo is disgusted with Solomon for being a Jew and trying to convert his son to Judaism.

> He was a Jew innate, an impostor,—a wretch, who, drawing sustenance from the bosom of our holy mother the church, had turned her nutriment to poison, and attempted to infuse that poison into the lips of his son. I was but a fugitive from the Inquisition,—a prisoner, who had a kind of instinctive and very venial dislike to giving the Inquisitors the trouble of lighting the faggots for me, which would be much better employed in consuming the adherent to the law of Moses. (249)

Alonzo is not thankful to Solomon for sheltering him; he merely sees the situation as a contract that mutually protects them. Furthermore, he feels jealousy toward the Jew whom he believes is far more deserving of punishment than himself. The scene may not reflect Maturin's own feelings, of course, but depict Alonzo's own overly pious adherence to Catholicism despite his persecution by those of his own religion. As a Protestant minister, Maturin was probably as disgusted with Catholicism as Judaism.

When the Inquisition suspects that Alonzo is hiding in Solomon's house, Solomon helps Alonzo escape by a secret underground passage. Here Alonzo finds himself in a subterranean maze that leads him to a large apartment filled with extraordinary furniture, maps and globes, anatomical instruments, four human skeletons, other giant bones and stuffed animals, a few books and scrolls, and even an electrifying machine (262-3). Alonzo here encounters an old Jewish man, Adonijah, who explains that Solomon had promised to bring Alonzo to him to work as a scribe until it was safe for Alonzo to leave the city. Adonijah further explains that all the Jews in Madrid have their homes connected by subterranean passages so they can visit each other without arousing the Inquisition's suspicions; Solomon had intended for Alonzo to escape through these tunnels, but the Inquisitors appeared before he could tell Alonzo about them. Alonzo is frightened by Adonijah's curious appearance, although Adonijah explains that he does not have the supernatural powers often falsely attributed to Jews. Adonijah does, however, have an extended life. He tells Alonzo he has lived in this underground apartment for over sixty years, and he is one hundred and seven years old (265-7).

Adonijah's protracted life and Jewish identity make him the Wandering Jew's literary descendant. Furthermore, Adonijah is a typical Gothic wanderer because he has been punished for seeking forbidden knowledge. He explains to Alonzo that he sought knowledge of the legendary Melmoth who was damned for seeking forbidden knowledge:

> In the days of my childhood, a rumour reached mine ears, even mine, of a being sent abroad on the earth to tempt Jew and Nazarene, and even the disciples of Mohammed....I listened to the tale, and mine ears received it, even as the soul of the thirsty drinketh in rivers of water, for my mind was full of vain fantasies of the Gentile fables, and I longed, in the perverseness of my spirit, to see, yea, and to consort with, yea, and to deal with, the evil one in his strength. Like our fathers in the wilderness, I despised angel's food, and lusted after forbidden meats, even the meats of the Egyptian sorcerers. And my presumption was rebuked as thou seest:—childless, wifeless, friendless, at the last period of an existence prolonged beyond the bounds of nature, am I now left, and, save thee alone, without one to record its events....I took in my hand the pen of a scribe, and vowed by a vow, that this lamp should not expire, nor this seat be forsaken, nor this vault untenanted, until that the record is written in a book, and sealed as with the king's signet. (269-70)

Roberts points out that Adonijah's quest for forbidden knowledge has been punished by an extended life that can only end when he has completed transcribing the manuscripts that bear Melmoth's story (*Gothic* 135). It should be noted, however, that Adonijah inflicts this punishment upon himself, for he is the one who makes the vow. Adonijah feels his work is more of a duty than a punishment, for he will produce the book that will warn the world about Melmoth. Because Adonijah has an extended life like Melmoth and he attempts to subvert Melmoth's power, he serves as a type of supernatural double of Melmoth. His life is perversely intertwined with that of Melmoth, for his existence is dependent upon recording Melmoth's existence, thus reflecting the relation and interdependence of good and evil.

Like Melmoth, Adonijah is equally tired of his extended life, and he fears he will never be allowed to die because his task is so overwhelming. He has prayed that God would send him one of the infidel Christians to assist him in his task, and he believes Alonzo is the answer to that prayer (271). Adonijah now orders Alonzo to transcribe the manuscripts for him. Alonzo fears he may lose his soul by reading and recording the tales of a being so horrible as Melmoth, but once he fixes his eyes on the manuscript, he is unable to remove them until his work is completed. This control over Alonzo's eyes by Melmoth's tale recalls the Wedding Guest's inability to move until he has heard the Ancient Mariner's story. The rest of the novel is almost completely Alonzo's reciting to John Melmoth of the tales he has read about Melmoth the Wanderer.

Maturin disappoints the reader by never stating what became of Adonijah after Alonzo finished transcribing the stories. Before Alonzo finishes reciting the many tales, Melmoth suddenly appears, leading to the novel's tragic conclusion. The novel's hasty resolution makes the reader feel cheated by the lack of a long deserved denouement that fills in the gaps of Melmoth, Alonzo, and Adonijah's stories. Maturin may have felt his novel was long enough at this point, or he may not have known how to explain Alonzo's departure from the subterranean passage. Perhaps Maturin even intended that his sequel would complete Alonzo's story and describe what became of Adonijah, besides explaining what became of Melmoth after the devils carried him over the cliff. Because of the novel's ambiguous ending, like the Wandering Jew, the characters have no true sense of closure to their lives but continue to wander in our memories as stories not quite completed. We can at least assume that Alonzo did finish transcribing the manuscripts and so Adonijah was finally allowed his rest. If Adonijah is allowed to die, he becomes a subversive version of the Wandering Jew who is forbidden to rest until Christ's return.

The Wandering Jew would make many more appearances in nineteenth century literature, although these appearances are neither Gothic nor significant in their additions to his depiction. Most of the later works that feature the Wandering Jew are historical treatments like George Croly's *Salathiel* (1828) or Lew Wallace's *The Prince of India* (1893). Other novels would contain anti-Semitic treatments of Jewish characters such as

Svengali in George DuMaurier's *Trilby* (1894) who retains the Wandering Jew's hypnotic powers, but he is not supernatural like his literary predecessor. The Gothic would borrow the Wandering Jew's attributes of wandering, an extended life, and hypnotic eyes for other Gothic wanderer characters such as Rosicrucians and vampires to continue the discussion of what is a transgression and whether transgression can lead to the reestablishment of Eden upon earth.

Chapter IV – The Rosicrucian Gothic Wanderer

The Rosicrucian novel, as a Gothic subgenre, attempts to rewrite *Paradise Lost* by using elements from the Rosicrucian legend, and it often combines these elements with the legends of the Wandering Jew and the vampire. While the Wandering Jew is a fictional character, the Rosicrucians' origins are a strange mix of history and myth. Rosicrucian societies still exist today, although their origins are shrouded in mystery, and it is questionable how much the present day societies are based upon their historical predecessors. The Gothic depicted the Rosicrucians as transgressive Gothic wanderers because they possessed secret knowledge that the Gothic interpreted as meaning they had achieved forbidden knowledge. The primary aspects of Rosicrucianism that were important to Gothic novelists were the attributed possession by the Rosicrucians of the philosopher's stone that could transform lead into gold, and the knowledge of the elixir of life by which they could perpetuate their youthful appearance and extend their lifespans. This second gift was especially conducive to Gothic treatment since it resembled the extended life suffered by the Wandering Jew. The Rosicrucian legend was transformed by Gothic novelists to create Gothic wanderers who seek the forbidden knowledge of the elixir of life and the philosopher's stone. By possessing these secrets, Rosicrucian Gothic wanderers believe they can reestablish a paradise upon earth in which they can be autonomous from God. The result of this transgression is the discovery that the very implements they thought would be a blessing to them, only increase their misery. A brief overview of the Rosicrucians' allegedly historical origins will help us to understand how the Gothic adapted the Rosicrucian as a figure of transgression.

The Rosicrucians' Origins

The Rosicrucians' history is very complex and their origins difficult to pinpoint because they may not be historically true but the result of a fantastic hoax. The Rosicrucian Brotherhood's intense secrecy has only increased speculation as to its fictitious origins. The Rosicrucians' existence was first proclaimed to the world in two manifestoes published in 1614-1615 entitled *Fama Fraternitas* and *Confessio Fraternitas*. The society's symbols were the Rose and the Cross, which were combined to form the Rosicrucian name, as well as the name of the Brotherhood's alleged founder, Christian Rosencreutz. From their beginnings, the Rosicrucians have claimed to be a Christian sect, as reflected in their founder's first name and the Rose and Cross both being familiar Christian symbols. The manifestoes proclaimed that the Rosicrucian Brotherhood's purpose was to revitalize Christianity by making apparent the compatibility of science, philosophy, and religion as explained in the *Book of Nature*, which their founder Rosencreutz had compiled (Findlay 138). The manifestoes also supplied the history of Rosencreutz and his founding of the Brotherhood.

Christian Rosencreutz was allegedly born to a noble family in 1378. He entered the monastery at age five. When an adult, he went on a pilgrimage to the Holy Land, and while he was in Damascus, he met a wise man who said he had expected him. This prophetic beginning made Rosencreutz yearn for knowledge. After mastering Arabic, he translated into Latin the mysterious *Book M*, which was said to contain the universe's secrets. Rosencreutz was also led to study the Cabala and other occult sciences. Eventually, he attempted to proclaim his knowledge to the learned of Europe, with the hope of benefitting humanity, but his efforts were only ridiculed. In response, Rosencreutz formed his own secret society which would strive for human betterment by compiling all knowledge into *The Book of Nature* so it would be available when the world was ready for such knowledge. Until that time, the knowledge would be kept secret, so the eight founding members wrote in a coded language of their own creation to protect their knowledge from acquirement by non-members (Roberts, *Gothic* 3). The society was to remain a secret one hundred years after Rosencreutz's death before professing their knowledge to the world. In 1604, Rosencreutz's disciples opened his tomb and then began preparing to announce his secrets, which were declared a decade later in the manifestoes (Roberts, *Gothic* 4).

Although the Gothic novelists would depict Rosicrucianism as a movement in opposition to God and Christianity, the second manifesto, *Confessio Fraternitas*, actually declared that only by knowing God and receiving His approval could the secrets of nature be unlocked. The Rosicrucian Brotherhood stated that they had not sought these secrets for their own selfish gain but to benefit humanity. The manifesto even attempted to dissociate the group from those who sought the philosopher's stone and the elixir of life, which the Rosicrucians viewed as selfish quests by people whom God had not deemed worthy to receive such knowledge. Furthermore, one could only come into contact with a member of the Rosicrucian Brotherhood if he were chosen by God (Roberts, *Gothic* 7). Despite this proclaimed devotion to Christianity, the Rosicrucians were condemned for indulging in the occult, and shortly after the manifestoes' appearance, the Brotherhood was accused of blasphemous crimes (Roberts, *Gothic* 9-10). In 1623, an anonymous pamphlet claimed the Rosicrucians had signed a pact of blood with a necromancer named

Raspuch, while the demon Astaroth witnessed the event. In exchange for selling their souls, the pamphlet alleged that the Rosicrucians were granted the gifts of invisibility, dematerialization, and the ability to speak fluently in every language, which would allow them to spread their secrets to all races (Roberts, *Gothic* 10).

In contrast to these fantastic accusations of transgression against God's natural laws, the Rosicrucians actually intended to benefit people, primarily by using their knowledge to redeem humanity from death. The Rosicrucians believed they could achieve human immortality by freeing the world of disease (Roberts, *Gothic* 10). Mankind would even be able to overcome bodily exhaustion so sleep would no longer be necessary (Roberts, *Gothic* 29). The body would be immune to all that prevented it from immortality, save death brought on by physical accidents. The manifestoes proclaimed that humanity could achieve all this if it were reconciled with Nature (Roberts, *Gothic* 12).

Christianity condemned the Rosicrucians for their desire to be immortal because earthly immortality was a blasphemy that denied Christ's redemption of humanity as the only means to salvation. To achieve immortal life on earth would be a defiance of God because it would reverse God's decree that humans must die as punishment for the transgression committed in Eden, and it would allow people to be autonomous rather than dependent upon God's plan for human salvation (Roberts, *Gothic* 137). Because of these condemnations, a Lutheran theology student, Johann Valentin Andreae (1586-1654), admitted to writing the manifestoes as a joke (Findlay 138-9). Scholars have noted that Andreae may have been inspired with the idea of the Rosicrucian brotherhood because his family insignia was a rose and cross (Roberts, *Gothic* 2-3). The veracity of Andreae's confession, however, is equally questionable. He may have felt forced to lie by confessing because of the severe disapproval exhibited by the religious authorities toward the Rosicrucian Brotherhood (Findlay 138-9).

Whether Andreae did fabricate the Rosicrucian Brotherhood, his confession could not hinder the society's popularity. Within a short time, Rosicrucian societies were formed as well as other secret societies based upon ideas similar to Rosicrucianism. Among these societies was the Invisible College, a scientific association that sought the secrets of the philosopher's stone and the elixir of life. The Invisible College would eventually become the basis for the Royal Society, which would reject the quest for occult secrets in favor of more rational scientific pursuits (Roberts, *Gothic* 5). Despite the manifestoes' rejections of the quest for the elixir of life and the philosopher's stone, these items became associated with the Rosicrucians, especially in Gothic literature.

The Rosicrucian Brotherhood's popularity resulted in the Gothic novelists finding Rosicrucianism an easily adaptable subject for their treatment of the quest for forbidden knowledge. Ignoring the supposed

Christian origins of the Rosicrucian Brotherhood, the Gothic depicted Rosicrucians as transgressors who sought autonomy from God by questing for forbidden knowledge. The quest for immortality was especially popular because of its timing in regard to the French Revolution. Paul Lewis Landsberg argues that the consciousness of death is deeply felt during historical periods of social chaos (Roberts, *Gothic* 21). The Reign of Terror and the Napoleonic Wars resulted in a high mortality rate that may have made people long for certainty that their own lives would continue. The Rosicrucian quest for extended life reflected this desire. Ironically, Rosicrucian characters are committing a transgression in seeking forbidden knowledge, so the quest can only result in tragedy. Consequently, Rosicrucian novels are typically tragic masculine Gothics that follow the pattern of the failed quest. In such works, the protagonist crosses the threshold into forbidden knowledge, but he seeks this knowledge for the wrong reasons; therefore, when forbidden knowledge is acquired, it becomes meaningless upon the hero's return to the ordinary world (DeLamotte 54).

Upon return to the ordinary world, the Rosicrucian discovers his forbidden knowledge is useless because it has alienated him from humanity and typical human concerns in life. This alienation transforms the life the Rosicrucian sought to extend into a type of "living death" in which life becomes purposeless and thereby tedious (Roberts, *Gothic* 126). The Rosicrucian repeats the Fall because like Eve, he sought forbidden knowledge to better himself, but when that forbidden knowledge is achieved, he is punished for possessing it (Roberts, *Gothic* 12). His alienation from humanity is the punishment for his transgression. Alienation results from the Rosicrucian's extended life and limitless wealth, separating him from the human concerns of survival by working and avoiding danger. Furthermore, extended life results in boredom because life's multitude of possibilities becomes exhausted. Finally, extended life results in all relationships with others becoming meaningless because all others will die while the Rosicrucian Gothic wanderer will live on, suffering grief and loneliness from the loss of his loved ones (Roberts, *Gothic* 12). The Gothic novelists attempted to analyze the miseries of such an extended life as punishment for transgressing against God.

In the remainder of this chapter, the reader must remember the distinction between Rosicrucianism and the Gothic novel's depiction of the Rosicrucian wanderer, which does not always comply with the Rosicrucian tenets, but is rather subjected to the Gothic novelists' personal agendas. The Rosicrucian novel does not provide an accurate depiction of Rosicrucianism, but only how Gothic novelists imagined Rosicrucians as transgressors against God and the family. As Roberts comments "The Rosicrucian novel of the nineteenth century was a faint echo of the reform movement heralded by the Brotherhood of the Rosy Cross" (*Gothic* 212). The Gothic Rosicrucian novels were not intended to create accurate depictions of the Rosicrucians or to enlighten humanity about the Brotherhood. Rather, the novels use the Rosicrucian as a literary tool for creating revisions of *Paradise Lost* that dealt with the question of humanity's right to forbidden knowledge.

Unlike the Romantic poets, the Gothic novelists are conservative in their treatment of *Paradise Lost* so the Rosicrucian wanderer as a satanic figure of transgression is not intended to be admirable. Like Satan, the Rosicrucian wanderers are selfish, often to the point where they are blind to their own selfishness in their pretense that they seek to benefit others. Eventually, the selfish desire for forbidden knowledge results in the Rosicrucian wanderer's regret that he received the immortality he sought. Consequently, extended life is without happiness for Rosicrucian wanderers because, as Roberts observes, "they have lost the ability to recreate perpetual goals and therefore, find meaning in life" (*Gothic* 208-9). Once life becomes meaningless, death is the only release from it. The Rosicrucian wanderer, like the Wandering Jew, finds that his extended life makes him long for death, but he now must wait longer for death before he can achieve the true immortality that God intends for the human soul. In the afterlife, everyone is immortal so there will be no sense of meaninglessness or alienation as is experienced on earth by one immortal among the multitudes of the mortal human race. The Gothic, therefore, suggests that it is better to wait for the immortality of the afterlife than to seek life-extension upon earth when such a state is a transgression against God.

St. Leon: Rosicrucianism and the Evolution of Reason

William Godwin's *St. Leon* (1799) was the first novel to introduce the Rosicrucian Gothic wanderer into British literature. Godwin chose to blend the Rosicrucian legend with Gothic elements to create a vehicle for expressing his philosophical ideas. In the original "Preface" to *Caleb Williams*, Godwin spoke of how a story or novel can be more successful in teaching a "valuable lesson" than a philosophical work because novels are more widely read by the general public (xxiv). For this reason, Godwin turned to the Gothic novel form in *St. Leon* to comment upon the French Revolution, to revise *Paradise Lost* by focusing upon reason rather than Christianity, and to reflect his own theories for humanity's regeneration. Godwin's atheism centered on the idea that man could achieve a form of earthly paradise rather than wait for a promised Christian afterlife. Instead of believing in a superstitious God and religion, Godwin believed man could use his reason to solve problems and thereby perfect himself (Ellis, *Castle* 163-4). While reason could not perfect an individual man, eventually Godwin believed the human race would evolve by the use of reason to achieve longer and better lives.

In *St. Leon*, Godwin created the title character as a symbol of the human race and how it could evolve from superstition and selfishness to using reason to benefit the common good. St. Leon's early life represents the opposite of Godwin's beliefs, but through his experiences and mistakes in using the Rosicrucian secrets, St. Leon eventually learns to be reasonable rather than selfish when he helps others, and he comes to understand the value of democracy over hierarchy and religious superstition. Godwin makes St. Leon a sixteenth century French aristocrat to provide a statement of the abuses of the aristocracy prior to the French Revolution. Godwin felt the sixteenth century, the age of the Reformation, was a "heroic age" of revolution like that of the 1790s (Kelly 118). Tysdahl states that *St. Leon* serves as a reply and attack upon Edmund Burke's 1790 essay *Reflections on the French Revolution* (85-6). Burke feared the French Revolution would result in the loss of chivalry and manners, in which France, and especially its aristocracy, set the European standard: "France has always more or less influenced manners in England; and when your fountain is choked up and polluted, the stream will not run long, or not run clear with us, or perhaps with any nation" (47). *St. Leon* attacked Burke's notion of the aristocracy as composing the center of a chivalrous, idyllic world. Although St. Leon is a likable character at times, he is also a negative depiction of an aristocrat who is both irresponsible and foolish, seeking merely to satisfy his desires to live a grand life. The novel reacts to Burke's notions of chivalry when St. Leon informs the reader that his early life was concerned with chivalry, culminating in his experiences at the Battle of Pavia. Rather than achieving glory, the entire French army suffered a great defeat in the battle. St. Leon mourns over this catastrophe:

> ...many persons of the highest distinction perished in the battle: many were made prisoners by the enemy. France by this event found the list of her noblesse considerably reduced in numbers; add to which, those whose loss she sustained, were almost all of them taken from among the most distinguished and meritorious in the catalogue. (25)

St. Leon concludes that the result of this horrible battle "may, perhaps, be considered as having given a deadly wound to the reign of chivalry, and a secure foundation to that of craft, dissimulation, corruption, and commerce" (26). Godwin makes chivalry fall at Pavia, just as Burke claims it would fall with the French Revolution. However, for Godwin, the fall of chivalry is inevitable because it is false and corrupt in its ideals.

After the battle, St. Leon retains his chivalric notions, hoping to reestablish the aristocratic world he had once known. He attempts to reestablish a type of paradise the chivalric world had offered him, but these attempts only increase his suffering. His depression over the battle makes St. Leon try to forget his sadness at the gaming tables. In these scenes, Godwin depicts St. Leon as a frivolous aristocrat to show the aristocracy's depravity and its failure to contribute to society. St. Leon's marriage could be his contribution to society by raising a family, but instead, St. Leon neglects his family to continue gambling, and thus, increasing his debts until his family is forced to emigrate in disgrace to Switzerland. While in Switzerland, St. Leon will gain the Rosicrucian secrets, hoping to use them to retain his aristocratic status.

Godwin's idea for St. Leon's acquisition of the Rosicrucian secrets was inspired by his reading of Dr. John Campbell's *Hermippus Redivivus* (1734), a work containing numerous stories about life-extension. One tale is of a man who lives over a century and a half by inhaling the breath of young women (Roberts, *Gothic* 49). Another tale is of Nicholas Flamel, described as a "well-known Rosicrucian sage." Flamel's story is highly similar to St. Leon's because Flamel learns alchemical secrets in a town named Leon. Flamel, like St. Leon, is also French, and he must seek refuge with his wife in Switzerland (Roberts, *Gothic* 51-2). Finally, the tale of Signor Gualdi in *Hermippus Redivivus* is used by Godwin in his preface to *St. Leon*. Signor Gualdi is an example of a person who has not yet found his immortality tiresome; however, like the Wandering Jew, he is forced to wander continually from town to town so people do not question why he never ages. *Hermippus Redivivus* also contains a possible source for St. Leon's name because there is a reference to a Leonicus, whose longevity extended to ninety-six years (Roberts, *Gothic* 39-40). Another possible source for St. Leon's name is Moses de Leon, the author of an important Cabalistic text associated with the Rosicrucians (Roberts, *Gothic* 39). Roberts suggests that Godwin may also have chosen to make St. Leon of aristocratic birth from rumors that the Rosicrucians originated in either the Knights Templar or the Red Cross Knights of the Crusades (*Gothic* 40).

St. Leon's aristocratic birth makes him long for what he has lost, and because he is a believer in privilege, he only considers how the Rosicrucian secrets can benefit him, while giving no thought to the problems they might cause, or how they might be used to benefit others. St. Leon's selfishness is, in Godwin's view, the ultimate example of human egotism (Roberts, *Gothic* 30). The character of St. Leon, therefore, becomes a study in the experiences of one selfish individual. The need to be selfish and in control is a neurosis in itself, and Godwin adds to this exploration the further neurosis that would result from perpetual life (Roberts, *Gothic* 8). As the novel progresses, St. Leon evolves from a selfish neurotic individual as he comes to realize that each disaster he and his family experience is the result of his selfishness, until he gradually becomes wiser and more reasonable.

St. Leon, therefore, is not punished for committing a transgression against God. Instead, his miseries result from his failure to be guided by reason in using the Rosicrucian secrets. Godwin, himself, believed that life-extension was possible for humanity, but it could not be acquired by superstitious secrets like the elixir of life. Instead, Godwin believed that by the power of the human mind, people could prevent the aging process; he argued that people age because of life's trials and tribulations, but if the human mind learns to overcome these boundaries that affect health, the human lifespan could be extended (Roberts, *Gothic* 28). The Rosicrucian theories were of interest to Godwin because he saw the Rosicrucians as, like himself, believers in reason, who sought logical ways to overcome the power of death. Roberts observes that while it was a scientific belief at the time that such immortality could be achieved, Godwin rejected the possibility of immortality achieved by scientific endeavor, in favor of life-extension occurring by the natural course of human evolution and an increase in human reason (*Gothic* 27). *St. Leon*, therefore, is not a Gothic novel that warns against a desire for autonomy from God (because for Godwin there is no God); rather, the novel warns against trying to achieve immortality by means other than the natural one of the human evolution of reason (Roberts, *Gothic* 47).

Godwin was severely criticized by Thomas Malthus for these philosophical theories. Malthus dismissed Godwin as having merely secularized Christianity by creating a theory that would establish a heavenly state upon the earth (Roberts, *Gothic* 31-2). Malthus thought earthly human immortality was impossible because if human lifespans were extended, it would result in the earth becoming overpopulated, which in turn would cause a food shortage. Godwin refuted this argument by stating that as people became more reasonable, they would be less bestial and more responsible, so not only would birth control become more frequent, but people would lose interest in sexual activity (Roberts, *Gothic* 31). Malthus, nevertheless, disagreed with this explanation because as a member of the clergy, he was opposed to birth control (Roberts, *Gothic* 31).

St. Leon is the nemesis of Godwin's belief in a rational man. St. Leon refuses to consider the consequences of using the Rosicrucian secrets, only thinking how they can benefit himself. Even when Zampieri, who gives St. Leon the secrets, warns him of the dangers he will encounter, St. Leon's greed and selfishness dominate his reason, making him blind to any possible consequences. Roberts argues that *St. Leon* reads almost as a case history of how the individual is destroyed by greed when he could better himself by using his resources to benefit others (*Gothic* 9). St. Leon believes his new knowledge will free him from the restraints of society, but instead, he is only restrained further because his new knowledge makes him a fugitive from the Church and government. These institutions pursue him, not only for the religious reason that he is subverting the laws of mortality as ordained by God, but also because his ability to create fabulous wealth threatens the entire socio-economic structure. People become suspicious of his newly acquired wealth, and the Church suspects St. Leon of being a sorcerer. Soon his family is persecuted for his crimes, and an angry and fearful mob burns down St. Leon's house. This scene is symbolic of the attack upon Versailles, during which the royal family were escorted back to Paris and eventually imprisoned. Just as the French monarchy were attacked for hoarding wealth, so St. Leon is attacked for engaging in a crime that includes having advantages over the common people because he has greater, although supernatural, resources. As the result of St. Leon's behavior and the persecutions that result from it, his wife dies of grief and his son abandons him. St. Leon then abandons his remaining daughters so they will no longer be persecuted for their association with their father. St. Leon's desire for wealth and power has now caused his isolation from his family. Like other Gothic novelists, Godwin believed that life's true meaning exists in the value of human relationships, so he condemns whatever may sunder them. In 1797, Godwin had expressed these democratic beliefs in his essay, "On Awakening the Mind" where he stated: "Man is a social being. In society, the interests of individuals are intrusted with each other, and cannot be separated" (Flanders 537). This statement reveals Godwin's democratic beliefs in equality and how people must work together in harmony for the general good.

St. Leon is next arrested by the Spanish Inquisition and held in their prisons which gives him plenty of time to reflect upon his past selfish behavior. When he finally escapes from the Inquisition, he realizes he has a chance to be a better man by using his wealth and knowledge to benefit others.

Ironically, to accomplish his more humanitarian goals, St. Leon must now further isolate himself. Before, he had only used the philosopher's stone to increase his wealth, but now he feels he must use the elixir of life to disguise himself so the Inquisition will not find him again. He realizes that by using the elixir he will further isolate himself from humanity, but he feels he has little choice. His situation reflects Godwin's belief that life-extension should only be acquired by human evolution so no one person would experience an isolated protraction of life. St. Leon meditates upon the changes the elixir brings to him when he first drinks it:

> I had long known, as far as reflection could assure me of it, that I possessed the elixir of immortality. But never till now had I felt the julep tingling in my veins, and known the effects of it in every joint and articulation of my frame. I before believed, I now felt, that I was immortal. The consequence of this intimate persuasion was not without its portion of melancholy. I still bore the figure and lineaments of a human creature; but I knew that I was not what I seemed. There was a greater distance between me and the best constructed and most consummate of the human species, than there is between him and an ant or a muskito, crushed by the accidental tread, or consumed by the first spark wafted by the wind. I can no longer cheat my fancy; I know that I am alone. The creature does not exist with whom I have any common language, or any genuine sympathies.

> Society is a bitter and galling mockery to my heart; it only shows in more glaring colours my desolate condition. The nearer I attempt to draw any of the nominal ties of our nature, the more they start and shrink from my grasp. From this moment I could not shake off the terrible impression of my loneliness; no, not for an hour. Often does this impression induce me to regard my immortality with loathing indescribable; often do I wish to shelter myself from it in the sweet oblivion of the grave. From this hour I had no passions, no interests, no affections; my heart has never expanded with one natural emotion; I have never delivered myself up to the repose of one genuine amusement. If at any time I have had a glimpse of pleasure, it has irritated, only to deceive; it has increased the appetite, while it displayed in stronger colours my impotence to gratify it. What is worse, every added year has still subtracted something from the little poignancy and relish which the bowl of human life continued to retain. I have the power of assuming a youthful and glossy appearance whenever I think proper; but this is only a bitter mockery of the furrows ploughed in my heart. (355-6)

St. Leon's feelings of isolation recall to him the selfishness that has caused his misery. He retains his wish to change his ways by benefitting others, so he travels to Hungary, hoping there to perform some good. St. Leon chooses Hungary as the place to perform his benevolence because the country has recently been torn apart by civil war, and he believes he can use the philosopher's stone to help relieve the resulting poverty. He hopes the philosopher's stone can become a blessing for others although it has only been a curse for him. Even in his desire to be benevolent, however, St. Leon's motives remain questionable. By using the philosopher's stone, he is still using an unorthodox means of creating wealth. Furthermore, his desire to help others with the stone may only be a way for him to rationalize his keeping it, which reflects how little he has learned from his past sufferings. His desire to become Hungary's benefactor is less from a loving desire to help others than from a desire for himself to be widely praised and loved. Godwin is still depicting St. Leon as immature in his reasoning. Godwin once stated, "Every benefactor of mankind is more or less influenced by a liberal passion for fame" (qtd. in Tysdahl 79). St. Leon's character explores the possibility that all good intentions could stem from selfish motives, and for St. Leon it is selfishness that continues to motivate his actions, but now he convinces even himself that the facade of benevolence behind which he hides his selfishness is his true and changed character.

Whatever his true intentions, St. Leon does attempt to do good. Despite his time in the Inquisition's prisons, he retains a belief in Christianity and the value of its tenets. He desires to help the Hungarians because they are at "the great frontier of the Christian world,—the theatre upon which the followers of Mahomet contended against the followers of Jesus for destruction and for empire" (368). Furthermore, having witnessed the horrors of war at the Battle of Pavia, St. Leon feels a sympathy for the suffering Hungarian people. He wishes to restore a type of Eden to Hungary by repairing the nation's economy. Nevertheless, his benevolence remains combined with his selfishness as reflected in the following passage:

> Determined as I was to open at once all the stores of my wealth, I thought I could not find a nobler scene for its display. I resolved to pour the entire stream of my riches, like a mighty river, to fertilise these wasted plains, and revive their fainting inhabitants. Thus proceeding, should I not have a right to expect to find myself guarded by the faithful love of a people who would be indebted to my beneficence for every breath they drew? This was the proper scene in which for the possessor of the philosopher's stone to take up his abode. He who could feel his ambition satisfied in a more straitened field would, by so doing, prove himself unworthy of the mighty blessing. (369)

What St. Leon believes will be a great act of benevolence, is also clearly in his mind, a means of protecting himself, by making an entire nation love him for that benevolence. By gaining the nation's love, St. Leon is also aware that he will obtain power, for if the people are indebted to him "for every breath they drew," he will undoubtedly possess the people's love and loyalty. Rather than selfishly hoard his riches, St. Leon is trying to buy love to compensate for the love lost with his family's demise.

Unlike his motives, St. Leon's program for helping the country appears very reasonable. He refuses to become involved in a dispute over whether the land is ruled by Christians or Muslims; he merely wishes to relieve the common people's suffering. His religious tolerance or indifference may reflect Godwin's own atheism and his democratic ideals of equality. St. Leon's discussion of how he will use his wealth to assist the Hungarian people reflects the evolution of his reason as he comes to realize that people are more important than wealth or social status.

> I easily saw that, if I would confer a substantial benefit on this unfortunate nation, I had scarcely any other means for the purpose, than that of reviving among them a spirit of industry. I was aware that, in the strictness of the term, money was not wealth; that it could be neither eaten nor drunk; that it would not of itself either clothe the naked or shelter the houseless; and that it was unable, but by a circuitous operation, to increase the quantity of provisions or commodities that the country afforded. It was my business therefore not to proceed idly in the

distribution of gold, but to meditate seriously my plan of operations. (372)

St. Leon's plans appear completely generous because he is not interested in receiving any material reward, although he does desire fame, love, and gratitude; however, St. Leon is also well aware of the dangers of gratitude: "I was not anxious to convert a nation or an army of men into my personal adherents and retainers: I was rather desirous to avoid this as a dangerous source of obloquy" (374). Nevertheless, there is a false note in this statement, as if he does desire fame and adoration, but declaims these desires so he may retain the reader's good opinion. If St. Leon were truly selfless in his desire to help the Hungarian people, he could have been an anonymous benefactor, but instead, he wishes the entire nation to believe in his generosity. He becomes torn between a true desire to help others and a selfish desire for love. There are moments when he does act completely selfless as when he gives money "anonymously to persons, whose dignity of birth or whose proud independence would have been too grievously wounded if they had known their benefactor" (374). But he also finds great pleasure in knowing that the Hungarian people feel affection for him. He is pleased to know he is:

> ...regarded as a phenomenon which could not be too much admired, or too loudly extolled. Wherever I appeared, the people followed me with their gratitude and blessings; ballads were written in my praise; the very children were taught with their infant tongues to lisp the virtues of the savior of Hungary. My doors were besieged; my steps were watched; I could move no where without public observation. I was importuned with petitions without end; yet, if any petitioner showed himself presumptuous and intrusive, the whole multitude of bystanders was ready to repress his indiscretion, and teach him the respect that was due to their generous benefactor, who never refused any thing, but what it would be improper and injurious to grant....I desired neither lordships nor estates, neither elevation of rank, nor extension of prerogative. Sufficient to myself, if I effected the happiness of the people, and they confessed me their benefactor, my every passion would then be gratified. The utmost boundary of my personal wishes proceeded no farther than this, that I might be honoured and loved. What I desired, I obtained...it was these things, that I felt within as the balsam of my life, and the ambrosia of heaven. (376-7)

These last lines suggest that St. Leon's intention is still the typical Gothic wanderer's desire to restore a lost paradise—in the past he tried to restore paradise by gambling or by the Rosicrucian secrets, but now he realizes happiness exists in relationships. He fails, however, to understand how to achieve such happiness because he believes he can buy the love of the people. He continues to act against the laws that govern society and Nature, remaining concerned with his own happiness, and willing to benefit others provided that such actions will benefit him as well.

As a benefactor, St. Leon grows proud of his actions that allow him to act autonomously in a godlike manner. He even dares to compare himself to God, but the comparison makes him realize the isolation he continues to feel because his power separates him from humanity's general concerns.

> I was not content; I wanted a friend. I was alone amidst the innumerable multitudes of those I had blessed. I knew no cordiality; I could repose no confidence; I could find no equal. I was like a God, who dispenses his bounties profusely through twenty climates, but who at the same time sits, separate, elevated, and alone, in the highest heaven. The reader may, if he pleases, despise me for the confession; but I felt that I was not formed for the happiness of a God. (377)

St. Leon's contradictory feelings about his godlike state reflect the typical irony faced by the Gothic wanderer who unorthodoxly achieves autonomy from God, only to find autonomy means alienation from humanity. St. Leon now feels how his wealth and extended life, in conjunction with his human nature, displaces him from communion with God or man.

St. Leon's loneliness makes him realize he cannot be both autonomous and happy. His happiness is dependent on personal relationships, for which even a nation's love cannot compensate. Furthermore, St. Leon soon learns how fickle the general population can be. The Hungarian people praise St. Leon when all is well, but they equally blame him for any problems that arise. Longing for someone who can relate to his situation, St. Leon befriends Bethlem Gabor, who is himself a type of Gothic wanderer. Gabor appears to be a compatible friend for St. Leon because their pasts and their present situations are somewhat parallel. Like St. Leon, Gabor has also lost his family, which was murdered during the religious wars. St. Leon describes how Gabor was affected by his family's deaths, suggestive that Gabor is a type of Gothic wanderer.

> He disbanded the body of men he had formed, and wandered a solitary outcast upon the face of his country. For some time he seemed to have a savage complacence in conceiving that the evil he had suffered was past all remedy, and in spurning at those palliations and disguises with which vulgar souls are accustomed to assuage their woe. Yet the energy of his nature would not suffer him to rest: he wandered an outcast; but every day engendered some new thought or passion: and it appeared probable that he would not yet quit the stage of existence till he had left behind him the remembrances of a terrible and desolating revenge. (396)

While Gabor's wandering and isolation make him appear similar to St. Leon, Gabor is less a Gothic wanderer than a Gothic villain. Unlike St. Leon, who is exiled from humanity because he possesses the Rosicrucian secrets, Gabor's exile is self-imposed, and his desire for revenge reflects a selfish cruelty that far surpasses the transgressions committed by St. Leon. Gabor's transgression is his defiance of God following his family's death: "He cursed their murderers; he cursed mankind; he rose up in fierce defiance of eternal Providence; and your blood curdled within you as he spoke" (397-8). Godwin's atheism is not offended by Gabor's religious rebellion, but Godwin does view Gabor's anger and cruel behavior as transgressions against reason. While St. Leon has evolved rationally throughout the novel, Gabor's evolution has been stunted.

For a short while, St. Leon feels a kinship and admiration for Gabor: "I could not help admiring him: his greatness excited my wonder and my reverence; and, while his manners awed and overwhelmed me, I felt an inexplicable attachment to his person still increasing in my bosom" (398). St. Leon also believes Gabor's military strength and fearful reputation will protect him from his detractors. The friendship, however, soon causes St. Leon to indulge in the anger and melancholy that Gabor feels.

> Fated each to be hereafter for ever alone; we blended ourselves the one with the other as perfectly as we could. Often over our gloomy bowl we mingled groans, and sweetened our draught as we drank it with maledictions. In the school of Bethlem Gabor I became acquainted with the delights of melancholy—of a melancholy, not that contracted, but that swelled the soul—of a melancholy that looked down upon the world with indignation, and that relieved its secret load with curses and execrations. We frequently continued whole nights in the participation of these bitter joys; and were surprised, still at our serious board, by the light of the morrow's sun. (398)

The sharing of their bitter joys makes St. Leon naively believe a bond exists between Gabor and him, but he soon learns that Gabor lacks the integrity St. Leon expects in a friend. Gabor's motivation for befriending St. Leon is soon revealed as purely selfish. At first, Gabor enjoys reaping the benefits of St. Leon's wealth, but soon he desires the wealth for himself. Eventually, Gabor realizes St. Leon possesses the philosopher's stone. He tries to force St. Leon to give him the secret of the stone by imprisoning St. Leon in his castle's underground dungeon, but St. Leon refuses to reveal the secret.

Betrayed by Gabor, St. Leon realizes how completely he is alienated from humanity, and he longs for death.

> Let me lie down and die!—I reasoned with myself. Why should I wish to live? I am nothing to any human being: I am alone in the boundless universe; I have no tie to existence. St.

> Leon has no wife; St. Leon has no child; he has neither connection nor friend in the world. Even in this wretched vision of the philosopher's stone, have I not tried it enough? have I any hopes from it? is it not time that I should throw away that and existence together? (413)

Once again, St. Leon has sought happiness only to experience misery as a result. He now realizes that wealth cannot buy love or happiness, but locked in prison, he despairs of ever making up for his mistakes.

Fortunately for St. Leon, the castle is soon attacked by Gabor's enemies. Realizing he will die in the attack, Gabor relents by freeing St. Leon. He tells St. Leon to escape by travelling through the castle's underground passages until he is outside the castle walls. When St. Leon is once again at liberty, he reflects upon the relationship he has had with Gabor, and he sincerely mourns the loss of his former friend.

> I may be mistaken; but this appears to me to have been a great and admirable man. He had within him all the ingredients of sublimity; and surely the ingredients of sublimity are the materials of heroic virtue. I have much cause of complaint against him; he conceived towards me an animosity the most barbarous and unprovoked; but, in writing this narrative, I have placed my pride in controlling the suggestions of resentment, and I have endeavoured to do him justice. (428)

St. Leon sympathizes with Gabor because suffering destroyed Gabor's humanity, making him a prisoner of social oppression and driving him to hate mankind (Clemit xxi). Gabor serves as a lesson to St. Leon of what he may become if he does not learn to act selflessly. As he emerges from the underground passages, St. Leon symbolically evolves from a darkened mind to enlightenment about what is truly valuable and meaningful—human relationships. In the novel's resolution, he finally learns to act upon this knowledge.

When St. Leon emerges from the underground passages, he is greeted by one of the soldiers attacking Gabor's castle. Realizing St. Leon has been Gabor's prisoner, the soldier takes St. Leon to the army's captain, who turns out to be St. Leon's son, Charles. Charles does not recognize his father because of St. Leon's youthful appearance from drinking the elixir of life. Keeping his identity secret, St. Leon befriends Charles, believing the situation is an opportunity to use his wealth to bring about Charles' happiness, thus making reparation for his past crimes against his own family. St. Leon anonymously arranges for Charles' fiancée, Pandora, to inherit a fortune, which will make her and Charles financially secure when they become man and wife. St. Leon has finally repaired the crime he committed against his family by accomplishing a selfless act.

In the novel's final pages, St. Leon expresses his reasons for narrating his life, beginning by warning, "Let no man, after me, pant for the acquisition of the philosopher's stone!" (466). He realizes that his transgression in using the Rosicrucian secrets has been to destroy his human relationships, and consequently, he warns the reader of the frailty of relationships and the need to value and protect them.

> Friendship is a necessity of our nature, the stimulating and restless want of every susceptible heart. How wretched an imposture in this point of view does human life for the most part appear! With boyish eyes, full of sanguine spirits and hope, we look round us for a friend; we sink into the grave, broken down with years and infirmities, and still have not found the object of our search. We talk to one man, and he does not understand us; we address ourselves to another, and we find him the unreal similitude only of what we believed him to be. We ally ourselves to a man of intellect and of worth; upon further experience we cannot deny him either of these qualities; but the more we know each other, the less we find of resemblance; he is cold, where we are warm; he is harsh, where we are melted with the tenderest sympathy; what fills us with rapture, is regarded by him with indifference; we finish with a distant respect, where we looked for a commingling soul: this is not friendship. We know of other men, we have viewed their countenances, we have occasionally sat in their society: we believe it is impossible we should not find in them the object we sought. But disparity of situation and dissimilitude of connections prove as effectual a barrier to intimacy, as if we were inhabitants of different planets. (447)

St. Leon finally realizes the irony of the human condition where everyone longs for companionship, yet it is ultimately impossible for two people to connect completely. He concludes that the best anyone can do is to work to strengthen the bonds between people, as difficult as it may be. For this reason, St. Leon's final act in the novel has been to act benevolently so Charles and Pandora can be united in a loving marriage. St. Leon exalts in having brought happiness to this idyllic couple, even if he has been denied such happiness for himself.

> I was the hero's father!—but no! I am not blinded by paternal partiality;—but no! he was indeed what I thought him, as near the climax of dignity and virtue as the frailty of our nature will admit. His virtue was at length crowned with the most enviable reward the earth has to boast,—the faithful attachment of a noble-minded and accomplished woman. I am happy to close my eventful and somewhat melancholy story with so pleasing a termination. Whatever may have been the result of my personal experience of human life, I can never recollect the fate of Charles and Pandora without confessing

with exultation, that this busy and anxious world of ours yet contains something in its stores that is worth living for. (478)

Marie Roberts summarizes the novel's ultimate philosophical goal of showing the value of family over all other pursuits and desires:

> Godwin's exposure of the hollow tyranny of the philosopher's stone in *St. Leon* is calculated to show that the secret of alchemical transmutation and eternal life are futile goals for which domestic affection and inner peace have been needlessly sacrificed, and that limitless wealth, freedom from disease, weakness and death are unimportant compared to the domestic affection of human life. (*Gothic* 37)

While Roberts uses the term "domestic affection," the novel values all forms of human relationships from marriage to parenthood and friendship. Relationships become necessary for personal happiness because without communication between people, existence becomes meaningless. Over the course of the novel, St. Leon's reason has slowly evolved until he has absorbed this lesson. Furthermore, St. Leon has forsaken his selfishness and learned how to use the Rosicrucian secrets to benefit humanity as the Rosicrucian Brotherhood had originally intended. While readers may ask why St. Leon does not relinquish the Rosicrucian secrets, as for example, Shakespeare's Prospero relinquishes his magic at the end of *The Tempest*, Godwin closes the novel without informing the reader of St. Leon's later experiences. Since St. Leon does not state that he has abandoned the secrets, the reader may assume he continues to use them, but St. Leon will now use them to benefit others as the Rosicrucians originally intended. The novel's happy ending is remarkable considering that Godwin's other male contemporary novelists wrote tragic masculine Gothics. The Gothic novels influenced by *St. Leon*, notably *St. Irvyne*, *Frankenstein*, and *Melmoth the Wanderer*, would in contrast all be tragic in their depictions of Rosicrucian Gothic wanderers. Only Edward Bulwer-Lytton's *Zanoni*, published over forty years later, would also depict the possibility of one who possesses the Rosicrucian secrets as capable of living a meaningful and benevolent life.

St. Irvyne: Rosicrucianism and the Rejection of Atheism

Percy Shelley's *St. Irvyne or, The Rosicrucian: A Romance* (1811) reflects the extent to which Godwin's *St. Leon* impressed itself upon the young Shelley's mind. *St. Irvyne* also demonstrates Shelley's early interest in Gothic novels and his attempt to be a novelist. The novel is a juvenile work, surprisingly poor in expression and organization, especially considering its author would become one of England's greatest poets. Even the novel's multiple plots border upon incoherence and fail to connect. What makes this juvenile novel interesting is the punishment visited upon the character Ginotti for transgressing to gain the Rosicrucian secrets and his attempt to make Wolfstein share his guilt.

Early in the novel, Ginotti saves Wolfstein's life; in return, he demands that when he becomes a destitute wanderer, Wolfstein must hear his tale and bury him so his soul can rest. Wolfstein agrees to this compact. Later Ginotti reappears in Wolfstein's life and he informs Wolfstein, "every event in your life has not only been known to me, but has occurred under my particular machinations" (170). Ginotti informs Wolfstein that he has been preparing him for his future. Ginotti now reveals his past. He once sought Nature's mysteries because he did not want to die, and he did not believe in God (181). During his search, Ginotti met a mysterious stranger, who forced him by violence to swear to be his. Ginotti awoke to find he had been dreaming, but from the dream he had learned the secret of eternal life. Ginotti tells Wolfstein that he may only pass the secret on to one person, and when he does, he will no longer himself possess it. Wolfstein is anxious to learn the secret, until Ginotti tells him he must first deny God before he can have it. When Wolfstein rejects this condition, Satan appears and gives Ginotti the eternal life he sought, but only as a skeleton. Ginotti's "endless existence" is to be "a dateless and hopeless eternity of horror" (199). Because Satan has no power over Wolfstein's soul, Wolfstein simply dies and the novel ends. Shelley concludes with the moral that one should only seek eternal life "from Him who alone can give an eternity of happiness" (199).

The novel has another, less obvious Rosicrucian context because of the failed rape the character Nempere attempts against Eloise, Wolfstein's sister. The third Rosicrucian manifesto, *The Chemical Wedding*, expressed a belief in the marriage of the male and female principles (Roberts, *Gothic* 105). The Rosicrucian symbol of the rose on a cross reflects the fusion of these male and female principles to create androgyny, although there was some privileging of the male (Roberts, *Gothic* 104). The rape scene in *St. Irvyne* may represent a failed attempt to create this androgynous fusion, a fusion often associated with the principles of turning lead into gold. Rape in *St. Irvyne*, as in *The Monk*, is a display of the masculine principle becoming detrimentally over-dominant and thus weakening itself. While this idea is poorly executed in *St. Irvyne*, Shelley would use it again in *Prometheus Unbound* (1820), where M.H. Abrams remarks, the union of Prometheus and Asia is a:

> ...love union between the masculine earth and the feminine moon—possibly, Shelley's adaptation of the alchemical marriage between the male and female contraries (symbolically represented as sun and moon, as well as king and queen) which consummates the hermetic quest for the principle that would transmute all elements to gold and all mankind to the age of gold. (*Natural* 306-7)

Roberts suggests the Rosicrucian quest has a similar sexual metaphor because the scientist or Rosicrucian is the male who penetrates female Nature (*Gothic* 104). The fusion, however, cannot be successful if forced as when Nempere rapes Eloise.

Most importantly, unlike Godwin's *St. Leon*, *St. Irvyne* depends upon Christian theology for its moral. While Shelley was an atheist like Godwin, in *St. Irvyne* he was a devout enough Christian to warn that one should not seek immortality except "from Him who alone can give an eternity of happiness" (199). While Godwin uses Rosicrucianism as a transgression against reason rather than against God, Shelley, like other Gothic novelists, depicted the quest for immortality as a transgressive attempt to be autonomous from God. Wolfstein refuses to deny God because he realizes it would be an act of transgression. Meanwhile, Ginotti's desired immortality is achieved as a curse because he must eternally exist as a skeleton.

Shelley never attempted to treat the Rosicrucian Gothic wanderer in a mature work, but he remained associated with Rosicrucianism throughout his life. In 1818, Thomas Love Peacock would satirize Shelley in *Nightmare Abbey* by making the Shelley-based character speak like a Rosicrucian (Roberts, "Mary" 61). That same year, Mary Shelley's *Frankenstein* would be published, a novel which also had Rosicrucian elements, and which Percy Shelley would assist his wife in editing.

Melmoth the Wanderer: The Sympathetic Rosicrucian

Charles Maturin's *Melmoth the Wanderer* (1820) would be the most extensive treatment of a sympathetic Gothic wanderer who is associated with the Rosicrucian secrets. Melmoth possesses knowledge and power, which are not specifically the Rosicrucian secrets—Maturin is vague concerning these details—but more importantly, Melmoth has acquired a form of forbidden knowledge. Maturin tells us that Melmoth received this knowledge on a trip to Poland where he became "irrevocably attached to the study of that art which is held in just abomination by all 'who name the name of Christ'" (498), and so, "Melmoth attached himself to those impostors, or worse, who promised him the knowledge and the power of the future world—on conditions that are unutterable" (499). Melmoth himself declares: "Mine was the great angelic sin—pride and intellectual glorying! It was the first mortal sin—a boundless aspiration after forbidden knowledge!" (499). Melmoth is referring to the first sin of Adam and Eve in eating the apple, as well as the angelic sin, which refers to Satan's sin of pride, thus providing Melmoth with sources in both the Bible and Milton's *Paradise Lost*. Melmoth's quest for knowledge is primarily based upon the Rosicrucian legends, although Loregy notes that Melmoth is also a Faustian character, for like Faust, he agrees to give up his soul for forbidden knowledge and power. While St. Leon made no contract to receive the Rosicrucian secrets, in *St. Irvyne*, Wolfstein could only receive them on the condition of denying God. Similarly, Melmoth must make a contract to receive the knowledge he craves—he trades his soul for knowledge, and the contract cannot be revoked unless Melmoth can find someone to take his place in the approximately one hundred and fifty years of extended life allotted to him.

Roberts argues that in Melmoth's creation, Maturin moved the Rosicrucian novel into "the realms of theological controversy" (*Gothic* 121). Melmoth lives out the Rosicrucian tradition that was first portrayed in Cornelius Agrippa, who believed man could transcend mortality, thus elevating himself to the equal of God (Roberts, *Gothic* 136). Melmoth's crime, furthermore, just like that of Ambrosio in *The Monk*, is an attachment to the world when he should be striving to achieve an afterlife in Heaven (Howard Anderson xv). Ironically, as with St. Leon, who thought great wealth would make him and his family happy, Melmoth believes happiness is achieved by autonomy from God, but he soon discovers the miseries of extended life and how being subordinate to God is preferable (Kramer 98). Melmoth's crime is not only against God but it is a misuse of the Rosicrucian secrets because Melmoth does not attempt to benefit humanity with his knowledge. Instead, he seeks to destroy men's souls, although ironically, he only succeeds in damning his own (Roberts, *Gothic* 130). Edgar Allan Poe was not impressed with how Melmoth "labours indefatigably through three octavo volumes, to accomplish the destruction of one or two souls, while any common devil would have demolished one or two thousand" (Roberts, *Gothic* 139). Poe's assessment of Melmoth as a poor devil is fair, but he is ignoring Maturin's theory that Melmoth cannot find someone to replace him because no person would willingly forsake his soul for forbidden knowledge. Furthermore, Maturin's theme depends upon Melmoth not finding a replacement so the reader understands how horrible would be a prolonged separation from God. Maturin believed such a depiction of misery would make readers reform to prevent themselves from a similar separation from God and an eternity in Hell.

Like *St. Leon*, *Melmoth the Wanderer* also emphasizes the importance of human relationships and how transgressions destroy those relationships. Melmoth longs to acquire a female companion to share his isolation. He believes that if he can find such a companion, the curse will be more bearable: "he cursed himself; and then, with the selfishness of hopeless misery, he felt that the curse might, by dividing it, be diminished" (353). Melmoth is selfish in his desire for female companionship, and consequently, when Immalee marries him, she suffers by being cast into the Inquisition's prisons. When both Immalee and the child she gives birth to die in prison, Melmoth feels guilty because his selfishness has resulted in his beloved's destruction. The novel details Melmoth's other attempts to find female companionship, but each time there are equally unsuccessful results. Melmoth's selfishness in pursuing forbidden knowledge has only resulted in his own isolation and the destruction of those he loves.

Conclusion

The Rosicrucian theme was of great interest to Gothic novelists because it served as a means for them to revise *Paradise Lost* by further discussing the fate of those who seek forbidden knowledge. The Rosicrucian theme is particularly relevant to the Gothic because Gothic novels thrive upon human fears and anxieties. Roberts states that in the Rosicrucian Gothic wanderer, a "microcosm of the individual unfolds the macrocosm of the species" (*Gothic* 143). In this case, the individual Rosicrucian represents the human fear of death as the end of existence and there being no eternal afterlife. Rejecting God's plan for human salvation and eternal life, the Rosicrucian wanderer symbolizes how man tries to cling to life as long as possible (Roberts, *Gothic* 209-10). In seeking immortal life on earth, man is attempting to be autonomous by no longer needing to follow the laws of God, Nature, or humanity. Once the Rosicrucian secrets are achieved, the Gothic wanderer believes he can do whatever he pleases, no longer having human concerns. Ironically, the Rosicrucian Gothic wanderer soon realizes that while he is freed from life's negative aspects, he is also separated from humanity and all meaning because he is no longer truly human by his immortality. Ultimately, the Rosicrucian Gothic wanderer symbolizes Christ's words that whoever seeks to save his life will lose it. Consequently, the Rosicrucian novel becomes a message of how man must reconcile himself to his humanity and its limits. While *St. Leon* is an exception with its emphasis on reason over religion or superstition, the Rosicrucian novel also demonstrates that it is best to trust in God for human salvation because transgressions that lead to extended lives on earth only result in lives of protracted alienation and sorrow.

By the Victorian period, depictions of Rosicrucians would vastly change within the Gothic novel. Most strikingly, Edward Bulwer-Lytton's *Zanoni* (1842) would depict how characters who possess extended life can use it as a blessing for humanity. Bulwer-Lytton's novel would be highly influenced by both *St. Leon* and *Melmoth the Wanderer*, but it would operate from a different theme by depicting the selflessness of its main character. Bulwer-Lytton treats his subject seriously without including Gothic elements. *Zanoni* would then influence Charles Dickens' *A Tale of Two Cities* (1859), a novel whose Rosicrucian subtext has long been ignored by critics. Both these Victorian novels will be explored in Chapter IX as demonstrations of how the Gothic wanderer figure, and by extension the Rosicrucian, would be transformed into positive figures who illustrate the power of redemption rather than punishments for transgression.

Chapter V – Gambling as Gothic Transgression

While the gambler's role in Victorian literature has received critical attention, the importance of gambling in early nineteenth century Gothic novels has been largely ignored. Gambling is not only a recurring vice among Gothic wanderer figures, but it is often the most severe transgression for which they are punished—their sentences being alienation from their families and humanity. The gambling Gothic wanderer typically believes that gambling will allow him to amass enough wealth to bring himself a material form of paradise, much as the Rosicrucian Gothic wanderer attempts to create a material paradise with the philosopher's stone. Gothic wanderers indulge in gambling in nearly every Gothic novel hitherto discussed, and they all suffer the consequences of such indulgence. In *The Mysteries of Udolpho*, both the villainous Montoni and the pseudo-heroic Valancourt gamble, making Emily fear Valancourt is another Montoni. In *St. Leon*, the title character ruins his family as a result of his gambling. In *St. Irvyne*, Wolfstein gambles and then blames Ginotti for his losses. In Polidori's *The Vampyre*, Lord Strongmore spends much of his time at a casino, seeking victims to drain of blood as the casino drains its patrons of their money. In Polidori's *Ernestus Berchtold*, the title character sinks into debt by gambling, and he is urged to destruction by his benefactor, Doni. In Balzac's *Melmoth Reconciled*, Castanier feels he must trade his soul to Melmoth in exchange for great wealth, the contract largely having to do with Castanier's need to pay his gambling debts. In a later chapter, I'll explore in detail Mary Shelley's *The Last Man*, in which gambling causes Lionel Verney's father to fall into debt and to be exiled from the royal court, a plot Mary Shelley most likely borrowed from her father's depiction of gambling and isolation in *St. Leon*.

Gothic fiction used gambling as a central focus of its plots because gambling was viewed in the nineteenth century as either a social or a moral transgression. As a social transgression, gambling often served as a metaphor for capitalism. Both gambling and certain forms of capitalism were considered unorthodox and a threat to the social hierarchy because instant wealth would allow for a person's social advancement without either birth or merit. The commercial man who rose by hard work was considered heroic because the nineteenth century still retained a belief in a Protestant Work Ethic. Calvinist predestination theories had viewed the wealthy as favored by God, and consequently, anyone who worked hard and had God's approval could become wealthy. In contrast, those who sought instant wealth by risky investments and other means outside the traditional spheres of trade and commerce were equated with gamblers. Such gambles with one's investments could result in wealth that was not the result of labor but of Chance—the direct opposite to God's plan of predestination (Zemka 304-5). Any form of gambling, in investments or at the gaming tables, was viewed as a transgression. Gambling was deceitful to society because one could not know where another gained his wealth, meaning that wealth could no longer be interpreted as a sign of one's moral character and God's favor. Consequently, society became more concerned with class-stratification and the differentiation between acceptable and "immoral" ways to achieve wealth. While capitalism was transformed from a social transgression into a socially acceptable source of income, gambling became not only a social but a moral transgression.

Gambling was defined as a moral transgression against God because the gambler seeks to acquire wealth so he can be autonomous from seeking God's approval. To advance up the social ladder through chance via gambling rather than by birth or merit was to declare autonomy from society and the need for God's approval. Nevertheless, a gambler is never autonomous because instead of relying upon God, he relies upon the fickle whims of Chance to bring about his earthly paradise. Chance is usually cruel, so rather than bringing riches and self-advancement, gambling usually causes the Gothic gambler to experience moral self-ruin and financial impoverishment.

The concept of gambling as a transgression against God originated in ancient religious ceremonies. The Hebrews used a form of gambling to determine God's will when they cast lots, known as the Urim and Thummin. Outside of religious ceremonies, it was considered a sin against God to cast lots because it could provide a person with knowledge of the future, allowing an individual to have dishonest advantages (Jeffrey Franklin 921).

Similar religious attitudes toward gambling were held by the middle class in the eighteenth and nineteenth centuries. While gambling had long been a vice of the aristocracy, only when the middle class began to gamble was it perceived as a major social threat. The middle class had always largely disapproved of the aristocracy's perceived lack of morals, so when members of the bourgeoisie indulged in such aristocratic vices as gambling, they frequently became outcasts of their own class; however, as gambling increased among the middle class, more specific forms of action were needed to fight against it, resulting in a large amount of anti-gambling literature that reinterpreted gambling as a transgression against God. Anti-gambling tracts condemned gambling in the context of Chance, work ethic, and class issues. Gamblers were depicted as transgressors against the traditional work ethic, thereby threatening the social structure because gambling provided them with the opportunity to rise from the class of their birth to the one above them (Zemka 305). Such rises of fortune were viewed as crimes against God's chosen plan for each individual as reflected in the class into which a person was born.

The changing financial world of the nineteenth century necessitated a means to differentiate between legitimate financial speculation, such as the stock market, and illegal speculation, such as gambling. Different ways of obtaining money became categorized as moral or immoral. In Anthony Trollope's Victorian novel *The Duke's Children* (1880), the Duke explains to his son the differences between what are moral and immoral means to acquire wealth:

> Money is the reward of labour...or rather, in the shape it reaches you, it is your representation of that reward. You may earn it yourself, or, as is, I am afraid, more likely to be the case with you, you may possess it honestly as prepared for you by the labour of others who have stored it up for you....There is nothing so comfortable as money,—but nothing so defiling if it be come by unworthily....If a man have enough, let him spend it freely. If he wants it, let him earn it honestly. Let him do something for it, so that the man who pays it to him may get its value. But to think that it may be got by gambling...— that I say is to have left far, far behind you, all nobility, all gentleness, all manhood! (qtd. in Jeffrey Franklin 911)

In this passage, gambling is not even equated with a religious viewpoint, yet it retains an association with immorality and dishonesty. Interestingly, the speaker is a duke, a member of the aristocracy who is shunning a vice usually associated with the upper class. Furthermore, the duke is counseling his son and heir, reflecting the duke's concern for the preservation of his family's fortune, and consequently, his son's stature.

The Gothic depicts gambling as both a social and moral transgression, but depictions of gambling are not wholly condemnatory. The Gothic wanderer, despite his transgressive nature, usually retains the reader's sympathy, and consequently, gambling is understood as an attempt to escape from life's grim realities. While gambling may be interpreted as a greedy desire for wealth, most people do not gamble out of a love for money, but because they desire the security and enjoyment that money can bring. By gambling, a person can escape from life's daily concerns to fantasize about the life he wishes to live. Alan Wykes gives an excellent analysis of this motivation:

> ...the gambler masochistically enjoys his fear of losing and continues it as long as possible, because when he leaves the table or race course to take up ordinary life some really intolerable fear awaits him, the smaller fear of losing his money

is by comparison a pleasure. The mock struggle is a sublimation of a real struggle. (qtd. in Cordery 45)

Wykes' description of gambling helps us understand why Gothic novelists continually use the gambling motif. The Gothic's concern with social criticism allowed gambling to be understood as a means of escape from the boredom and anxieties of daily life. Cordery's statement that gambling covers up an "intolerable fear" of ordinary life is related to the daily concern of trying to support oneself, and consequently, the fear that one will not be able to do so in the future. Gothic novels capitalize upon the fear of the unknown, and the Gothic wanderer who gambles is attempting to prevent the unknown future from being unpleasant by amassing wealth as a means of protection. Gambling, therefore, becomes an attempt to secure one's own future rather than to rely upon God for such security.

Wykes' focus on the masochism associated with gambling is parallel to the ironic downfalls experienced by the Gothic wanderer who searches for forbidden knowledge and immortality. Like other Gothic wanderers, the gambler discovers that the happiness he hoped to achieve only results in further unhappiness. Gambling seemingly promises the possibility of financial security, but ironically, it is the least reliable means for bringing about such security, and the vast majority of gamblers come away from the gaming table with less money than when they began. Against all odds, the gambler hopes to win, but instead he continues to punish himself by believing one more game will bring him the goal he desires; the masochistic repetition of gaming only moves him farther and farther from the goal he foolishly continues to pursue. Gambling becomes a form of suicide, for if one loses everything by gambling, there is no longer the fear of slipping into poverty. Poverty becomes less of an evil than the fear of poverty, and the unknown future becomes the immediate present, thus ending a great deal of anxiety. The gambler may know a sense of peace once all hope is lost and he is impoverished.

While Gothic novels conservatively reacted against gambling by defining it as a transgression against God, the Gothic also treated gambling as a transgression against the family and human relationships. While the gambler may masochistically risk his wealth and life by gambling, the Gothic reveals that gambling has repercussions upon the gambler's family. The gamblers in Gothic novels are typically aristocratic men with families. Consequently, when the gambler falls into poverty, he risks both his family and his social status. The Gothic creates aristocratic gamblers because their social status allows them to be born into an earthly form of Eden. Consequently, the gambler must attempt to return to that former paradise. Some gamblers fail in this attempt by continuing to view gambling as a means to restore their personal Edens. Other gambling Gothic wanderers learn that it is not in wealth but the family and human relationships that paradise exists. Unfortunately, even these enlightened

Gothic wanderers generally learn this lesson only after their gambling has destroyed their families, ending any hope of restoring a paradise.

The Mysteries of Udolpho: Gambling as a Threat to Love

The Mysteries of Udolpho is the first Gothic novel in which gambling is important to the plot and theme. Here, gambling threatens the family as represented by the romantic couple of Emily and Valancourt, and it contributes to the characters' status as Gothic wanderers. Emily, we have seen, is already a Gothic wanderer because of her transgression against her father's command not to read the secret papers. Valancourt is a Gothic wanderer not only because he is a second son, but also because he gambles. Although Montoni gambles more frequently than Valancourt, he is less truly a Gothic wanderer than a Gothic villain for whom the reader feels no sympathy. Valancourt is the novel's true Gothic wanderer because his hopes for domestic happiness are threatened by his gambling, while Montoni was never interested in acquiring domestic happiness.

Gambling first becomes an issue in *The Mysteries of Udolpho* when Montoni takes Emily and her aunt to Venice. At this time, Montoni becomes so addicted to gambling that he indulges in the vice throughout the night. His gambling addiction provides the first clues to the true depravity of his character.

> ...his soul was little susceptible of light pleasures. He delighted in the energies of the passions; the difficulties and tempests of life, which wreck the happiness of others, roused and strengthened all the powers of his mind, and afforded him the highest enjoyments, of which his nature was capable. Without some object of strong interest, life was to him little more than a sleep; and, when pursuits of real interest failed, he substituted artificial ones, till habit changed their nature, and they ceased to be unreal. Of this kind was the habit of gaming, which he had adopted, first, for the purpose of relieving him from the languor of inaction, but had since pursued with the ardour of passion. (182)

Montoni takes the frivolous pastime of gambling and makes it vastly serious. His original reason for gambling supports Wykes' argument that people indulge in gambling to escape the boredom of life. Yet Montoni soon turns his means of entertainment into a serious stake for which he masochistically risks his fortune on the chance of acquiring larger sums of money. Soon, the reader and Emily will learn that Montoni is also suffering from anxieties about gaining control of his new wife's fortune to further his evil plots of robbery. Until he can further these plots when they reach the Castle of Udolpho, he seeks to relieve his anxiety by passionately enjoying the lesser anxieties of the gaming tables.

Montoni's addiction to gambling becomes a metaphor for his constant willingness to gamble with life. Montoni saw his marriage to Emily's aunt as a sure gamble because he believed her to be wealthy. Instead, he finds himself deceived by her pretensions to wealth, thus ironically placing himself in the position of the Gothic wanderer by attempting to better himself, only to bring about his further degradation. Montoni's gambling with life is also obvious in his being the leader of banditti; he gambles with disobeying the law, believing the wealth he steals from innocent travelers is worth the risk of being caught for his criminal actions. At the novel's conclusion, Emily will learn that Montoni also lost this gamble by being arrested and thrown into prison where he soon dies.

Montoni's behavior causes Emily to associate gambling with immorality; consequently, when she learns of Valancourt's gambling, she fears he has fallen to Montoni's base level. Her concerns are enhanced when Valancourt tells her he is no longer worthy of her love (505). Although Valancourt is too ashamed to divulge his reasons for such feelings, Emily is informed by Count de Villefort of rumors regarding Valancourt:

> ...he had formed an acquaintance with a set of men, a disgrace to their species, who live by plunder and pass their lives in continual debauchery....I soon learned, that these, his associates, had drawn him into a course of dissipation, from which he appeared to have neither the power, nor the inclination, to extricate himself. He lost large sums at the gaming-table; he became infatuated with play; and was ruined....I afterwards learned, that, in consideration of his talents for play, which were generally successful, when unopposed by the tricks of villainy,—that in consideration of these, the party had initiated him into the secrets of their trade, and allotted him a share of their profits. (505-6)

Radcliffe uses not only gambling here to associate Valancourt with Montoni, but she adds for Valancourt the disreputable companions, and the willingness to cheat people for profit. Although Emily does not wish to believe these rumors, she feels they are confirmed by Valancourt's own statement that he is unworthy of her love. Worst of all, the Count adds of Valancourt's behavior:

> ...the Chevalier's extravagance has brought him twice into the prisons of Paris, from whence he was last extricated, as I was told upon authority, which I cannot doubt, by a well-known Parisian Countess, with whom he continued to reside, when I left Paris. (507)

Overcome by this news, Emily faints from astonishment and sadness. That Valancourt has become a womanizer, who openly lives in sin, completes the equation in Emily's mind between Montoni and Valancourt. Emily now feels she has only one option:

> She must part from Valancourt, therefore, for ever—for what of either happiness or tranquillity could she expect with a man, whose tastes were degenerated into low inclinations, and to whom vice was habitual? whom she must no longer esteem, though the remembrance of what he once was, and the long habit of loving him, would render it very difficult for her to despise him. (509-10)

Emily's feeling that there can be no happiness in marriage to a gambler, especially one who also indulges in other vices, is a recurrence of the Gothic theme of transgression destroying domestic happiness. Here gambling becomes more than just a game: to gamble at the gaming table is to gamble with one's life and one's relationships. Fortunately for Valancourt, Emily soon learns that Valancourt is innocent of much with which he is charged.

Because Mrs. Radcliffe is setting Valancourt up as a double to Montoni, the narrator soon after tells us that Montoni has been captured by the Venice senate and imprisoned for his crimes, although Emily remains ignorant of this turn of events (522). By Mrs. Radcliffe's deletion of Montoni's threat to society, she is preparing the reader for an end to the circumstances that also threaten Emily and Valancourt's relationship. When Emily later learns that Montoni has died in prison, probably from being poisoned, she is able to repossess her aunt's estates, which provide her with the financial power to support herself and a husband. Emily soon after discovers the truth about Valancourt's actions: he was only in prison for his gambling debts, and he only indulged in gambling as a way to bear his separation from Emily while she was in Italy—another example of how the gambler indulges in a lesser anxiety to forget a greater one. All the more malicious rumors against Valancourt are false, and in addition, Emily hears of his kind acts: when Valancourt was released from prison, he gambled one last time to win enough money to free a fellow prisoner and restore him to his wife. Here, Radcliffe almost condones gambling if done with the right intentions, and so consequently, the gambling transgression can bring about good as well as ill, as here where it promotes domesticity by reuniting a married couple. As a feminine Gothic novel that does not condemn the search for knowledge, *The Mysteries of Udolpho* allows for the possibility of good arising from the evils of gambling. Gambling now seizes to be a threat to happiness when Valancourt makes "a solemn vow never again to yield to the destructive and fascinating vice of gaming" (653). Valancourt realizes that the vice has nearly made him lose Emily, and he is wise enough not to take such a risk again. Because *The Mysteries of Udolpho* is a feminine Gothic novel, there is a happy ending. Most Gothic gamblers, however, are depicted in masculine Gothic novels as being punished for their transgressions by experiencing domestic tragedies.

St. Leon: Gambling Destroys the Family

Although the focus in *St. Leon* is upon the title character's acquisition of the Rosicrucian secrets and their effects upon him, emphasis needs to be placed upon the fact that all of St. Leon's problems originally stem from his gambling addiction, and as with Montoni, a character's participation in gambling foreshadows worse transgressions to be committed. St. Leon becomes addicted to gambling in an attempt to forget how he witnessed the death of chivalry at the Battle of Pavia. As Wykes explained, gambling is a vice indulged in by people who wish to escape the mundanity of life and to release anxiety by masochistically indulging in a lesser form of anxiety (Cordery 45). St. Leon understands the sordidness of gambling, as he explains, but nevertheless, he indulges in the vice to provide release from his painful past.

> It was with hesitation and reluctance that I entered into this habit. I saw it as it was, and as every ingenuous and undebauched mind must see it, base and sordid. The possession of some degree of wealth I regarded, indeed, as indispensable to a man who would fill a lofty and respectable character in the world; a character that, by uniting the advantages of exterior appearance with the actions of a hero, should extort the homage of his species. But, in the picture I drew of this man in my mind, I considered wealth as an accident, the attendant on his birth, to be dispensed with dignity, not to be adverted to with minuteness of attention. (28-9)

Here, St. Leon morally condemns gambling; his opinion is not unlike that of Trollope's duke. But being an aristocrat who was born into wealth, St. Leon is careless about money, saying it was an "accident" and not to be given great attention to but to be "dispensed with dignity." Dispensing of wealth in a dignified manner suggests being charitable, but St. Leon dispenses of it by indulging in the undignified vice of gaming. Having been born into wealth, St. Leon does not consider the full necessity of possessing money to maintain his luxurious lifestyle; his wealth has separated him from the ordinary struggles of humanity to survive in an often cruel world, so he cannot understand the desperation that would lead someone to stake everything upon gambling. St. Leon gambles solely for amusement and to forget the past rather than to provide for the future. As St. Leon continues to discuss gambling, his tone is high, moral, and condemnatory:

> Deep play is certainly sufficiently inconsistent with this character. The direct purpose of the gamester is to transfer

> money from the pocket of his neighbour into his own. He rouses his sleepy and wearied attention by the most sordid of all motives. The fear of losing pierces his heart with anguish; and to gain—to obtain an advantage for himself which can scarcely exceed, and which seldom equals, the injury his competitor suffers,—is the circumstance which most transports his heart with delight. For this he watches; for this he calculates. An honourable gamester does not seize with premeditation the moment when his adversary is deprived, by wine or any other cause, of his usual self-possession. He does not seek with sober malice to play upon his passions. He does not enter with avidity into the contest with an unpractised but presuming rival: but he cannot avoid rejoicing, when he finds that accident has given him an unusual advantage. I have often thought that I could better understand how a man of honour could reconcile himself to the accursed and murderous trade of war, than to the system of the gaming table. In war, he fights with a stranger, a man with whom he has no habits of kindness, and who is fairly apprised that he comes against him with ruinous intent. But in play, he robs, perhaps, his brother, his friend, the partner of his bosom; or, in every event, a man seduced into the snare with all the arts of courtesy, and whom he smiles upon, even while he stabs. (29)

Despite his moral disapproval of gambling, St. Leon does allow that there are rules of conduct that provide a higher status for the honest gambler than for one who cheats or takes advantage of his opponent. Yet, even the honest gamester's morals are questionable in his willingness to take money from his acquaintances. St. Leon's use of the words "his brother, his friend, the partner of his bosom" are words Godwin wisely chose as a means to emphasize how gambling destroys domesticity and human relationships.

St. Leon now turns to discussing the consequences of his own gambling addiction, which because of his protracted lifespan, he has had years to reflect upon.

> I am talking here the mere reason and common sense of the question as it relates to mankind in general. But it is with other feelings that I reflect upon the concern I have myself individually in the subject. Years roll on in vain; ages themselves are useless here; looking forward, as I do, to an existence that shall endure till time shall be no more; no time can wipe away the remembrance of the bitter anguish that I have endured, the consequence of gaming. It is torture! It is madness! Poverty, I have drained thy cup to the dregs! I have seen my wife and my children looking to me in vain for bread!

> Which is the most intolerable distress?—that of the period, in which all the comforts of life gradually left me; in which I caught at every fragment of promise, and every fragment failed; in which I rose every morning to pamper myself with empty delusions; in which I ate the apples of purgatory, fair without, but within bitterness and ashes; in which I tossed, through endless, sightless nights, upon the couch of disappointment and despair?—or the period, when at length all my hopes were at an end; when I fled with horror to a foreign climate; when my family, that should have been my comfort, gave me my most poignant agony; when I looked upon them, naked, destitute, and exiles, with the tremendous thought, what and who it was that had caused their ruin? Adversity, without consolation,—adversity, when its sting is remorse, self-abhorrence and self-contempt,—hell has no misery by which it can be thrown into shade or exceeded. (29-30)

This passage, besides the intense anguish it displays, makes a clear connection between gambling and transgression. Gambling is equivalent to eating the "apples of purgatory" which taste of "bitterness and ashes," words which echo *Paradise Lost* (Clemit 482), where the fallen angels "fondly thinking to allay / Their appetite with gust, instead of fruit / Chewed bitter ashes" (X, 564-6). The reference to fruit also recalls the apple that caused humanity's fall. Eating the fruits of forbidden knowledge and indulging in gambling are parallel in St. Leon's mind because both are transgressive attempts to be autonomous from God. Gambling is an attempt to satisfy an appetite for happiness without trusting that God will fulfill one's needs; consequently, the only result is the taste of "bitterness."

As he concludes his discussion of gambling, St. Leon now explains exactly what fascinated him about the vice:

> It appeared to my distempered apprehension to be only a mode in which for a man to display his fortitude and philosophy. I was flattered with the practice of gaming, because I saw in it, when gracefully pursued, the magnanimity of the stoic, combined with the manners of a man of the world; a magnanimity that no success is able to intoxicate, and no vicissitude to subvert. I committed my property to the hazard of the die; and I placed my ambition in laughing alike at the favours of fortune and her frowns. In the sequel, however, I found myself deceived. The fickle goddess sufficiently proved that she had the power of making me serious. But in her most tremendous reverses, I was never influenced to do any thing that the most scrupulous gamester regards as dishonourable. (30)

St. Leon indulges in gambling as a means to overcome the boredom of life and to erase his horrible memories of the Battle of Pavia. He has stated that the battle caused the end of chivalry, but in gambling, he finds an occupation as potentially enticing and gentlemanly as chivalry because it provides for the stoicism that he believes is the mark of true nobility. St. Leon, however, should have learned from his past that chivalry's stoicism did not prevent it from being destroyed. Similarly, the stoicism St. Leon feels while gambling will not remain once he sees his family impoverished and suffering because of his own addictive vice.

The novel's use of the gambling motif extends to the emphasis upon the philosopher's stone. Even prior to obtaining the stone, St. Leon was willing to gamble for its attainment. He informs the reader that he once gave money to an alchemist who claimed he could turn lead into gold (144). St. Leon was too ignorant to realize that the alchemist was a con-artist, who would not have needed St. Leon's money if he had been able to perform the deed. St. Leon is again willing to gamble for the stone when he meets Zampieri. Despite Zampieri's story of the continual harassment he has suffered because he possesses the philosopher's stone, St. Leon willingly gambles his life on the chance that his own experiences with the stone will not be as horrendous. More importantly, as Ellis argues, the philosopher's stone represents capitalism's ability to multiply money (*Castle* 163). Godwin sets the novel in the sixteenth century when capitalism was just emerging to create an intentional parallel between capitalism and the philosopher's stone. Capitalism eventually resulted in the increased social mobility of millions of people, and as noted above, it was perceived as a threat to the economy and especially to the social hierarchy. Godwin uses the philosopher's stone to symbolize this capitalistic threat; people view St. Leon's possession of the stone as a threat to religion and the economy. Use of the philosopher's stone, therefore, becomes a rebellion against the patriarchal hierarchy by turning lead into gold so one can escape the economic laws that govern society and determine one's class status.

Finally, while the philosopher's stone is a way to gamble and rise in society, it threatens the family, and hence, the patriarchal structure. St. Leon thinks the stone will return his family to its former noble splendor, but instead, it leads to the death of his wife and his alienation from his children. When St. Leon refuses to explain to his son, Charles, how he came by his wealth, Charles is so infuriated that he rejects his father, exclaiming, "I am no longer your son!....By your dishonour you have cut me off from the whole line of my ancestors. I cannot claim affinity with them, without acknowledging my relation to you. You have extinguished abruptly an illustrious house" (192-3). The philosopher's stone, therefore, has overthrown the aristocratic family, as capitalism threatened to overthrow the aristocracy's position of power. In addition, the stone causes the displacement of each family member, just as capitalism increased social and physical mobility, resulting in the breakdown of the extended family in favor of the nuclear one. Gambling in *St. Leon*, therefore, results in an increased alienation for the Gothic wanderer because it can destroy his family and all his relationships. In the later chapter on Mary Shelley, I will demonstrate how Shelley's *The Last Man* was influenced by her father's novel to depict a similar situation where the indulgence in gambling by Lionel Verney's father causes the displacement of his children from their aristocratic birthright.

The Vampyre: Money Circulating Like Blood

John Polidori's personal experiences are reflected in his use of the gambling motif in *The Vampyre* (1819) and *Ernestus Berchtold* (1819) to depict gambling as a transgression that destroys the family and upsets the social class structure. Polidori's gambling eventually resulted in his own suicide because he could not pay his gambling debts, an example of how gambling was not only a literary motif but a real threat to society and the individual; therefore, when Polidori emphasizes the horrors that result from gambling, he speaks from firsthand experiences that strengthen the creation of his characters.

In *The Vampyre*, Polidori uses gambling as a metaphor for the vampire, Lord Strongmore. Macdonald and Scherf accurately describe this symbolic connection: "Lord Strongmore is addicted to the aristocratic vice of gambling, and he drains some of his victims of cash at the faro table much as he drains others of blood after dark" (3-4). Strongmore is not interested in whether he wins or loses, but only "in keeping money in circulation, like blood" (4); he gambles not to win, but merely to make others lose. At times, Strongmore possesses the same stoic gambler attitude that St. Leon admired:

> He betted and always gambled with success, except when the known sharper was his antagonist, and then he lost even more than he gained; but it was always with the same unchanging face, with which he generally watched the society around. (36)

Lord Strongmore's stoicism does not last, however, when he sees an easy victim. Then he becomes the very embodiment of evil in the way he will manipulate and mercilessly destroy the most vulnerable person who dares to play against him.

> It was not, however, so when he encountered the rash youthful novice, or the luckless father of a numerous family; then his very wish seemed fortune's law—his apparent abstractedness of mind was laid aside, and his eyes sparkled with vivid fire. In every town, he left the formerly affluent youth, torn from the circle he adorned, cursing, in the solitude

of a dungeon, the fate that had drawn him within the reach of this fiend; whilst many a father sat frantic, amidst the speaking looks of mute hungry children, without a single florin of his late immense wealth, wherewith to buy even sufficient to satisfy their present craving. Yet he took no money from the gambling table; but immediately lost, to the ruiner of many, the last gilder he had just snatched from the convulsive grasp of the innocent. This might but be the result of a certain degree of knowledge, which was not, however, capable of combatting the cunning of the more experienced. (36)

Lord Strongmore epitomizes the ruthlessness of the unsympathetic gambler, who is completely lacking in the nobility St. Leon believed some gamblers possess. In addition, Lord Strongmore's behavior connects the vampire and gambling to the fear that capitalism can completely ruin people who foolishly invest their money, especially people like the youth and the father who cannot afford to lose, yet risk everything at the gaming tables. Macdonald argues that the vampire-gambler metaphor is especially effective because gambling is a repetitive and compulsive activity, just as the vampire must repetitively drain people's blood and move from place to place to seek fresh blood (208). The vampire's bloodsucking is inherent in his nature and he cannot overcome it, just as the gambler has an addiction he cannot break.

Polidori extends his metaphor of gambling as a form of vampirism to depict the threat posed to the class hierarchy by capitalism and the rising middle class. Because Lord Strongmore is based upon Lord Byron, Polidori may have felt offended by Lord Byron's own upper class snobbery, so he chose to debase Byron's character in the figure of Lord Strongmore. Polidori comments on class struggle by innovatively making his vampire an aristocrat (Macdonald 192-3) and by making Lord Strongmore's victims those who are at the bottom of the upper class. Strongmore specifically preys upon youths and fathers because he can easily wipe out their funds and force them into the lower class. As a member of the aristocracy, he is protecting his social stature by redirecting class mobility as solely a downward movement. Strongmore's merciless despisal of the lower class is further reflected in his willingness to manipulate card games that will strike a blow to the family unit, causing a father's loss to result in his family's impoverishment and his children's starvation. This blow is intentional because the family was viewed by the middle class as the seat of its morality and virtues, so the family had to be preserved at all costs. Lord Strongmore, therefore, is an embodiment of the aristocracy's immorality and its tyrannical repression of the middle class' upward mobility. It should be noted, however, that while Strongmore may assist in the middle class family's destruction, the transgressive father is most at fault for choosing to gamble. Lord

Strongmore enforces a perverted justice that punishes those who commit the social transgression of gambling to elevate their class status.

Ernestus Berchtold: Gambling and Incest

In *Ernestus Berchtold*, Polidori creates a character, probably not unlike himself, who becomes the victim of his gambling addiction, and by a strange twist, his gambling assists in destroying his entire family. When Ernestus saves the Olivieri's life, he is repaid by Olivieri's father, Doni, by being adopted into the family. Unknown to all the characters, Ernestus and his sister Julia are actually a half-brother and half-sister to Olivieri and his sister, Louisa. The mother of these four siblings had left her first husband, Doni, and then had two more children by another man. The result of the mother's marital transgression is that incest will develop among the half-siblings who do not realize their relationship. Gambling becomes the vehicle to carry out this incestuous plot.

Ernestus becomes addicted to gambling shortly after he and Julia become members of Doni's family. When Ernestus falls in love with his unknown half-sister, Louisa, she tempts him into gambling. For several nights, Ernestus is successful at the gaming tables and gives his winnings to Louisa. Then his fortunes change. Even though his losses become severe, he cannot resist his gambling addiction, and he is enticed on by Louisa, before whom he does not wish to appear cowardly by refusing to risk further losses. In addition, Ernestus is well supplied with money by his foster-father, Doni.

> I was so profusely supplied with money by the kind friend who called me son, that I did not at first heed my losses. I had given all I gained to the syren, who still urged me on: I lost every franc I had. She then supplied me; I was ashamed to take it of her, though it was what I myself had gained; but I hoped my luck would change; I lost the whole. She then began to exert her more baneful powers, she led me from folly to vice, in search of what she assured me was an antidote to memory; I joined the libertine and the desperate. I was ashamed of letting Doni know that he, whom he had pointed out as a model of virtue to his son, had sunk into the lowest debauchery....often I threw myself deeper into the sinks of vice, in hopes that such reflections would not pursue me thither. (90)

Ernestus, in correlation with Wykes' statement for why people gamble, becomes enticed into the vice, partly from shame and partly because he hopes it will help him forget the sadness of his past, it being an "antidote to memory." Louisa is herself only an instrument of her brother, Olivieri. Olivieri is an example of the Gothic concern with legitimacy because as Doni's true son, Olivieri is jealous of his father's preference for Ernestus, which defies the laws of inheritance being determined by legitimacy. In retaliation against his father, Olivieri wishes to expose Ernestus' weaknesses by further tempting Ernestus to gamble.

> He [Olivieri] also excited me to gamble, lent me money himself when I had none, and gathered round me every incentive to vice. He had been mortified at his father's holding me up as a pattern of strength against temptation; he was revenged, he exposed my weakness. (90)

Olivieri, although not a vampire, shares Lord Strongmore's delight in preying upon the weak, whether it be at the gaming tables or by seducing women. While he destroys Ernestus by addicting him to gambling, Olivieri is also seducing Julia. Ernestus is so intensely transfixed with gambling that he never guesses the additional assault Olivieri is preparing against him by seducing and then abandoning his sister.

As Ernestus falls further into debt, Doni gives him monetary presents. Doni achieves this money by supernatural means because he has acquired control over spiritual beings who must obey his commands. Doni intends to be kind, but his monetary gifts only further ruin Ernestus. Rather than using this money to pay off his gambling debts, Ernestus also loses it at the gaming tables. Soon, Ernestus feels his situation has turned into a Gothic nightmare, his guilt creating a Hell within him in the form of his compulsive gambling addiction.

> It was now quite useless to think of retreating, I fell again into my former life, with more than double energy. I was at times surprised to find that great sums were paid to several of my creditors, I could not learn by whom; I imagined it was Olivieri's father; this did not stop me. My vicissitudes were great, but I could never entirely extricate myself, so that I was always either lured by hope or urged by despair.
>
> I need not describe to you the progress of my other vices; debauched women, men of whom one is ashamed, and wine, are generally the attendants upon gambling. I could not seek the house of Doni, nor of virtue; I threw myself into every haunt of desperate characters like myself, and learnt to boast alike of the smile of the prostitute, or of the tear of the debauched virgin; when losing, I stupified my mind with wine, and was glad to fall from my chair, provided memory failed with my senses. Noted cheats, and men proscribed from society for their low dissoluteness, often seized upon my arm on the Corso, as if I were one of their equals, and I dared not repel their familiarity, for I was in their power. Once Louisa saw me in this situation, she never again rode out on the Corso; I had the maddened impudence to bow to her. I at last became mad, and once, was induced to aid in depriving a young novice of all his wealth, by means of false dice. I could not however stand by and see his

horrible despair, he had beggared a wife and two lovely babes. I had just then been lucky, I confessed my participation to him, and gave him the whole amount of his loss; it became known, and I was laughed at; but for once I could withstand ridicule. (93)

Ernestus has become an outcast because of his gambling. Louisa is now ashamed to see him, and he has become known to associate with the lowest type of men, thus casting him from good society. Rather than achieve social elevation by gambling to increase his wealth, Ernestus becomes impoverished and the companion to the lowest people. His position becomes a mixture of the typical Gothic wanderer and the Gothic villain. Like Montoni, Ernestus cheats people, yet like St. Leon, he retains enough decency to feel guilt over his criminal acts. He is trapped in a nightmarish situation—ironically imprisoned by the very activity he thought would help him escape his negative memories. Furthermore, as with all Gothic transgressors, Ernestus has destroyed his hope for domestic happiness—he is rejected by Louisa, who now loves another man. This knowledge so depresses Ernestus that he "wandered about alone" and finds himself "fatigued with wandering" about the city (94), thus placing himself in the characteristic Gothic wanderer role.

Self-absorbed by his troubles, Ernestus is blind to his sister's situation, leaving her no protection from seduction by Olivieri. When he learns of his sister's fate, Ernestus feels intensified guilt, stating: "My sister was dead....I was the source of all...my example in the career of vice were the causes of her fault—her death" (112). As Julia's brother, Ernestus should have been both protector and moral guide to her, but his indulgence in vices instead served as an encouragement for Julia also to indulge, resulting in Olivieri seducing her. Ernestus, therefore, blames his gambling for his sister's ruin. Later he will learn that by neglecting his sister, not only has he helped bring about the loss of her virginity, but he has also assisted in her becoming a participant in incest because Olivieri was her unknown half-brother.

Like *St. Leon, Ernestus Berchtold* also connects gambling to the supernatural by the use of fantastic means to achieve wealth, which like the philosopher's stone, also serve as a commentary upon capitalism. Doni raises spirits so they may bring him great wealth, thus improving his family's financial situation. When Ernestus becomes aware of Doni's illegal sorcery, he sees how Doni's illicit acts destroy his health. When Doni emerges from his secret room after performing his supernatural tasks, Ernestus is struck by his foster-father's physical appearance: "his face was, or I imagined it to be, pale; his eyes wandered, and then seemed to fix their angry glance at times upon us; but whether this were imagination or reality, I could not decide" (101). Polidori's emphasis upon Doni's eyes suggests the supernaturalism associated with the Wandering Jew. Doni's knowledge of the supernatural and his ability to have great wealth as a result, makes Doni, like the Wandering Jew, displaced from humanity's normal concerns. Ernestus remains troubled by Doni's appearance, but he soon dismisses it in consideration of what Doni is able to achieve by his use of the supernatural.

> I went to bed, but not to sleep, the thoughts of having seen an unembodied being, the tales of my foster-mother, of power, of wealth, arising from the communication with beings of another world, arose before me. Obtaining such a power, it seemed as if I might learn the things hidden in the earth's deepest recesses, the ocean's depth; I even thought, that by such a power, I might tear away the veil which the first Cause has thrown over itself. (101)

Ernestus is willing to gamble for the advantages that may be gained by transgressing into the supernatural world, ignoring the risks to his health and soul. By wishing to "tear away the veil which the first Cause has thrown over itself," he is, like most Gothic wanderers, willing to transgress to restore paradise. Polidori, however, rather than allowing Ernestus to indulge in the supernatural, now ends the novel with Doni's death. Doni leaves behind him a manuscript that details his personal history. Besides the horrible revelation that the four siblings have committed incest, Doni also explains the conditions by which he could use the supernatural to achieve wealth.

> I could only call for a certain sum at a time, and that at each time, some human domestic infliction, worse than the preceding, would fall upon me, or that, I at once, could gain unlimited power, and constant domestic prosperity, on the condition of giving myself up for ever to the will of a malignant being....I laughed in my own mind at domestic happiness....I bound myself to the first condition. (137)

Doni's willingness to sacrifice domestic happiness for wealth and supernatural powers exhibits the recurring Gothic depiction of transgression as a threat to the family's stability. Because of Doni's willingness to gamble with domestic happiness, the supernatural being has manipulated events to bring about the end of Doni's marriage, his murdering of his father-in-law, and now the incest between his children and their half-siblings. Gambling in *Ernestus Berchtold* becomes a metaphor for the transgressor's willingness to gamble with domestic happiness and his own soul.

Conclusion

The recurrence of the gambling metaphor in Gothic novels demonstrates the serious stigma attached to gambling in the nineteenth century as a severe transgression against God and His pre-ordained social hierarchy. The Gothic depicts the gambler as one who seeks to elevate his social position by gambling, but ironically, his transgression results in his financial and moral destruction. The nineteenth century concern with gambling as a dishonest way to achieve social elevation is reflected in the Gothic's punishment of the gambler as a means to maintain the status quo. This punishment also reflects the nineteenth century concern over capitalism's threats to social hierarchy. The Gothic's conservative promotion of middle class values is generally not in opposition to social mobility, but it does disapprove of illegitimate forms of social advancement as represented by gambling, and to a lesser extent, by capitalism. Ultimately, while gambling was perceived in the nineteenth century as a threat to the social class structure, the Gothic primarily condemned gambling for its destruction of the family. While the Gothic concerns itself with all forms of transgression, those transgressions that threaten the family and human relationships are most to be condemned, even over transgressions against God. Gambling is always a transgression against the family, and therefore, the gambler is always severely punished.

PART II - Subversive Gothic Wanderers

Chapter VI – "A Wandering Jewess": Fanny Burney's *The Wanderer* as Gothic Novel

Since its republication in 1988, Fanny Burney's *The Wanderer: or, Female Difficulties* (1814) has been read both as an early feminist text and as a response to Romanticism. No critic, however, has fully explored the text's place in the Gothic novel tradition. In *The Wanderer*, Burney uses Gothic elements to depict how patriarchal society views women's employment as a form of transgression. The novel's subtitle "Female Difficulties" refers not only to the difficulties of working women but patriarchal society's overall mistreatment of women. Burney uses the Gothic theme of female confinement to depict how women are confined by misogynistic, patriarchal codes. Burney's title alludes to the wanderers of Romantic poetry, but Burney also intends the reader to associate it with the figure of the Gothic wanderer. Burney's wanderer heroine, Juliet, as I will show, becomes a symbolic "wandering Jewess" to serve as a feminist response to the Gothic and Romantic wanderer traditions.

Critics might argue that *The Wanderer* cannot be classified as a Gothic novel, but merely as a novel with occasional Gothic elements. Such an argument, however, limits the definition of Gothic to those novels with conventionally supernatural Gothic atmospheres. While a Gothic atmosphere only exists in a few of the novel's scenes, Burney utilizes numerous other Gothic elements throughout *The Wanderer*, blending them with elements from the sentimental novel and novel of manners genres to create a Gothic novel that is a direct piece of social criticism. Burney's decision to use Gothic elements in *The Wanderer* resulted from the Gothic's growing popularity, and its successful use of female confinement plots. Burney understood that these plots served as metaphors for the patriarchal oppression women often encountered. Burney bravely updated the Gothic novel by setting *The Wanderer* in contemporary England to emphasize how the oppressiveness of England's patriarchal society can be as frightening for women as the foreign lands and pseudo-historical past where Gothic novels are usually set. Burney also builds upon the English fear of the French Revolution by suggesting that the oppression of women and all of England's second-class citizens may result in a similar catastrophe in England. Burney's direct commentary upon the French Revolution is progressive beyond her Gothic predecessors who simply used the Gothic as a metaphor for the French Revolution. Burney, therefore, was the first novelist to depict contemporary England as a place of potential Gothic horror.

The Wanderer as a Revision of *Evelina*

Despite *The Wanderer*'s remarkable achievements and its literary importance, it was condemned by the critics for its feminist theme, so Burney's present fame rests mostly upon her first novel *Evelina* (1778). To read solely *Evelina*, however, is to have only a rudimentary understanding of both Fanny Burney's powers as a novelist and her opinions regarding the role of women in her society. *Evelina*'s plot has several similarities to *The Wanderer*, but it is devoid of major Gothic elements. A brief comparison of the two novels emphasizes Burney's growth as a novelist and her wise decision to write *The Wanderer* as a Gothic novel to express more fully her opinions regarding women's oppressive situations.

While *Evelina* is far from being Gothic, it contains latent social criticism upon the situation of women which would become Burney's dominant subject in *The Wanderer*. *Evelina* belongs to the tradition of eighteenth century sentimental novels that frequently revolve around plots of female abduction and confinement, plots upon which the Gothic would later draw. Such plots reflect eighteenth century women's experiences when their suitors, husbands, brothers, or fathers treated them as property or a form of wealth to be claimed, hoarded away, sold in marriage, or simply displayed as their male "owners" saw fit (DeLamotte 161). Women who did not "belong" to a man were viewed as available to any man who wished to claim them (Cutting-Gray 95). Evelina experiences such a situation at Marybone Gardens when she finds herself separated from her friends. Seeing her alone, "a young officer, marching fiercely up to me, said, 'You are a sweet pretty creature, and I enlist you in my service;' and then, with great violence, he seized my hand. I screamed aloud with fear, and, forcibly snatching it away, I ran" (233). In further describing the experience, Evelina relates that she felt "great terror" and was "frightened" (233). The scene may not be Gothic in atmosphere, yet Evelina experiences a terror similar to that of Gothic heroines. Such situations where women were victimized by men were found easily adaptable by Gothic novelists. Margaret Anne Doody has remarked that "It is in the Gothic novel that women writers could first accuse the 'real world' of falsehood and deep disorder" ("Deserts" 560), but already here in *Evelina*, Burney was making such an accusation by revealing how dangerous the world could be for women. Burney chose to write *The Wanderer* as a Gothic novel to emphasize more directly such mistreatment of women within patriarchal society.

Burney understood that even if women did not suffer physical confinement, they were always imprisoned within patriarchal society by a code of feminine conduct. Women lived in continual uncertainty of their social status because if they deviated or were thought to deviate from this patriarchal code, they could become social outcasts. Ellen Moers was the first critic to explore how both novels of manners and Gothic novels similarly treated this fearful uncertainty in women's situations:

> The perils that threaten A Young Lady's Entrance into the World (the subtitle of *Evelina*) seem to issue from the same grim realities of eighteenth-century girlhood that inspired Mrs. Radcliffe's Gothic: the same unjust accusations and uncaused severities; the same feminine malice and masculine cruelty; the restraints on her freedom, all the way to actual imprisonment; the mysterious, unexplained social rituals; the terrible need always to appear, as well as always to be, virtuous; and over all, the terrible danger of slippage from the respectable to the unrespectable class of womanhood. (136)

Moers' comparison of Burney and Mrs. Radcliffe can be used to illustrate the difference between *Evelina* as a novel of manners and *The Wanderer* as a Gothic novel. *The Wanderer* builds upon the same social criticism as *Evelina*, but where *Evelina* implies criticism of a society that places women in such roles of uncertainty, *The Wanderer* is explicit in its denouncement of the social injustices women endure. By utilizing the Gothic in *The Wanderer*, Burney combines her earlier sentimental novel tradition with Mrs. Radcliffe's Gothic tradition to create a new form of Gothic that is used for direct social criticism. *The Wanderer*'s Gothic elements, therefore, make the novel a more direct and mature expression of the social criticism that Burney offered in *Evelina*.

In both *Evelina* and *The Wanderer*, Burney uses themes common to both the sentimental and Gothic genres—inheritance and identity. Burney uses the inheritance theme to criticize the patriarchal establishment's treatment of women as second class citizens to men. Evelina is distressed because her father, Sir James Belmont, refuses to acknowledge her as his legitimate daughter. Without such acknowledgment, Evelina feels she has no real identity. Because inheritance and identity plots were also popular in the Gothic novel, Burney recreated a similar situation for Juliet. Juliet's father dies without acknowledging her, so Juliet must gain the acceptance of her uncle and siblings if she is to claim her rightful social position and inheritance. Burney's use of the inheritance plot in both cases reflects her awareness of the injustices of female children being treated differently than males, as evidenced in the works of male novelists. Like Evelina and Juliet, Henry Fielding's Tom Jones and Tobias Smollett's Humphry Clinker seek the acknowledgement of their families; ironically, when the true parentages of these male characters are revealed, they are warmly accepted by those families, despite their both being of illegitimate birth. In contrast, Evelina and Juliet are both legitimate children and known to their fathers, yet their existences are considered shameful so their fathers refuse to acknowledge them. This discrimination against female children largely existed because a son rather than a daughter typically carried on the family name. In the absence of legitimate children, an illegitimate son could be acknowledged as an heir to perpetuate his father's surname. There were cases, of course, where there were no sons and only daughters. In such cases, a son-in-law might be required upon marriage to take his wife's surname, or to hyphenate her name with his own. Even when Evelina is acknowledged by her father, she becomes merely an extension of his identity by taking his name. Later, by her marriage to Lord Orville, Evelina trades her identification with her father for identification with her husband. In neither case is Evelina's situation ideal. The one benefit she gains is the safety of her father or husband's protection.

In *The Wanderer*, Juliet's situation is even more extreme than that of Evelina. Juliet finds herself, unlike Evelina, not even having the benefit of a male guardian. Consequently, Juliet is forced to struggle alone in a patriarchal world. *The Wanderer*, therefore, becomes a dramatic revision of *Evelina*, using Gothic elements to emphasize the full "horror" of Juliet's situation. The most important Gothic element Burney employs in *The Wanderer*, reflected in the title, is to make her heroine, Juliet, a Gothic wanderer. Burney then blends numerous other Gothic elements into the novel, all of which revolve around Juliet's wandering status. The novel's Gothic elements and themes are:

1. Issues of legitimacy and inheritance, reflected in Juliet's position as unacknowledged daughter of an earl.
2. Juliet's mysterious identity—she must keep her identity a secret for her own safety and that of her friends who are imprisoned in France. Through most of the novel, even the reader is ignorant of Juliet's true identity because Burney creates a unique narrative strategy to enhance the novel's suspense.
3. Juliet's metaphorically supernatural powers by suggesting that Juliet can metamorphose herself into various people, ages, and races. These metamorphoses also build upon the frequent Gothic motif of immortality.
4. Female abduction and confinement plots, particularly in the forest scenes where Juliet continually hides from a male villain while simultaneously fearing rape or murder from everyone she encounters.
5. Gothic architecture—Burney innovatively uses Gothic architecture by applying Gothic elements to her description of Stonehenge.

These numerous Gothic elements reflect that Burney envisioned herself as writing within the Gothic novel tradition. The similarities between *Evelina* and *The Wanderer* illustrate Burney's belief that the Gothic provided an effective metaphor for the oppression of women and was the best means within fiction to protest against the injustices women daily suffered in eighteenth and early nineteenth century England.

Juliet as Female Gothic Wanderer

Burney's most daring and important use of the Gothic is to depict Juliet as a wanderer. Specifically, Burney links Juliet to the Wandering Jew when one of the characters refers to her as "a wandering Jewess" (485). Juliet's wandering status associates her with transgression and social alienation. Critics have generally interpreted *The Wanderer*'s title as a response to Romanticism and the wanderer figures in the works of Wordsworth, Byron, and Shelley. Burney was certainly aware of her Romantic contemporaries' use of the wanderer figure, and she does respond to Romanticism in the novel, but her wanderer is actually a female version of the Gothic wanderer. Burney chooses to make Juliet a Gothic rather than Romantic wanderer because Romantic wanderers notoriously choose to rebel and they celebrate their wandering status. Burney wishes to demonstrate that for women, there is nothing heroic about wandering, but rather it is a position society forces upon them and ostracizes them for. Furthermore, a woman who wandered was defying the social code of what was proper feminine behavior (Perkins 70, 74). Women writers were fully aware that wandering was a taboo activity for women in the early nineteenth century. Ellen Moers has remarked that an entire history of literary feminism can be found in the treatment of women who walk or travel in novels (*Literary* 130). For example, in *The Mysteries of Udolpho*, Emily's aunt disapproves of her taking solitary walks before breakfast from fear that she is indecorously spending time with Valancourt. Jane Austen's heroines, despite considerable time spent walking, almost always walk in groups and with male accompaniment. When a woman walks alone, she is frowned upon as unladylike, as occurs in *Pride and Prejudice* when Elizabeth takes a solitary walk to Netherfield to visit her ill sister Jane. Elizabeth's reception by the Bingley sisters is quite memorable:

> She [Elizabeth] was shown into the breakfast-parlor, where all but Jane were assembled, and where her appearance created a great deal of surprise. That she should have walked three miles so early in the day, in such dirty weather, and by herself, was almost incredible to Mrs. Hurst and Miss Bingley; and Elizabeth was convinced that they held her in contempt for it. (34)

Later, when Elizabeth is absent, the Bingleys comment upon her walk. The passage reflects how a minor act such as walking alone can become an indecorous and even offensive deed, potentially ruining a woman's reputation. The passage begins with Mrs. Hurst's comments.

"She [Elizabeth] has nothing, in short to recommend her, but being an excellent walker. I shall never forget her appearance this morning. She really looked almost wild."

"She did, indeed, Louisa. I could hardly keep my countenance. Very nonsensical to come at all! Why must she be scampering about the country because her sister has a cold? her hair, so untidy, so blowsy!"

"Yes, and her petticoat; I hope you saw her petticoat, six inches deep in mud, I am absolutely certain; and the gown which had been let down to hide it not doing its office."

"Your picture may be very exact, Louisa," said Bingley; "but this was all lost upon me. I thought Miss Elizabeth Bennet looked remarkably well when she came into the room this morning. Her dirty petticoat quite escaped my notice."

"You observed it, Mr. Darcy, I am sure," said Miss Bingley; "and I am inclined to think that you would not wish to see your sister make such an exhibition."

"Certainly not."

"To walk three miles, or four miles, or five miles, or whatever it is, above her ankles in dirt, and alone, quite alone! what could she mean by it? It seems to me to show an abominable sort of conceited independence, a most country-town indifference to decorum." (37)

Such intense condemnation over such an innocent activity as a solitary walk is humorous to modern readers, but while Jane Austen intends there to be light humor in this scene, she is also fully aware of the situation's seriousness. The Bingley sisters see Elizabeth's walking as an indecorous and even scandalous behavior that separates her from them. Ellen Moers correctly remarks that Jane Austen uses walking in her novels as a means for her female characters to display their independence (*Literary* 130). While independence is desirable for men, this scene depicts the double standard in action where a woman who seeks to be independent can destroy her entire reputation. The Bingley sisters here support the patriarchal system by conforming to it when they condemn Elizabeth, thus hoping to maintain their own superiority and social acceptance.

A more frightening example of the dangers of a woman walking alone occurs in Jane Austen's *Emma* (1816) where Harriet Smith and Miss Bickerton are attacked by gypsies during one of their walks. Miss Bickerton flees before the gypsies confront her, but Harriet is unable to follow due to a leg cramp and she is soon "assailed by half a dozen children, headed by a stout woman and a great boy" (300). In fear, Harriet gives them money, then tries to walk on, but they surround her, wanting more coins. At this point, Harriet is fortunately rescued by Frank Churchill, but the event has terrified Harriet indescribably, not so much for what has happened as the possibility of what could have happened had

Mr. Churchill not appeared. While the gypsy children and woman are less threatening, the "great boy" could well have assaulted Harriet's virtue, claiming her physically as his property. Simply that Harriet feels intimidated into giving up her money shows that her right to claim her own property is taken from her because she is a single woman, unable to defend herself. Such a scene shows how single women were viewed as unclaimed property available to any man who wished to possess it. Consequently, had Mr. Churchill not appeared in time, Harriet's moral reputation might have been ruined by further assault.

If walking alone could endanger a woman's moral reputation, then a woman who dared to be independent enough to work in a man's world was close to being considered a prostitute. In *The Wanderer*, Juliet's need to support herself results in her holding various employment situations, all of which reflect how women who work are morally misjudged by men. Nancy Armstrong remarks that in the eighteenth and nineteenth centuries, "the figure of the prostitute could be freely invoked to describe any woman who dared to labor for money" (qtd. in Perkins 74). Pam Perkins argues that Burney goes even farther than this idea by suggesting that any woman who needs money may be interpreted by men as a woman willing to be paid for her sexual favors (74). In Burney's time, most novels depicted women who labored as suffering punishment for their pride or folly (Perkins 80). Burney rejects this notion in *The Wanderer* by showing how women need money to support themselves, and they should not have to be dependent upon men for this money. Nor should women be treated as morally degraded for seeking to be self-supportive (Perkins 80). If the feminine Gothic is revising *Paradise Lost* to show that Eve's transgression to obtain forbidden knowledge was not a sin, then Fanny Burney is declaring that women who choose to be independent or who must work to support themselves are not committing a transgression and should not be treated as social outcasts for their independence. Burney's novel rejects the patriarchal notion that all women are transgressors simply for being born female, and that as transgressors, women must conform to patriarchal laws or be punished with social ostracism.

The relation between wandering and transgression was so well understood by Burney and her contemporaries that it became standard in depictions of the fallen woman. Several of Burney's contemporaries had already used wandering as a metaphor for the fallen woman. Conservative novelist Jane West in *Letters to a Young Lady* (1811) asks the reader to take pity upon "the poor night-wanderer who offends for bread" (Perkins 74), a suggestion that the woman prostitutes herself out of hunger, thus making her situation more sympathetic. In William Alexander's *History of Women* (1779), a girl who loses her "virtue" becomes a "hapless wanderer." In two American novels, Susannah Rowson's *Charlotte Temple* (1794) and Hannah Webster Foster's *The Coquette* (1797) friends of the fallen heroines mourn the loss of their respective "dear wanderer" and "deluded wanderer" (Perkins 74). When the word "wanderer" was applied to a woman, therefore, it had negative connotations which were the far opposite of more positive uses of the word for male wanderers of Romantic literature.

Because a "female wanderer" was considered a definite threat to a patriarchal society, Burney realized that such a figure was the perfect symbol of transgression for a Gothic novel. A female wanderer, because of her attributed sexual deviance, would serve as a major threat to patriarchy and its concerns over legitimacy, the preservation of hereditary lines, and family stability, all of which were frequent Gothic themes. By linking Juliet to the Wandering Jew, Burney exposed the myth that women are transgressors because they are descended from Eve who committed the first sin, just as the Wandering Jew unfairly symbolizes the Jewish people as transgressive murderers of Christ. Readers who sympathized with Juliet would realize that she does not morally transgress against patriarchy, but rather, she is unfairly accused of transgression simply because she is a woman who must work to support herself. The only transgression Juliet commits is against the arbitrary codes of femininity that patriarchy cruelly imposes upon women.

Burney's treatment of the Gothic wanderer figure, therefore, is innovative because she creates a female Gothic wanderer who is not a transgressor but is blamed for something beyond her control. Burney is more innovative in her use of the female wanderer than even her novelist successors, such as Gaskell and Eliot, who continue to equate female wandering with sexual transgression, as is the case with Esther in *Mary Barton* (1848) and Hetty Sorel in *Adam Bede* (1859). In contrast, Burney makes the reader fully aware that Juliet is morally impregnable and would not consider committing a sexual transgression. Juliet's innocence emphatically reveals the extent of society's discrimination against women, showing that the true transgressor is the patriarchal society because it discriminates against women and then condemns them for not conforming to impossible codes of femininity.

Female Identity

Juliet's role as wanderer results from her father's refusal to acknowledge her. Burney creates a plot that centers on the Gothic themes of inheritance and legitimacy to raise serious questions about female identity in patriarchal societies. Juliet's own individual identity is erased by the wanderer role placed upon her by her society when she becomes a victim of the French Revolution's events. Juliet is the unacknowledged daughter of an English earl by an earlier "unsuitable" marriage (645). Prior to the novel's opening, Juliet's father has died, and her half-brother and half-sister are unaware of her existence. Her father's desire to keep Juliet's existence a secret resulted in her upbringing in France and her father's agreement to make a financial settlement upon her when she marries.

When the Reign of Terror began, Juliet's guardian, a bishop, was arrested by a French commissary. The commissary discovered a promissory note for Juliet's inheritance upon her marriage. Because a woman's property belongs to her husband, the commissary forced Juliet to marry him, with the threat that he would execute the bishop if she would not. Juliet's victimization by patriarchy is then twofold: her father would not accept her, and she was forced into the confinement of an undesirable marriage. Immediately after the wedding ceremony, Juliet succeeds in escaping to England, but there she must keep her identity secret until she is assured of the bishop's safety and her marriage's illegality.

The novel opens with Juliet crossing the channel to England. The reader, however, is not informed of Juliet's name, history, or reason for fleeing France. Burney creates a unique narrative strategy by keeping Juliet's identity a secret throughout the first three of the novel's five volumes with the narrator referring to Juliet as "the Incognito" or "Ellis," a name a character mistakenly gives her because of a letter she receives addressed to "L.S." Critics have argued that this narrative strategy is unrealistic because Burney's third person limited point of view narration is restricted only to Juliet's thoughts, and these thoughts are restricted only to the present and future so Juliet never recalls her past. Critics McMaster and Adelstein both harshly criticize the novel's delay in revealing Juliet's true identity. Even when Juliet's real name is finally revealed in volume three, McMaster complains that Juliet's full identity remains hidden until the novel's final pages (27). Adelstein, in agreement with McMaster, remarks that *The Wanderer*'s melodramatic plot could have made it an exciting novel, but Burney ineffectively handled the point of view. Burney's earlier novels always provided the heroine's unrestricted thoughts, either by first person letters in *Evelina*, or by an omniscient narrator in *Cecilia* and *Camilla*. Burney's restriction of Juliet's thoughts to only the present or future is not only unnatural as a narrative point of view, but also unnatural for a real person. Adelstein argues that Burney's decision to keep Juliet's identity a complete secret until the novel's denouement was, therefore, an unfair attempt to build suspense (123). Adelstein concludes that Burney should have revealed Juliet's situation early in the novel so the reader could then share Juliet's anguish, distress, and frustration while dramatic irony would have compensated for any lost suspense (124).

Critics, however, have failed to understand Burney's full reasons for creating this unique narrative strategy. The primary purpose behind the point of view is not to build suspense over Juliet's true identity, but to subsume her personal identity into her role as a symbolic Everywoman. Burney intends Juliet's role as wanderer to symbolize the displacement of all women in patriarchal society. To sustain this ambitious theme, Burney wanted a point of view that would effectively display an individual's thoughts, yet place that individual in numerous situations to signify the thoughts and experiences of various women. Juliet's role as Everywoman is evident by the difference in *The Wanderer*'s title when compared to Burney's earlier novels. *Evelina* (1778), *Cecilia* (1782), and *Camilla* (1796) all have a woman's name for a title. *The Wanderer* is not only without the main character's name, but neither does it identify the main character's gender. Each of Burney's earlier novels also had the respective subtitles: "The History of a Young Lady's Entrance Into the World," "Memoirs of An Heiress," and "A Picture of Youth." All the subtitles contain "A," to identify each novel as the story of a single, female main character. Although "The" in *The Wanderer* suggests one main character, the novel's subtitle "Female Difficulties" suggests collective female experiences. The difference in titles and point of view enhances Juliet's role as representative of the female sex, while subordinating the importance of her individual identity. While the novel's characters disdain Juliet because of her obscure identity, the reader is asked to set aside the social assumption that a woman's background and class must be known to determine her character (Doody, *Frances* 324; Cutting-Gray 89).

Burney uses an omniscient third person narration so Juliet's thoughts of the past are also restricted; the restriction of Juliet's memory frees her from identifying herself as the commissary's possession. Her greatest fear is that he will find and reclaim her, but she represses this fear throughout most of the novel, thus successfully achieving her own individual and independent identity. Juliet's repression of her memories results in the reader's ignorance of Juliet's past through the majority of the novel. Consequently, the reader can only judge Juliet by her actions and not her background. The reader is placed in the same situation as the characters, continually wondering about Juliet's identity and being surprised by her various metamorphoses. Unlike the other characters, however, the reader becomes knowledgeable enough to understand that Juliet is not intentionally deceitful; rather, she must keep her identity a secret for her own protection. The reader sympathizes with Juliet's situation, trusting her until the time when her full identity will be revealed at the novel's conclusion. By willingly suspending disbelief, the reader becomes all the more curious about Juliet's metamorphoses, which in turn builds the narrative suspense and allows Burney's symbol of Juliet as Everywoman to be the more persuasive.

Burney's theme of identity is enhanced by Juliet not revealing her name and the other characters feeling the need to identify her by naming her. Shortly after she arrives in England, Juliet is employed by Mrs. Maple and Elinor. During this time, she receives mail addressed to L.S. While the novel never explains what these initials represent, Margaret Anne Doody suggests they stand for the first two symbols of the old British currency, namely L.s.d. Burney may have intended to associate Juliet with monetary units to show that men view women only in economic terms as forms of currency, exchange, or property (*Frances* 329). Doody's argument is supported by the fact that both Juliet's uncle and the commissary view her merely as a piece of property, as evidenced by the promissory note of six thousand pounds to be given her upon her marriage. Characters in the novel, disconcerted by Juliet's lack of identity, assume the initials represent Juliet's name. Miss Bydell, when hearing Juliet referred to as "L.S.," makes the mistake of calling Juliet "Elless," a name suggesting the French word for woman "Elle" plus "less" to show Juliet is less than a woman because she has no identity. It is Elinor, the novel's champion of women's rights, however, who changes the name to "Ellis" (suggestive of "Elle is"), meaning "She exists" or "Woman is Alive" (Doody, Introduction xvi). Burney has made a dramatic leap here between her first and last novel in identifying her female characters. Evelina Anville's name suggests "Eve in a Veil" or that woman's identity is hidden and unknown (Doody, *Frances* 40). If it is "Eve in a Veil," it suggests that all women continue to suffer by hiding their true identities as a result of the transgression committed by Milton's Eve. "Elle" can also be found in the names of Cecilia and Camilla. If Evelina means Eve in a Veil, and Elless means Woman is Less or Nobody, Burney is reusing a theme she expressed first in her diary which she addressed as "Nobody."

Often in her diaries and novel prefaces, Burney would revoke her identity and authority by referring to herself as Nobody, and asking "must a female be made Nobody? Ah! my dear, what were this world good for, were Nobody a female?" (Cutting-Gray 109). If nobody or no one were a female, there would be no human race. Burney believes women are as equally important and necessary as men, yet she and her female characters are devalued by a patriarchal world that both denies them their identity by treating them as property, and consequently, prevents them from supporting themselves because they cannot claim possession of their own bodies. Burney is also showing that a person's identity is not merely psychological, but it is also dependent upon gender, race, and one's social class. Although a person may cultivate his or her own identity, ultimately, identity is dependent upon the culture into which one is born and how that culture labels people. Gallagher remarks that Burney's statement in her diary regarding woman as "nobody" is Burney's attempt to divorce herself imaginatively from these "particulars of time, place, sex, class, and age" that no real person can escape, and therefore, people need their imaginations to liberate them so they may have some control over their identities, despite the strictures placed upon their identities by their culture (*Nobody* 206). While Juliet's hidden identity makes her appear as a Nobody to the other characters, the name Ellis proclaims that woman exists and must and will be recognized. Juliet/Ellis uses her namelessness to determine her own identity, free of a man's control because she can belong to herself rather than having a name that proclaims her possession by a man. While Juliet hides her identity to protect herself, her lack of identity also suggests her attempt to escape her past and the commissary's claim to possess her so she can be an independent woman. Her imaginative self-denial of her past provides Juliet with the strength to be independent and self-sufficient in a constrictive patriarchal world.

Women's Employment as Gothic Horror

When Juliet arrives in England, she has no friends or fortune, so she must support herself. Burney places Juliet in nearly every work situation available to a woman in the late eighteenth and early nineteenth century to depict thoroughly the various "horrors" faced by women who try to support themselves. Burney reveals that none of the employment positions available to women offer them freedom or independence (Doody, Introduction xv). While a Gothic atmosphere or conventional Gothic elements are not used in most of the scenes detailing Juliet's work experiences, Burney realized she did not need to exaggerate descriptions of the working world for women because it was already comparable to the horrors of Gothic novels.

Juliet's first position is as a household servant; she then becomes a music teacher, a self-employed seamstress, an employee in a milliner's shop, a seamstress for a mantua maker, and finally, a lady's companion. Later, Juliet witnesses the experiences of farmers and shepherds' wives. Consequently, Juliet is familiar with nearly every employment position available to a middle-class woman in the eighteenth and early nineteenth century, only to find each situation exhausting and demeaning. She is mistreated as Mrs. Maple's servant because of her mysterious identity. As a music teacher, her pupils are too inconsiderate to pay promptly for their lessons; money is not something Juliet's wealthy pupils worry over, so they seldom consider its importance to others. While a self-employed seamstress, Juliet works all day with little sleep and no rest or exercise; she suffers continual exhaustion, yet she can barely earn an income. When employed as a seamstress in a shop, her speed makes her hated by the other workers, and she finds that by working quickly, she runs out of work, causing her own unemployment. Hardest of all for Juliet is that she can find no mental stimulation nor any pride in her work. Doody argues that Burney, in her depiction of Juliet's working experiences, is the first novelist to explore the "alienation" caused when workers feel no personal participation in their tasks. Instead of having control over or a creative input in the work, the worker suffers the monotony of routine tasks that are degrading to the mind (*Frances* 356). The worker merely becomes a type of automaton, losing his or her identity. Ironically, Juliet's identity is already hidden from the reader, so these scenes only further express the impossibility in a patriarchal society for a woman to be anything other than the extension of a man's identity. Menial employment situations leave Juliet barely able to remain financially independent; furthermore,

Juliet finds that while physical labor may grant her financial freedom, it does not provide true independence when it exhausts the body so that the mind is too fatigued to function freely. Juliet summarizes this sad truth by remarking, "ah! what is freedom but a name, for those who have not an hour at command from the subjection of fearful penury and distress?" (473-4).

Juliet's position as paid companion to Mrs. Ireton further exemplifies the difficulty a woman faces in trying to be independent both financially and mentally. Being a paid lady's companion is the most genteel position Juliet occupies, yet it is simultaneously the most degrading; Juliet must fulfill Mrs. Ireton's every whim, continually serving and entertaining her. By living merely to please Mrs. Ireton, Juliet demeans herself by becoming a mere extension of her employer. She is treated as a nonentity, a person without her own personality, and Mrs. Ireton increases this demeaning fact by believing that as a lady's companion, Juliet should "never think of taking such a liberty as to give her own opinion" (524). As Doody observes, in this scene Juliet has sold her identity to feed her body (*Frances* 358). Only when Juliet's personality reasserts itself does Juliet's employment with Mrs. Ireton end. In a dramatic scene, she departs from Mrs. Ireton's presence without permission. Mrs. Ireton accosts her by saying, "permit me to enquire who told you to go?" (526). Juliet responds, "A person, Madam, who has not the honour to be known to you,—myself!" (526). Juliet has asserted her ability to reason for herself, and consequently, the right of a woman to have and to cultivate her own identity (Cutting-Gray 100). Nevertheless, even if a woman does assert her identity, it can only work against her. After her comments to Mrs. Ireton, Juliet finds herself again unemployed.

Juliet's Metamorphoses and Immortality

While a Gothic atmosphere is absent from the descriptions of Juliet's various employment situations, Burney does suggest that the shifts Juliet makes from one job to another are almost supernatural, as if Juliet metamorphoses herself each time she changes her position. Her employment changes are, however, the least remarkable of Juliet's metamorphoses throughout the novel. More striking contrasts in her situation occur when she first disguises herself as a black woman to escape from France. Burney uses Juliet's black identity to symbolize how women are treated like slaves in patriarchal society. When she arrives in England, Juliet transforms herself from a black woman into a white. Juliet is also of English blood, yet she speaks English with a French accent. She holds lower class employment positions, yet at the novel's end, she is revealed to be of aristocratic birth. These contrasts, or metamorphoses, are what make Juliet's character cross the racial, national, and class barriers that separate women. Margaret Anne Doody observes that because Juliet's metamorphoses allow her to relate to all women throughout history, Juliet becomes an Everywoman.

> The heroine thus arrives as a nameless Everywoman; both black and white, both Eastern and Western, both high and low, both English and French. She unites but does not resolve contradictions....she persists in being 'an Aenigma', the 'Incognita', or Unknown. She sustains her role of Everywoman throughout the novel, as is indicated by the name she adopts or has thrust upon her (Introduction xv).

Burney has turned Juliet into an Everywoman by not revealing her name and by restricting her thoughts from the past. Had Juliet's true identity and upper class background been revealed at the novel's beginning, the reader would have judged Juliet according to her social background; then, as she passes from one demeaning position to another, sympathy for Juliet would arise from her being an aristocrat fallen on hard times, and the reader might have paid less attention to the important theme of the working woman's plight. By divorcing us from Juliet's personality and thoughts of the past, Burney asks the reader to suspend disbelief and participate in Juliet's wanderings to experience fully the difficulties that exist for all women, regardless of class, position, age, or race.

Juliet's continual transformations from employment positions and races make the other characters suggest she really does have the supernatural power to metamorphose herself. Her employer, Mrs. Ireton, first suggests Juliet's supernatural ability when she discovers that Juliet, whom she had thought to be black, is really white:

> You have been bruised and beaten; and dirty and clean; and ragged and whole; and wounded and healed; and a European and a Creole, in less than a week. I suppose, next, you will dwindle into a dwarf; and then perhaps, find some surprising contrivance to shoot up into a giantess. There is nothing that can be too much to expect from so great an adept in metamorphoses. (46)

Mrs. Ireton later comments again upon the possibility of Juliet's supernatural state by suggesting she may be immortal and thereby directly linking Juliet to the Wandering Jew.

> Pray, if I may presume so far, how old are you?—But I beg pardon for so indiscreet a question. I did not reflect upon what I was saying. Very possibly your age may be indefinable. You may be a person of another century. A wandering Jewess. I never heard that the old Jew had a wife, or a mother, who partook of his longevity; but very likely I may now have the pleasure of seeing one of his family under my own roof? That

red and white, that you lay on so happily, may just as well hide the wrinkles of two or three grand climacterics, as of only a poor single sixty or seventy years of age. However, these are secrets that I don't presume to enquire into. Every trade has its mystery. (485-6)

Juliet's suggested immortality allows her to transcend time and to be linked to all women throughout history, suggesting that women have always been Gothic wanderers because patriarchal culture has labeled them as transgressors. Furthermore, Mrs. Ireton's comments reflect the discomfort felt by those characters with stable identities for Juliet's continually shifting identity. Juliet is placed in the role of transgressor because she is a woman capable of change, and therefore, her real identity is difficult to determine. Her continually shifting identity adds to the difficulty of defining or categorizing her so she remains ambiguous and all the more threatening to a stable patriarchal culture.

When Juliet is dismissed from the irate Mrs. Ireton's service, she travels to London to be with her friend, Gabriella, another émigré from France. During her short stay with Gabriella, Sir Jaspar tells Juliet that if she reveals her identity to him, he will protect her so she no longer needs to "wander" (628). Juliet, however, still fears to reveal her true identity. Sir Jaspar then whimsically asks, "Has any one presumed to give you a human genealogy? Are you not straight descended from the clouds? without even taking the time to change yourself first into a mortal?" (629). Sir Jaspar's comments coincide with Mrs. Ireton's suggestion that Juliet can metamorphose herself, and more specifically, that she may be immortal.

Juliet's time with Gabriella is short because she now learns that the French commissary is in England searching for her so he can force her to return to France as his wife. In terror, Juliet flees from London and again takes up her wandering life in the most Gothic moments of the novel where she fully plays the role of Wandering Jewess by continually having to wander to hide from the commissary. First, Juliet takes a stage to Salisbury and then to Ramsey because she reads newspaper inquiries for information about her. These scenes may have been inspired by William Godwin's *Caleb Williams*, where Caleb discovers his story is being sold in narrative form on the streets, and he is described as a criminal so he must remain a fugitive and conceal his identity by disguising himself as a Jew. Already symbolically a Wandering Jewess, Juliet similarly disguises herself by exchanging clothes with various women she meets. These women are often of dubious chastity, resulting in Juliet being misrecognized as a woman of free morals. These scenes emphasize Burney's theme of the impossibility for women to be Romantic wanderers in a patriarchal society. Juliet remarks of this experience "is it only under the domestic roof,—that roof to me denied!—that woman can know safety, respect, and honour?" (666).

Juliet now attempts to hide by entering the forest. Here Burney again emphasizes Juliet's metamorphoses in the most Gothic moments of the novel. Throughout these scenes, Juliet must continually move from place to place to avoid being identified, just as the Wandering Jew is unable to rest but must continually wander from one location to another. Juliet is further linked with Gothic wanderers who, by virtue of their immortality, are the Wandering Jew's literary descendants. Like the Rosicrucians who gain life-extension by drinking the elixir of life, Juliet metaphorically becomes a Gothic immortal when she begs for food and drink at a cottage. Exhausted, hungry and thirsty, she greatly appreciates the few moments of rest and nourishment, and "in quaffing her milk and water, believed herself initiated in the knowledge of the flavour, and of all the occult qualities, of Nectar" (669). She then receives food, "And if her drink had seemed nectar, what was more substantial appeared to her to be ambrosia!" (671). Burney specifically makes these references to ambrosia and nectar because they are the nourishment of the gods, and if mortals partake of them, they have immortality conferred upon them. Furthermore, by metaphorically acquiring immortal life, Juliet has symbolically transgressed because to seek immortal life is to seek autonomy from God's plan for human salvation. During her wandering in the forest, Juliet will have her great epiphany by realizing true immortality can only be found in God's plan for human redemption. While Gothic wanderers generally seek forbidden knowledge, Juliet will gain knowledge in the form of religious faith. Unlike forbidden knowledge, Juliet's strengthened faith is something she may return with from her wanderings and use to improve her society.

Gothic Forest Scenes and Anti-Romanticism

The Wanderer's forest scenes are the novel's most traditionally Gothic moments. Burney uses these Gothic moments to comment directly upon social problems including the plight of the poor, the situation of women, and humanity's spiritual needs. The forest scenes provide for Juliet both a horrifying experience and a metaphoric return to the Garden of Eden. Once in the forest, Juliet feels herself surrounded by the beauties of an Edenic Nature, and while admiring Nature's beauty, she feels that "all paradise was opened to her view" (676). Burney incorporates Romantic ideas of Nature into the novel by making Juliet feel refreshed and strengthened by the sight of Nature.

> Here, for the first time, she ceased to sigh for social intercourse: she had no void, no want; her mind was sufficient to itself; Nature, Reflection, and Heaven seemed her own! Oh Gracious Providence! she cried, supreme in goodness as in power! What lesson can all the eloquence of rhetoric, science, erudition, or philosophy produce, to restore tranquillity to the

> troubled, to preserve it in the wise, to make it cheerful to the innocent,—like the simple view of beautiful nature? so divine in its harmony, in its variety so exquisite! Oh great Creator! beneficient! omnipotent! thy works and religion are one! Religion! source and parent of resignation! under thy influence how supportable is every earthly calamity! how supportable, because how transitory becomes all human woe, where heaven and eternity seem full in view! (676)

Burney is in agreement with the Romantics about the power of Nature's beauty to restore peace to the mind and soul; however, Burney also emphatically criticizes Romanticism for its elevation of Nature, when it is merely part of creation and God's gift to humanity. Burney believes Nature's beauty should be viewed as a reminder of God's promise of paradise for those who are faithful to Him. In this Christian perspective of Nature's restorative value, Burney is not only rejecting Romanticism, but she anticipates her Victorian successors who will use Christianity more directly in their treatment of the Gothic than had the earlier Gothic novelists.

Burney further criticizes Romanticism by condemning the falsity of its sentimental depictions of the poor who live among Nature. Juliet realizes that the poor she meets in the forest are largely indifferent to Nature's beauty rather than allowing it to ennoble their minds and spirits.

Numerous examples are used by Burney to depict just how spiritually depraved are the poor. When Juliet begs for shelter at a cottage, she is turned away, until she offers a half-crown to pay for food and a night's lodging. The experience leaves Juliet "mortified that so mercenary a spirit could have found entrance in a spot which seemed fitted to the virtuous innocence of our yet untainted first parents" (678). Nature is not Eden, and it is not sufficient to elevate the mind or cultivate kindness in the soul. Burney criticizes Romanticism's elevation of Nature further by showing that although Juliet's hosts live amidst Nature, they are less an innocent Adam and Eve than possible Gothic villains. As Juliet prepares for bed, she hears her hosts whispering and glancing at her in a manner that makes her fear they intend her harm. Their strange behavior makes her wonder, "Have I fallen into a den of thieves?" (679). During the night, her fears increase as she hears unfamiliar voices and strange movements about the house. While she is not harmed, she suspects her hosts are plotting hideous crimes of theft and murder. When the house is finally quiet, Juliet decides she will try to escape. The scene that follows is as terrifying as any in a Gothic novel.

> Raising her head, next, to view the door, which, the preceding night, had escaped her notice, she espied, close to its edge, a large clot of blood.

Struck with terrour, she started up; and then perceived that the passage from door to door was traced with bloody spots.

She remained for some minutes immovable, incapable either to think of her danger, or to form any plan for her preservation; and wholly absorbed by the image which this sight presented to her fears, of some victim to murderous rapacity.

Soon, however, rousing to a sense of her own situation, she determined upon making a new attempt to escape. She listened beneath the trap-door, to ascertain that all was quiet, and received the most unequivocal assurances, that fatigue and watchfulness had ended in sound sleep. Still, however, she could find no key; but, while fearfully examining every corner, she remarked that the low door was merely latched.

Should she here seek some out-let? She recoiled from the sight of the blood; yet it was a sight that redoubled her earnestness to fly. Whatever had been deposited would certainly be concealed: she resolved, therefore, to make the experiment, though her hand shook so violently, that, more than once, it dropt from the latch ere she could open the door.

Trembling she then crossed the threshold, and found herself in a miserable outer-building, without casements, and encumbered with old utensils and lumber. She observed a large cupboard which was locked, but of which, from the darkness of the place, she could take no survey. To the outward door there was no lock, but it was doubly bolted. She opened it, though not without difficulty, and saw that it led to a small disorderly garden, which was hedged round, half planted with potatoes, and half wasted with rubbish. She examined whether here were any opening by which she might enter the Forest; and discerned a small gate, over which, though it was covered with briars, she believed that she could scramble.

Nevertheless, she hesitated; she might be heard, or presently missed and pursued; and the vengeance incurred by such a detection of her suspicions and ill opinion, might provoke her immediate destruction. It might be better, therefore, to return; to rise only when called; to pay them another half-crown; and then publicly depart.

Accidentally, while thus deliberating, she touched the handle of a large wicker-basket, and found that it was wet: she held out her hand to the light, and saw that it was besmeared with blood.

She turned sick; she nearly fainted; she shrunk from her hand with horrour; yet strove to recover her courage, by ejaculating a fervent prayer.

> To re-enter the house voluntarily, was now impossible; she shuddered at the idea of again encountering her dreaded hosts, and resolved upon a flight, at all risks, from so fearful a dwelling. (682-3)

Juliet flees from the cottage and stumbles through the forest, hoping to find someone to whom she can reveal the horrendous murders she suspects, but everyone she meets only serves further to frighten her. She comes to a cottage occupied by an elderly couple, only to detect from their comments that they are friends and accomplices to the family from whom she has just fled. Keeping her secret to herself, she continues to wander through the forest.

At first, Burney might be accused of creating this Gothic moment for sensation, but later, it is revealed as an example of social criticism when Juliet learns that the blood she discovered was from animals. Her host's secrecy results from his having to poach to support his family. This incident helps Juliet to realize that the poor are too busy trying to support themselves to contemplate Nature's beauty. The novel has turned poaching into a potential Gothic moment to highlight how the patriarchal system, controlled by the aristocracy, not only oppresses women but all levels of society.

Juliet soon after finds shelter with a farm family and then two shepherds and their wives. These experiences make Juliet realize how difficult survival is for the poor who are also afflicted by the aristocratic patriarchy. Juliet finds the shepherds to be kind and she respects the usefulness of their occupation, but she cannot imagine their vocation to be spiritually fulfilling or intellectually stimulating. She finds their isolated existence to be especially disturbing, for after her long wanderings as an outcast, she realizes there is nothing pleasant in being separated from society.

> ...she sought vainly to content herself with their uncultured society; and soon saw, with regret, how much the charm, though not the worth, of innocence depends upon manners; of goodness, upon refinement; and of honesty upon elevation. There was much to merit her approbation; but not a point to engage her sympathy; and, where the dominion of the character falls chiefly upon the heart, life, without sympathy, is a blank. The unsatisfied soul sighs for communion; its affections demand an expansion, its ideas, a development, that, instinctively, call for interchange; and point out, that solitude, sought only by misery, remorse, or misanthropy, is as ungenial to our natural feelings, as retirement is salubrious. (700)

Like the Romantics, Burney can admire these simple people and honor them for their work, yet she does not find intellectual stimulation among them; nor does she see anything ideal about pastoral life despite its depictions in literature. She becomes highly critical of Romantic writers who glorify the lives of the poor without experience of those lives.

> She had here time and opportunity to see the fallacy, alike in authors and in the world, of judging solely by theory. Those who are born and bred in a capital; who first revel in its dissipations and vanities, next, sicken of its tumults and disappointments, write or exclaim for ever, how happy is the country peasant's lot! They reflect not that, to make it such, the peasant must be so much more philosophic than the rest of mankind, as to see and feel only his advantages, while he is blind and insensible to his hardships. Then, indeed, the lot of the peasant might merit envy!
> But who is it that gives it celebrity? Is it himself? Does he write of his own joys? Does he boast of his own contentment? Does he praise his own lot? No! 'tis the writer, who has never tried it, and the man of the world who, however murmuring at his own, would not change with it, that give it celebrity. (700)

Burney goes on to remark how Juliet has become meditative from her many experiences. Her desire to understand all she sees has made her experiences productive for her, so she is able to judge accurately such situations rather than write blindly about the happiness of country life as do most authors.

> She looked with an intelligent desire of information, upon every new scene of life, that was presented to her view; and every class of society, that came within her knowledge: she now, therefore, with equal clearness and concern, saw how false an idea is conceived, at a distance, not only of the shepherd's paradise, but of the general happiness of the country life;—save to those who enjoy it with a large family to bring up; or with means not alone competent to necessity, but to benevolence; which not alone give leisure for the indulgence of contemplation, and the cultivation of rural taste, of literature, and of the fine arts; but which supply means for lightening the labours, and softening the hardships of the surrounding poor and needy. Then, indeed, the country life is the nearest upon earth, to what we may conceive of joys celestial! (700)

Burney is above all a realist. If people are to be happy on earth, they must have the independence, provided by money and time, to pursue their interests. Those who labor continually in the country do not have time to enjoy Nature's beauty, but find their relationship to Nature is conditioned by its effect upon their tasks. Juliet is again critical of Romanticism's belief that the beauty of Nature makes peasant and country life ideal in the following passage:

> The verdure of the flower-motleyed meadow; the variegated foliage of the wood; the fragrance and purity of the air, and the wide spreading beauties of the landscape, charm not the labourer. They charm only the enlightened rambler, or affluent possessor. Those who toil, heed them not. Their eyes are upon their plough; their attention is fixed upon the harvest; their sight follows the pruning hook. If the vivid field catches their view, it is but to present to them the image of the scythe, with which their labour must mow it; if they look at the shady tree, it is only with the foresight of the ax, with which their strength must fell it; and, while the body pants but for rest, which of the senses can surrounding scenery, ambient perfumes, or vocal warblers, enchant or enliven? (700-1)

Having now lived among the poor and country people, Juliet is better able to give an accurate depiction of them to the reader. She again speaks out against those writers who ignorantly depict ideal versions of country life, and she declares that we should appreciate these simple people, not because they provide fruit for the creation of picturesque or romantic literary subjects, but for the integral needs of society that they fulfill at the expense of their own enjoyment and well-being.

> O ye, she cried, who view them through your imaginations! were ye to toil with them but one week! to rise as they rise, feed as they feed, and work as they work! like mine, then, your eyes would open; you would no longer judge of their pleasures and luxuries, by those of which they are the instruments for yourselves! you would feel and remark, that yours are all prepared for you; and that they, the preparers, are sufferers, not partakers! You would see then, as I see now, that the most delightful view which the horizon can bound, affords not to the poor labourer the joy that is excited by the view of the twilight through which it is excluded; but which sends him home to the mat of straw, that rests, for the night, his spent and weary limbs. (701)

The Wanderer's long commentary upon rural life and literature's misconceptions of it reveals the extent of Burney's desire to depict realistically the flaws of her entire society. By setting *The Wanderer* during the French Revolution, Burney intends for her commentaries upon the English poor to resonate in the minds of her readers and warn them of possible class upheaval that might occur in England as it already has in France. Workers, whether metropolitan or rural, male or female, must be treated better if England is to avoid revolution. At the novel's end, Juliet will herself set an example of how the upper class must be socially aware of such injustices and attempt to remedy them if England is to maintain political and economic stability. Once accepted by her family and married into the upper class, Juliet rewards the poor people of the forest who assisted her, despite their own poverty. "No one to whom Juliet had ever owed any good office, was by her forgotten, or by Harleigh neglected. They visited, with gifts and praise, every cottage in which the Wanderer had been harboured" (872).

Juliet now contemplates how Nature's beauty is a proof of God's existence. She reacts against the currently popular atheism of the French Revolution, which her friend Elinor believes in. Juliet believes that anyone who contemplates Nature's magnificence cannot possibly doubt that God exists and that He is benevolent to humanity by granting immortality in the afterlife.

> Oh that Elinor, she cried, escaping from the pressure of her passions, would expand her feelings by contemplating the works of God! Oh Father of All!—Who can reflect, yet doubt, that Man, placed at the head of these stupendous operations, lord of the earthly sphere, can fail to be destined for Immortality? Yet more, who can examine and meditate upon the uncertain existence of thy creatures,—see failure without fault; success without virtue; sickness without relief; oppression in the very face of liberty; labour without sustenance; and suffering without crime;—and not see, and not feel that all call aloud for resurrection and retribution! that annihilation and injustice would be one! and that Man, from the very nature of his precarious earthly being, must necessarily be destined, by the All Wise, and All Just, for regions that we see not; for purposes that we know not;—for Immortality! (702)

This speech may well be the most powerful and important passage in the entire novel. While the book's first three quarters have depicted Juliet's plight as symbolic of women's oppression, now the novel has expanded Juliet into a symbol of all who suffer within the patriarchal society. Although Burney is writing at the Romantic period's height, with its emphasis on the individual, she returns to eighteenth century literature's emphasis upon the universal to make Juliet's story relevant to the common experiences of all people. This universalism extends to the acknowledgement that we are all God's children so we are all destined for immortality. Juliet's speech also reflects Burney's agreement with her Gothic predecessors that the Gothic wanderer figure ultimately must reject an extended life upon earth in favor of eternal life in Heaven. Seeking autonomy from God can only bring unhappiness, while submitting to His plan for salvation is the way to immortality and spiritual freedom. Burney is more direct than her Gothic predecessors by asserting this Christian theology, whereas earlier Gothic novelists had indirectly made their novels reworkings of *Paradise Lost* and the Christian belief system. Burney is a precursor here to the Victorians who will use the Gothic to promote Christian values by transforming the Gothic wanderer into a symbol of Christian redemption.

Soon after these philosophical thoughts, Juliet is captured by the French commissary, who attempts to take her back to France. Instead, the commissary is himself arrested, leaving Juliet free from fear and able to reveal her true identity. Sir Jaspar informs Juliet that her brother and sister have learned she is their sister and they fully acknowledge her. Sir Jaspar then offers to escort Juliet to where her family awaits her. Juliet and Sir Jaspar travel by carriage across Salisbury plain, where they stop at Stonehenge. The Stonehenge scene is the novel's climax and a microcosm of the wanderer theme and the emphasis upon the soul's immortality. Burney uniquely uses the Gothic in this scene by describing Stonehenge as a piece of Gothic architecture where forgotten secrets are revealed for human enlightenment.

Stonehenge: Symbol of the Immortal Soul

Like Juliet, Stonehenge's true identity is a secret. Just as Burney presented Juliet for three volumes before naming her, now Burney describes Stonehenge for two pages before presenting its name, and then it is Sir Jaspar who finally names it. Doody argues that for Sir Jaspar, Stonehenge is a masculine place whose stones are erect on Salisbury plain like phallic symbols (*Frances* 366). In addition, Sir Jaspar links the monument to the male world by mentioning the druids and the giants Gog and Magog (766). Before Sir Jaspar makes these connections, however, Juliet has already noticed Stonehenge's circular pattern (765). The circle represents the feminine and motherhood, recalling an earlier scene in the novel when Juliet's friend, Gabriella, placed sticks upright in a circle to mark her dead son's grave (Doody, *Frances* 366). While Sir Jaspar and Juliet both interpret the monument's appearance according to their own genders, Stonehenge's original purpose has been forgotten by time, leaving it to stand as a monument to a forgotten people and culture. Similarly, when Gabriella dies, the world will no longer remember her child or what the sticks at his grave represent because his name and identification are not recorded there. While the novel uses Stonehenge as an image of those forgotten by history, it also makes clear that it does not matter whether it was a place of worship or the throne of kings; it was built by laborers, who are equally forgotten just as are women, the poor, and the other outcasts of Juliet's time who are the foundation of a patriarchal society that devalues them (Doody, Introduction xxxvi).

Despite the novel's concern with female identity, during the Stonehenge scene, the novel transcends issues of gender. Juliet has known poverty and suffering, and she has learned that they afflict both sexes. No longer is

Juliet Everywoman, or even Everyman, but now she becomes Everyperson. Cutting-Gray observes that by the novel's end, Juliet's name, history, and identity are unimportant. The reader, who has suffered with Juliet throughout the novel and who has doubtless suffered in his or her own life, is the one who now gives Juliet her identity by identifying with her. The reader takes Juliet's suffering upon him or herself, and thus Juliet is "named" (108). Her name is now Everyperson because her story is humanity's story. All people are wanderers on this earth, and the way for each person to learn his or her own identity is to understand others' pain (Doody, *Frances* 367).

At this point, Juliet's earlier thoughts upon immortality are reasserted and concluded. Juliet realizes the immortal presence of Stonehenge, seeing how the upright stones "were so ponderous that they appeared to have resisted all the wars of the elements, in this high and bleak situation, for ages" (765). Similarly, the spirit of the human race has resisted falling into utter despair throughout history. Burney now connects the emphasis upon the human spirit to Juliet's role as Everyperson by reintroducing Juliet's ability to metamorphose. While at Stonehenge, Riley, a witness of Juliet's meeting with the commissary, comes to inform her that the commissary has returned to France and she is completely safe. Riley, surprised to learn Juliet is married to the commissary, then repeats Mrs. Ireton's earlier suggestion that Juliet can metamorphose herself.

> "What a rare hand you are, Demoiselle," cried Riley, "at hocus pocus work! Who the deuce, with that Hebe face of yours, could have thought of your being a married woman! Why, when I saw you at that old Bang'em's concert, at Brighthelmstone, I should have taken you for a boarding-school Miss. But you metamorphose yourself about so, one does not know which way to look for you. Ovid was a mere fool to you. His nymphs, turned into trees, and rivers, and flowers, and beasts, and fishes, make such a staring chaos of lies, that one reads them without a ray or reference to truth; like the tales of the Genii, or of old Mother Goose. He makes such a comical hodge podge of animal, vegetable, and mineral choppings and changes, that we should shout over them, as our brats do at a puppet-shew, when old Nick teaches punchinello the devil's dance down to hell; or pummels his wife to a mummy; if it were not for the sly rogue's tickling one's ears so cajolingly with the jingle of metre. But Demoiselle, here, scorns all that namby pamby work."
>
> Sir Jaspar tried vainly to call him to order; the embarrassment of Juliet operated but as a stimulus to his caustic humour.
>
> "I have met with nothing like her, Master Baronet," he continued, "all the globe over. Neither juggler nor conjuror is a

match for her. She can make herself as ugly as a witch, and as handsome as an angel. She'll answer what one only murmurs in a whisper; and she won't hear a word, when one bawls as loud as a speaking-trumpet. Now she turns herself into a vagrant, not worth sixpence; and now into a fine player and singer that ravishes all ears, and might make, if it suited her fancy, a thousand pounds at her benefit: and now, again, as you see, you can't tell whether she's a house-maid, or a country girl! yet a devilish fine creature, faith! as fine a creature as ever I beheld,—when she's in that humour! Look but what a beautiful head of hair she's displaying to us now! It becomes her mightily. But I won't swear that she does not change it, in a minute or two, for a skull-cap! She's a droll girl, faith! I like her prodigiously!" (771)

Riley's lengthy comments upon Juliet's metamorphoses again emphasize her agelessness as he feels she looks too young to be a married woman. His comments recall Mrs. Ireton's earlier suggestion that Juliet may be far older than she appears, and hence, be a Wandering Jewess. Riley also summarizes many of the metamorphoses Juliet has passed through in the novel, including being single and married, a maid, country girl, singer, and actress. In addition, she has been black and white, English, French, and Jewish, and her supernatural abilities are comparable to either a witch or an angel. Juliet has become the ultimate universal symbol for every possible branch of humanity, thus celebrating the uniqueness as well as solidarity of the human race and its immortal spirit.

Burney chooses Stonehenge as the scene for the culmination of this universal theme by connecting it to the ancient architecture of the Gothic novel. Eugenia DeLamotte has remarked that Gothic architecture represents the lost secrets of a place and the threat that the heroine's identity and virtues will also be lost (15). As the most ancient monument in England, Stonehenge stands as a symbol of the past, its origins and purpose forgotten and open to speculation. Gothic architecture frequently symbolizes a family house, both the physical home and the family itself. As Anne Williams has stated, "Gothic plots are family plots; Gothic romance is family" (22-3). Stonehenge, therefore, symbolizes the home of the human family because it is an immortal monument. The family secret lost in its Gothic walls is the human race's immortality. Juliet has discovered this secret and been reconfirmed in her belief that, "Man, from the very nature of his precarious earthly being, must necessarily be destined, by the All Wise, and All Just, for regions that we see not; for purposes that we know not;—for Immortality!" (702). Immortality is the ultimate secret, but it is not forbidden knowledge. It is the knowledge of God's plan for human salvation that everyone must learn and believe in if one is to end his or her earthly wanderings and gain true immortality. Juliet, having learned this knowledge, is now no longer an outcast, but able to return to society. She will bring with her the knowledge she has gained, and she will use this knowledge to begin bettering her society and freeing it from its patriarchal oppression.

Following the Stonehenge scene, Juliet is still nervous about meeting her brother and sister, so Sir Jaspar takes her to a village where she can rest from her experiences before claiming her familial and social place and inheritance. While staying in the village, Juliet wanders "in the vicinity of Milton-abbey; of which she never lost sight from distance, though frequently from intervening hills and trees" (774). Burney is here paying tribute to John Milton, by metaphorically informing the reader that she has never lost sight of Milton and *Paradise Lost* as a major influence upon *The Wanderer* and the Gothic novel tradition. Like other Gothic novelists, Burney is responding to *Paradise Lost* by creating a Gothic wanderer; however, her response is both more radical and more conservative than her Gothic predecessors. As a feminine Gothic novel, *The Wanderer* has reacted against the domination of men over women, and it vindicates Milton's Eve by showing that women are not transgressors, but rather they are transgressed against by an unfair patriarchal society. Juliet has acquired knowledge about women's situations and their oppression by patriarchy. Now, restored to her social birthright, she realizes she has the knowledge and the power to relieve the injustices of the patriarchal system.

Restored to her true identity and free from fear, Juliet is able to marry the man she loves, Harleigh. This marriage plot ending is common in feminine Gothic novels where the good are rewarded and the evil are punished. Critics have complained, however, that Juliet's marriage is an unsatisfactory conclusion, for while Juliet may be rescued from her plight, the novel does not solve the problems of working women, but instead, it has a fairy tale ending that ignores the social problems it has raised. McMaster has even suggested that Juliet's marriage to Harleigh is not the solution but part of the problem (248). Such an interpretation of the novel's conclusion, however, ignores the text's final paragraphs that painstakingly describe what happens following Juliet's marriage.

While Juliet's acceptance by her family and her marriage to Harleigh do allow her to assimilate into the patriarchy, this assimilation does not mean that Juliet simply conforms to patriarchal society. Critics have blindly failed to realize that Juliet's "assimilation" is simply her final metamorphosis into a member of the patriarchal society so she can continue to commit subversive acts of "transgression" and even enlist her husband in those actions. Juliet acts subversively by using her social position to reward and assist those people she suffered with and who, despite their own afflictions, assisted her. The novel's final paragraphs make clear that Burney does not merely affix a fairy tale marriage ending to an otherwise realistic piece of social criticism. Instead, Burney suggests that Juliet's story is an example of how women can improve their situations. Burney declares that Juliet has been:

> ...a being who had been cast upon herself; a female Robinson Crusoe, as unaided and unprotected, though in the midst of the world, as that imaginary hero in his uninhabited island; and reduced either to sink, through inanition, to nonentity, or to be rescued from famine and death by such resources as she could find, independently, in herself.
>
> How mighty, thus circumstanced, are the DIFFICULTIES with which a FEMALE has to struggle! Her honour always in danger of being assailed, her delicacy of being offended, her strength of being exhausted, and her virtue of being calumniated! (873)

Burney's final paragraphs prove that she has not forgotten her novel's original purpose. While all women may not have such happy endings as Juliet, Burney suggests that Juliet exemplifies how women can support themselves in a harsh world and improve their situations. Like Robinson Crusoe, women must learn how to survive by their own resources. Although women's imprisonment within patriarchal society makes it appear that women are denied any resources, Burney declares that women have inner resources to draw upon just as Juliet did.

> Yet even DIFFICULTIES such as these are not insurmountable, where mental courage, operating through patience, prudence, and principle, supply physical force, combat disappointment, and keep the untamed spirits superiour to failure, and ever alive to hope. (873)

Burney heads her list of women's resources with "mental courage," perhaps the most important, for it is by her wit and imagination that Juliet has survived her ordeal. Her imaginative ability to identify with and metamorphose herself into various women, while subsuming her individual identity, has allowed her to gain a realistic view of women's situations in the patriarchal society. With her newfound knowledge, Juliet commits a subversive transgression in her final metamorphosis by becoming a member of the patriarchal establishment so she can use her knowledge to reform the system from within and to improve women's situations. The novel has exposed the need for reform in England among women and the poor; Juliet becomes a model of how that reform can be accomplished from within the system, so that unlike France, England can improve its social problems without a revolution. While *The Wanderer*'s Gothic elements might suggest that the novel is more fantasy than realism, ultimately, the Gothic elements emphasize the realities that render women's lives horrible. Once these "Gothic" realities are realized, social reform can occur, even if it only begins on an individual level.

While Burney's conclusion is subtle in depicting Juliet's actions to reform society's ills, Burney must have felt that a more aggressive conclusion would have been rejected by the reading public. Even as subtle as the ending was, the critics condemned the novel, ending its sales and making it fall into literary obscurity until its republication in 1988. Nevertheless, the novel remains a remarkable achievement in its original and complex use of the Gothic to create a subversive text that offers hope to women for the improvement of their situations so they no longer have to be Gothic wanderers in a male-dominated world.

Chapter VII – The Existential Gothic Wanderer: Mary Shelley's *Frankenstein* and *The Last Man*

Mary Shelley, like Fanny Burney, was a female novelist who responded to the Gothic wanderer figure and created variations of it, particularly in her novels *Frankenstein* (1818) and *The Last Man* (1826); however, unlike Burney, Shelley cannot be as easily classified as a feminine or feminist Gothic novelist. The tragic endings of her two Gothic novels and their male rather than female main characters make both novels more closely aligned to the masculine than the feminine Gothic tradition. Mary Shelley also expands a dimension of the earlier masculine Gothic by focusing not on the guilt of the transgressive Gothic wanderer, but upon the psychology of those victimized by transgression. While Godwin's *St. Leon* is written from the point of view of the transgressive title character, in *Frankenstein*, Mary Shelley presents the voice of both the transgressor, Victor Frankenstein, and the victim of that transgression, the Monster. In *The Last Man*, Shelley is even more innovative in writing the entire novel from the perspective of Lionel Verney, who is the victim of others' transgressions. Shelley's concentration upon the victims of transgression emphasizes her interpretation that the only real transgressions are those against the family unit, which Shelley held sacred to an even greater extent than her Gothic predecessors. *Frankenstein* and *The Last Man* create existential worlds where God may not exist, but if He does, He is clearly not interested in human affairs, so people have no hope that a Divine intervention will correct the transgressions they commit. Furthermore, without a God who concerns Himself with humanity, Shelley believes that transgressions are not against God but solely against the human family. Both *Frankenstein* and *The Last Man* reject Christian theological reasons to avoid transgression, in favor of a more practical warning that transgression is an irredeemable crime, which once committed, is irreversible and can have indefinite and unforeseen consequences.

Frankenstein: Critical History and Position in the Gothic Wanderer Tradition

Along with *Dracula*, *Frankenstein* is the only novel in this study that has become a household word and part of popular culture. Nevertheless, like most nineteenth century Gothic novels, *Frankenstein* received little critical attention until the last few decades. The earliest criticism of the novel was primarily negative. Upon its initial publication, William Beckford complained that it was poorly written and "perhaps the foulest Toadstool that has yet sprung up from the reeking dunghill of the present times" (Roberts, "Mary" 60; Lowe-Evans 14). *Frankenstein*'s 1831 edition received the condemnation of "disgusting" from Henry Crabb Robinson, who argued that the novel should have been set in the medieval rather than modern period (Lowe-Evans 15). Robinson failed to perceive that the novel's modern setting suggested the possibility that the misuse of modern science could create real-life Gothic horrors for contemporary people. Other critics complained that it was disgusting to think a woman could create such a nightmarish story (Roberts, *Gothic* 105), or they insisted that Percy Shelley must be the real author, or at least a major collaborator whose ideas Mary Shelley simply copied into the novel (Blumberg 2). While Percy Shelley did assist his wife in the capacity of editor, the extent of his assistance has been grossly exaggerated; consequently, Mary Shelley has received less credit than she deserves for her imaginative creation.

Even in the twentieth century, *Frankenstein* was generally dismissed by critics, despite its sustaining popularity. In *The Romantic Agony* (1933), Mario Praz coldly remarked of the novel: "All Mrs. Shelley did was to provide a passive reflection of some of the wild fantasies which, as it were, hung in the air about her" (114). In 1965, Harold Bloom was somewhat kinder although still derogatory of the novel by stating:

> ...what makes *Frankenstein* an important book, though it is only a strong, flawed novel with frequent clumsiness in its narrative and characterization, is that it contains one of the most vivid versions we have of the Romantic mythology of the self... *Frankenstein* affords a unique introduction to the archetypal world of the Romantics. (613)

By reading the novel in conjunction with Romanticism, much can be gained, but to limit readings of the text to its place in the Romantic Movement is to ignore the points where Shelley drastically differs from and even rejects Romanticism. Furthermore, critics like Praz and Bloom ignored the novel's Gothic elements, the Gothic then being regarded as a lesser literary form, so consequently, the full extent of Shelley's innovations of Romantic and Gothic literature and her own unique vision were misunderstood and ignored. Only in the 1970s, when feminism led to a rediscovery of many women writers, did *Frankenstein* begin to receive the critical attention it richly deserves. Since the 1970s, an overwhelming amount of material has been published about the novel, exploring all aspects of its literary and historic value. My discussion will explore *Frankenstein*'s place within the Gothic wanderer tradition by emphasizing its use of the Rosicrucian figure, its revision and rejection of *Paradise Lost*, and Shelley's formulation of an existential theme that only receives mature expression in her later Gothic novel, *The Last Man*.

Rosicrucian Elements in *Frankenstein*

At *Frankenstein*'s core is Victor's quest for forbidden knowledge, which Shelley intends to be analogous to the Gothic wanderer's quest for the Rosicrucian secrets. Rosicrucian elements in the novel are apparent beginning with the title and main character's name. Marie Roberts lists several possible sources for the novel's title, including a Castle Frankenstein, which was the alleged home of an eighteenth century alchemist, Johann Konrad Dippel. Dippel was known to sign his name as Frankenstein, since he owned the castle of that name. Dippel claimed to have found the elixir of life, and he was also a body snatcher who believed it would be possible to reanimate the dead ("Mary" 64; *Gothic* 99). Another possibility for Frankenstein's name is as a combination of Benjamin Franklin and Wolfstein's names, the latter being the main character of Percy Shelley's *St. Irvyne*. Benjamin Franklin's studies in electricity would be comparable to Victor's studies in electro-magnetism to reanimate the dead, and Percy Shelley's Wolfstein, like Victor Frankenstein, is tempted to pursue the Rosicrucian secrets (Roberts, *Gothic* 101). Either of these sources is possible, and Mary Shelley may have intended for the name of Frankenstein to have several layers of association.

Another Rosicrucian link to the novel exists in Shelley's choice to have Victor attend college at Ingoldstadt. In 1776, Ada Weishaupt founded at Ingoldstadt the Bavarian Illuminati, a secret society rumored to be responsible for bringing about the French Revolution in their desire to better man and increase human knowledge at any cost (Paulson, "Gothic" 546). The secrecy of societies like the Bavarian Illuminati and the Rosicrucians made them highly suspicious, and in the years following the French Revolution, such secret societies were associated with conspiracy theories against the former French monarchy. These conspiracy theories made their way into nineteenth century Gothic novels in scenes where characters swear secret oaths that readers would have understood as reflecting secret societies supposedly involved in the French Revolution (Macdonald 191-2). Readers, therefore, might associate Victor's attendance at Ingoldstadt with such secret societies. Later, the Monster's murderous rampage is suggestive that Victor has helped to create a conspiracy or revolution of which he has now lost control.

Rosicrucianism equally may have influenced Shelley's creation of the Monster. Marie Roberts suggests that Shelley saw the 1804 exhibition at the Royal Academy where Fuseli displayed a painting of a mechanical being who guards the tomb of Christian Rosencreutz. The painting may have ignited Shelley's childhood imagination and remained in her memory until she used it in her creation of the Monster, who is himself a type of mechanical being because of his reanimation by electrical means ("Mary" 63-4). These examples strengthen *Frankenstein*'s position in the dialogue of the Gothic wanderer and the novel's incorporation of Rosicrucian elements.

The novel's most significant relation to Rosicrucianism is Victor's quest to reanimate the dead. This quest originates in his youthful interest in pursuing the Rosicrucian secrets.

> I entered with the greatest diligence into the search of the philosopher's stone and the elixir of life, but the latter soon obtained my undivided attention. Wealth was an inferior object, but what glory would attend the discovery, if I could banish disease from the human frame, and render man invulnerable to any but a violent death! (35)

Victor's Rosicrucian interests are eventually transformed into more scientific pursuits of how to reanimate the dead. His change in interests results from the grief he experiences over the loss of his mother.

> I need not describe the feelings of those whose dearest ties are rent by that most irreparable evil, the void that presents itself to the soul, and the despair that is exhibited on the countenance....These are the reflections of the first days, but when the lapse of time proves the reality of the evil, then the actual, bitterness of grief commences. Yet from whom has not that rude hand rent away some dear connection? And why should I describe a sorrow which all have felt, and must feel? (39)

Victor finds his mother's death traumatic because it has opened the "void" of grief which will only open farther as his life continues and more of his loved ones die. Shortly after his mother's death, Victor leaves for school with the intention that his studies will teach him how to return the dead to life. He becomes interested in animating lifeless objects, believing this study will teach him how to prevent death: "if I could bestow animation upon lifeless matter, I might in process of time (although I now found it impossible) renew life where death had apparently devoted the body to corruption" (53). Despite his changed interests, Victor retains similarities to Gothic wanderers who quest for the Rosicrucian secrets because he still seeks a forbidden knowledge he is not prepared to use properly. Victor longs to renew life so he can restore the Edenic family circle he knew prior to his mother's death. He believes that like the Rosicrucians, he can be a benefactor to society. Furthermore, he believes he can make humanity autonomous to natural causes including death just as the Rosicrucian Gothic wanderer seeks autonomy from God and Nature. Victor is unable to foresee that his creation of the Monster is merely a mockery of Nature's creation, and he fails to consider the repercussions of his actions or to be responsible toward his creation. When the creature destroys Victor's family, it is analogous to Adam and Eve's transgression resulting in the fall of their family, the human race (Roberts, *Gothic* 110).

Marie Roberts argues that Mary Shelley rejects earlier versions of the Gothic's treatment of the Rosicrucian: "Her fiction effectively freed the Rosicrucian preoccupation with immortality from Godwin's Enlightenment materialism and Percy Shelley's Germanic melodrama" (*Gothic* 115). Both William Godwin and Percy Shelley use the Rosicrucian wanderer figure to show the dangers of questing for forbidden knowledge, but they also use Rosicrucianism to validate their own belief systems. Godwin's *St. Leon* presents the disasters of the Rosicrucian quest to argue for human reason's evolution, and Percy Shelley's *St. Irvyne* uses the quest to depict the consequences of transgression against God. Mary Shelley rejects these theoretical interpretations of the Rosicrucian quest to show that humans must be responsible for their own actions because God does not guide humanity or repair human errors. *Frankenstein* becomes Mary Shelley's rejection of both her father and husband's theories of social evolution and millenarianism as well as the feminine Gothic revision of Eve that suggests transgressions can still have positive results.

Divorced from theological beliefs, Victor Frankenstein is an offspring of the Enlightenment who looks to science, not religion, for solutions (Dussinger 47). Victor's transgression cannot be redeemed by his own repentance, as occurs for other Gothic wanderers, because his transgression has effects he no longer has control over. His creation of the Monster, a being separate from himself, results in his loss of control over his creation and even his creation coming to control him. Victor's trust in science leaves no room for him to trust in God, so he is blind to the parallel between himself and God as creators, and he fails to understand that like God, he should be a loving father to his creation. *Frankenstein* becomes Shelley's imagining of an existential world where Victor's failure to care for his creation is a metaphor for a God, who if He even exists, has no concern for His creation. Whether Shelley herself believes there is no God is ambiguous. Victor never mentions whether he believes in God, but he informs us that he was raised not to believe in supernatural horrors: "In my education my father had taken the greatest precautions that my mind should be impressed with no supernatural horrors. I do not ever remember to have trembled at a tale of superstition, or to have feared the apparition of a spirit" (50). Consequently, Victor feels no fear for the dead or repulsion in his experiments with corpses. While Victor never mentions God, except in figures of speech, by the end of the novel he seems to realize the horror of existing in a world where man may be the most powerful being. In his quest to destroy the Monster, he longs for help from supernatural beings.

> I knelt on the grass and kissed the earth, and with quivering lips exclaimed, "By the sacred earth on which I kneel, by the shades that wander near me, by the deep and eternal grief that I feel, I swear; and by thee, O Night, and the spirits that preside over thee, to pursue the demon who causes this misery until he or I shall perish in mortal conflict....And I call on you, spirits of the dead, and on you, wandering ministers of vengeance, to aid and conduct me in my work. (245)

Later Victor remarks that he feels he is being helped by spirits.

> ...it was during sleep alone that I could taste joy. O blessed sleep! Often when most miserable, I sank to repose, and my dreams lulled me even to rapture. The spirits that guarded me had provided these moments, or rather hours, of happiness that I might retain strength to fulfill my pilgrimage. (247-8)

By this point in the novel, Victor borders on madness, longing to believe in anything that might help him. His failure to destroy the Monster, however, suggests that no supernatural beings exist to help him. Shelley creates an existential world where God does not involve Himself in human affairs. The novel's radical revision of *Paradise Lost* is Shelley's most significant means for carrying out her existential theme because she depicts man in the position of God, and consequently, man fails to fulfill a divine role.

Frankenstein as Existential Revision of *Paradise Lost*

Like her Gothic predecessors, Mary Shelley also intended her Gothic novel to respond to and revise the myth of *Paradise Lost*. *Frankenstein*, more than any other Gothic novel, is layered with references to and symbols from *Paradise Lost*. Both Victor and the Monster are repeatedly placed in the various roles of God, Satan, Adam, and Eve, but Shelley also refuses to let her characters merely repeat these roles. Shelley's revision of *Paradise Lost* places Victor in the role of God, so he lives in an existential world where the transgressions he commits are against himself and humanity as the highest levels of being. Victor fails as a god because he cannot provide salvation and he cannot offer redemption for transgressions, unlike Milton's depiction of God as promising Adam and Eve that humanity will eventually be redeemed. The novel's existential treatment of Victor's transgression is Shelley's rejection of the Gothic and Romantic traditions which are hope-affirming despite their depictions of transgression. Robert Hume states that *Frankenstein*, because of its rejection of Romanticism, is an example of Negative Romanticism, which he defines as "the outlook of those who have rebelled against static mechanism but not yet arrived at faith in organicism" (109). While Shelley does reject Romanticism, Hume's statement is not completely adequate in describing Shelley's position. To consider *Frankenstein* as an example of Negative Romanticism is to suggest it is somehow inferior to Romanticism because it has "not yet arrived at faith in organicism" as if the faith of Romanticism is a progression beyond Negative Romanticism. While Romanticism may be such a progression, Mary Shelley, having lived her life among the Gothic and Romantic literati, was certainly aware of Romantic faith, and therefore, she did not fail to progress to such a faith, but rather, she firmly rejected it. Because she outlived most of the Romantics, it might be fair to consider Shelley as progressing beyond their beliefs, as more adequately represented in *The Last Man*. Because Hume sees Negative Romanticism as a stage before Romanticism, I prefer the term Existential to describe Shelley's novel, a term Hume also applies to *Frankenstein* without directly distinguishing between but rather seemingly equating Existentialism and Negative Romanticism. Hume says *Frankenstein* expresses an "Existential Agony" because "The central form of Dark Romanticism is essentially an acute perception of evil with little move toward either solution or escape" (123). In *Frankenstein*, Victor himself has this perception of evil as existing in the Monster. He makes no real attempt to solve the problem he has created because he fails to take responsibility for his creation and instead blames the Monster for faults that are essentially his own. Victor's world is existential because he never seeks forgiveness for his transgression in creating the Monster or failing to care for it. He has no religious belief to make him question his own actions, and his attempt to rely on himself for the solution to his problems only increases his agony. Shelley's version of *Paradise Lost* in the form of *Frankenstein*, therefore, is an existential vision that makes her revision not inferior but rather different from Romanticism and other Gothic novels. The novel's reversal of themes and character roles in *Paradise Lost* best illustrates Shelley's existential viewpoint.

Frankenstein's relation to *Paradise Lost* has long been recognized by critics, but there has been division between whether the novel merely retells *Paradise Lost* in a more modern context, or whether it subversively attempts to rewrite Milton's epic. Critics who first read the novel as simply a retelling of *Paradise Lost* include Harold Bloom, Pollin, Mays, Gardner, and Tannenbaum, while the new interest in Shelley as a feminist writer led to readings of *Frankenstein* as a subversive version of *Paradise Lost* by Gilbert and Gubar, McInerny, Sherwin, Jacobus, Oates, Homans, Baldick, and Lamb (Lamb, "Mary" 304n).

My reading is intended to demonstrate that while straightforward parallels exist between *Frankenstein* and *Paradise Lost*, Shelley's novel is deeply subversive because it rejects the entire Christian theology of *Paradise Lost* in favor of a more existential viewpoint. Furthermore, *Frankenstein* is not part of the feminine Gothic tradition because it does not seek to vindicate Eve by suggesting that benefits may result from the quest for forbidden knowledge. The novel's subversion goes beyond that of the feminine Gothic to divorce the characters from strict gender roles and to create a form of androgyny in the two main characters by allowing them both to play the role of Eve as well as that of the male characters in *Paradise Lost*. John Lamb has suggested that *Paradise Lost* splits people up, so that the reader is not sure whether to identify with God, Adam, or Satan (and I would add Eve); therefore, the novel creates a cultural "schizophrenia, a disruption of the self's relation with the world and with itself" ("Mary" 307). The novel continually combines, breaks down, or questions gender roles for the characters. To accomplish this diminishment of gender roles, Shelley places both Victor and the Monster in the roles of all the major characters of *Paradise Lost*. This character repositioning also displays the paradoxical composition of people who are never solely good or evil as they tend to be represented in Milton's poem; the good and evil in Victor Frankenstein and the Monster make them more fully rounded characters who both repulse the reader yet gain the reader's sympathy because of their human emotions, virtues, and flaws.

The most important deviation from *Paradise Lost* is Victor's positioning as God because he creates the Monster. In creating life, Victor is attempting autonomy from God, so humanity no longer need depend upon God or Nature for the creation or sustenance of life. Victor is originally depicted as having benevolent intentions of preventing human death in a manner similar to God's plan for human salvation. Victor fails in his role as God, however, when he is overcome by revulsion for his creation and fails to be responsible for it. The moment Victor rushes from the room in disgust, thus abandoning his creation, he has fallen from his godlike status. At this moment, Victor becomes a typical Gothic wanderer whose discovery of forbidden knowledge has led to his personal suffering.

Victor simultaneously plays the role of Satan because his pride makes him believe he can create life and achieve godlike status (Tannenbaum 106). When the Monster begins to destroy Victor's family, Victor learns that his pride has resulted in the creation of death, a situation similar to Satan's pride resulting in the literal creation of the characters Sin and Death. Similarly, as Satan regrets his rebellion against God, Victor regrets having creating the Monster, blaming himself for the Monster's destruction of his family. When Victor realizes the full extent of his transgression and the horror that has resulted from it, he becomes like Satan in his feelings of guilt and despair (Bloom 617). After the deaths of his family, Victor feels lonely and desolate and dreams he "wandered in flowery meadows and pleasant vales with the friends of my youth, but I awoke and found myself in a dungeon" (240). Victor dreams of returning to the Edenic innocence he knew, but like Satan, he cannot reverse the transgressions he has committed so he cannot hope to return to his former happy and innocent state (Pollin 104).

Tannenbaum argues that at the novel's conclusion, Victor remains like Satan because he still refuses to take responsibility for his actions; Victor shifts all the blame onto the Monster for his family's destruction just as Satan blames God for his fallen condition (105). Victor fails to understand the reasons why he failed in his quest for forbidden knowledge, and he believes the quest might still be achieved by another. His egotistic beliefs and goals make him dazzling to Walton, who thinks of Victor in terms reminiscent of Milton's Satan. Walton describes Victor as "noble and godlike in ruin" (256), thus echoing Milton's description of Satan when addressing his legions as "Majestic though in ruin" (II, 305). Walton also refers to Victor as a "divine wanderer" (20), reflecting Victor's literary ancestry as a Gothic wanderer descended from Satan. While Walton is dazzled by Victor, he fails to understand the full implications of Victor as a Satan figure, but Victor presents the equation by stating "like the archangel who aspired to omnipotence, I am chained in an eternal hell" (256). When Walton asks for Victor's knowledge of how to reanimate life, Victor wisely refuses to reveal the forbidden knowledge he possesses, instead warning Walton "Learn my miseries and do not seek to increase your own" (255). Victor, however, fails to heed his own advice; he realizes his quest for forbidden knowledge has caused his miseries, but his pride makes him continue to blame the Monster rather than himself and to believe the Monster's destruction will solve everything. Like Satan, Victor knows the difference between right and wrong but his pride prohibits him from admitting defeat because of his own faults (Tannenbaum 105).

Victor's role as Satan is connected with his role as Eve because both characters are transgressors in Milton's text. Although neither Victor nor the Monster are female, Sandra Gilbert and Susan Gubar base their feminist reading of *Frankenstein* largely on the idea that "the part of Eve is all the parts" (230). The first connection made between Victor and Eve occurs when Victor explains to Walton how his father objected to his quest for arcane knowledge (231). Just as Satan convinces Eve that God's prohibition against eating the apple is without reason, so Victor finds his father's reasons for objecting to his occult studies to be ambiguous, and therefore, insufficient to make him desist from them. Never willing to take responsibility for his own actions, Victor believes that if his father had explained why such knowledge was forbidden, he never would have transgressed.

> If...my father had taken the pains to explain to me that the principles of Agrippa had been entirely exploded....It is even possible that the train of my ideas would never have received the fatal impulse that led to my ruin. (33-4)

Victor is responsible for his own choice to transgress, but like Satan and Eve, he prefers to blame the father figure for his own faults. Selfishness motivates both Eve and Victor in their transgressions. Eve wishes to better herself and become Adam's equal while Victor wishes to benefit the human race by preventing death and, thereby, himself becoming a hero. Victor and Eve both overlook the consequences of their transgressions by convincing themselves that their actions are morally acceptable. Because Victor never thinks of religion, he fails to consider that his actions might be transgressions against God or Nature.

By creating the Monster, Victor's association with Eve is enhanced. As Milton equates Eve with the character Sin, because Eve's transgression results in giving birth to death for the human race, so Victor's transgression gives birth to death when the Monster destroys Victor's family. Shelley further emphasizes Victor's association with Sin and Eve by describing Victor in feminine terms when he creates the Monster. Victor's scientific labors to create the Monster are equivalent to the labor of a woman in childbirth. Victor's work is described as "days and nights of incredible labor and fatigue" (51) and "a work of inconceivable difficulty and labor" (52) which makes Victor feel "dizzy with the immensity of the prospect" (51) (Gilbert and Gubar 232). Victor's transgression is ultimately less against God or Nature than against the family. His decision to create a life without the help of a female is a rejection of the family unit and an attempt to be autonomous from the feminine.

As creator, Victor is the only character to play the role of God, which positions the Monster into the roles of Satan, Adam, and Eve. The Monster begins his existence in the role of Adam, innocent and ignorant of the world into which he is born. Shelley, however, radically deviates from *Paradise Lost* by setting up parallel opposites between God's treatment of Adam and Victor's treatment of the Monster. Victor's abandonment of the Monster is a cruel contrast to God's acknowledgment of Adam and His concern for Adam's education and well-being. Milton wrote *Paradise Lost* to justify God's ways to man, but Shelley reverses *Paradise Lost* by forcing the Monster/Adam to justify his actions to his creator, Victor (Tannenbaum 108). Never does Victor feel a need to justify himself to the Monster or to take responsibility for his own actions as a creator.

Gilbert and Gubar note that *Frankenstein* contains several passages that depict the Monster as the reverse of how Adam is depicted in *Paradise Lost*. The Monster describes his first moments of life: "I was a poor, helpless, miserable wretch; I knew and could distinguish nothing; but feeling pain invade me on all sides, I sat down and wept" (117). In contrast, Adam awakens to life, feeling that:

> all things smil'd,
> With fragrance and with joy my heart o'erflowed.
> Myself I then perus'd, and Limb by Limb
> Survey'd, and sometimes went, and sometimes ran
> With supple joints, as lively vigor led: (VIII, 265-9) (Gilbert and Gubar 236).

The Monster describes his first attempt to speak: "Sometimes I wished to express my sensations in my own mode, but the uncouth and inarticulate sounds which broke from me frightened me into silence again" (118). Adam's first attempt to speak is far more successful: "To speak I tri'd, and forthwith spake, / My Tongue obey'd and readily could name / Whate'er I saw" (VIII, 271-3) (Gilbert and Gubar 236). Finally, both the Monster and Adam question their existences. The Monster despairingly asks, "What was I? The question again recurred to be answered only with groans" (141), while Adam elatedly feels "who I was, or where or from what cause, / Knew not....And feel that I am happier than I know" (VIII, 270-1, 282) (Gilbert and Gubar 236). Soon after his creation, Adam sleeps and in a dream is told that he is the "First Man, of Men innumerable ordain'd" (VIII, 297); in contrast the Monster remains "absolutely ignorant" (139). Adam is told the meaning of his existence, but the Monster must seek out the answers for himself, which is only accomplished after he learns to read and discovers the answers to his questions in Victor's journal. Not surprisingly, the Monster reads *Paradise Lost* and becomes aware of the striking differences between Adam and himself. Realizing the happiness and the divine plan God has given to Adam, the Monster only feels his misery intensified when he learns of his own maker's irresponsibility and apparent abandonment of him. Bloom argues that because the Monster is able to realize his creator's faults, he is more intellectual and emotional than Victor just as a modern reader may feel the character of Adam excels that of God in *Paradise Lost*. Ironically, therefore, the Monster becomes "more human" than Victor (613).

The Monster seeks moral guidance similar to the guidance Adam receives from Raphael, and he believes he will find such help from the DeLaceys. When he is brave enough to reveal his existence to the blind old man, the Monster remarks, "You raise me from the dust by this kindness" (158), a remark that recalls Adam's creation from dust. Sadly, the moment the Monster feels raised, he is discovered by the rest of the family and driven away, thus immediately experiencing his first fall (Tannenbaum 109). Rather than falling because of a transgression, however, the Monster falls precisely because he is a monster. Because Victor created him as monstrous, the Monster becomes the victim of Victor's transgression.

That Victor is the novel's true transgressor and the Monster merely the victim of that transgression is clear from the novel's epigraph from *Paradise Lost*: "Did I request thee, Maker, from my clay / To mould me Man, did I solicit thee / From darkness to promote me?" (X, 743-5). This epigraph emphasizes the Monster's mistreatment by an irresponsible creator in comparison to Adam's relationship with God. Lamb argues that the Monster's predicament thus shows that people never choose their own natures, but that an individual's nature is a cultural construct dependent upon the situation into which a person is born ("Mary" 318). The Monster has not chosen his environment, his grotesque form, or to be a social outcast; the mistreatments the Monster experiences are what motivate his revenge against Victor by the destruction of Victor's family. At this point, the Monster is transformed from a completely sympathetic character to one who takes on the role of Satan for he chooses to hurt Victor indirectly just as Satan revenges himself against God by attacking Adam and Eve (Soyka 171).

The Monster's transformation into a Satan figure occurs when his rejection by the DeLaceys makes him feel cast forth from paradise. In anger, he compares himself to Satan: "I, like the arch-fiend, bore a hell within me and, finding myself unsympathized with, wished to tear up the trees, spread havoc and destruction around me and then to have sat down and enjoyed the ruin" (160-1). Similarly in *Paradise Lost*, several of the fallen angels wreak havoc upon Nature as they "Rend up both Rocks and Hills, and ride the Air / In whirlwind" (II, 540-1). Other devils discuss philosophy only to be "in wand'ring mazes lost" (II, 562) as the Monster finds himself wandering through the forest and philosophizing upon the meaning of his existence. Like Satan, the Monster now declares war on the human race (Pollin 104). The Monster states, "from that moment I declared everlasting war against the species and, more than all, against him who had formed me and sent me forth to this insupportable misery" (161). The Monster then feels a "hellish rage and gnashing of teeth" (167). Satan's declaration "Evil be thou my good" (IV, 110) has become the Monster's philosophy (Mays 152).

When God punishes Lucifer for his transgression, He gives Lucifer a new identity as Satan. Similarly, after the Monster murders William, Victor refers to him as a "devil" (112, 114). Victor himself realizes the parallel of the Monster to Satan, and he interprets the Monster's story as that of a Satanic fall (Lamb, "Mary" 311). The Monster realizes Victor is incorrectly using *Paradise Lost* to interpret their present situation, explaining to Victor, "I ought to be thy Adam, but I am rather the fallen angel" (113), and the Monster tries peacefully to convince Victor to acknowledge him, "Let your compassion be moved and do not disdain me. Listen to my tale" (114). He then warns Victor that he will only act as Satan if Victor refuses to acknowledge him as his own created Adam.

> Do your duty toward me, and I will do mine toward you and the rest of mankind. If you will comply with my conditions, I will leave them and you at peace, but if you refuse I will glut the maw of death, until it be satiated with the blood of your remaining friends. (112)

Victor acknowledges the Monster's position as an Adam when he agrees to create a female monster to serve as the Monster's Eve. Victor fails to complete the task, however, because he is revolted by the possibility that the two monsters might together create a monstrous race that will threaten humanity: "children, and a race of devils would be propagated upon the earth who might make the very existence of the species of man a condition precarious and full of terror" (199). Victor destroys the female monster, believing his actions make him humanity's benefactor. He remains selfish in this act, however, because his main motive is concern for how he will be remembered: "I shuddered to think that future ages might curse me as their pest, whose selfishness had not hesitated to buy its own peace at the price perhaps of the existence of the whole human race" (199). The Monster is infuriated by his future bride's destruction and tries to control Victor by calling him "Slave" and declaring, "You are my creator, but I am your master. Obey!" (201). When Victor still refuses, the Monster warns Victor in words that recall Satan's form as a snake in Eden: "I will watch with the wiliness of a snake that I may sting with its venom" (202). The Monster then threatens that he will be with Victor on his wedding night.

The Monster's attack upon Elizabeth is the final destruction of Victor's paradise. Because Victor has denied the Monster his own Eve, the Monster now denies Victor equivalent happiness. The Monster's decision to murder Elizabeth rather than Victor reflects Satan's decision to tempt Eve, as the weaker sex, rather than Adam (Mays 152). The Oedipal conflict in the scene also provides a role reversal as the Monster tries to dominate his creator, just as Satan tried to overthrow God. As Victor's creation, the Monster is Victor's son, so when he breaks into his father's bridal chamber and ravages his father's wife, he is symbolically raping his mother. By taking his father's wife, the Monster becomes the father, reducing Victor to the child. Victor's discovery of the dead Elizabeth and the Monster leering through the window is a symbolic primal scene of the son witnessing his parents' intimacy. In murdering Elizabeth, the Monster has proven himself the master, leaving Victor helpless and impotent, both in his inability to defeat the Monster and in his inability to have intercourse with Elizabeth, thus destroying his hopes for domestic happiness. Unlike Satan, who fails in his rebellion against God, the Monster has successfully overpowered his creator.

Throughout the novel, the Monster also plays the role of Eve from *Paradise Lost*. Just as God treats Eve as inferior to Adam, so the Monster feels he is an inferior creation. The first reference in *Frankenstein* to the Monster's equation with Eve occurs shortly after the Monster is born when he sees a vision of himself in a pool and gazes at his own reflection. Similarly, upon birth, Eve is fascinated with her own reflection (IV, 456-65). Also like Eve, the Monster does not receive his instruction from his creator, but he has a mediated form of knowledge from books as Eve receives God's instructions from Adam (Gilbert and Gubar 239). This parallel suggests that God, like Victor, was not adequately responsible for his creation and treated it as inferior from the beginning. Finally, the Monster's physical deformity can be equated with Eve's moral deformity which, after her sin, also becomes equated with physical deformity

(Gilbert and Gubar 241). In both cases, the creator may be charged with creating the character's deformity. As discussed in the earlier chapter upon *Paradise Lost*, Milton equates Eve to Sin, and the character of Sin is deformed in her genital region, which is associated with sin and filth. Eve is considered deformed in her genital region because she will undergo the pain of childbirth. The Monster's physical deformity equates him with the female deformities of Eve and Sin. Since Victor thinks of women as deformed versions of men, he believes that a female monster will be even more deformed than the male one. Furthermore, Victor fears that the Monster will be only further angered if the female rejects it because of its grotesqueness.

> The creature who already lived loathed his own deformity and might he not conceive a greater abhorrence for it when it came before his eyes in the female form? She also might turn with disgust from him to the superior beauty of man; she might quit him and he be again alone, exasperated by the fresh provocation of being deserted by one of his own species. (198-9)

Victor's fear that the female Monster might reject her mate's grotesqueness reflects the scene in *Paradise Lost* when Eve, after having seen her own beauty reflected in a pool, thinks herself more attractive than Adam and prefers to gaze at her own image rather than look at him (IV, 477-80). Victor may also fear that the female monster, not finding her mate attractive, will turn to human males instead. While the female monster's extensive deformity will make her repulsive to men, she is a sexual threat to them because her physical strength may allow her to rape them. Furthermore, Victor's equation of deformity with the female already places the deformed Monster in a female role, so Victor may intellectually find it impossible for the feminine Monster to have a female mate (Homans 106).

Shelley's comparison of Victor to Eve is to link him to Eve the sinner. However, Shelley's use of Eve as parallel to the Monster reflects Shelley's use of the Monster as a symbol of how the "inferior" creation (i.e. woman) is mistreated by humanity. Like Fanny Burney, Shelley was well aware of the position of women in her society and how women receive identification from a man (father or husband) who gives a woman his name. By making Victor reject his creation, Shelley was making the Monster an unacknowledged and hence an illegitimate and bastard child. Mary Shelley knew that to be a bastard was to be nameless, for she had an illegitimate sister, Fanny Imlay, and Shelley herself gave birth to a bastard child who died nameless at two weeks old (Gilbert and Gubar 241-2, Homans 115). The Monster's position as bastard child to Victor results in his also remaining nameless throughout the novel. To name a child is to acknowledge you are the child's parent, but the only names Victor gives the Monster are "demon" and "devil." Because the Monster is nameless, feminine, and illegitimate, he is a threat to patriarchy. Consequently, the Monster symbolizes the oppression of women in the nineteenth century (Homans 109). Shelley is more subtle than Burney in her female subversiveness because the Monster remains male, despite its feminine equations. Shelley is radical, however, in allowing the Monster to rebel against and to destroy its male creator. Had Shelley created a female Monster, one can only imagine how far more brutal her critics would have been, if the novel had even achieved publication.

The Monster's final role from *Paradise Lost* is that of Christ, but he never completely fulfills this role. Christ is God's legitimate son, causing Satan to rebel out of jealousy toward Christ for receiving God's favor. Similarly, the Monster is the son of Victor, but because he is not acknowledged as Victor's son, he cannot play the role of Christ as Victor plays the role of God. Nevertheless, the Monster's creation is similar to that of Christ because both births do not result from human procreation, and the Monster's existence as a reanimated corpse parodies Christ's resurrection from the dead (Homans 117). Joyce Carol Oates suggests that the Monster has a Christ-like role because he is continually sinned against by everyone he meets, while he is originally innocent; therefore, the Monster's decision to destroy himself becomes a type of sacrifice for humanity's benefit (547). The Monster's failure to fulfill his Christ role and to redeem himself or anyone in the novel stems from his never receiving love, and therefore, being unable to give it (Tannenbaum 110). Mary Shelley purposely chose to prohibit the Monster from fulfilling the Christ role because she was against the Romantic tendency to secularize Christianity as a way to rewrite the Christian myth. As the novel's many analogues to *Paradise Lost* display, Shelley rejects the Christian myth in her revision of *Paradise Lost*, thus creating an existential world where there is no Divine intervention to redeem or solve human errors. Mary Shelley's rejection of Christianity and its secular versions is equally a rejection of the Miltonic idea that good can come from evil, as Adam and Eve's transgression results in Christ's sacrifice for human salvation. In Shelley's world, people must be responsible for their actions and suffer the consequences of their transgressions.

Shelley not only rejects the possibility of evil leading to good, but she questions goodness in itself and the motivation behind benevolent deeds. Victor becomes an example of the ambiguity of good intentions. *Frankenstein*'s subtitle "The Modern Prometheus" reflects Victor's lack of responsibility in his blind belief that he is doing good by attempting to conquer death. The name Prometheus means "forethought," but Victor lacks forethought in creating the Monster, as Shelley suggests that God lacked forethought in creating a world where evil was allowed to enter in (Soyka 167). The novel also shows Victor's lack of forethought in his belief that he could make humanity autonomous from God by allowing it to overcome death (Oates 552). Victor intends to perform a benevolent deed, but he fails to realize that he needs not only knowledge, but the wisdom to use that knowledge properly (Rauch 243). Like other Gothic wanderers, Victor fails to see that his own benevolence is actually an arrogant desire to be godlike and esteemed by all; this selfishness is apparent when he dreams that, "A new species would bless me as its creator and source. Many happy and excellent natures would owe their being to me. No father could claim the gratitude of his child so completely as I should deserve theirs" (53). His pride results in the opposite of his intentions when his creation curses rather than blesses him. Ultimately, Victor is responsible for his own position as outcast and wanderer, while the Monster has unfairly been forced into this position by his selfish creator.

The French Revolution, Illegitimacy, and the Family in *Frankenstein*

As seen with previously discussed Gothic novels, ultimately the Gothic wanderer's transgression leads to destruction of the family unit, the most sacred institution in the Gothic genre. Victor's transgression is to have created a bastard creature whose illegitimacy ultimately brings about the destruction of the Frankenstein family. The Monster's jealousy at not being treated as Victor's legitimate child is a typical example of the Gothic emphasis upon the crimes of the patriarchal system. Numerous critics have interpreted the Monster's anger over the denial of his rights as a symbol of lower class resentment toward the aristocracy, thus making the novel a commentary upon the French Revolution. Robert Paulson states that Victor's attempt to create a new man symbolizes the French Revolution's "attempt to recreate man and the disillusionment and terror that followed" ("Gothic" 545). Fred Botting points out that Burke referred to France during the Revolution as "a world of monsters" while Wollstonecraft responded to Burke by declaring that the aristocracy was the true monster (52). Shelley depicts how both authority and rebellion can be monstrous. Victor becomes a monster when he fails in his responsibility toward his creation and discriminates against the Monster as an inferior being. The Monster, denied human rights, burns the DeLaceys' home and kills Victor's family in a rage suggestive of the lower class' destruction of aristocratic homes and the guillotining of aristocrats during the French Revolution (Heller 36). At the same time, Victor's attempt to better the world by creating life results in the Monster destroying life; in opposition to Godwin and Percy Shelley, Mary Shelley here points out that revolutionary activity cannot bring about an Eden on earth because such an Eden is simply not possible. Humanity is by nature tainted and unable to reach perfection on earth. That Victor creates his new life form out of dead body parts reflects that his mission is already bound to fail, just as humanity's attempt to perfect itself by revolution must fail (Blumberg 49).

Mary Shelley utilizes the common Gothic motif of legitimacy by making humans "legitimate" and "aristocratic" while the created Monster is rejected because he was not legitimately born into a human family. This legitimacy theme is most evident in the structure of the Frankenstein family. As Victor's creation, the Monster believes he should have the same rights as would Victor's son, but Victor refuses to acknowledge the Monster as his legitimate child. Because his illegitimacy denies him acceptance by his father and his family, the Monster seeks revenge against Victor and all those who are legitimate because they bear the Frankenstein name. When the Monster meets William, Victor's younger brother, the Monster has no desire to murder him until William reveals his class and name—"My papa is a Syndic—he is M. Frankenstein" (168). The Monster resents the privileges William receives from the Frankenstein family, declaring, "Frankenstein! You belong then to my enemy—to him toward whom I have sworn eternal revenge. You shall be my first victim" (168) (Heller 34-5, Gilbert and Gubar 243). The Monster's next victims are Justine and Elizabeth, who like William, are accepted members of the Frankenstein family. Tamar Heller points out that the three Frankenstein women, including Victor's mother, Caroline Beaufort, are socially inferior to the Frankenstein family but have been adopted into it (33). If the Frankensteins can adopt socially inferior women into their family, then Victor's refusal to acknowledge the Monster is all the more unjust.

The Monster's murderous acts are inflicted against the family from a sense of the patriarchal system's injustices, but because the Monster is Victor's creation, ultimately, Victor is responsible for his family's deaths and his transgression is primarily against the family. In the novel's "Preface," Shelley states that one of her chief concerns in the novel was "the exhibition of the amiableness of domestic affection" (4). Victor realizes the importance of domesticity only after his transgression has resulted in its destruction. He warns Walton:

> A human being in perfection ought always to preserve a calm and peaceful mind, and never to allow passion or a transitory desire to disturb his tranquility. I do not think that the pursuit of knowledge is an exception to this rule. If the study to which you apply yourself has a tendency to weaken your affections, and to destroy your taste for those simple pleasures in which no alloy can possibly mix, then that study is certainly unlawful, that is to say, not befitting the human mind. If this rule were always observed, if no man allowed any pursuit whatsoever to interfere with the tranquility of his domestic affections, Greece had not been enslaved. Caesar would have spared his country. America would have been discovered more gradually and the empires of Mexico and Peru had not been destroyed. (55-6)

Victor realizes now the value of the family and human affections, but earlier, he abandoned the family for his own selfish pursuits. He left his family soon after his mother's death because of his devotion to science, and even while he intended to study science to prevent the deaths of other family members, he chose to study so he could purposely isolate himself from his family. Similarly, Walton leaves his sister and her family to travel far away to the North Pole. William Day interprets both Walton and Victor's actions as examples of the male superego that wishes to distance itself from the domestic which is equated with the feminine (140). Victor realizes the value of the family, yet his desire for self-reliance and power makes him reject any alliance with the feminine and its connection to domesticity. When the Monster begins its destructive acts, Victor realizes that it may be acting out his own unconscious desires for domestic destruction by describing the Monster as "my own vampire, my own spirit let loose from the grave, and forced to destroy all that was dear to me" (83) (Oates 547, Soyka 168). As vampires traditionally prey upon members of their own family, so the Monster, as Victor's illegitimate child, preys upon his own family by destroying the Frankensteins.

Mary Shelley contrasts Victor and Walton's ambiguous feelings toward the domestic with examples of domestic affection that reflect the nineteenth century's growing interest in the future of marriage and Shelley's own concern with her marriage and the unorthodox relationships of her friends and relatives (Lowe-Evans ix). Of all the couples in the novel, it is Felix and Safie whom Shelley presents as having the most idyllic relationship, and the hint of their future marriage implies that their union will be successful. Kate Ellis argues that the DeLacey family represents a type of "Paradise Regained" where men and women learn together and gender roles are not really distinctive, as opposed to the gender hierarchy Milton imposes on Adam and Eve in *Paradise Lost* (*Castle* 183-4). While feminine Gothic novels would have ended with the domestic bliss of a couple such as Felix and Safie, Mary Shelley emphasizes the importance of domesticity by showing the extreme defeat of Victor who rejects and fails to achieve the paradise of domestic happiness (Ellis, *Castle* 183-4). Besides the bliss of Felix and Safie, Victor's parents are depicted as being happily married, and Victor hopes for happiness when he marries Elizabeth. Victor's hopes for domestic bliss, however, are shattered by his mother's death, making Victor wish to replace his mother by having Elizabeth fulfill her role; this desire is evident from Victor's dream of Elizabeth being transformed into his mother's corpse. The dream makes Victor subconsciously fear Elizabeth as representing his incestuous and Oedipal desires, and he also fears a repetition of the grief over his mother's death should Elizabeth die. Victor's refusal to dwell on his grief—"I need not describe the feelings" (39)—reflects Victor's discomfort with showing his weaknesses, which he may also equate with being feminine. Ultimately, Victor finds himself trapped between a desire for domesticity, and the fear that domestic life will make him feminine and weak.

Victor's torn feelings about domesticity result in his disastrous marriage. When Victor destroys the female monster, the Monster declares it will be with Victor on his wedding night. Victor naively interprets this threat to mean that the Monster will kill him rather than Elizabeth. Lowe-Evans rightly questions how Victor could so misinterpret the Monster's threat (61). Subconsciously, Victor must be aware of the Monster's intentions, for the parallel between the murders of the female monster and Elizabeth should be obvious enough for Victor to foresee. Earlier, Victor had postponed his marriage to Elizabeth so he could create the female monster and then marry without fear of the Monster's vengeance. Victor's postponement of the marriage may be simply an unwillingness to marry, and now, with the Monster's threat in his thoughts, Victor expresses a further unwillingness to marry, "I would rather have banished myself forever from my native country, and wandered a friendless outcast over the earth, than have consented to this miserable marriage" (231). Victor's belief that the Monster will kill him on his wedding night is unreasonable since the Monster has had numerous opportunities to murder Victor, so subconsciously, Victor may realize that by destroying the female monster, he will indirectly be destroying Elizabeth when the Monster kills her. On the wedding night, Victor leaves the bridal chamber to "protect" Elizabeth, but his absence only provides the Monster with a better opportunity to commit the murder, while Victor does not have to feel guilt because his absence left him unable to defend her. Elizabeth's murder, therefore, is Victor's final and ultimate, even if indirect, transgression against the family. Victor's quest for forbidden knowledge has now resulted in domestic extermination.

Frankenstein's Existential Ending

The novel concludes with Victor's narration of his story to Walton, whose own narrative serves as the novel's frame. This multi-layer narrative frame causes interpretive difficulties in determining Mary Shelley's position in response to *Paradise Lost* and her Gothic predecessors' treatments of the Gothic wanderer. Peter McInerney argues that the novel is concerned with presenting separate autobiographies of Walton, Victor, and the Monster. Despite one autobiography being presented in another, thus raising questions of accuracy, McInerney states that each autobiography is intended to be reliable, as reflected when Victor reads over Walton's recording of his story because Victor does not wish "that a mutilated one should go down to posterity" (255) (McInerney 458). These multiple, first person autobiographies also serve to create "dramatic irony" by presenting various viewpoints and creating ambiguous meanings, a general attribute of masculine Gothic, while feminine Gothic typically limits its narration to a third person point of view (Williams 102). Masculine Gothic thrives upon this ambiguity to create a tragic conclusion, which is all the more tragic in *Frankenstein* because the ambiguity reinforces Shelley's existential viewpoint. In contrast, feminine Gothic novels end with marriages that reinforce the value of the family and domesticity. Shelley's ending also emphasizes the value of the family by uniquely depicting the depravity of those who are unable to maintain family relationships. While marriage symbolizes the human race's future regeneration, *Frankenstein*'s tragic ending prevents any continuance of the Frankenstein family.

The novel's tragic conclusion emphasizes Shelley's existential theme that people must be responsible for their own deeds rather than depend on a benevolent God to solve the problems they create. Shelley rejects both Christianity and the philosophical millennialism of her father and husband to demonstrate that human beings must learn to solve their conflicts and control their transgressions if the human race is to endure. Shelley's refusal to offer any resolution for Victor's transgressions is intended to make the reader more fully realize the extensive danger of such actions. Victor's transgressions are so severe that he refuses to take responsibility for them even on his deathbed. He warns Walton against committing similar transgressions, then immediately contradicts himself.

> Farewell, Walton! Seek happiness in tranquility and avoid ambition, even if it be only the apparently innocent one of distinguishing yourself in science and discoveries. Yet why do I say this? I have myself been blasted in these hopes, yet another may succeed. (264)

Walton, like Victor, is too obsessed with his goals to heed any warnings, but fortunately for Walton, his crew refuses to travel farther so Walton is forced to return home.

Victor now dies and the Monster appears to mourn the death of his creator. Dussinger states that Victor's death places the Monster in the role of man without God to guide him, so that "man himself has been abandoned by his Maker and left a victim of his uncontrollable nature" (53). Being left without a guide or a creator, the Monster retains no hope of achieving the love and acceptance he craved; believing that to continue his life is pointless, the Monster informs Walton of his plan to destroy himself.

> "But soon," he cried, with sad and solemn enthusiasm, "I shall die, and what I now feel be no longer felt. Soon these burning miseries will be extinct. I shall ascend my funeral pile triumphantly and exult in the agony of the torturing flames. The light of that conflagration will fade away. My ashes will be swept into the sea by the winds. My spirit will sleep in peace or if it thinks it will not surely think thus. Farewell."

> He sprang from the cabin window as he said this upon the ice raft which lay close to the vessel. He was soon borne away by the waves and lost in darkness and distance. (271)

While the Monster claims he will destroy himself, the death is not witnessed by the reader. Perhaps Mary Shelley felt she could not adequately depict the Monster's final self-destruction so she placed the scene off-stage, but it is also possible that the Monster does not kill himself but merely tells Walton he will do so to prevent anyone from pursuing him. If the Monster chooses to remain alive, his intentions cannot be known. This ambiguity makes the novel's eerie conclusion more disconcerting because the reader is left without assurance of the Monster's ending; however, such ambiguity may only strengthen Shelley's novel by refusing an easy solution to the difficult issues explored in the text. The lack of closure suggests that there is no end to the consequences of transgression. *Frankenstein*, therefore, in its creation of an existential world without hope for transgressors or their victims becomes the most emphatic treatise against the quest for forbidden knowledge in the Gothic wanderer tradition.

The Last Man: The Rejection of Romanticism

The Last Man is a more mature expression of the existentialism Shelley developed in *Frankenstein*, yet it has received less critical attention, largely because the critics condemned it upon its publication in 1826. After the 1833 second edition, the novel was out of print until 1965. One of the major criticisms against the novel was that it merely mouthed the Romantic theories of Percy Shelley, a charge also made against *Frankenstein*. A close reading of the novel, however, reveals that Mary Shelley did not use the novel to express her husband's theories, but rather, she created her own uniquely existential and anti-Romantic vision of the future. Written shortly after the deaths of John Keats, Percy Shelley, and Lord Byron, *The Last Man* mourns the passing of the great Romantic poets and their ideas, but simultaneously, it exposes the severe flaws of Romanticism and its natural supernaturalism. The novel's negative and apocalyptic vision of the twenty-first century is a repudiation of Romantic millennialism. Shelley further rejects the possibility of God, Nature, or some divine and benevolent force that orders the universe and directs it toward some glorious goal. Even more so than *Frankenstein*, *The Last Man* emphasizes that even if God exists, He is not concerned in human affairs and has no plan for human salvation. Shelley's rejection of a possible hopeful future for humanity is best evidenced in her inversion of the Romantic myth of consciousness. All the Romantic poets had their own versions of this myth which purports that people pass from a stage of innocence in childhood into experience as adults; once in the stage of experience, people long to return to the stage of innocence, but this return is impossible. Most people remain in the stage of experience, while a few progress into wise innocence where they can acquire what Wordsworth termed the "philosophic mind" ("Intimations" 184) to reconcile themselves with the past and use experience for their benefit. Shelley inverts this Romantic belief system in the stages of the main character's life. Lionel Verney's childhood begins in the stage of experience where he is an orphaned outcast and wanderer. Lionel passes into a happy stage of innocence as an adult when he marries and has friends; however, he returns to experience when a plague wipes out the human race, leaving him the sole survivor. He is then unable to find innocence again because of the misery he has known and the lack of other humans to console him. Shelley's inversion of the Romantic myth of consciousness displays her rejection of Romanticism and her existential belief that there is no future happiness for people because there is no divine plan or order to the universe. This perspective, distinct from Shelley's Romantic contemporaries, reveals that she had her own intellectual abilities and literary talents rather than merely being the mouthpiece of her husband and friends' Romantic beliefs. Shelley also adapts the Gothic wanderer figure, as in *Frankenstein*, by creating a main character who is innocent yet suffers from others' transgressions. Lionel Verney becomes the ultimate example of the existential Gothic wanderer who is isolated in a world without meaning.

The Sibyl: Immortality and Prophecy

The charge that Shelley was her husband's mouthpiece stems from critical overemphasis upon the extent to which Percy Shelley assisted his wife in editing *Frankenstein*. While her husband was dead by the time Shelley wrote *The Last Man*, critics have pointed to the "Author's Introduction" as proof of Percy Shelley's influence upon the novel. In the introduction, Mary Shelley creates a fictional source for the novel by using the Gothic mode of discovering a fragmented manuscript which she has merely edited (Mishra 162). Shelley claims that she and her companion (Percy Shelley) came upon this manuscript while visiting the Sibyl's cave near Naples. The manuscript was a collection of unorganized narrative fragments written on leaves that Mary Shelley had to arrange and decipher. The writing was in numerous languages including "ancient Chaldee, and Egyptian hieroglyphics, old as the Pyramids. Stranger still, some were in modern dialects, English and Italian" (3). The leaves contain prophecies, names of famous people, exultations of victory or woes of defeat (3). From the leaves, Shelley collects all those that detail Lionel Verney's eyewitness account of how the human race became extinct because of a plague during the last years of the twenty-first century. These leaves are assembled to form the novel's text.

Shelley uses the Sibyl's cave as the tale's source because the Sibyl's immortality makes her symbolic of a Gothic wanderer. Traditionally, the

Sibyl was punished for rejecting Apollo's sexual advances by being condemned to eternal life without eternal youth and constantly being forced to prophesy the future (Smith 48). As with the Gothic wanderer who achieves life-extension, the Sibyl finds that her extended life is only extended misery. The Sibyl becomes the novel's doppelganger of Lionel Verney who remains alive while the rest of the human race dies from a plague. While Lionel does not prophesy like the Sibyl, his story of the future is inexplicably found in the Sibyl's cave three centuries before the occurrence of the events described. Steven Goldsmith has argued that the Sibyl represents Mary Shelley because the Sibyl had Apollo's prophecies breathed into her as Apollo's medium. Similarly, Shelley was the medium for her husband's Romantic vision, which she was attempting to prolong by writing *The Last Man* (275-7). I believe Shelley did not intend such a symbolic comparison, but instead, she merely compared herself to the Sibyl because she had outlived her Romantic friends. In addition, like the Sibyl, Shelley felt she was prophetic because she was writing about the future. Shelley's pessimistic prophecy rejects the Romantic belief that the human race will eventually evolve into a state of millennial happiness. Instead, Shelley believed in a form of existentialism in which life is without meaning so no future state of happiness will be likely or lasting. Shelley's existential ideas are best reflected in her depiction of Lionel Verney's life as an inversion of the Romantic myth of consciousness.

Lionel Verney as Gothic Wanderer

The Last Man begins with Lionel Verney's childhood in the stage of experience as opposed to the Romantic belief that childhood is the stage of innocence. Shelley draws on the Gothic tradition by depicting Lionel as a wanderer and social outcast because his father committed the social transgression of gambling. Shelley possibly drew upon her father's *St. Leon* to depict Lionel's father as a gambler who impoverishes his family because of his vice. Lionel's father was not born a noble, but he worked his way up in society until he became the King of England's closest friend; however, Mr. Verney became addicted to gambling and fell into debt. Mr. Verney's adversities were relieved by the king in exchange for promises that he would mend his ways. Mr. Verney failed to keep these promises because "his social disposition, his craving for the usual diet of admiration, and more than all, the fiend of gambling, which fully possessed him, made his good resolutions transient, his promises vain" (6). The king remained indulgent toward his friend, but the queen disapproved of her husband's friendship. Eventually, the king grew tired of his wife's complaints and made one last attempt to reform Lionel's father by paying off his debts. Mr. Verney ruined this final chance for his salvation, as Lionel explains:

> ...as a pledge of continued favour, he received from his royal master a sum of money to defray pressing debts, and enable him to enter under good auspices his new career. That very night, while yet full of gratitude and good resolves, this whole sum, and its amount doubled, was lost at the gaming-table. In his desire to repair his first losses, my father risked double stakes, and thus incurred a debt of honour he was wholly unable to pay. Ashamed to apply again to the king, he turned his back upon London, its false delights and clinging miseries; and, with poverty for his sole companion, buried himself in solitude among the hills and lakes of Cumberland. (6-7)

During this exile, Lionel's father married a lowly cottage-girl and became the father of Lionel and his sister, Perdita. Soon after his children's births, Mr. Verney died of debt, leaving his children as "outcasts, paupers, unfriended beings" (8).

Lionel grows up in this wilderness exile, himself becoming practically a wild man. He feels victimized by his father's gambling which has resulted in his being denied his rightful social position. Lionel also hates the royal family for not having further assisted his father. Lionel's youth is spent as an outcast.

> Thus untaught in refined philosophy, and pursued by a restless feeling of degradation from my true station in society, I wandered among the hills of civilized England as uncouth a savage as the wolf-bred founder of old Rome. I owned but one law, it was that of the strongest, and my greatest deed of virtue was never to submit. (9)

Lionel's sister grows up in a similar fashion, indulging in "self-created wanderings" inspired by her fancy as a means to escape from her dull common life (10).

Lionel's existence in this stage of experience ends when he seeks revenge by poaching on royal land. When he is caught for his crime, Lionel is brought before Adrian for punishment. Adrian, who is based on Percy Shelley, is the son of the late king, who abdicated his throne and agreed to the monarchy's abolishment; however, Adrian retains social prominence with the title Earl of Windsor, and the royal family remains much respected in England. Consequently, while both Adrian and Lionel have been disinherited from their birthrights, Adrian does not feel the same extreme displacement as Lionel. Upon their introduction, Adrian immediately greets Lionel as the son of his father's friend, thus acknowledging a bond between them. When Adrian asks Lionel, "will you not acknowledge the hereditary bond of friendship which I trust will hereafter unite us?" (17), Lionel feels an instant restoration to his rightful, hereditary position at court, remarking "I trod my native soil" (18). Lionel and Adrian's friendship thus reestablishes a sort of lost Eden experienced by their fathers. Lionel now enters the stage of innocence, remarking, "I now began to be human. I was admitted within that sacred boundary which divides the intellectual and moral nature of man from that which characterizes animals" (20). Lionel's happiness culminates in his marriage to Adrian's sister and his sense of belonging to a family.

The Existential Plague

Lionel remains in the stage of innocence for several years until he is thrust back into experience when a worldwide plague begins to eliminate the human race. As the plague sweeps across the globe, the novel's main characters watch the world's population rapidly diminishing. Realizing their own chances of survival are slim, they gamble with the plague by attempting to escape from it. Adrian decides to lead the few remaining English people to Switzerland where the healthy climate may best protect them from the plague's power. While the journey will have enormous risks and hardships, and the odds are completely against them, the English people agree to make the exodus.

The plague serves as the novel's vehicle for expressing its existential philosophy. Shelley displays the lack of meaning in human existence by repeatedly showing the impossibility of defining or interpreting the plague. There is no order or reason to the plague's choice of victims as it kills young and old, rich and poor, wicked and innocent. At the same time, the earth undergoes tumultuous weather suggestive of an apocalypse, but natural events continually resist all attempts to interpret them. An example of the impossibility of interpreting events occurs when the English people are about to cross the English channel. The exodus of the English severely differs from the biblical exodus of the Israelites because the English do not have God to guide them, although they wish to believe God is controlling events. When the English arrive at the channel, rather than the water splitting apart for them to walk across on dry land, the sea is in a furious tumult and burning globes fall from the sky. The people try to interpret these globes as a sign of God's intention to destroy humanity (270-1). While the people succeed in crossing the channel into France, they remain severely frightened of the supernatural events occurring, and their fears only increase with their inability to read meaning in these events. If God does intend to destroy humanity, He is being inconsistent with Christian belief for He destroys both the evil and the good, thus differing from biblical accounts of the apocalypse.

The plague becomes the ultimate Gothic villain in the novel because the inability to understand it makes it all the more frightening. Continually, characters find that their interpretations are incorrect; what are believed to be supernatural occurrences are rationally explained in the manner of Mrs. Radcliffe (Birkhead 167). For example, a Black Spectre is sighted by the party travelling to Switzerland. The people think they are witnessing a supernatural warning of their approaching deaths, but the Spectre is later revealed to be merely a French nobleman on a horse (299). The explanation for these minor supernatural occurrences only increases the Gothic horror of the plague whose meaning continues to be indeterminable. Most characters continue to interpret the plague as the instrument of God's wrath to destroy humanity, but the text continually rejects any Christian interpretation of events. The voice of religion in the novel turns out to be that of a fanatic who preaches that the plague will end if humanity repents for its sins. This man gains many followers who protect themselves by hiding in a compound in Paris. The plague enters the compound and kills everyone except the religious leader. The leader then commits suicide after confessing that he knows of no divine plan associated with the plague, and he was merely trying to manipulate people to gain power.

While such scenes demonstrate the plague's resistance against all attempts to define it, critics have nevertheless insisted upon attaching symbolism to the plague, thus overlooking Shelley's existential purpose. Barbara Johnson has interpreted the plague in relation to democracy and the French Revolution by calling it "a nightmarish version of the desire...to spread equality and fraternity throughout the world" (264). Johnson cites a minor scene in the novel where a high born girl, Juliet, loves a man from the lower class. Juliet's father separates the couple, but the plague then kills Juliet's family, allowing her to be with her lover, and symbolically breaking down class lines. Johnson's reading is unconvincing because eventually the plague kills Juliet, her beloved, and their child. Johnson argues further that the plague is "lethal universality" and that it "deconstructs" boundaries between countries and people (264). While the plague appears to spread equality, ironically, when it ceases, the three people left alive are members of the English nobility. Steven Goldsmith and Sandra Gilbert and Susan Gubar have tried to depict the plague as a feminist protagonist who wishes to wipe out human history because men have denied women a voice (Goldsmith 313, Gilbert and Gubar 247). This argument weakly rests upon the novel's female authorship. The text fails to support this feminist interpretation because not only is human history not erased, but it is a man, Lionel Verney, who writes down the end of human history to preserve it.

Shelley's use of the plague is best described as a symbol of existentialism that allows for the elimination of the entire human race except for Lionel Verney. Mary Shelley felt total isolation after the death of her husband and friends, so she felt she could best express her feelings by depicting one man alone in the world as she felt herself to be alone; consequently, she needed a way to eliminate all but one human, and the plague was a logical means for human extinction. Shelley may have derived the idea of the Last Man from contemporary poems that had used the theme, including Byron's "Darkness" (1816), Thomas Campbell's "The Last Man" (1823), and Thomas Hood's "The Last Man" (1826).

The Gothic Wanderer: From Transgression to Redemption 155

Anne Mellor remarks that all these works "invoke a Judaeo-Christian framework and the possibility of a finer life elsewhere, either on earth or in heaven. Mary Shelley explicitly denies such theological or millennial interpretations of her plague" (Introduction xvi). Paley in agreement, adds, that death and the plague both exist in *The Last Man* "somewhere between personification and myth in a borderland where causality seems nonexistent" (120). Mary Shelley intends the only meaning of the plague to be its meaninglessness, so that its destruction of humanity will reflect life's futility.

The plague's mode of operation is as inexplicable as its meaning. The only people who survive the plague are Adrian, Clara, and Lionel—all English, noble, and related by marriage or blood. Of these three, Lionel is the only one to catch the plague and recover, while Adrian and Clara remain immune. Surprisingly, Lionel catches the plague from a black man, although he is in England and could easily receive it from a multitude of English people. The event occurs during a scene of Gothic horror as Lionel returns home to his family after a long journey. As he enters the house, he hears a groan and,

> ...without reflection I threw open the door of the first room that presented itself. It was quite dark; but, as I stept within, a pernicious scent assailed my senses, producing sickening qualms, which made their way to my very heart, while I felt my leg clasped, and a groan repeated by the person that held me. I lowered my lamp and saw a negro half clad, writhing under the agony of disease, while he held me with a convulsive grasp. With mixed horror and impatience, I strove to disengage myself, and fell on the sufferer; he wound his naked festering arms round me, his face was close to mine, and his breath, death-laden, entered my vitals. For a moment I was overcome, my head was bowed by aching nausea; till, reflection returning, I sprung up, threw the wretch from me, and darting up the staircase, entered the chamber usually inhabited by my family. (245)

Why Shelley chooses to have Lionel receive and then become immune to the plague is hard enough to explain, since no one else who acquires it gains immunity. Even less comprehensible is why Lionel receives the plague from a negro. Perhaps being plague-stricken and black makes the negro a double outcast who foreshadows the intense isolation Lionel will later know. Of the few critics who have written upon the novel, none have succeeded in providing convincing interpretations of this scene. Vijay Mishra suggests it is Lionel's compassion that causes him to receive the plague and his recovery is a symbol of Christ's passion and resurrection (177-8). However, because Shelley rejects the Christian myth, and Lionel is never able to redeem anyone, he is an unlikely character to associate with Christ. Furthermore, Lionel's treatment of the negro is completely lacking in compassion. Anne Mellor argues that "From this unwilling but powerful embrace of the racial other (significantly, this is the only time that a 'negro' is specifically mentioned in the novel), Verney both contracts and, recovering, becomes immune to the plague" (Introduction xxiv). Mellor's statement attempts to find a racial purpose in the scene, but she fails to elaborate upon her statement that the scene is significant, suggestive that she is unsure of its significance. The negro is never mentioned again, but on the same page, Lionel's son dies, so the negro's black skin may equate him with the blackness of Death that has entered Lionel's home. Lionel's lack of compassion in the scene should not be read as bigotry but rather as fear of catching the plague. He is so frightened after inhaling the negro's breath that he may automatically assume he caught the plague when in reality, he merely suffers from exhaustion. Lionel is only ill for a few days, so he may have merely needed rest and not contracted the plague after all. Whether Lionel ever actually contracts the plague, the scene further emphasizes the inexplicable purpose of the plague and the existential world in which it operates.

The Gamble with Death

After the plague completes its rampage, leaving only Clara, Adrian, and Lionel alive, the novel again uses the gambling motif to depict Lionel as a Gothic wanderer victimized by others' transgressions. The remaining three characters realize they have outlived the plague by the time they reach Venice. Because Adrian and Clara are not blood relatives, they are the only two people who are capable of repopulating the earth. Shelley's interest in rewriting *Paradise Lost* is reflected, therefore, in her placing Adrian and Clara in the potential position of a new Adam and Eve. Shelley then revises the Eden story by making Adrian and Clara feel no responsibility or desire to create a new human race. Rather than a God or an angel to warn them against sin, Adrian and Clara are warned by Lionel against foolhardiness when Clara wishes to travel to Greece where her parents are buried. The easiest way to make the journey from Venice would be by boat, but Lionel objects to the dangers of travelling by sea rather than land. His companions nevertheless persuade him to make the journey with them. They are willing to gamble with their lives, and consequently, the future of the human race, for the mere whim of visiting Greece, and subconsciously perhaps, from a desire to die. At the same time, they believe their survival of the plague may mean that Fate has preserved them for some future purpose, so their lives are charmed against potential harm. Even when a storm arises while they are at sea, Clara, like a typical gambler, denies the possibility of losing her life by refusing to consider the seriousness of the danger. She remarks, "Why should I fear? neither sea nor storm can harm us, if mighty destiny or the ruler of destiny does not permit. And then the stinging fear of surviving either of you, is not here—one death will clasp us undivided" (321). Despite the continual failure of attempts to find meaning in events, Clara retains a belief in destiny and the order of the universe. Similarly, a gambler convinces himself of his chance to win despite the odds being that he will lose. Lionel is aware that Clara and Adrian's past success in surviving the plague has transformed them into gamblers who are unwilling to believe they can tempt Fate and lose. Lionel himself experiences the gambler's numbness at moments of great risk when he is surrounded by the dangers of the storm at sea.

> ...resignation had conquered every fear. We have a power given us in any worst extremity, which props the else feeble mind of man, and enables us to endure the most savage tortures with a stillness of soul which in hours of happiness we could not have imagined. A calm, more dreadful in truth than the tempest, allayed the wild beatings of my heart—a calm like that of the gamester, the suicide, and the murderer, when the last die is on the point of being cast—while the poisoned cup is at the lips,—as the death-blow is about to be given. (322-3)

Lionel applies the gambling metaphor to the many choices and risks in life. Clara and Adrian allow the gambler's resignation to descend upon them because they feel that it can hardly matter if they die since the plague has so drastically changed the world. If there is meaning to life or some intended destiny for them, then they believe they have nothing to fear. As with most gambles, they lose when the ship sinks, and they both drown. Lionel manages to swim to shore, realizing he is now the Last Man upon earth.

This conclusion brings the novel full circle by its repetition of the gambling motif. Earlier Lionel had been exiled from his birthright because of his father's gambling; now he has become exiled from all humanity because others were willing to gamble with their lives, never considering his own happiness. In both cases, gambling has destroyed the family unit. Clara and Adrian, as a new Adam and Eve, bring about a second fall of humanity, but this time the fall is more serious, for while Adam and Eve's transgression introduced death for humanity, Clara and Adrian's transgression results in human extinction.

Lionel's solitary position marks his return into a stage of experience that completes Shelley's inverse of the Romantic myth of consciousness. Lionel acknowledges that he has returned to the earlier stage of his life by comparing the present to his youth and feeling his burden will be easier to bear because he long ago learned to survive without depending upon others (338). Nevertheless, Lionel mourns the loss of the human race. To assuage his loneliness, he writes the history of the end of humanity, which becomes the novel. When the novel is completed, he decides he will wander the earth on the small chance of finding another human who has also survived the worldwide plague. Clara and Adrian's gambling transgression has resulted in Lionel's return to his childhood role of Gothic wanderer as he recognizes, "A solitary being is by instinct a wanderer, and that I would become" (341). Lionel differs from earlier Gothic wanderer characters, however, because he wanders as the result of others' transgressions rather than his own.

Lionel's final isolation reflects Mary Shelley's personal grief over the deaths of her husband and Lord Byron. Adrian's drowning is a direct parallel to the drowning of Percy Shelley (Mishra 185), and earlier in the novel, Lionel's sister, Perdita, had drowned herself because her husband, Lord Raymond, was dead, a scene reflecting Shelley's own wish for death so she might join her husband (Mellor, Introduction xi). Shelley might also have chosen for Clara and Adrian to die together as a way to rewrite her own life, herself taking on Clara's role so she could die with her husband. Shelley, however, identified most fully with the main character, Lionel Verney, as evident from her journal entry of May 14, 1824: "The last man! Yes I may well describe that solitary being's feelings, feeling myself as the last relic of a beloved race, my companions extinct before me" (Paley 109). The grief Shelley feels for her former companions inspired her to write *The Last Man*, as Lionel Verney, to solace the grief of his solitary existence, records the events that resulted in his complete isolation.

The End of Human History: Deconstructing Lionel's Manuscript and Shelley's Novel

Lionel Verney's manuscript is the history of his life and an eyewitness account of how the plague destroyed humanity. He writes without an audience to read his work, yet his act of writing assumes he will have readers since the purpose of writing is to communicate (Paley 121; Mellor, Introduction xiv). Lionel realizes no one will ever read his work, yet he attempts to remain positive by stating that he will write on the chance that the world will be re-populated by people of whose existence he may not know, and someday, they will want to learn how earlier humanity had become extinct (339). In writing the final chapter of human history, Lionel seeks to make history's end memorable and meaningful to the reader even if in essence, his task is pointless because his work will not be read. Lionel attempts to enforce meaning upon his experience, but the more he writes and tries to explain what has happened, the more unclear the meaning of the plague becomes. He questions why he should live and considers suicide, but then rejects it, choosing instead to believe that there is some reason for why he is the only human survivor.

> But this [suicide] I would not do. I had, from the moment I had reasoned on the subject, instituted myself the subject to fate, and the servant of necessity, the visible laws of the invisible God—I believed that my obedience was the result of

> sound reasoning, pure feeling, and an exalted sense of the true excellence and nobility of my nature. Could I have seen in this empty earth, in the seasons and their change, the hand of a blind power only, most willingly would I have placed my head on the sod, and closed my eyes on its loveliness for ever. But fate had administered life to me, when the plague had already seized on its prey—she had dragged me by the hair from out the strangling waves—By such miracles she had bought me for her own; I admitted her authority, and bowed to her decrees. (337-8)

Against all hope, Lionel continues to insist that there is a reason why he has not been destroyed by the plague, and since Fate has saved him, he must obey her. When Lionel finishes his history and decides to write no more, but rather to search for other survivors, it marks the defeat of language and meaning because he has told his story to himself and is now left without anyone else to communicate. Lionel remains hopeful that there are other survivors who will read his manuscript, but in this hope, he is seeking to delude himself rather than to be realistic. Even if his writing is meaningful because it consoles Lionel, without other readers, the work will be worthless when he dies. The end of Lionel's writing demonstrates that meaning only exists in communication and human relationships (Paley 121; Mellor, Introduction, xiv, xxii). Mellor interprets the novel as a reflection of Derrida's theory that human history is dependent upon language. While Lionel continues to live, human history has not ended, but there is no reason to record it because without Lionel being able to communicate his story to others, it can have no meaning (Introduction xii). Mellor suggests that the futility of Lionel's writing makes *The Last Man* the first example of a work that is fully conscious of how its language can be deconstructed as it continually attempts to place meaning upon what is meaningless (Introduction vii). Mellor concludes that the novel suggests "all conceptions of human history, all ideologies, are grounded on metaphors or tropes which have no referent or authority outside of language" (*Mary* 164). The novel becomes Shelley's rejection of the Romantic belief in imagination's ability to create lasting meaning.

Lionel's return to the stage of experience is the final step in Shelley's rejection of Romanticism. While the novel is partially written to mourn the loss of the great Romantic poets, it also clearly reveals the flaws in Romantic theories. Shelley rejects the belief of her father, William Godwin, that human life could be extended by the evolution of reason, as he expressed in *St. Leon*. Shelley's novel reveals the inability of reason to fend off accidents and disease which cannot be prevented or explained logically. Shelley also rejects Godwin and Percy Shelley's belief in millennialism, which argues that the human race slowly evolves and progresses. Mary Shelley completely erases this possibility by causing the human race to become extinct. Shelley most harshly criticizes

Romanticism's exaltation of Nature as having salvific value for people. Wordsworth believed that with Imagination, one could interpret Nature as benevolent. Early in *The Last Man*, Lionel uses his imagination to see Nature as benevolent, but he is already aware that it is his imagination that so defines Nature. "So true it is, that man's mind alone was the creator of all that was good or great to man, and that Nature herself was only his first minister" (5). By the novel's conclusion, however, Lionel realizes the danger of the human imagination's distortion of Nature. Mellor notes that here Shelley criticizes the two main points of Romanticism: "that nature can be the source of moral authority and that the human mind can create meanings of permanent value" (*Mary* 164). Lionel experiences Nature's sadistic personality when the plague destroys all but one member of the human race, yet allows other creatures to survive in multitudes upon the earth. In despair, Lionel exclaims, "Shall I not bestow a malediction on every other of nature's offspring, which dares live and enjoy, while I live and suffer?" (334). Yet Lionel still attempts to believe in a Romantic Nature that is benevolent. In words reminiscent of the Ancient Mariner's blessing of the sea serpents, and Wordsworth's blessing upon the creatures in the "Intimations Ode," Lionel declares his love for the earth's remaining creatures.

> Ah, no! I will discipline my sorrowing heart to sympathy in your joys; I will be happy, because ye are so. Live on, ye innocents, nature's selected darlings; I am not much unlike to you. Nerves, pulse, brain, joint, and flesh, of such am I composed, and ye are organized by the same laws. I have something beyond this, but I will call it a defect, not an endowment, if it leads me to misery, while ye are happy. (334)

However, Lionel's moment of Romantic sensibility is immediately destroyed.

> Just then, there emerged from a near copse two goats and a little kid, by the mother's side; they began to browze the herbage of the hill. I approached near to them, without their perceiving me; I gathered a handful of fresh grass, and held it out; the little one nestled close to its mother, while she timidly withdrew. The male stepped forward, fixing his eyes on me: I drew near, still holding out my lure, while he, depressing his head, rushed at me with his horns. I was a very fool; I knew it, yet I yielded to my rage. I snatched up a huge fragment of rock; it would have crushed my rash foe. I poized it—aimed it—then my heart failed me. I hurled it wide of the mark; it rolled clattering among the bushes into dell. My little visitants, all aghast, galloped back into the covert of the wood; while I, my very heart bleeding and torn, rushed down the hill, and by the

violence of bodily exertion, sought to escape from my miserable self. (334)

Lionel's intense emotions reflect that even the Romantic belief in Nature is contrary to Lionel's experiences of reality. Nature cannot be a solace to him, so he decides, "I will not live among the wild scenes of nature, the enemy of all that lives. I will seek the towns" (335). By declaring that Nature is the enemy of all that lives, Lionel has completely rejected Romanticism's value of Nature, in favor of the value of human relationships, although he cannot benefit from them. Lionel leaves the country and travels to Rome where the buildings still proclaim the one time existence of humanity; it is the only environment where Lionel can retain any sense of meaning because it retains the memories of those with whom he once communicated.

Despite all he has suffered, Lionel continues to long for an explanation of his situation. He still wonders whether other human beings live or whether a God exists. In the novel's final paragraph, Lionel sets off in his boat, alone save for a dog he has befriended, describing his future as "Thus around the shores of deserted earth, while the sun is high, and the moon waxes or wanes, angels, the spirits of the dead, and the ever-open eye of the Supreme, will behold the tiny bark, freighted with Verney—the LAST MAN" (342). Paley suggests that Lionel's solitary journey is a reference to Coleridge's Ancient Mariner (121). Shelley cruelly parodies the Ancient Mariner's continuous need to tell his story, by placing Lionel in a position where he writes from a desire to communicate, although there is no one to read or hear his tale. Consequently, unlike the Ancient Mariner, Lionel will never even know momentary relief of telling his story. Lionel's reference to the Supreme as existing and even having an "ever-open eye" suggests his hope that he will still someday understand the miseries he has endured. His desire to continue hoping is a refusal to acknowledge what he fears, that there is no meaning and there is no God.

The novel's opening epigraph from *Paradise Lost* foreshadows this conclusion: "Let no man seek / Henceforth to be foretold what shall befall / Him or his children" (XI, 770-2). These words are spoken by Adam after the Fall when Michael, showing Adam the future, reveals to him the flood that will destroy humanity. Shelley focuses upon this moment in *Paradise Lost* because it foretells the future, but fails to foresee God's divine plan of salvation for humanity by Christ's death and resurrection. By using this reference to the Flood, Shelley is suggesting that human extinction is the eventual future of humanity. Lionel realizes humanity is fated for extinction, yet to the end he continues to hope, only to be tortured with memories of the happiness he once knew but now has lost forever (Paley 114-5). Lionel's final quest marks his role as a Gothic wanderer alienated from the world. His determination against all hope to find other humans represents the continual human need to search for meaning and to have someone with whom that meaning can be communicated.

Conclusion

Both *Frankenstein* and *The Last Man* provide unique existential treatments of the Gothic wanderer figure. Their uses of *Paradise Lost* and Gothic and Romantic elements reflect Shelley's immersion in the literary culture of her family and friends, but her revision and rejection of such elements proves that she was more than just a mouthpiece for her husband or friends' theories. Shelley uses existentialism to show that because God does not exist, life has no meaning or purpose, save for what human imagination interprets for it. Consequently, the only form of transgression is an act that destroys the human relationships in which all meaning resides. However, Shelley's existential Gothic is not simply a pessimistic view of the world—it is a strong warning that people are responsible for their own actions. If a person transgresses, there is no God to redeem the transgressor or protect the innocent from the effects of those transgressions. Transgressions have indeterminate and far reaching effects that must constantly be guarded against. Shelley's philosophical interpretation of transgression and her original treatment of the wanderer figure make her a major contributor to the Gothic tradition.

PART III -
From Transgression to Redemption

Chapter VIII – Teufelsdrockh as Gothic Wanderer and Everyman: Carlyle's *Sartor Resartus*

Sartor Resartus (1838) is the first Victorian treatment of the Gothic wanderer, and the work that was most significant in transforming the Gothic wanderer figure in the second half of the nineteenth century. In *Sartor Resartus*, Thomas Carlyle reminds us that we are all wanderers. The novel's main character, Diogenes Teufelsdrockh, passes from Gothic wanderer to Everyman figure by undergoing the universal spiritual crisis experienced in different degrees by everyone who gives some thought to life's meaning. Carlyle uses Teufelsdrockh's spiritual crisis to display how crisis can reaffirm order and meaning if people learn to accept their places in the universe and work for humanity's betterment. In transforming a Gothic wanderer into an Everyman figure, Carlyle resembles Fanny Burney; however, while Burney's *The Wanderer* is a rediscovered text that is valued today, it had little influence in the nineteenth century. I have chosen *Sartor Resartus* as the first Victorian Gothic text for discussion because its use of the supernatural and the Wandering Jew theme would influence later Gothic novels in their depiction of the Gothic wanderer. Beginning with *Sartor Resartus*, Victorian novels would transform the Gothic wanderer from a figure of transgression who deserves damnation into a character who deserves mercy and is capable of redemption and salvation.

Besides making the novel's protagonist, Teufelsdrockh, a Gothic wanderer figure, Carlyle adapts numerous other Gothic elements in *Sartor Resartus*. He uses the supernatural by converting it into "Natural Supernaturalism" to make the Gothic a part of the everyday world; this change would allow Victorian novelists to utilize the Gothic as a direct form of social criticism. Carlyle would also employ a typically Gothic narrative strategy by using the multiple narrators of Teufelsdrockh and Teufelsdrockh's Editor. Carlyle inserts the Editor as someone who must piece together the fragmented manuscript of Teufelsdrockh's life, the fragmented manuscript being a typical Gothic device. In addition, Teufelsdrockh's writing style is often complex and disorderly. Consequently, the book's fragmentation and disorder become as complicated and labyrinthian as the passages of a Gothic castle. The chaotic structure symbolizes the chaos and seeming meaninglessness of life, but by the Editor's piecing together of the fragmented narrative, order and meaning are eventually achieved. By creating meaning out of chaos, Carlyle transforms Teufelsdrockh from his role as Gothic wanderer into Everyman the Hero, a symbol of survival amid life's "Gothic" experiences.

Teufelsdrockh's Christian Origins

Although the wanderer theme is most emphasized in the four famous chapters of Book II: "Sorrows of Teufelsdrockh," "The Everlasting No," "Centre of Indifference," and "The Everlasting Yea," from the very beginning of *Sartor Resartus*, Carlyle sets up the image of Teufelsdrockh as a wanderer and an outcast because of his enigmatic origins. Teufelsdrockh, as a foundling baby, is brought to the town of Entepfuhl by a mysterious stranger who leaves the baby with Andreas and Gretchen Futteral, charging them to raise the child. With the baby is a baptismal certificate on which nothing but the child's name is decipherable. This beginning presents Teufelsdrockh as a typical hero with mysterious origins, but also as a displaced person because he is raised by parents other than his own. G.B. Tennyson remarks that the mysterious stranger who brings the foundling to the Futterals is obviously an emissary from Heaven (218), for no one but the Futterals have ever seen him, and they hear no further word about him. Carlyle intends the reader to interpret Teufelsdrockh as a person with heavenly origins because the narrative states that the Heavens smiled on the Futterals' endeavors to raise Teufelsdrockh (85). The main character's oxymoronic name, Diogenes Teufelsdrockh, means "God begotten Devil's dung." The last name, Teufelsdrockh, symbolizes the suffering and doubt the main character will pass through, while the first name, Diogenes, confirms order and meaning (Waring 57). Walter Waring points out that the dualism of good and evil in Teufelsdrockh's character is further suggested by his being brought to the Futterals' home on the autumn equinox, the midpoint between summer and winter and by extension between light and dark, good and evil; light and dark will become recurring images throughout *Sartor Resartus*. Beginning with Teufelsdrockh's name and origins, Carlyle is preparing the reader for the process of despair and wandering that Teufelsdrockh must pass through to reach a state of enlightenment.

Despite the Futterals' kindness to him, Teufelsdrockh's mysterious birth makes him grow up wondering about his unknown father, and he feels a sense of displacement with his foster-parents. Already, he equates his true father with God, as he informs the reader,

> Hadst thou, any more than I, a Father whom thou knowest? The Andreas and Gretchen, or the Adam and Eve, who led thee into Life, and for a time suckled and pap-fed thee there, whom thou namest Father and Mother; these were, like mine, but thy nursing-father and nursing-mother: thy true Beginning and

Father is in Heaven, whom with the bodily eye thou shalt never behold, but only with the spiritual. (86)

This statement is the reader's first clue that Teufelsdrockh is a Christ figure. Like Christ, he is raised on earth by a foster-father, while acknowledging that his true father is in Heaven. Because his name suggests equal portions of good and evil, we can also equate him with being half-god and half-man, as Christ is God and man. If Heaven is Teufelsdrockh's rightful home, then he is displaced upon the earth, just as Christ remarked that he had no home upon the earth. Both Christ and Teufelsdrockh must wait to rejoin their Father in Heaven, and both have a mission to fulfill before they can return to Heaven. Teufelsdrockh is also correlated to Adam because of his human nature, and because Adam, being the first man, also had no human father, so he was also a Son of God. From a Christian perspective, all humans are children of God, and consequently, they are displaced from their heavenly home, being forced to wander upon the earth until their return to Heaven. Therefore, Adam, like Teufelsdrockh and Christ, is a mixture of the human and the godlike. Adam's human nature became dominant over his spiritual, godlike half when he transgressed against God, resulting in his wanderer status when forced to leave Eden, as depicted in *Paradise Lost* (XII, 648-9).

By linking Teufelsdrockh to Adam, Carlyle follows his Gothic predecessors by rewriting *Paradise Lost*. Carlyle's revision of Milton's epic reflects his belief that Christianity must be revised and revitalized for modern man. Teufelsdrockh remarks that there is some of the "old Adam, lodged in us by birth" (183), meaning we are all capable, like Adam, of committing transgressions. G.B. Tennyson distinguishes Teufelsdrockh from Adam by remarking, "Teufelsdrockh is another Adam; yet he is set down not in Eden but in the barren desert of modern life" (292); this modern desert may be equated with the wilderness where Christ had to face his temptations before he began his ministry. Teufelsdrockh will himself face the temptations of modern life, but like Christ, rather than Adam, he will resist temptation. Once Teufelsdrockh conquers the temptations of modern life, he will, also like Christ, be able to minister to humanity.

Teufelsdrockh's temptations begin as he grows up and becomes more involved in worldly concerns, resulting in his giving less thought to his heavenly origins. Teufelsdrockh's change in attitude that accompanies his transition from childhood to adulthood is the passing from innocence into experience that all must undergo. For Teufelsdrockh, this transition occurs when he falls in love. Teufelsdrockh makes his beloved Blumine the center of his world, placing all his hopes of happiness upon their romance. Then when he finds Blumine with another man, he loses faith in her and eventually, in the universe, believing all his hopes for happiness have vanished. Brookes describes Teufelsdrockh's romance with Blumine as "being lured into the false Eden of romantic love" (117). Teufelsdrockh, like the traditional Gothic wanderer, has transgressed by seeking to recreate a paradise on earth, in this case by romantic love. He placed all his faith in romantic love, forgetting to have faith in God's promise of eternal happiness in a heavenly paradise. When Teufelsdrockh's false paradise ironically leads to his misery and despair, the light of Heaven seems most distant to Teufelsdrockh, but this moment also marks the beginning of his journey back to his heavenly origins.

Teufelsdrockh's despair replaces his hopes for happiness. He remarks, "Man is, properly speaking, based upon Hope, he has no other possession but Hope; this world of his is emphatically the 'Place of Hope'" (158-9). Feeling that his chance for earthly happiness is now impossible, Teufelsdrockh believes that life and the universe are only chaotic and disordered. The Editor of Teufelsdrockh's story remarks that "If what thou namest Happiness be our true aim, then are we all astray" (160). It is not the universe but Teufelsdrockh who is confused because he has placed his hope in earthly happiness where hope does not belong. His inability to achieve happiness causes Teufelsdrockh to lose faith in God, and without this faith, he knows he can never be happy, as he remarks, "for man's well-being, Faith is properly the one thing needful" (159). The Editor remarks, "it will be clear that, for a pure moral nature, the loss of his religious Belief was the loss of everything" (159). Teufelsdrockh even begins to question the existence of God: "Is there no God, then; but at best an absentee God, sitting idle, ever since the first Sabbath, at the outside of his Universe, and seeing it go?" (159). This spiritual crisis plunges Teufelsdrockh into a circle of doubt, despair, and indifference.

Carlyle's Theory of Symbols

Like Teufelsdrockh, Carlyle would himself feel moments of despair. The author remarked that his own personal despair arose from excessive faith in symbols that create false expectations (Gaull 279). Among these symbols was Christianity, which Carlyle lost faith in. Carlyle realized that symbols eventually fail, for they will "wax old" (224) and lose their mystique, but such symbols, Christianity being an example, can still be useful because their "significance will ever demand to be anew inquired into, and anew made manifest" (224). Carlyle believed "the Poet and inspired Maker...Prometheus-like, can shape new Symbols, and bring new Fire from Heaven to fix it there" (225). In *Sartor Resartus*, Carlyle intended to shape such new symbols for people to rely upon as a means for dealing with the crises of modern life. In reshaping old symbols, Carlyle also revised the tradition of the Gothic wanderer.

Frank Kermode, in his book, *The Sense of an Ending*, discusses fictional endings in much the same terms that Carlyle discusses symbols. Kermode believes that, just as Teufelsdrockh places all his hope in romantic love, all humans create symbols that they believe will lead them to happiness. This creation of symbols, in Kermode's terms, comes from the human inability to know what one's end will be. No one can know when or how he or she will die, but people console themselves about death by creating fictional endings for themselves. To believe in these fictional endings is to brainwash oneself into believing happiness can be achieved at some future time in life if a specific goal is achieved. Similarly, the Gothic wanderer continually trusts in a false symbol of happiness by believing his transgression will restore a lost paradise and provide him with personal autonomy. These false symbols always fail, resulting in unhappiness and despair. Kermode argues that the way people pull themselves out of this despair is, ironically, by creating new fictional endings for themselves. People look toward a new future goal, thereby trusting in the same type of fictional ending that earlier deceived them. When these new fictions also fail, people invent yet more fictional endings to replace the earlier ones because as Teufelsdrockh remarks, "Man is, properly speaking, based upon Hope" (158).

Carlyle's discussion of symbols is much the same as Kermode's theory of fictional endings. When Teufelsdrockh's fictional ending of romantic love fails, he enters into despair, and then he must decide whether to allow this despair to destroy his life, or if he will find some way to overcome the despair and reconstitute hope for himself. Teufelsdrockh's journey to overcome his despair will become a model for Victorian treatments of the Gothic wanderer. Influenced by Carlyle, Gothic novelists will create transgressors who will transcend the guilt and remorse of transgression to be redeemed and to become a model of hope for others.

Teufelsdrockh as Gothic Wanderer

Teufelsdrockh's reaction to being deceived in love is to lift up his pilgrim or wanderer's staff and begin "a perambulation and circumambulation of the terraqueous Globe" (147). At this point, not only has Teufelsdrockh lost his faith in symbols, but Carlyle now turns his main character into a symbol of both the Romantic and the Gothic wanderer by drawing upon the wanderings of Romantic figures including the Byronic hero as well as upon the Gothic figure of the Wandering Jew. In *Sartor Resartus'* four central chapters, from "Sorrows of Teufelsdrockh" to "The Everlasting Yea," Carlyle tirelessly depicts Teufelsdrockh as a wanderer. In fact, some form of the word "wander" appears twenty times in these four chapters, eleven of these occurrences in the chapter "Sorrows of Teufelsdrockh." Intermixed with the repetitive wanderer image are descriptions of Teufelsdrockh as a pilgrim. Generally, a distinction exists between these two words, wandering being aimless, while pilgrimages imply a journey to a specific place, usually for a religious purpose. Occasionally, Teufelsdrockh's wanderings do have a momentary purpose as when he seeks a remedy from his sorrows by visiting fountains and saints' wells (154), but even these moments are disappointments in what is overall a long physical and spiritual wandering. However, Carlyle generally seems to equate the meanings of "wanderer" and "pilgrim"; Teufelsdrockh's walking stick is called a "Pilgerstab," translated from German as a pilgrim staff, but a Pilgerstab is the regular "property" for wanderers in German literature (Harrold 147n), so there seems to be no contradiction in Carlyle's mind when he refers to Teufelsdrockh as both a wanderer and a pilgrim.

Teufelsdrockh's connection to the wandering writers and characters of the Romantic age and the Gothic tradition is based upon a mutual loss of hope. For the Romantics, despair occurred in the years following the French Revolution when they felt their dream of a millennial age was destroyed. Like Teufelsdrockh, the Romantics fell into despair and needed a way to reconstitute hope. Carlyle draws upon various Romantic writers and characters to depict Teufelsdrockh's own struggles to reconstitute hope for himself.

A major influence upon the depiction of Teufelsdrockh was Goethe's *The Sorrows of Young Werther* (Tennyson 208-9). In Goethe's novel, Werther despairs and commits suicide because the woman he loves instead loves another. Like Goethe's Werther, Teufelsdrockh also considers suicide, but remarks "From Suicide a certain aftershine (Nachschein) of Christianity withheld me: perhaps also a certain indolence of character; for, was not that a remedy I had at any time within reach?" (165). This aftershine of Christianity makes Teufelsdrockh realize it would be a transgression against God to take his own life. The act of suicide implies a lack of faith in God's goodness and ability to order the universe, and a disbelief in God's plan for human salvation. That Teufelsdrockh does not commit suicide reflects that he has not yet completely transgressed by disbelieving in God's eternal plan. Nevertheless, his despair has distanced him from God.

Teufelsdrockh's other literary sources include British Romantic poets and their literary creations. The Editor of *Sartor Resartus* remarks of Teufelsdrockh, "what a Gehenna was within; that a whole Satanic School were spouting, though inaudibly, there" (148). Gehenna is, of course, another word for Hell, so like Milton's Satan, Teufelsdrockh has a "Hell within," and his being placed in a state of Hell emphasizes the novel's supernatural aspects. "Satanic School" refers to the Romantic school of poetry as practiced by Byron and Shelley, thus linking him to Romantic wanderer figures. Teufelsdrockh's wanderings about the globe recall Byronic heroes, such as Childe Harold, who travels about Europe, visiting famous and remote places of interest while speculating upon the mysteries of human experience, government, war, literature, social institutions, and history. Throughout Byron's work, Childe Harold is greatly depressed and melancholic, trailing his "bleeding heart" across the page for his readers (Harrold xliv). Similarly, Shelley's Alastor visits the deserts, ruins, and ancient places of the earth, and Goethe's Meister wanders through romantic mountain scenery (Harrold xliv). The list of Romantic writers who pass through personal experiences and crises similar to those of Teufelsdrockh may also include William Blake, Samuel Taylor Coleridge, William Wordsworth, and John Keats, who all experienced states of despair and felt a need to restore hope in life (Gaull 279).

Most specifically, Carlyle equates Teufelsdrockh with the Wandering Jew. As the Wandering Jew is forever unable to rest from his wanderings, Teufelsdrockh can find no rest from his despair (Tennyson 206). Teufelsdrockh is described as being "in the temper of ancient Cain, or of the modern Wandering Jew, save only that he feels himself not guilty and but suffering the pains of guilt" (156). His guilt and despair cause Teufelsdrockh, like the Wandering Jew, to be isolated from humanity: "it was a strange isolation I then lived in" (163). His despair is "bitter protracted Death-agony, through long years" (165), reflecting how the Wandering Jew must live a protracted lifespan, longing for a death that will never come. As he wanders the globe, the Wandering Jew inexplicably appears to witness such great historical events as the sack of Rome, the crusades, and decisive Napoleonic battles (Tennyson 212). Like the Jew, Teufelsdrockh visits many famous places and meets several great men. He travels to ancient cities, the wells of saints, and churches (170-1). He witnesses several battles including that at Wagram where Napoleon defeated the Austrians (173). He reads in most public libraries including those of Constantinople and Samarcand (176), and he visits such famous ancient sites as the ruins of Babylon and the Great Wall of China (177). Teufelsdrockh even meets the famous men of his time: he has heard Goethe and Schiller's conversations and known such men as Byron, Napoleon, and Pope Pius (176-8).

The equation between Teufelsdrockh and the Wandering Jew is most apparent in the four chapters of Book Two where Teufelsdrockh undergoes his depression, but throughout *Sartor Resartus*, there are images to equate Teufelsdrockh to his Gothic predecessors. Early in the novel, we are told that Teufelsdrockh became a professor at Weissnichtwo: "He was a stranger there, wafted thither by what is called the course of circumstances" (17). Because no one in Weissnichtwo knows Teufelsdrockh's origins or dares to question him about them, the wits of the town:

> ...spoke of him secretly as if he were a kind of Melchizedek, without father or mother of any kind; sometimes, with reference to his great historic and statistic knowledge, and the vivid way he had of expressing himself like an eye-witness of distant transactions and scenes, they called him the Ewige Jude, Everlasting, or as we say, Wandering Jew. (17)

Carlyle's reference to Melchizedek resembles a passage in *St. Leon* where the main character compares himself to Melchizedek after achieving the elixir of life: "A man who, like Melchisedec, is 'without end of life,' may well consider himself as being also, like him, 'without father, without mother, and without descent.'" (165). Such a similarity shows Carlyle's great familiarity with the Gothic Wanderer tradition and his desire to build upon such depictions of the Wandering Jew.

Carlyle expands on the Wandering Jew theme in such moments as when the Editor remarks that Teufelsdrockh appears in the North Cape. G.B. Tennyson suggests that here Carlyle may be borrowing from stories that the Wandering Jew appeared at the North Pole (208). The text does not explain, however, how Teufelsdrockh reaches the distant North Cape. This absence of explanation reflects Carlyle's purposeful use of a fragmented structure to enhance the symbolism of his main character. If the Editor is piecing together Teufelsdrockh's biography from assorted fragments, then there must be gaps in the manuscript that the full text would have explained. These fragments allow Teufelsdrockh's visit to the North Cape to resemble a mysterious appearance the Wandering Jew might make.

Even at the conclusion of *Sartor Resartus*, when Teufelsdrockh has ended his wanderings, there is still some correlation made between him and the Wandering Jew. The Editor reports to us that Teufelsdrockh has suddenly disappeared from Weissnichtwo; similarly, the Wandering Jew often vanishes without explanation. Before his disappearance, Teufelsdrockh has been heard repeating "Es geht an (It is beginning)" (296). The Editor speculates upon these words as meaning that Teufelsdrockh has gone to Paris to witness the Revolts of 1830, and the birth of a new society, just as the Jew is commonly present at great historical moments.

Teufelsdrockh's Despair

During his wanderings, Teufelsdrockh attempts to reconcile himself with his despair. He gradually passes through stages of despair, negation, disbelief, and indifference before he finally finds meaning in life when he reawakens to his spiritual side and renounces himself. In his self-renunciation, he will return to a belief in the glories of the universe, which will lead him to a greater understanding and appreciation of himself (Waring 53). The process that brings about this greater understanding begins in "The Everlasting No" chapter. Teufelsdrockh is depicted as an extreme version of the Wandering Jew, who unlike the Israelites who wandered for forty years in the wilderness, has "no Pillar of Cloud by day, and no Pillar of Fire by night" (161) to guide him. Nevertheless, amid this chaos, Teufelsdrockh finally asks himself "What art thou afraid of? Wherefore, like a coward, dost thou forever pip and whimper, and go cowering and trembling? Despicable biped! what is the sum-total of the worst that lies before thee? Death?" (16). Once he shakes this fear from him, Teufelsdrockh becomes emotionally stronger: "I shook base Fear away from me forever. I was strong, of unknown strength; a spirit, almost a god. Ever from that time, the temper of my misery was changed: not Fear or whining Sorrow was it, but Indignation and grim fire-eyed Defiance" (167). By renouncing fear, Teufelsdrockh has also renounced concern for himself. This self-renunciation is the first step in his realization that there is more in the universe than just himself; eventually, this moment will lead to his concern for others and how to benefit them. Walter Waring astutely observes that Carlyle depicts Teufelsdrockh's crisis as "the neurotic in-grown personality slowly turning outward, beginning to right itself" (54). Neurotics are generally self-involved, always wanting to be loved, wondering why no one will love them, and then becoming depressed as a result and blaming the world for their troubles when they should instead learn to see their own selfishnesses and take responsibility for their own situations. In asking what right he has to be happy, Teufelsdrockh realizes that his self-concern is trivial in a universe filled with larger, more demanding concerns. When Teufelsdrockh finally overcomes his self-concern, he transcends himself and reaches a state where he can feel "almost a god" (167). In fact, it is only by no longer catering to his childish whims that Teufelsdrockh truly learns to love others and to do what is best for himself. He now realizes that even if he is never happy, he will have a more fulfilling life if he does something worthwhile and productive for the good of the world. Waring remarks that:

> ...annihilation of self or renunciation is necessary to spiritual or material leadership. It is the one thing to which every hero must attain and without which no man can qualify as a true leader. It is prerequisite to sincerity, without which heroism is impossible. (54)

It is when Teufelsdrockh renounces himself that he can come out of his despair and follow the path that leads him to becoming a hero and leader or helper of men.

As Teufelsdrockh enters "The Everlasting Yea," he has transcended his inner fallen Adam by having survived his temptations in the wilderness. "Temptations in the Wilderness... Have we not all to be tried with such? Not so easily can the old Adam, lodged in us by birth, be dispossessed" (183). Teufelsdrockh realizes that because we are all the sons of Adam, we are all tempted to transgress as was our ancestor. To experience temptation is the universal human condition. Teufelsdrockh's personal temptation was to desire happiness, and when that happiness was not achieved, to reject God as indifferent or even non-existent. Once Teufelsdrockh has experienced unhappiness, he has also been tempted to seek knowledge for why man is not happy (Harrold xliv-v). All of these temptations have arisen from selfish desires, but when Teufelsdrockh renounces himself and his desires, he overcomes his temptations. The phrase "Temptations in the Wilderness" equates Teufelsdrockh's experience to Christ's own temptations, which He had to undergo before He could begin His ministry on earth. Similarly, it is only after Teufelsdrockh emerges from temptation that he can become a heroic Christ figure by working for the common good. Teufelsdrockh declares, "Work thou in Welldoing, lies mysteriously written, in Promethean Prophetic Characters, in our hearts; and leaves us no rest, night or day, till it be deciphered and obeyed" (183-4). It is only by renouncing the selfish Adam inside us that we can cease our wanderings. Rest is achieved by the realization that freedom lies in willing acceptance of one's earthly tasks. Teufelsdrockh remarks, "Our Life is compassed round with Necessity; yet is the meaning of Life itself no other than Freedom, than Voluntary Force" (183). The early Gothic wanderers believed that by achieving autonomy from God, they would be free, but they always failed to achieve freedom. Teufelsdrockh's character is a progression beyond his Gothic predecessors because he has learned that freedom lies in acceptance of one's duty.

By rejecting earthly necessities to concentrate on God's mandates, Teufelsdrockh has once again achieved connection with his spiritual origins, which have all along fought against and refused to be controlled by his earthly desires. "Man's Unhappiness, as I construe, comes of his Greatness; it is because there is an Infinite in him, which with all his cunning he cannot quite bury under the Finite" (190). Wordsworth's "Ode: Intimations of Immortality" similarly expresses that there is a divinity in people that they tend to forget during their earthly exiles. This divinity is what makes people dissatisfied with life in a fallen world, and eventually, turns their hopes toward a future heaven. Teufelsdrockh realizes now that even when it is forgotten, the spiritual nature of humanity continues to work within: "So spiritual (geistig) is our whole daily Life: all that we do springs out of Mystery, Spirit, invisible Force; only like a little Cloud-image, or Armida's Palace, air-built, does the Actual body itself forth from the great mystic Deep" (172). Teufelsdrockh now fully recalls his spiritual origin as a child of God. "The Universe is not dead and demoniacal, a charnel-house with spectres; but godlike, and my Father's!" (188). Upon realizing he is a Son of God, Teufelsdrockh is ready, like Christ, to suffer upon earth, await his reunion with his Father in Heaven, and most importantly, to perform his prophetic mission.

The Metamorphosis from Wandering Jew to Everyman

At this point, Carlyle allows Teufelsdrockh to transcend his characterization as the Wandering Jew to become an Everyman much as Fanny Burney transformed her Wandering Jewess into an Everywoman. Rather than merely equating Teufelsdrockh with the Wandering Jew, Carlyle treats the Wandering Jew theme as yet another symbol that must be renewed, and this renewal occurs by Carlyle's exploitation of the Wandering Jew figure to create and define Teufelsdrockh's character (Tennyson 204). Already there is a hint of the Everyman character in

Teufelsdrockh through his connection to Adam. As the father of humanity, Adam's descendants have spread throughout the world; therefore, Teufelsdrockh's connection to Adam allows him to be connected to the entire human race. However, the use of the Wandering Jew theme is Carlyle's primary vehicle to turn Teufelsdrockh into an Everyman. As a Wandering Jew figure, Teufelsdrockh has travelled around the globe, as well as having experienced all time periods from contemporary events, like the Napoleonic wars, to ancient history by visiting ancient cities and ruins. Those places and events he could not experience for himself, he becomes acquainted with by reading about in the great public libraries. Through these historical connections, Teufelsdrockh becomes a type of eternal character, familiar with all history and races. Gerry Brookes states that Carlyle here attempts "to give Teufelsdrockh's voice the authority of universal knowledge" (109). Furthermore, because the Wandering Jew has lived for centuries and can never die, Carlyle has embodied in Teufelsdrockh the universal experiences, knowledge, and history of the entire human race, which transform Teufelsdrockh into an Everyman.

As a Christ-figure and Everyman, Teufelsdrockh can relate to all people, for he knows they experience the same wandering from faith in God and the same questioning of life that he has undergone. Teufelsdrockh's shared experiences with humanity allow him to call all men his brothers, "Poor, wandering, wayward man! Art thou not tired, and beaten with stripes, even as I am?....O my Brother, my Brother, why cannot I shelter thee in my bosom, and wipe away all tears from thy eyes!" (188). When Teufelsdrockh realizes that his work is to comfort the rest of humanity, he has closed his Byron and opened his Goethe (192). He has passed from the stage of idle self-pity that Byron indulged in, to assisting the universe, the primary teaching in Carlyle's Gospel of Work (Sanders 98). Teufelsdrockh remarks that there is an Evil that "arises in every soul, since the beginning of the world; and in every soul, that would pass from idle Suffering into actual Endeavoring, must first be put an end to" (189). Teufelsdrockh has now put an end to his idle suffering by renouncing himself and learning to work for the world's betterment. His lesson is one all Gothic wanderers who selfishly transgress must learn, but which none of Teufelsdrockh's Gothic predecessors, excepting St. Leon, could achieve. Carlyle's depiction of Teufelsdrockh's transition beyond selfishness marks the transformation in the Gothic wanderer figure and its equation with that of all humanity.

That all men must struggle with such selfishness also adds to the depiction of Teufelsdrockh as an Everyman. Carlyle quotes Goethe, by saying, "Man is properly the only object that interests man" (87). Teufelsdrockh, therefore, interests the reader because he is an Everyman, and like Teufelsdrockh, all people embrace "The Everlasting No," "The Center of Indifference," and "The Everlasting Yea." Waring remarks,

"Only the hero can sort out and reject the negative elements of life, overcome indifference, and move steadily to affirmation" (57). If Teufelsdrockh as Everyman is such a hero, then every human has the heroic capacity to achieve the same goals. Simply by going on with life, despite all its tribulations, is a heroic endeavor. Teufelsdrockh's statement that "From Suicide a certain aftershine (Nachschein) of Christianity withheld me" (165) can be broadened to say that the reason people do not end their lives is because they have faith in their spiritual and godlike origins. Waring remarks that Carlyle believed in hero worship because "Hero worship is loyalty to the godlike in man" (50). While all people have the potential to become Gothic wanderers, Carlyle's Teufelsdrockh symbolizes that all people who endure life equally have the capacity to be heroic.

Natural Supernaturalism: Reinventing the Gothic

In discussing humanity's spiritual struggles, Carlyle reinvented the Gothic's use of the supernatural by equating the supernatural with the spiritual. Carlyle begins to make this shift in the famous chapter "Natural Supernaturalism." The much-quoted passage regarding Samuel Johnson may be the best example of how Carlyle converts the supernatural into the spiritual for a Christian perspective of humanity. Dr. Johnson reputedly longed all his life to see a ghost. Carlyle reprimands Dr. Johnson for his blindness:

> Foolish Doctor! Did he never, with the mind's eye as well as with the body's, look round him into that full tide of human Life he so loved; did he never so much as look into Himself? The good Doctor was a Ghost, as actual and authentic as heart could wish; well nigh a million of Ghosts were travelling the streets by his side. Once more I say, sweep away the illusion of Time; compress the three-score years into three minutes: what else was he, what else are we? Are we not Spirits, shaped into a body, into an Appearance; and that fade away again into air, and Invisibility? This is no metaphor, it is a simple scientific fact. (264)

Carlyle builds upon Goethe's statement that, "All men make up mankind" by suggesting we are all ghosts who contribute to make up the spiritual world. Carlyle believes there is unity among humanity because we all possess spirits hidden by our fleshly garments. Unfortunately, our bodies are what blind us from our spiritual unity. Harrold summarizes Carlyle's point by stating that people exist "in union because of similar necessities and obligations; in division because the flesh-garment prevents any man from wholly knowing or sympathetically identifying himself with another" (xlvii). Carlyle believes that if our earthly garments could be removed, humanity would be completely united. Unfortunately, the earthly garment remains and prevents even Dr. Johnson from seeing a person's full spiritual potential.

Carlyle has reinvented the Gothic by defining the supernatural not as something terrifying, but as a manifestation and reconfirmation of Christianity. While critics have argued about the extent of Carlyle's Christian belief, he did frequently use Christian terminology, and if Carlyle was not himself an orthodox Christian, his use of Christian terminology is supportive of the religion. After passing through the Everlasting Yea, Teufelsdrockh feels that God, rather than Hell, is within him. As Carlyle states, "where else is the GOD'S PRESENCE manifested not to our eyes only, but to our hearts, as in our fellow-man?" (66) and later, quoting Novalis, "There is but one Temple in the world...and that Temple is the Body of Man. Nothing is holier than this high Form. Bending before men is a reverence done to this Revelation in the Flesh. We touch Heaven, when we lay our hands on a human body" (239). Carlyle's implication is that God resides within people's supernatural natures. Teufelsdrockh's reawakening to his spiritual side is his transition from Gothic wanderer into Christlike being. His redemption offers hope for all humanity, and it will inspire future depictions of Gothic wanderers as likewise able to achieve redemption and salvation.

Gothic Structure and Narrative Strategy

Now that Teufelsdrockh has achieved the heroic status of a Christ and Everyman figure, he serves as a model of how to succeed in the struggle against temptation and despair; consequently, in instructing others, Teufelsdrockh now takes upon himself the mantle of prophet. Teufelsdrockh, like Christ, has had to pass through his temptation in the wilderness, before his apostolic work could begin (185). The Wandering Jew theme is again used, for Judaism is allied with the Old Testament, while the New Testament is the result of the coming of Christ. For Teufelsdrockh to complete his transformation from a Wandering Jew into a Christ figure, he must create a New Testament (Tennyson 201, 210). Carlyle's belief in the need to recreate symbols is dominant in this section. As the New Testament replaced the Old, so now Carlyle feels a Newer Testament is needed to replace the New Testament that itself has become old. For Christianity to remain a useful religion, it must be renewed for the present generation. Teufelsdrockh says of Christianity, that we need "to embody the divine Spirit of that Religion in a new Mythus, in a new vehicle and vesture, that our Souls, otherwise too like perishing, may live" (194).

Just as Carlyle believed that Christianity needed revision and a new "vesture," so he allows Teufelsdrockh's wandering text to be reclothed by the Editor into the text of *Sartor Resartus* to show how chaos can be formed into meaning. Many critics have argued for and against the possibility that Carlyle intended the style and structure of *Sartor Resartus* to be part of the theme. Some critics have even been brutal enough to argue that the book's disorder is the result of Carlyle's own disordered mind and thought process (Brookes 90). Other critics have argued that the style is simply natural to Carlyle and resembles the way he spoke (Harrold lx). Both suggestions are too derivative and simplistic because they overlook the marvelous complexity the novel contains by applying the process of writing as analogous to the condition of Everyman.

Carlyle's writing style has most accurately been described by V.S. Pritchett as a revolution against the eighteenth century classical prose style, and that nothing was "more calculated to break the smooth classical reign than this Gothic and Gaelic confection" (qtd. in Goldberg 164). By calling Carlyle's prose "Gothic," Pritchett is referring to the fragmented and often convoluted sentence structures, and Pritchett's use of the word "confection" implies the combination of diverse narrative strategies. Besides the unique writing style given to Teufelsdrockh, from which the Editor must make sense, Carlyle deliberately makes Teufelsdrockh's wisdom and stories a collection of fragments. Teufelsdrockh had written a manuscript entitled "Die Kleider, ihr Werden und Wirken (Clothes, their Origin and Influence)" (8). This manuscript was badly damaged and now only exists in fragments. Carlyle creates the character of the Editor, who must "sew" it back together, and who renames the work, *Sartor Resartus*, meaning "The Tailor Retailored." Simply by renaming a literary work, Carlyle is exhibiting his belief in the necessity to renew the past and recreate symbols, just as he has renewed the Gothic Wanderer figure, the use of the supernatural, and is attempting to renew Christianity. The Editor must read and impose order upon six bags of fragments from Teufelsdrockh's original book, an undertaking that mirrors Carlyle's notion of how the mind must read the symbolic universe to find order in it (Brookes 91). The bags of fragments may well be Carlyle's allusion to Mary Shelley's *The Last Man*, for the Editor complains that various anecdotes "often without date of place or time, fly loosely on separate slips, like Sibylline leaves" (78), a passage that recalls how Shelley claims to have found Lionel Verney's story scattered among the leaves in the Sibyl's cave. However, Carlyle's theme is the extreme opposite of Shelley's because Teufelsdrockh's manuscript achieves meaning while Lionel Verney's story only proves a lack of meaning.

Throughout Book I of *Sartor Resartus*, the Editor complains about the chaos of Teufelsdrockh's writing, which allows him often to rail at the style, structure, and ideas of Teufelsdrockh as if there is no order or point to the work. These complaints allow the reader to join the Editor in questioning the work, and they give readers the chance to form their own opinions about the message's worthiness. By presenting the reader with both Teufelsdrockh's views, and the Editor's views of Teufelsdrockh's views, the reader is ultimately given both opinions to judge from, a structure not unlike *Frankenstein*, which presents both Victor and the Monster's narratives, thus allowing the reader to sympathize and understand the situation of both characters. However, Carlyle rejects the possibility of as open an interpretation as *Frankenstein* allows because the Editor's opposing viewpoint is ultimately negated when the Editor is converted to Teufelsdrockh's views. Despite his railings against the circumlocutions, jargon, and repetitions, the Editor continues in his task of bringing order to the work, and by the end of *Sartor Resartus*, he appears sympathetic and perhaps even admiring of Teufelsdrockh, showing that even the Editor has found meaning and order in the book's chaos.

Critics have been unfair in stating that Carlyle allows the book to wander about without purpose. Had Carlyle not purposely wanted the book to appear chaotic, he would have simply written the book as Teufelsdrockh's *Die Kleider ihr Werden und Wirken*. Instead, Carlyle goes through the trouble of writing a fragmented book within a book so Teufelsdrockh's character will be enigmatic. As mentioned above, the fragments add to Teufelsdrockh's caricature as a Wandering Jew by allowing him to appear mysteriously at the North Cape, when this seemingly mysterious appearance would have been understandable had the whole manuscript been intact. More importantly, the fragments add to Teufelsdrockh's role as a Christ figure. The Editor is piecing together the life and sayings of Teufelsdrockh just as the apostles wrote gospels, or biographies, of Christ, leaving huge gaps in his biography. Christ never wrote a book but left the task for his disciples. Similarly, Teufelsdrockh has to depend on the Editor to finish his book for him; the Editor is placed in the role of Teufelsdrockh's apostle who transforms Teufelsdrockh's book into a modern gospel. As the apostles wrote Gospels that brought a renewal of spirituality in the spreading of Christianity, so "the Editor, in his labors of reconstructive editing, carries out in fictional, symbolic terms the necessary work that Carlyle sees as the solution to the historical and social dilemma of his era" (Franklin 39). The Editor, therefore, has created a new Christianity in creating *Sartor Resartus*, the new Gospel of Work.

The Editor also becomes a symbolic Everyman because he has to decipher the book's fragments as Everyman must decipher life's various experiences and try to find some purpose or meaning in them. The Editor, himself a character in *Sartor Resartus*, cannot see the overall plan of the god-like author, Carlyle. Similarly, man cannot see the overall plan of God, the author of the universe. The Editor is the reader's equal for both are trying to piece together the fragments and find some sense of unity among them (Tennyson 227). The Editor instructs the reader to search for meaning among the chaotic text: "Successive glimpses, here faithfully imparted, our more gifted readers must endeavour to combine for their own behoof" (185). Consequently, everyone involved with the novel, whether it be Carlyle, Teufelsdrockh, the Editor, or the reader, becomes involved in its writing process. The Editor and the reader are both trying to create unity and meaning by reading the fragments. Meanwhile, Teufelsdrockh writes the original book, which then must be rewritten, so that it serves only as a type of rough draft for the later version. Teufelsdrockh's own life even serves as a yet cruder rough draft; it is his wanderings and personal confusion that will be turned into the rough draft he himself writes, and which later becomes fragmented.

Finally, the last pages of "The Everlasting Yea" affirm that *Sartor Resartus* is purposely fragmented and disordered to show that the writing process can be a symbol of how meaning may be found in the chaos of life. Teufelsdrockh states that every era of mankind must deal with the question of suffering and solve it in its own way:

> In every new era, too, such Solution comes-out in different terms; and ever the Solution of the last era has become obsolete, and is found unserviceable. For it is man's nature to change his Dialect from century to century; he cannot help it though he would. (189)

The only way that suffering can be dealt with and a new solution be achieved is by creativity and imagination. Harrold discusses how Carlyle always believed in the supremacy of the imagination and moral insight over analytical reasoning; therefore, *Sartor Resartus* is "a brilliant imaginative delineation of the world as an embodiment of mind, as essentially psychical" (lii). Carlyle reaffirms Romanticism by rejecting ideas, like those of Mary Shelley, that imagination distorts reality. Carlyle believes imagination can be used to shape reality and change the future.

When Teufelsdrockh becomes a type of prophet at the end of "The Everlasting Yea" he must spread the message that he has learned, a message that has become known as Carlyle's Gospel of Work. Teufelsdrockh declares that the "God-given mandate" is "Work thou in Welldoing" (183). Man must know what work he can do and then perform that work because it is man's duty and the best way to love God (192).

The work Carlyle, Teufelsdrockh, and the Editor can all do is literary, and the product of their work is *Sartor Resartus*. Walter Read remarks that the process Teufelsdrockh undergoes is not a religious conversion so much as an "imaginative creation, a symbolic action worked out in literary form" (416). Harrold states that *Sartor Resartus* shows the individual's need to find his capabilities and happiness in creative production (lv). Support for *Sartor Resartus* serving as a means for Carlyle to discuss the writing process appears within the text. When Teufelsdrockh remarks on "the folly of that impossible Precept, Know thyself; till it be translated into this partially possible one, Know what thou canst work at" (163), he is saying that man cannot know himself until he knows and does his work. For Carlyle, writing is the process to self-knowledge. Even the Editor acknowledges that order will be achieved from the chaotic book when the whole work is completed, and the entire product is seen: "his mad Pilgrimings, and general solution into aimless Discontinuity, what is all this but a mad Fermentation; wherefrom, the fiercer it is, the clearer product will one day evolve itself?" (158). Modern composition theory discusses writing as a process from which evolves a product. It seems no accident that the Editor chooses to say the disorder will lead to a "product" rather than simply meaning or order, for a literary work is a product. Teufelsdrockh later picks up this vocabulary in the final, powerful paragraph of "The Everlasting Yea." "I too could now say to myself: Be no longer a Chaos, but a World, or even Worldkin. Produce! Produce! Were it but the pitifullest infinitesimal fraction of a Product, produce it, in God's name!" (197). For Carlyle and Teufelsdrockh, what they can produce is literature. Even when he is in the Centre of Indifference, Teufelsdrockh realizes the value of writing. He calls books one of the "Visible and tangible products of the Past" (172), and he remarks that he who can write a book should not envy a "City-builder":

> Thou too art a Conqueror and Victor; but of the true sort, namely over the Devil: thou too hast built what will outlast all marble and metal, and be a wonder-bringing City of the Mind, a Temple and Seminary and Prophetic Mount, whereto all kindreds of the Earth will pilgrim. (173)

Therefore, the best way to renew the symbols of the past and resolve the problem of suffering is to write about it. In that way, others who have similar experiences can read of past sufferings and be strengthened by knowing that such sufferings can be overcome. In his journal, Carlyle would write, "Every man that writes is writing a new Bible; or a new Apocrypha; to last for a week, or for a thousand years: he that convinces a man and sets him working is the doer of a miracle" (Tennyson 291). While *Sartor Resartus* preaches that man's way to deal with suffering should be to work, for Teufelsdrockh, the work he needs to do is to spread the message that man must work, and the Editor conveys this message by editing Teufelsdrockh's writings. Work provides a goal and future hope. Later Gothic wanderers, modeled after Teufelsdrockh, would equally turn from self-concern to self-sacrifice, working to better humanity.

Sartor Resartus brings order out of chaos by depicting the life experience of Everyman, embodied in the story of Teufelsdrockh. Carlyle saw his own age as wandering about in a loss of faith, so he felt it necessary to bring new faith to the modern age by creating in Teufelsdrockh's story a "symbolic myth" to guide himself and his own society. By depicting the transformation of Teufelsdrockh from a Gothic Wanderer into a Christ-figure, Carlyle makes Everyman a Son of God who only has to wander the earth until he joins his Heavenly Father. While Carlyle supports the conservative Gothic tradition that transgression is wrong, he also shows God's mercy because by Teufelsdrockh's transgression, just as with that of Adam and Eve, ultimately Christ may enter the world and a person's life. In *Sartor Resartus*, Carlyle created a new pattern for faith, which would become the classic Victorian pattern of doubt, denial, and affirmation (Tennyson 291-2). Carlyle reinvented the Gothic wanderer figure, and his Victorian successors would follow his example by focusing upon how the Gothic wanderer could become a symbol of redemption rather than transgression.

Chapter IX – The Gothic Wanderer Redeemed: Edward Bulwer-Lytton's *Zanoni* and Charles Dickens' *A Tale of Two Cities*

Thomas Carlyle's *Sartor Resartus* had such a widespread influence upon its contemporary readers that hardly any writer in the first decades of the Victorian period could claim not to hold a debt to Carlyle. George Eliot remarked in 1855 that "there has hardly been an English book written for the last ten or twelve years that would not have been different if Carlyle had not lived" (Oddie 14). In agreement, Harriet Martineau stated that Carlyle:

> ...infused into the mind of the English nation a sincerity, earnestness, healthfulness, and courage which can be appreciated only by those who are old enough to tell what was our morbid state when Byron was the representative of our temper, the Clapham Church of religion, and the rotten-borough system of our political morality. (Oddie 16)

Carlyle's influence created many literary disciples, including Edward Bulwer-Lytton and Charles Dickens. Like Carlyle, Bulwer-Lytton and Dickens transformed the Gothic wanderer from a figure of transgression into one of Christian redemption while adding their own original characteristics.

Both Bulwer-Lytton and Dickens wrote enormous bodies of work and they deserve separate chapters if not complete books devoted to their largely ignored but innovative applications of the Gothic tradition. Because my focus, however, is to trace the development of the Gothic wanderer throughout the nineteenth century, I will limit my discussion to one work by each novelist. Bulwer-Lytton's *Zanoni* (1842) and Dickens' *A Tale of Two Cities* (1859) are comparable works for discussion because both reflect Carlyle's influence, while also drawing upon earlier Gothic novels, especially Charles Maturin's *Melmoth the Wanderer*. To a great extent, *A Tale of Two Cities* is a revision of *Zanoni*, while *Zanoni* is a revision of Maturin's novel. While critics have commented upon the similar endings in Bulwer-Lytton and Dickens' novels, critics have ignored how Dickens pervasively uses Rosicrucian coloring throughout *A Tale of Two Cities*, for which he was also indebted to Bulwer-Lytton's novel. Both

Bulwer-Lytton and Dickens' novels create Rosicrucian heroes who are not symbols of transgression, but examples of how anyone can achieve redemption and salvation.

Zanoni and *A Tale of Two Cities* are also comparable because they are both set in France during the French Revolution. While the Gothic novels of the Romantic period were understood by their audiences to be commentary upon the French Revolution, that Revolution was never directly depicted in the novels—even Burney's *The Wanderer* is set in England and does not depict the Revolution's events directly. Bulwer-Lytton and Dickens, writing their novels respectively fifty-three and seventy years after the fall of the Bastille, could set their novels in France during the Revolution because they were far enough distanced by time not to recall personally the Revolution's terrors or to fear its immediate repercussions upon England. Both novelists' interest in the French Revolution primarily resulted from their admiration for Carlyle's *French Revolution: A History* (1837), which would become an important source for both *Zanoni* and *A Tale of Two Cities*. These novels equally owe a debt to *Sartor Resartus* in their treatment of the Gothic wanderer as redeemable. Ultimately, however, both novels are original works within the Gothic tradition.

Zanoni: Redemption of the Rosicrucian

Edward Bulwer-Lytton's *Zanoni* (1842) is the last significant treatment of the Rosicrucian figure in the Gothic wanderer tradition. *Zanoni* is original to the tradition because it rejects earlier depictions of the Rosicrucian as a transgressor against God who seeks autonomy in the form of earthly immortality. The novel vindicates Rosicrucianism by presenting it as beneficial to those who are trained to be wise in the use of its secrets. While Bulwer-Lytton knew earlier Rosicrucian novels including Godwin's *St. Leon* and Maturin's *Melmoth the Wanderer*, *Zanoni* radically differs from these works in theme and content. Robert Lee Wolff remarks that *Zanoni* is only similar to *Melmoth the Wanderer* because Zanoni and Viola, like Melmoth and Immalee, live for a short while on an uninhabited island (226). I believe, however, that *Melmoth the Wanderer*'s conclusion inspired the final scene of *Zanoni*, although Bulwer-Lytton dramatically altered the meaning of the scene. *Zanoni*'s ending is an affirmation of Christianity because Bulwer-Lytton wished to depict Rosicrucianism in a positive light. As a member of a revived Rosicrucian society, Bulwer-Lytton rejected the Gothic depictions of Rosicrucians as opponents to Christianity; he wrote *Zanoni* to express the true tenets of Rosicrucianism that were in agreement with Christianity as reflected in the society's symbolic name meaning the Rosy Cross. *Zanoni*, therefore, has a Christian theme that affirms God's power over humanity, and the novel's immortal characters are true Christians in their practice and belief, despite their contact with the supernatural and their life-extensions. As the immortal character Mejnour states regarding Christianity, "Knowledge and atheism are incompatible. To know nature is to know that there must be a God!" (255).

Zanoni also differs from earlier Rosicrucian novels because it is not a tale about the quest for the elixir of life. Upon the novel's opening, the title character is already an immortal who possesses great knowledge, and who belongs to a mystical society that is even older than the Rosicrucians. Zanoni's role in the novel is to open the eyes of the other characters to hidden knowledge. Bulwer-Lytton's philosophical theory behind the novel is that the air is peopled with invisible intelligences, whose deeds influence human actions; some of these intelligences are hostile while others are benevolent to humanity. In addition, Bulwer-Lytton believes, more scientifically than supernaturally, that there are certain plants that are able to prevent the natural decay of the body, thus allowing for earthly immortality, or at least, prolonged lifespans (Birkhead 80). Bulwer-Lytton's theories on the increased lifespan of humanity recall those of William Godwin, who also believed that the human lifespan would gradually increase by natural processes. The character Mejnour explains that the purpose of his mystical sect is to use its knowledge about Nature to create a dominant race who will be the true lords of the earth:

> ...a race that may proceed, in their deathless destinies, from stage to stage of celestial glory, and rank at last amongst the nearest ministrants and agents gathered round the Throne of Thrones? What matter a thousand victims for one convert to our band? (176).

Mejnour's statement is somewhat elitist, for he is determined that only the most deserving will be part of this race, but similarly, Christianity only allows for the most deserving to enter Heaven. By creating immortal characters who are satisfied with their state and who seek to bring about a superior order of human beings, Bulwer-Lytton is refusing to degrade Rosicrucianism for the purpose of creating selfish characters whose sole purpose is to manipulate a fabulous plot. Compared to Godwin's selfish St. Leon, who discovers that immortality is a curse, Zanoni and Mejnour are types of Supermen who embody the virtues to which all people should aspire (Lytton, *Bulwer* 82). Bulwer-Lytton rejects completely the earlier Rosicrucian novel plot and instead creates a tale inspired by his own interests and knowledge of Rosicrucianism and its metaphysical mysteries.

Besides its innovative use of the Rosicrucian theme, *Zanoni* reflects a large influence by Carlyle. Prior to *Zanoni*'s publication, Carlyle felt that Bulwer-Lytton was a "poor fribble" of a writer (Campbell 117), but he had great praise for *Zanoni*:

> I confidently gather that it will be a liberating voice for much that lay dumb imprisoned in many souls; that it will shake old deep-set errors loose in their rootings, and through

such chinks as are possible let in light on dark places very greatly in need of light! (Lytton, *Bulwer* 84-5)

Carlyle's praise attests to *Zanoni*'s agreement with his own theories regarding the human need to transcend and liberate ourselves from old traditions and to seek out new systems. Like *Sartor Resartus*, Bulwer-Lytton's novel promotes a Christian theme of love while emphasizing the soul's need to be renewed and released from the chains that imprison it. Once released, people can strive for humanity's betterment, as Zanoni does throughout the novel, most dramatically by sacrificing his life.

Carlyle and *Sartor Resartus'* influence upon *Zanoni* is also apparent in the novel's structure. Christensen states that both works are anti-novels because they often work against the typical novel form (109). *Sartor Resartus'* restructured yet fragmented narrative makes it difficult for the reader to abstract its definite meaning. *Zanoni* is equally difficult to classify because it purposely plays with the barriers between fiction and reality. In the novel's opening section, Bulwer-Lytton describes his meeting with one of the novel's characters, Glyndon, who has acquired philosophical secrets so that he has scarcely aged, despite the passing of fifty years since the novel's primary action. By his personal meeting with Glyndon, Bulwer-Lytton has placed himself within his own fictional world, thereby making the lines between reality and fiction become ambiguous and the impossible appear to be reality.

Like *Sartor Resartus*, *Zanoni* is also a novel that needs an editor. Bulwer-Lytton receives a manuscript from Glyndon, who is dying and wants his writing to be preserved for posterity. The manuscript is Glyndon's history of Zanoni and Glyndon's involvement with him. Rather than being a fragmented manuscript, as in *Sartor Resartus*, the manuscript is written in a hieroglyphic cipher and is accompanied by a dictionary to the hieroglyphics. Bulwer-Lytton claims that he only translated a small portion of the manuscript which he published as *Zicci* (1838). The public's interest in *Zicci* encouraged him to toil further so the entire manuscript was translated and could appear as *Zanoni* (xiv-xv, Campbell 115). While Bulwer-Lytton does not have to assemble fragments like the Editor in *Sartor Resartus*, nevertheless, he realizes he not only has to translate but also to edit the manuscript so it will be acceptable to the public. Consequently, he states that "if, reader, in this book there be anything that pleases you, it is certainly mine; but whenever you come to something you dislike,—lay the blame upon the old gentleman!" (xx). *Zanoni* and *Sartor Resartus*, according to Christensen, both use the metaphor of translation for what is really the novelist's "natural-supernatural creation" (108). This textual literary game, by which the text continually reflects upon the method of composition, is intended to emphasize the magical power of creation that is overlooked in the everyday world. By this theory, Bulwer-Lytton demonstrates that life is a text perpetually being created by humanity. Consequently, people can use their imaginations to determine how their individual lives or texts can lead to a comprehension of their own divine missions (Christensen 108-9). Like *Sartor Resartus*, therefore, *Zanoni* is a novel written to bring about a spiritual revival among its readers.

Zanoni's interest in spirituality makes it both a Rosicrucian and a Christian novel. At the novel's opening, the immortal Glyndon tells Bulwer-Lytton that the Rosicrucians are true Christians: "no monastic order is more severe in the practice of moral precepts, or more ardent in Christian faith" (xiv). Glyndon himself has matured beyond the foolish character depicted in the main story of the novel because he has spent the past fifty years, not seeking occult knowledge, but living as a devout Christian (Campbell 115). Glyndon began as a typical Gothic wanderer who desired forbidden knowledge, but he eventually learned that man's true mission upon earth is to work for the benefit of others, a mission resembling that of Carlyle's Teufelsdrockh. This Christian perspective makes *Zanoni* deviate from a typical Gothic plot to emphasize that the Rosicrucian novel need not be simply a fantastic adventure story, but it can become a medium for studying metaphysical questions. Campbell argues that *Zanoni* should not even be considered a "Rosicrucian romance" but rather a parable based upon occult concepts of the Chaldeans and Platonists (Campbell 116). In fact, the novel does not even contain a Rosicrucian character. The two immortal characters, Zanoni and Mejnour, are members of a much older cult from which the Rosicrucians are a later branch. The characters' only connection to Rosicrucianism is that Zanoni and Mejnour are willing to make Glyndon their pupil because one of his ancestors had been a Rosicrucian (Wolff 185, 207).

Glyndon is the only character in the novel who can be described as a true Gothic wanderer. While Zanoni and Mejnour are immortals, they are not transgressors and do not consider their immortality to be a form of suffering. Instead, they view extended life as a blessing that gives them time to use their knowledge for humanity's benefit as declared in the original Rosicrucian manifestoes. Zanoni and Mejnour make Glyndon their pupil, believing because he has a Rosicrucian ancestor, he has qualities that will benefit their sect. Mejnour takes Glyndon to his castle and begins to teach him the elementary knowledge of his mysterious order. Glyndon, however, hungers for the greater knowledge he has not yet advanced enough to receive. This desire for forbidden knowledge leads Glyndon to a transgression that makes him a typical Gothic wanderer figure.

Mejnour had earlier warned Glyndon that certain types of knowledge are fruitless to seek: "Not in the knowledge of things without, but in the perfections of the soul within, lies the empire of man aspiring to be more than men" (192). Mejnour further informs Glyndon: "thy first task must be to withdraw all thought, feeling, sympathy from others. The elementary stage of knowledge is to make self, and self alone, thy study and thy world" (195). Mejnour trains Glyndon with the intent that Glyndon will discover his true nature and learn self-control rather than selfishness so he will be prepared to use wisely the more advanced knowledge he will eventually receive. Despite these warnings, Glyndon succumbs to his curiosity and seeks out the knowledge he is temporarily forbidden. When Mejnour goes on a journey, Glyndon is free to give into temptation by drinking the elixir of life. Mejnour had warned Glyndon that he must slowly build up a tolerance to the elixir by first splashing it on his face and smelling it. Glyndon, however, greedily imbibes the mysterious liquid, then instantly sees apparitions he longs to join, but they float away from him. He is next confronted by the apparition of a reptilian creature in what is the most Gothic scene in the novel. Glyndon is so frightened by this creature that "All fancies, the most grotesque, of Monk or Painter in the early North, would have failed to give to the visage of imp or fiend that aspect of deadly malignity which spoke to the shuddering nature in those eyes alone" (243). The creature's eyes have a "burning glare so intense, so livid, yet so living, had in it something that was almost human in its passion of hate and mockery" (243). When the creature speaks, it causes Glyndon's hair to stand erect while "his soul rather than his ear comprehended the words it said" (243). The creature states:

> "Thou hast entered the immeasurable region. I am the Dweller of the Threshold. What wouldst thou with me? Silent? Dost thou fear me? Am I not thy beloved? Is it not for me that thou hast rendered up the delights of thy race? Wouldst thou be wise? Mine is the wisdom of the countless ages. Kiss me, my mortal lover." And the Horror crawled near and nearer to him; it crept to his side, its breath breathed upon his cheek! With a sharp cry he fell to the earth insensible, and knew no more. (243)

Glyndon wakes to find himself in bed. Then in a letter from Mejnour, Glyndon is informed that because he succumbed to temptation, he is dismissed from further training. Mejnour also warns Glyndon that because he drank the elixir, he will have to battle continually with the demon, although the powers of the elixir may allow him to shine in the world of men. Glyndon's situation parallels that of Adam and Eve, for having tasted forbidden knowledge, he is thrust from a type of Eden where he could have become one with the immortals. The possibility that he may shine, however, suggests a hope for the future similar to God's promise to Adam and Eve that humanity would eventually be redeemed.

Before leaving the castle, Glyndon again encounters the Being, described as the "presence of the Nameless" (272). This time, Glyndon tries to overcome his fear:

With a violent effort that convulsed his whole being, and bathed his body in the sweat of agony, the young man mastered his horror. He strode towards the Phantom; he endured its eyes; he accosted it with a steady voice; he demanded its purpose and defied its power.

And then, as a wind from a channel, was heard its voice. What it said, what revealed, it is forbidden the lips to repeat, the hand to record. Nothing save the subtle life that yet animated the frame, to which the inhalations of the elixir had given vigour and energy beyond the strength of the strongest, could have survived that awful hour. Better to wake in the catacombs and see the buried rise from their cerements, and hear the ghouls, in their horrid orgies, amongst the festering ghastliness of corruption, than to front those features when the veil was lifted, and listen to that whispered voice! (272)

Despite his bravery in facing the creature, Glyndon now flees from Mejnour's castle. Nevertheless, he cannot erase from his memory either the demon or its words; by drinking the elixir, Glyndon has allowed the demon to enter inside him, just as Milton's Satan feels Hell burn within him because of his transgression.

Glyndon continues to have demonic visions throughout the remainder of the novel, but eventually, he comes to terms with them. Toward the novel's end, Zanoni explains to Glyndon that wherever men labor and aspire "everywhere cowers and darkens the Unutterable Horror. But there where thou hast ventured, alone is the phantom visible; and never will it cease to haunt, till thou canst pass to the Infinite, as the seraph, or return to the Familiar, as a child!" (376). This passage reflects Bulwer-Lytton's drawing upon the Romantic myth of consciousness: Glyndon's transgression places him in the stage of experience; unable to return to the innocence of childhood, Glyndon must learn how to achieve the "philosophic mind" that brings wise innocence. Glyndon tells Zanoni that he tries to resist the Specter by clinging to Virtue, which has made the Specter become faint. Zanoni replies that Resolve is the beginning of success in overcoming the terror and mystery of the Specter, so Glyndon can rejoice because eventually his exorcism will be complete (377). Bulwer-Lytton's use of the Specter, or Dweller of the Threshold, is a rejection of Gothic manifestations of the supernatural to show that humanity's true horrors are psychological and it is our inner selves with which we must wrestle. At the beginning of Glyndon's training, Mejnour had warned Glyndon that he must learn to overcome his true nature, and now Glyndon has succeeded by seeking virtue over his natural selfishness and the other inner demons that controlled him. Glyndon has achieved redemption as a Gothic wanderer.

While Glyndon is a more traditional Gothic wanderer because of his transgression and redemption, Zanoni is the most original wanderer figure in the novel and the one who learns the greatest lesson. Zanoni is never completely definable as a Gothic wanderer because, despite his immortality, he is neither a transgressor nor the victim of transgression. Zanoni is already immortal at the novel's beginning when he falls in love with the singer Viola. Zanoni and Viola marry and find happiness together by living solitary lives on an island, thus recreating an Eden where innocence can exist. Wolff notes that Zanoni and Viola's life on an island is similar to how Melmoth finds Immalee on an island (226). Bulwer-Lytton intentionally borrowed from *Melmoth the Wanderer* in creating Zanoni and Viola's relationship, but he also radically changes the relationship. Melmoth selfishly sought a partner to ease the burden of his cursed, prolonged existence. His selfishness resulted in his marriage to Immalee, followed by Immalee's imprisonment for allegedly engaging in occult behavior by marrying Melmoth. Consequently, both Immalee and her child die in the prisons of the Spanish Inquisition. Bulwer-Lytton adapts this love story by making Zanoni immortal, but not cursed like Melmoth. Zanoni seeks Viola as his partner out of love and a desire to confer immortality upon her so their bond can never be broken by her death. To obtain immortality for Viola and their child, Zanoni must go to the supernatural being, the Dweller of the Threshold, also known as Adon-ai. Because Adon-ai is the Hebrew word for God, we can assume Zanoni is a Christian and disciple of God. The Dweller of the Threshold agrees to Zanoni's request, but he also demands a price in return, not yet stating what that price will be (298).

Zanoni and his family now move to Paris where they witness the events of the French Revolution. During the Reign of Terror, Zanoni finds himself deeply interested in the people who die at the guillotine. In a letter to Mejnour, he theorizes that death can be good because he sees many people die at the guillotine to save a loved one. The novel's Christian theme is clearly expressed in Zanoni's description of these people's courage.

> Because such hearts live in some more abstract and holier life than their own. But to live forever upon this earth is to live in nothing diviner than ourselves. Yes, even amidst this gory butcherdom, God, the Everlasting, vindicates to man the sanctity of His servant, Death! (341-2)

Even Death can be benevolent because it brings people to God. Zanoni's reflections upon death foreshadow the novel's stunning climax.

Nicot, an enemy of Glyndon and Zanoni, now betrays them to Robespierre. Zanoni escapes arrest, but Glyndon, Viola, and her child are cast into prison (366). Zanoni manages to help Glyndon escape, but he is unable to rescue Viola, who is sentenced to death at the guillotine. Desperate to save his wife and child, Zanoni once again seeks help from the Dweller of the Threshold. The Dweller informs Zanoni that Viola and the child can be rescued if Zanoni takes their place because it is written that a sacrifice can always save. Whether the Dweller himself demands this sacrifice is unclear, but he also comforts Zanoni by telling him not to worry about Viola and the child after his death. The Dweller says Zanoni could not care for them any better than God now will:

> ...what, with all thy wisdom and thy starry secrets, with all thy empire of the past, and thy visions of the future,—what art thou to the All-Directing and Omniscient? Canst thou yet imagine that thy presence on earth can give to the hearts thou lovest the shelter which the humblest take from the wings of the Presence that lives in Heaven? Fear not thou for their future. Whether thou live or die, their future is the care of the Most High! In the dungeon and on the scaffold looks everlasting the Eye of HIM, tenderer than thou to love, wiser than thou to guide, mightier than thou to save! (393)

In the end, Zanoni's supernatural immortality is both powerless and ultimately meaningless when compared to his sacrifice of love that results in eternal life in Heaven. Zanoni now turns himself in to the French government and dies at the guillotine in place of Viola and their child. While Zanoni's sacrifice is admirable, the reader is left unsatisfied when Viola then dies of grief while yet in prison. Consequently, Zanoni has failed to save his wife, although Viola's death expresses the power of her love for him. Her death allows her to share in Zanoni's heavenly life as she had previously shared in his earthly immortality.

Despite Zanoni and Viola's deaths, the novel ends upon a note of hope, for the child left behind in prison is pitied by a woman who decides to care for him. The novel concludes with a priest remarking to the woman, "THE FATHERLESS ARE THE CARE OF GOD!" (419). *Zanoni*'s conclusion, therefore, has effectively revised the ending of *Melmoth the Wanderer* where Melmoth's selfishness results in the death of his wife and child. While Viola still dies, Zanoni is selfless, and their child remains alive as a symbol of hope. The orphaned child will have God as its father, thus suggesting it has a spiritual purpose in the future, much as Carlyle's orphaned Teufelsdrockh is depicted as the child of God.

The lessons of sacrifice and self-control that Zanoni and Glyndon respectively learn emphasize the novel's theme that people who receive special gifts must be responsible by using those gifts for the betterment of humanity (Punter, *Terror* 172). This assertion recalls Carlyle's belief in *Sartor Resartus* that people must work to better the world if they are to find personal fulfillment. Furthermore, while Bulwer-Lytton vindicates Rosicrucianism, he conservatively agrees with his Gothic predecessors that earthly immortality is undesirable in comparison to immortality in Heaven. Marie Roberts suggests that Zanoni's death liberates him into true immortality and he ascends to Heaven in a Dantean vision of the apocalypse (*Gothic* 181). Zanoni's death is also symbolic as a political and religious statement against political visionaries like the atheistic Robespierre, whose downfall occurs the day after Zanoni's death (Campbell 114; Roberts, *Gothic* 179). Consequently, Zanoni serves as the Christ-like sacrifice that frees France from its terror, as Christ freed humanity from its sins.

While Zanoni's death is his Carlylean work to better humanity, Glyndon's work more closely resembles that of Teufelsdrockh and *Sartor Resartus*' Editor. Like Carlyle's characters, Glyndon engages in literary work by writing the text of *Zanoni* to spread a Christian message to humanity. Prior to his meeting with Zanoni and Mejnour, Glyndon had aspired to being an artist; now he fulfills that aspiration by writing. Glyndon represents Bulwer-Lytton's statement that the purpose he sought to illustrate in *Zanoni* was: "the artist must not work in isolation but in society" (Campbell 112). Glyndon is now a better artist because his experiences have reformed him, thus preparing him to reform society by his art, with the understanding that art is only ideal when synonymous with religious faith (Campbell 115). Consequently, in writing Zanoni's story, Glyndon becomes the Christ-like Zanoni's disciple who writes a gospel.

Zanoni was largely condemned by the critics as being unreadable, but Bulwer-Lytton always felt it was his best novel. Harriet Martineau was so impressed with the novel that she told Bulwer-Lytton that if only one person read *Zanoni* for every one hundred who had read *St. Leon*, nevertheless, he must feel rewarded simply for having spent so many hours working out such a sacred philosophy (Lytton, *Life* 35). Martineau's enthusiasm for the novel extended to her writing a key to the philosophical meanings of the novel, which Bulwer-Lytton, greatly pleased, printed in subsequent editions of *Zanoni*. Martineau and Carlyle, however, seem to be the only recorded enthusiastic readers of the novel. One reader felt *Zanoni* was so ridiculous that he wrote a spoof entitled *The Dweller of the Threshhold* by Sir Ed-d L-tt-n B-lw-r. Today the novel is forgotten by all but literary historians because of the decline in Bulwer-Lytton's reputation. Nevertheless, the novel deserves a rediscovery and acknowledgment as a major work in the Gothic tradition. Furthermore, the novel attests to the widespread influence of Carlyle, and Bulwer-Lytton's own influence upon his contemporaries, most notably, Charles Dickens.

Dickens' Carlylean Gothic

Despite Charles Dickens' constant use of Gothic elements, his place in the Gothic tradition has not been adequately explored by critics. Dickens was a master novelist within the Gothic tradition, innovatively building upon Carlyle's natural supernaturalism to create grotesquely Gothic characters whose bodily disfigurements reflect the state of their souls.

While Dickens' use of the Gothic deserves a full-length study, a brief overview of his position in the Gothic tradition will display how he helped to transform the Gothic genre. My concentration upon *A Tale of Two Cities* will demonstrate Dickens' literary debts to his Gothic predecessors and his unique revisions of the Gothic genre to create a novel that is life-affirming and provides redemption for its Gothic wanderer characters. Early in his career, Dickens considered himself as writing within the Gothic tradition. In *The Old Curiosity Shop* (1841), Dickens' intention was to create a short Gothic story. Dickens recalled his original plan:

> ...it [had been] always in my fancy to surround the lonely figure of the child with grotesque and wild, but not impossible companions, and to gather about her innocent face and pure intentions, associates as strange and uncongenial as the grim objects that are about her bed when her history is first foreshadowed. (Coolidge 114)

While Dickens does not use the word "Gothic" here, he does use the word "grotesque," and throughout his works, the Gothic and the grotesque have the same definition, specifically in character descriptions. Claire Kahane has remarked that the "modern" Gothic "by its transformation of the unseen to the seen, moves the Gothic toward the grotesque" (351). Kahane uses the word "modern" to refer to twentieth century writers like Flannery O'Connor and Carson McCullers, but Dickens can be credited over a century earlier with equally moving the Gothic toward the grotesque.

Dickens' use of the grotesque to create Gothic situations was inspired by Carlyle's Natural Supernaturalism which expressed that the human soul is hidden by the body but if our souls were visible, we would all be recognized as ghosts and beings of the supernatural. Dickens adapted Natural Supernaturalism, blending it with allegory, to show that the state of one's inner soul is reflected by the state of one's visible, outer body. Consequently, Dickens' most Gothic characters are also the most physically grotesque because their souls lack spiritual nourishment and have practically died within them. Dickens uses these grotesque characters to criticize the society that makes them grotesque. While some individuals naturally tend toward evil, Dickens also realizes that society and its injustices contribute to the deformity of people's souls and by extension, their bodies. Dickens purposely depicts a selfish, money-grubbing character like Quilp in *The Old Curiosity Shop* as a dwarf to symbolize how Quilp's selfishness has stunted the growth of his moral character, reflecting Dickens' disapproval of an increasingly capitalist society that valued money over the well-being of the human spirit. In *Bleak House* (1853), Richard Clare becomes pale and drained because the Court of Chancery and its vampiric lawyers have sucked his life and energy from him by entwining him in a decades' long lawsuit. Also in *Bleak House*,

Tulkinghorn, the blackmailer of Lady Dedlock, is depicted as grotesquely devilish. Dickens creates numerous hints of Tulkinghorn's satanic nature. Tulkinghorn's name may be interpreted to mean "Old Horny" referring to the devil's horns. Tulkinghorn always wears black and his clothes "never shine" but are "irresponsive to any glancing light" (10), which recalls Milton's Satan whose "lustre" is "visibly impair'd" (IV, 850) and who has lost his former "transcendent brightness" (I, 86) only to have a "faded splendor wan" (IV, 870). In addition, Tulkinghorn's apartment resembles Hell because it is an "oven made by the hot pavements and hot buildings" (542-3) (Georgas 25). Such examples demonstrate that the grotesqueness of Dickens' characters reflects the state of their spiritual natures; such grotesque characters' allegorical implications attest to Dickens' Christian agenda in writing his novels.

Dickens' use of Carlyle's Natural Supernaturalism made him Carlyle's greatest literary disciple, as acknowledged by his contemporaries. In 1841, after reading *The Old Curiosity Shop*, Caroline Fox remarked of Dickens, "That man is carrying out Carlyle's work more emphatically than any other" (Oddie 1). Dickens himself told his son, Henry Dickens, that "the man who had influenced him most was Thomas Carlyle" (Oddie 3). Dickens and Carlyle first met in 1839, but it would not be until writing *The Chimes* in 1844 that Dickens would first feel he was working within a Carlylean tradition. Nevertheless, Dickens may have been unconsciously influenced by Carlyle in his earlier works, such as in *Oliver Twist* where clothing references suggest a debt to *Sartor Resartus* (Oddie 4). Carlyle was seldom a fan of Dickens' novels, but he greatly approved of *A Tale of Two Cities*, pleased with its expression of his own belief system. Carlyle also assisted Dickens with the novel by loaning him numerous works about the French Revolution. Carlyle's own history of the French Revolution, along with Bulwer-Lytton's *Zanoni*, became major sources of inspiration for *A Tale of Two Cities*.

Despite Carlyle's influence upon Dickens, there are notable differences between the philosophies of the two men as expressed in their writings. Carlyle's belief in the importance of heroes made it difficult for him to admire Dickens' lower-class characters as sympathetic or inspiring examples of the human spirit (Goldberg 16). William Oddie argues that Carlyle believed in a God of Vengeance, whereas Dickens believed in a God of Mercy. While Carlyle would try to show how men like Teufelsdrockh can be heroes by refusing to abandon themselves to despair, Dickens realized that many people face severe disadvantages that prohibit them from exerting such heroic strength. Dickens' compassion for such people was the result of his own impoverished childhood which taught him to sympathize with the lower classes, the oppressed, and the outcasts of society (29). While Dickens believed in affirming life and the strength of the human soul, he was also aware of the many social injustices that prevented people from cultivating their spirituality. Consequently,

Dickens' grotesque characters are not always Gothic in the sense that they are guilty of transgressions. Dickens realized that people become so focused upon the daily need to support themselves that they often neglect their spirituality, and eventually this neglect can result in a one-sided, fanatical interest in acquiring material possessions. While Dickens tends to become overly sentimental in depicting the plight of the poor in his novels, his use of the Gothic is revolutionary in such cases because it is sympathetic. Whereas Gothic horrors had been created by earlier novelists to cause terror for victimized characters, or to serve as a means of punishment for transgressions committed, Dickens used the Gothic to reflect the everyday horrors of the modern world and to sympathize with people who suffered from these modern day horrors. Dickens' Gothic worlds often become places of extreme nightmares from which good people can escape by their virtue, courage, and endurance. *A Tale of Two Cities* serves as a perfect example of how Dickens depicts the modern world as a place of terror where people can become Gothic wanderers, but where also the human spirit can rise above earthly concerns to achieve redemption and salvation.

A Tale of Two Cities: Rosicrucian Immortality and Christian Redemption

In *A Tale of Two Cities* (1859), Charles Dickens attempts to recapture the time of the French Revolution by transforming it into a scene of Gothic terror. While the Gothic novels of the 1790s were metaphors for the French Revolution, Dickens directly treats the French Revolution as a time of horror. Throughout the novel, Dickens draws upon the wanderer theme, returning to earlier depictions of the Gothic wanderer, particularly the Rosicrucian, but he adapts the Gothic tradition for the Victorian period. Critics have acknowledged *A Tale of Two Cities'* debt to *Zanoni*, but concentration has been solely upon the similar sacrifices of Zanoni and Sidney Carton. Critics have overlooked Dickens' borrowing of the Rosicrucian theme from *Zanoni* to create in Sidney Carton a type of Gothic wanderer and immortal who reverses the curse of damnation, exchanging it for eternal life in Heaven. Dickens, therefore, removes emphasis upon the Gothic wanderer as a transgressor to one capable of redemption.

Dickens' choice to write about the French Revolution was primarily the result of his fascination with Carlyle's *French Revolution* (1837), a work Dickens enthusiastically carried with him wherever he went (Lindsay 359). Dickens realized the French Revolution was an ideal historical background for tales of adventure and romance. Rather than writing a political novel, Dickens largely accepts Carlyle's philosophy of the French Revolution as resulting from upper class oppression and instead concentrates on his Christian theme (Oddie 63). William Oddie's thorough study of the influence Carlyle's *French Revolution* had upon *A Tale of Two Cities* attests to Dickens' lack of interest in the politics of the period, save to create dramatic effect. Oddie states:

> Dickens omits any reference to the political background of the events he describes: he is not interested in the historical assessments that can be seen as part of the fibre even of Carlyle's most fevered descriptions. Dickens is interested in sustaining the tension of his narrative. (71)

Consequently, *A Tale of Two Cities* is less a novel about the French Revolution than the tale of a group of English characters whose love and lives are threatened by the Revolution, thus making the Revolution itself subservient as part of the plot mechanics. The Revolution becomes the vehicle that motivates the characters' actions to bring about Carton's sacrifice and Christian redemption and to manifest the familiar Gothic emphasis upon the family's preservation.

Dickens' use of the Revolution is to provide a background in which he can work out his plot of sacrifice. While the Revolution is far enough in the past that few of his readers would remember it, Dickens reminds his readers that human nature, its desires and fears, remain the same, so the past and the present have many similarities. Readers, therefore, will find something relevant to their own lives in his historical tale. Dickens breaks down the gap between the past and present by creating an opening that reflects his story's timelessness.

> It was the best of times, it was the worst of times, it was the age of wisdom, it was the age of foolishness, it was the epoch of belief, it was the epoch of incredulity, it was the season of Light, it was the season of Darkness, it was the spring of hope, it was the winter of despair, we had everything before us, we had nothing before us, we were all going direct to Heaven, we were all going direct the other way—in short, the period was so far like the present period, that some of its noisiest authorities insisted on its being received, for good or for evil, in the superlative degree of comparison only.
>
> There were a king with a large jaw and a queen with a plain face on the throne of England; there were a king with a large jaw and a queen with a fair face, on the throne of France. In both countries it was clearer than crystal to the lords of the State preserves of loaves and fishes, that things in general were settled for ever.
>
> It was the year of Our Lord one thousand seven hundred and seventy-five. (1)

Dickens spends two full paragraphs making comparisons between the present and the historical setting of the novel before informing the reader of what year he is discussing. This introduction is intended to make the reader immediately see comparisons between the past and present. Dickens also creates an opening that prepares the way for his Christian theme by creating a sense of timelessness that is almost biblical and mythic in its symbolism. In *"Noah's Arkitecture": A Study of Dickens's Mythology*, Bert G. Hornback has exhaustively recorded Dickens' recurring use of biblical symbols in his novels. Hornback argues that Dickens' intense use of these recurring biblical images reflects his continual concern and questioning regarding the progress of human civilization and his theories of historical evolution. Dickens' novels symbolically begin in the mythic times of Genesis, especially, the Creation, Eden, and the Flood, and from there, they must evolve either into order or else move backward, in either case progressing toward or returning to an idyllic world (87-8). Dickens' use of the Edenic myth places him, like Carlyle and his Gothic predecessors, among those who wish to revise *Paradise Lost*; Dickens creates his own revision of Milton's epic by blending the Gothic and grotesque with biblical mythology to emphasize the need for human redemption and the importance of cultivating one's spirituality in a fallen world. The opening of *A Tale of Two Cities* uses this biblical mythology by comparing Light and Dark, which reflects Genesis and the times of Chaos and creation, suggesting that both the years 1775 and 1859 are such times of new beginnings as well as endings (Hornback 121). Hornback argues that Dickens' use of the myth "is to collapse all time into the crisis of the historical present" (122). Similarly, David Marcus suggests that the opening of *A Tale of Two Cities* is intended to confuse the reader, making time impossible to define just as it is impossible for people to understand the times in which they live (58). Dickens believes that all time periods are similar, whether the creation of the world, pre-French Revolution, or the mid-Victorian age because they are all confusing to those living within those periods. Consequently, while Dickens sets the novel during the French Revolution, the setting becomes symbolic and universal because the events of the novel could happen anywhere and anytime under the right conditions. George Lukacs concludes from this setting that the French Revolution becomes merely a "Romantic background" and the characters are historically displaced as a result (Goldberg 116-7). Hornback, in agreement, believes that because the biblical images collapse time, the characters' stories could easily have been told without the French Revolution as the setting (119).

More important than the novel's historical background is its typical Gothic emphasis upon the sanctity of the family and the need to preserve it. For Dickens, the family is where morals are learned and character is formed. Familial love rather than revolution is more productive in bringing about individual reform and redemption. Dickens uses the family as a place where reform occurs by allowing outcast characters like Carton to enter into the family and achieve a sense of belonging. The novel also depicts the broken family unit and how it can be repaired. The novel opens with an attempt to repair the broken unit of the Manette family. Lucie Manette travels to France to care for her father who has just been released from the Bastille. Dr. Manette is mentally wandering, but she hopes to restore his mind and health by establishing a home for the two of them. As the novel progresses, more broken families are introduced: the Evremondes, Defarges, and the solitary Sidney Carton, who is without a family but becomes an honorary member of the Darnays. The English families in the novel become restored and strengthened, while the broken French families serve as a contrast to emphasize the disaster resulting when the bonds of familial love are violated by society or a family member. The Gothic wanderers in the novel become the central focus within these families; consequently, to understand the importance of family structure in *A Tale of Two Cities*, one must understand the novel's three Gothic wanderers: Dr. Manette, Charles Darnay, and Sidney Carton.

Dr. Manette, the first Gothic wanderer introduced in the novel, is a victim of the aristocratic and patriarchal system of pre-revolutionary France. He is imprisoned because of his knowledge regarding a crime of rape and murder committed by the aristocratic Evremonde family. Because of their social status, the Evremondes are powerful enough to lock Dr. Manette in the Bastille so he cannot reveal the Evremondes' crimes. Dr. Manette's imprisonment is typical of the confinements of victims in Gothic novels, and the horror of his imprisonment ultimately results in his madness. Dickens had a source for Dr. Manette's imprisonment in Carlyle's *French Revolution*, and also in his 1842 American tour when he visited Pennsylvania's Eastern Penitentiary. At the penitentiary, Dickens saw prisoners who were forced to wear hoods so they could not see, thus separating them from the living world. Dickens would use this idea to describe Dr. Manette's incarceration as being "buried alive" because he is locked in his cell without access to the outside world or other prisoners (160-1). Dickens characterizes the Bastille as a Gothic prison, exaggerating the horrors that would have been faced by its prisoners to make Dr. Manette's situation all the more sensational and Gothic. Shawn Lyons points out that by the reign of Louis XVI, the Bastille's dungeons were no longer used. Furthermore, the Bastille had better government funds than other prisons in France because it frequently held important political prisoners. Because of their political influence, these prisoners could often bribe their jailors to bring them luxuries. Lyons suggests, therefore, that Dr. Manette could have had books or other intellectual pursuits in prison, rather than becoming a shoemaker (84).

Dr. Manette's role as Gothic wanderer is largely based upon the Wandering Jew. Dickens intentionally depicts Dr. Manette in prison as a shoemaker to link him with the Wandering Jew because Ahasuerus was also a shoemaker. Dickens' choice to make Dr. Manette a shoemaker also shows the severe mental degradation that prison has had upon his character. Like Satan who has Hell within him, Dr. Manette is never free from his memories of prison, even when he is physically free. The torture of being in prison becomes manifested in his worst moments when he reverts to his former occupation of making shoes. Dickens borrows from Mercier's *Tableau de Paris* the story of an old man who, when freed from imprisonment in the Bastille, recreated his cell in a room of his house; similarly after he is freed, Dr. Manette continues to make shoes in his own home when his madness comes upon him (Oddie 81n). At such times, he also wanders back and forth in his room, trying to shake off his madness like the Wandering Jew who continually wanders from place to place to hide his identity and escape persecution. Dr. Manette is further linked to the Wandering Jew when described as "a famished traveller, wearied out by lonely wandering in a wilderness" (35), suggestive of the biblical Hebrews' wanderings in the wilderness, and the Wandering Jew as symbol of the Jewish race. Dr. Manette metaphorically shares the Wandering Jew's extended life because he was practically dead while in prison and now he has been "recalled to life" and moves about like a supernatural being, as if he "were a Spirit moving among mortals" (256). Even Dr. Manette's attempts to speak begin with "first wandering" and forgetting his words (36). Dr. Manette remains displaced after his release, trying to adjust to a normal life, but often relapsing to his old state. The housekeeper, Mrs. Pross, describes his state as:

> ...his mind is walking up and down, walking up and down, in his old prison. She [Lucie] hurries to him, and they go on together, walking up and down, walking up and down until he is composed. But he never says a word of the true reason of his restlessness...they go walking up and down, walking up and down together, till her love and company have brought him to himself. (89)

For Dickens, love is what ultimately restores and redeems the Gothic wanderer. For Dr. Manette, it is Lucie's love that restores him to the fullest extent possible after his horrible experience.

Dickens bases Dr. Manette's imprisonment in the Bastille upon the historical imprisonment of King Louis XVI in the Bastille as described in Carlyle's *French Revolution*. Carlyle wrote that when the Bastille was attacked and searched, "its paper archives shall fly white. Old secrets come to view; and long-buried Despair finds voice" (Oddie 74). Carlyle records that among the papers discovered was a secret document concealed in the wall of the Tuilleries by Louis XVI with the aid of a locksmith. The discovery of this document was responsible for finally condemning the king to death. Similarly, the discovery of a document written by Dr. Manette will condemn his son-in-law, Charles Darnay. Dr. Manette is also connected to Louis XVI because during his imprisonment, Louis XVI would pretend he was a locksmith as a form of escapism from his imprisonment. Louis XVI actually learned the trade of locksmith from the man who helped him conceal his secret papers (Oddie 81n). Dickens uses this historical detail but changes Dr. Manette's occupation from locksmith to shoemaker in the Bastille to enhance the Gothic wanderer theme. Dickens rewrites his historical sources for his own purposes, then combines them with the Gothic device of the discovered manuscript. The manuscript reveals relationships between all of the novel's main characters as well as providing a history of family transgression, thus showing once more that Gothic plots are family plots.

Dr. Manette becomes a prisoner in the Bastille, and hence a Gothic wanderer, because he has unwillingly acquired forbidden knowledge about the Evremondes, and consequently, they punish him for having such knowledge. As recorded in the manuscript, the Evremonde brothers, Darnay's father and uncle, raped Madame Defarge's sister and murdered her brother. Dr. Manette was called upon to treat the wounded from this conflict, but his knowledge of the event results in the Evremondes imprisoning him for many years. During his imprisonment and when he is released, Dr. Manette, like other literary Gothic wanderers, notably immortal ones, takes on supernatural characteristics. When he is first seen by Mr. Lorry, he looks almost like a ghost. Mr. Lorry's role in assisting Dr. Manette is described as "He was on his way to dig some one out of a grave" (11). In his dreams, Mr. Lorry sees numerous prisoners' faces, all of which are the faces of Dr. Manette, with "sunken cheek, cadaverous colour, emaciated hands and figures" (11) and with a "ghostly face" (12). These descriptions suggest Dr. Manette has been dead or buried alive, and now he has been "recalled to life" (11), a phrase borrowed from *Paradise Lost* and spoken by Adam in reference to the human race's future redemption by Christ's sacrifice "yet recall'd / To life prolong'd and promis'd Race" (XI, 330-1). Dr. Manette's release from prison becomes another example of Dickens' use of the biblical myths of Creation and the Deluge, all myths of death and regeneration of life that foreshadow Christ's resurrection (Hornback 122). Dickens ties this biblical resurrection to the Gothic tradition by suggesting Dr. Manette is a reversal of Christ's resurrection, being almost more like a vampire or the living dead who returns to life pale or bloodless.

Released from his physical imprisonment, Dr. Manette, like Carlyle's Teufelsdrockh, realizes he can use his suffering to benefit humanity. When Darnay is imprisoned in France, Dr. Manette's reputation as a former prisoner of the Bastille makes him almost a superhero to the French people. Consequently, he uses his popularity to persuade the courts to free Darnay. Dr. Manette now realizes that the evil he suffered has brought about some good.

> ...the Doctor felt, now, that his suffering was strength and power. For the first time he felt that in that sharp fire, he had slowly forged the iron which could break the prison door of his daughter's husband, and deliver him. "It all tended to a good

end, my friend: it was not mere waste and ruin. As my beloved child was helpful in restoring me to myself, I will be helpful now in restoring the dearest part of herself to her; by the aid of Heaven I will do it!" Thus, Doctor Manette. (253)

By saving Darnay, Dr. Manette takes on the role of Christ, his suffering having been the sacrifice that redeems Darnay. Furthermore, Dickens, like Burney and Carlyle, transforms his Gothic wanderer into an Everyman figure, for the name Manette suggests Mankind, while the feminine ending of the name incorporates women as well as men into this role. Dr. Manette's sufferings are representative of the sufferings everyone must undergo in order to empathize with others and help them in their tribulations. In the novel's Preface, Dickens himself attested to this truth by realizing his own experiences made him able sympathetically to depict the events in the novel: "I have so far verified what is done and suffered in these pages, as that I have certainly done and suffered it all myself" (v).

The second Gothic wanderer character in the novel is Charles Darnay, a son and nephew to the Evremonde brothers who imprisoned Dr. Manette. Although innocent himself of committing crimes against the French people, Darnay is cursed as the result of his family's crimes, making him the victim of patriarchy despite his position as aristocratic heir to the family. Darnay has tried to escape his cursed family background by rejecting his aristocratic connections, changing his name from Evremonde to Darnay, and moving to England. Nevertheless, his family background continues to haunt Darnay. The name Evremonde, like Manette, is intended as a universal symbol. Michael Goldberg argues that Evremonde is a combination of the English word "every" with the French "tout le monde" meaning all the world. This combination results in a French word that would be equivalent to the English "Everyman" (118). Consequently, the evils of the Evremonde family become the evils of all humanity; therefore, Carton's sacrificial death to compensate for the evils of the Darnay/Evremonde family is equivalent to Christ's death to wash away Everyman or humanity's sins.

Dickens further expands upon the Everyman theme by connecting the Evremonde family with Gothic immortality because of the curse placed upon the family. Critics have overlooked the significance of this curse, which provides a literary link between the Evremonde family and the Wandering Jew, the curse of Cain, and the Rosicrucians. Dr. Manette records that the young man whom he medically assisted placed the curse upon the Evremonde brothers after he had fought for the honor of his violated sister. Darnay's father, by his aristocratic position, views the rape as his "droit du seigneur," while the girl's brother views the rape as a transgression against his family. Dr. Manette records that before dying, the young man cursed the Evremonde family.

> "'Marquis,' said the boy, turned to him with his eyes opened wide, and his right hand raised, 'in the days when all these things are to be answered for, I summon you and yours, to the last of your bad race, to answer for them. I mark this cross of blood upon you, as a sign that I do it. In the days when all these things are to be answered for, I summon your brother, the worst of the bad race, to answer for them separately. I mark this cross of blood upon him, as a sign that I do it.'
>
> "Twice, he put his hand to the wound in his breast, and with his forefinger drew a cross in the air. He stood for an instant with the finger yet raised, and, as it dropped, he dropped with it, and I laid him down dead. (305)

The cross placed upon the Evremonde brothers is a cross of blood to symbolize the murder they have committed. The cross is equivalent to the mark Cain received upon murdering his brother Abel. As noted earlier, the mark of Cain was transferred in literature to the Wandering Jew, who is usually depicted with a burning cross upon his forehead. Later in his narrative, Dr. Manette emphasizes the fatal result of this curse upon the Evremonde family.

> I believe that the mark of the red cross is fatal to them, and that they have no part in His mercies. And them and their descendants, to the last of their race, I, Alexandre Manette, unhappy prisoner, do this last night of the year 1767, in my unbearable agony, denounce to the times when all these things shall be answered for. I denounce them to Heaven and to earth. (310)

Dr. Manette defines the curse as extending to all the Everemondes' descendants, just as Cain's descendants were traditionally believed to be cursed by God until Judgment Day, and as the Wandering Jew, representative of the Jewish race, is traditionally depicted as cursed to wander the earth until Christ's Second Coming. While the color of the Wandering Jew's cross is not described, Dickens has the Evremonde family cursed with a cross of blood. While a red cross, symbolic of blood, may seem an obvious choice, it is used here to emphasize the novel's immortality theme by connecting the curse's cross with Rosicrucianism, whose symbol is a rose and a cross, and whose name means the Rosy Cross, suggestive that the cross is red. Evidence that Dickens was aware of the Rosicrucian implications of a red cross can be derived from his use of similar symbols in *The Mystery of Edwin Drood* where Hyrom Grewgious has in his rooms a doorway with tiles containing symbols of the Freemasons and the Rosicrucians (Burgan 295). The Freemasons themselves have been associated with the Rosicrucians in their origins (Burgan 257-8). Furthermore, because Dickens borrows the idea of Sidney Carton's sacrifice from Bulwer-Lytton's *Zanoni*, the Rosicrucian connection seems even more likely. As a friend of Bulwer-Lytton, Dickens would have been aware that there were Rosicrucian societies in existence and perhaps he was even knowledgeable about them.

As a member of the eternally cursed Evremonde family, Darnay is also a Gothic wanderer, representing how the sins of the father are visited upon the child. Abhorred by his family's crimes, Darnay rejects his ancestry and his place of power in the patriarchal system. This rejection results in his feeling guilty as if he had committed parricide, for his uncle, the patriarchal head of the aristocratic family, is murdered immediately after Darnay rejects the Evremondes (Eigner 151). Darnay's rejection of his family is his own attempt to redeem himself from the family curse. The new surname he chooses means "mender" (Eigner 155), suggestive of his attempt to make peace between his past and his new life with a different name and in a different country, as well as to compensate for the previous crimes of his family. When the French Revolution breaks out, Darnay feels he should return to France to aid his countrymen and to help prevent too much bloodshed. When he learns one of his former servants has been imprisoned, Darnay attempts to play the Christ-like role of savior by returning to France and striving for his servant's freedom. Ironically, while Darnay succeeds in rescuing his servant, he then finds himself imprisoned.

Dickens' emphasis on the importance of family bonds is evidenced by Dr. Manette now journeying to France to rescue Darnay. Dr. Manette has long since accepted that his son-in-law is a member of the Evremonde family that oppressed him, but both Darnay and Dr. Manette have forgotten the crimes of the past because they realize love and family sanctity are more important. Dr. Manette fails to save Darnay, however, because the document Dr. Manette hid in the Bastille is discovered and it condemns all the Evremondes including Darnay. Dickens uses the manuscript to endanger the family unit, then creates a non-family member, Sidney Carton, to make the ultimate sacrifice that preserves the family. While Dickens borrows the final scene of sacrifice at the guillotine from *Zanoni*, he rejects the death of one of the married couple in favor of a non-family member so the sanctity of the family unit can remain unbroken.

Sidney Carton's sacrifice makes him the novel's only character to fulfill successfully the role of savior. First, however, Carton plays the role of Gothic wanderer to become the most successful example in the Victorian period of how a Gothic wanderer can redeem himself by rejecting selfishness for self-sacrifice. Sidney Carton's role as Gothic wanderer is apparent from his first introduction to the reader as one who has no interest in life, is a near victim of despair, and consequently, like Dr. Manette, may be described as one of the living dead. Although still a young man, Carton feels his life is wasted; he realizes he could be ambitious and achieve great deeds, but lacking the motivation and purpose, he despairs of ever accomplishing anything of importance. The most moving depiction of Carton's despair occurs early in the novel when he assists in freeing Darnay from charges of treason as a spy because of their similar resemblances. Following the trial, Carton works late into the night, then returns home to feel overwhelmed by despair.

> Waste forces within him, and a desert all around, this man stood still on his way across a silent terrace, and saw for a moment, lying in the wilderness before him, a mirage of honourable ambition, self-denial, and perseverance. In the fair city of this vision, there were airy galleries from which the loves and graces looked upon him, gardens in which the fruits of life hung ripening, waters of Hope that sparkled in his sight. A moment, and it was gone. Climbing to a high chamber in a well of houses, he threw himself down in his clothes on a neglected bed, and its pillow was wet with wasted tears.
> Sadly, sadly, the sun rose; it rose upon no sadder sight than the man of good abilities and good emotions, incapable of their directed exercise, incapable of his own help and his own happiness, sensible of the blight on him, and resigning himself to let it eat him away. (82)

Carton feels unable to battle against despair and finds it easier to let it destroy him. His vision of a fair city and gardens suggests a desire to create a paradise or Eden for himself, but he despairs that he will never be able to accomplish such a goal. His despair is especially bitter for he has just met and fallen in love with Lucie Manette. Carton realizes that by saving Darnay, he has preserved his rival for Lucie's love; he immediately comes to hate Darnay for being preferred by Lucie. Eventually, no longer able to hide his emotions, Carton speaks to Lucie.

While expressing his love, Carton characterizes himself in words relevant to the Gothic wanderer figure. He remarks, "I am like one who died young" (138), suggesting that like Dr. Manette, he has died, but his body unnaturally lives on. In response, Lucie asks "can I not save you, Mr. Carton? Can I not recal [sic] you—forgive me again!—to a better course?" (138). Lucie's use of the word "recall" suggests that she would recall Carton to life as she has done for her father, but Carton believes that her concern and pity are insufficient to cure him, and only if she loves him could he be recalled to life. He then tells Lucie, "For you, and for any dear to you, I would do anything....I would embrace any sacrifice for you and for those dear to you....think now and then that there is a man who would give his life, to keep a life you love beside you!" (140-1). Unknown to himself, Carton has just spoken his own death sentence, but he has also begun his redemption by his willingness to sacrifice himself for one he loves, rather than focusing upon himself by demanding that love. Love is always the redeemer in Dickens' novels. Before Carton had been indifferent to life, but once he begins to love, "he finally emerges from the self-imposed prison of indifference" (Marcus 65) to be "recalled to life."

Carton proves the strength of his love for Lucie when he fulfills his vow and sacrifices his life to save Darnay, thus preserving the sacred family unit. In sacrificing himself, however, Carton also comes to save himself. Carton's sacrifice embodies Christ's statement that no man can gain his life unless first he loses it. In the novel's final scene, Dickens creates a vision of a person's full capacity to love selflessly. Carton's final words show his concern for Lucie, Darnay, and their daughter, as well as concern for the seamstress whom he befriends by holding her hand until the last moment (Timko 193).

Critics have argued about the extent to which Carton's death is to be interpreted as a Christian sacrifice. Wilson argues that Carton's death is pagan because it is motivated by romantic love for Lucie (267). However, Carton's sacrifice is not only for Lucie but for her entire family and friends. His death supersedes romantic love to become brotherly love, the love he comes to feel for Darnay and also for the seamstress. The final scenes break down boundaries of class and race as Carton joins hands with the lower class girl who is dying with aristocrats, and who is French while he is English, thereby again using Dickens' theme of universality and the common brotherhood of humanity.

Critics have overlooked the strongest evidence for reading Carton's sacrifice as Christian and himself as a Christ-figure: his death at the guillotine. Earlier in the novel, Dickens states that the Guillotine has come to replace the Christian Cross as an object of worship during the French Revolution, "La Guillotine....It was the sign of regeneration of the human race. It superseded the Cross. Models of it were worn on breasts from which the Cross was discarded, and it was bowed down to and believed in where the Cross was denied" (255). Consequently, if the guillotine has become the Cross, Carton's death at the guillotine is a symbol of Christ's crucifixion. Furthermore, Dickens here blends Christianity with the Gothic literary tradition, for the guillotine also represents Rosicrucianism; the guillotine is a red cross because it is bathed in its victims' blood. Carton's death by guillotine, therefore, is a Christian sacrifice by which he saves his loved ones from death, as well as saving his own soul and achieving eternal life in Heaven. His death, however, also assures for Carton a type of Rosicrucian immortality in the prolonged earthly existence of his name and memory because he foresees the Darnays naming their descendants after him.

Dickens' intention that Carton's sacrifice be interpreted as Christian is evidenced when Carton repeats Christ's words, "I am the Resurrection and the Life, saith the Lord: he that believeth in me, though he were dead, yet shall he live: and whosoever liveth and believeth in me shall never die" (351). Carton had been dead to life but by his selfless love for others, he has been resurrected to eternal life. Dickens further portrays Carton as a

Christ-figure when Carton comforts the seamstress, reminiscent of when Christ comforts the thief who is crucified with him (Lyons 49). Finally, like Christ, Carton has the gift of prophecy. This prophecy displays Dickens' theory of historical evolution:

> I see a beautiful city and a brilliant people rising from this abyss, and, in their struggles to be truly free, in their triumphs and defeats, through long years to come, I see the evil of this time and of the previous time of which this is a natural birth, gradually making expiation for itself and wearing out. (352)

Carton envisions the future of France and the good that can still arise from all the atrocities committed by the Reign of Terror, making the events of the present part of a historical process by which God brings about good for humanity despite transgression or original sin. Carton's vision reflects a positive Christian view of history that begins with Adam and Eve's transgression and ends with Christ's Second Coming, representing that good can come from evil. Consequently, the novel reflects the shared historical viewpoint of Dickens and Carlyle of history as a "God written apocalypse" (Goldberg 123-4), but for Dickens, the apocalypse results in the establishment of a new Eden upon the earth.

Carton also prophesies concerning the future of the Darnay family:

> I see the lives for which I lay down my life, peaceful, useful, prosperous and happy, in that England which I shall see no more. I see Her with a child upon her bosom, who bears my name. I see her father, aged and bent, but otherwise restored, and faithful to all men in his healing office, and at peace. I see the good old man, so long their friend, in ten years' time enriching them with all he has, and passing tranquilly to his reward.
>
> I see that I hold a sanctuary in their hearts, and in the hearts of their descendants, generations hence. I see her, an old woman, weeping for me on the anniversary of this day. I see her and her husband, their course done, lying side by side in their last earthly bed, and I know that each was not more honoured and held sacred in the other's soul, than I was in the souls of both. (352)

In this reflection, Carton realizes he has redeemed himself by loving and having that love returned both by the woman he loves and his rival for that love. Lyons remarks of this passage, "Carton, an outcast in the world, not unlike Christ Himself, accepts his fate of saving the new Adam and Eve willingly" (49). Carton envisions that he will be eternally remembered by Lucie and Darnay, the new Adam and Eve who will generate a new race. His memory will inspire them to teach their descendants about the love and honor Carton demonstrated. His sacrifice is so important in their memories that they will name their child after him.

> I see that child who lay upon her bosom and who bore my name, a man winning his way up in that path of life which once was mine. I see him winning it so well, that my name is made illustrious there by the light of his. I see the blots I threw upon it, faded away. I see him, foremost of just judges and honoured men, bringing a boy of my name, with a forehead that I know and golden hair, to this place—then fair to look upon, with not a trace of this day's disfigurement—and I hear him tell the child my story, with a tender and faltering voice. (352)

This paragraph contains a complex number of symbolic images. It reflects Dickens' debt to *Zanoni* by providing a final image of a child, although for a different purpose than Bulwer-Lytton had used. Lindsay argues that in *Zanoni* the child is the symbol of new life, while for Dickens it symbolizes the lovers' union (365). However, the lovers are passed over in Carton's vision to make the child the final emphasis. Because the Darnays represent the new Adam and Eve, the child symbolizes the future human race. Lyons suggests that this child, named for Carton, represents "the new apostle who will 'preach' the 'gospel' of Carton's life" (50). This child will grow up and tell Carton's story to his own child, making him a type of disciple to Carton. Consequently, Carton envisions his death as significantly influencing the future as Christ's death established the Christian church. In addition, Carton imagines Darnay's son bearing his own name, and that son also naming his child after Carton. Carton focuses primarily upon the immortal life of his soul, but he also remains concerned with his earthly immortality as it will be carried on by the Darnay descendants named for him. David Marcus argues, therefore, that Carton secularizes the Christian immortality theme for one of earthly "continuity of generations" (61). The Darnay child named for Carton will provide Carton with earthly immortality, reflecting his Rosicrucian life-extension. His death at the Rosicrucian, rosy cross of the guillotine gives him eternal salvation in Heaven, but also a form of Rosicrucian life-extension upon earth. Furthermore, Carton's death to preserve the family ensures that he will be an eternal part of that family by the children named in his memory.

Following this unique blending of literary symbolism, Dickens closes the novel with Carton's famous lines: "It is a far, far better thing that I do, than I have ever done; it is a far, far better rest that I go to than I have ever known" (352). With these words, Carton is able to go to his "rest," a word whose connotation is the exact opposite of "wandering." Sidney Carton has been transformed from a Gothic wanderer to an example of the Victorian theme of redemption, by which the transgressor can achieve not only eternal life in Heaven, but whose good deeds can also provide him with a form of earthly immortality.

Chapter X – The Gothic Wanderer at Rest: *Dracula* and the Vampiric Tradition

Throughout this book, little attention has been given to treatments of the vampire in nineteenth century Gothic fiction. I have reserved discussion of the vampire as a Gothic wanderer for the end because *Dracula* represents the culmination of the tradition, being the work in which the greatest number of attributes common to the Gothic wanderer are combined or echoed within one character. This chapter will trace the development of the vampire figure from myth and legend to its popularity in nineteenth century fiction. By reserving the vampire for the end, a discussion of its development will equally serve as a review of the transformation of the Gothic wanderer throughout the nineteenth century. *Glenarvon* (1816) presents a typical early treatment of the Gothic wanderer as damned beyond hope for his transgression. *Varney the Vampyre* (1847), by comparison, reflects the Victorian treatment, as evidenced also in Carlyle, Bulwer-Lytton, and Dickens, of the Gothic wanderer as redeemable; however, this "Victorian" redemption depends upon the Gothic wanderer's repentance for transgression and his willingness to forsake selfishness in favor of self-sacrifice. *Varney the Vampyre* is very Victorian in its exploration of the character's feelings of contrition and his desire for self-reform, although it denies Varney the redemption that less wicked Gothic wanderers like Sidney Carton are able to achieve. *Dracula* (1897) is a return to an early Gothic tradition with a setting among castles and coffins, but the novel is also a movement away from the Victorian emphasis upon the character's repentance as necessary for redemption. Dracula's resistance to repentance marks the novel as a product of the *fin de siecle* and the movement toward modernism because the character's restlessness and his transgressions cannot be as easily contained in the narrative as Victorian happy endings generally allow. The characters must force redemption upon Dracula, and they must convince the reader that this forced redemption, which requires Dracula's murder, is necessary and even desired by Dracula. This forced redemption declares that God is ultimately merciful and forgiving to the worst of sinners. Paradise is at last regained, but not by the Gothic wanderer's method of committing a new transgression to reverse the transgression of Adam and Eve. Instead, the Gothic asserts once more the value of the family as *Dracula* creates a new form of family for the new century to come, a family representative of the human race's ability to band together and overcome evil. The vampire figure's role in bringing about this conclusion to the Gothic wanderer tradition is best explained by tracing the vampire figure from his mythical origins through the major treatments of the vampire in the nineteenth century, which ultimately influenced the creation of *Dracula*.

Origins and Early Literary Uses of the Vampire Legend

The vampire legend has existed since ancient times with numerous sources for possible explanations of how people become vampires. The two most frequent and popular beliefs were that one was either born to be a vampire, though innocent at birth, or one became a vampire as the result of committing a transgression, usually some form of blasphemy. Innocent people could become vampires by a hereditary family tendency or by being born on an unlucky day. An example of the latter occurs in an old Greek rhyme that states that children born on Christmas Day become vampires as punishment for their mother's sin of being presumptuous enough to bear a child on the same day as the Virgin Mary (Jones 115). Such innocent vampires are of little influence or interest to the Gothic wanderer tradition, but transgressors who become vampires as a result of their evil deeds would inspire the imaginations of numerous poets and novelists, allowing the vampire to become a popular and familiar figure.

The belief that people could become vampires by guilt or transgression against God began as the result of a schism within the Christian Church. The Roman Catholic Church had declared that the bodies of saints did not decompose; in opposition, the Greek Orthodox Church declared that the only bodies that would not decompose were those of the wicked, unholy, and excommunicated (Jones 103). Catholic tradition stated that heretics were turned into werewolves, but the Greek Orthodox Church instead stated that those whose bodies did not decompose were actually vampires, whose punishment for their transgression was being forced to endure a prolonged lifespan (Jones 103). This punishment, of course, is not dissimilar to that of the Wandering Jew who, in representing the entire Jewish race, is forced to wander for denying Christ. Transgressors who are transformed into vampires are also forced to wander from place to place in search of new blood to consume. The influence of the Wandering Jew legend upon nearly all nineteenth century Gothic wanderers would become especially dominant in treatments of the vampire, whose Eastern European origins allowed him to become a vehicle for anti-Semitism in a more powerful, if less direct manner than Jewish characters in most Gothic novels. Echoes of the Wandering Jew occur in depictions of vampire characters in several Gothic novels.

The vampire shares with the Wandering Jew the inability to rest because he is cursed for his transgressions. While the Catholic Church would later relegate restless souls to Purgatory, the idea of vampires stimulated people's imaginations so that the vampire quickly emerged into legend and literature outside of the religious sphere. Numerous reasons besides heresy were developed for how one became a vampire, including such bizarre transgressions as working on Sundays, smoking on a Holy Day, and having sexual intercourse with one's own grandmother (Jones 115). The incest motif became a particularly frequent element of the vampire tradition because vampires were credited with only haunting members of their own families (Twitchell, *Living* 111). Because a vampire's victim was a member of its own family, the vampire's bloodsucking served as a metaphor for the act of intercourse, and consequently, of incest. Even the vampire's inability to rest was connected with incest because to be buried in the earth was equated with a return to the Mother's womb. Christians were freed from their burials being incestuous by their last rites freeing them from sin and by their being buried in holy ground. The vampire, however, because of his transgression, remains sinful and unable to enter the earth for his final rest (Jones 104). Suicide was another explanation for how one became a vampire; suicides were forbidden to be buried on holy ground, but were generally buried at the crossroads with a stake driven through their hearts to prevent their returning from the grave as vampires. Finally, one could become a vampire by being victimized by one (Gaull 249). Since vampires traditionally only haunted their relatives, an entire family could become vampires from generation to generation. Such victimization by a vampire was equivalent to suffering from a family curse, an idea similar to the Christian belief that one is born into original sin as a result of Adam and Eve's transgressions.

Three main reasons exist for why vampires were believed to haunt only their families: the undead person may wish to return and punish his family, he may desire to protect the family, or he wishes the family to join in his fate so the family will not be separated (Jones 99-100). Vampires were even believed to impregnate their former wives, thereby emphasizing the sexual nature of vampires, as does their bloodsucking (Jones 102). Consequently, whenever a vampire scare occurred in Eastern Europe, the widow of the most recently deceased person in the village was the first to be questioned since her deceased husband may have become a vampire and visited her (Jones 102).

Psychologists have attempted to explain the origins of vampire legends as arising from guilt-based dreams. Ernest Jones suggests that it is common for people to dream of deceased loved ones, and from such dreams, the vampire myth arose (102). A living person may be visited in dreams by the deceased, who asks the living to return with him to the grave. The death of a loved one is a reminder to people of their own mortality. Dreams of the dead, therefore, may be a manifestation of the dreamer's fear of death. Jones argues that a person who fears vampires may be suffering from guilt over still being alive while a loved one has died (113). While such psychological explanations exist, in Gothic literature the vampire is always depicted as a real supernatural being rather than simply a dream or hallucination. Consequently, vampire novels fall into the masculine Gothic tradition where the supernatural is part of reality. Psychological interpretations of vampires are significant, however, because they offer reasons for why vampires would haunt their own family members. Gothic novels depict vampires as haunting their families, as in *Varney the Vampyre* where the vampire claims to be a distant relative of the family he is haunting. The Gothic's emphasis upon family-centered plots makes the vampire a perfect symbol of how an individual's transgression can destroy his family.

While vampire legends originated in ancient times and were popular in Eastern Europe, there is scarcely a mention of vampires in England until they became popular fictional characters first in Romantic poetry and then in Gothic fiction. The Romantic poets showed some minor interest in the vampire, but they were often unsure how to treat him or what he could be used to symbolize. A few Romantic poems with vampires exist, notably Southey's *Thalaba the Destroyer* (1797) and Keats' "Lamia" (1820), but these had little if any influence upon the vampires of Gothic fiction.

One Romantic treatment of the vampire that may have influenced Gothic fiction was Coleridge's "The Rime of the Ancient Mariner" (1798). This work, as noted earlier, had a significant influence upon the Gothic tradition because of its title character's Wandering Jew attributes. Originally, Coleridge may have intended the Ancient Mariner to contain more references to vampires, but he appears to have removed these references from the final version. James Twitchell has set forth an argument for vampire references in "The Rime of the Ancient Mariner" that may explain some of the poem's ambiguities. Twitchell argues that Coleridge originally intended the work to be a vampire poem as evidenced by numerous passages, including when the Mariner bites his arm and sucks blood. Twitchell interprets the characters on the ship as Life in Death (suggestive of the vampire as the living dead), notes that the sun is blood red, and the crew works by moonlight (suggestive of vampires who are nocturnal and could be resuscitated by moonbeams). Twitchell also states that Coleridge originally intended for the crew to drink the Mariner's blood to make them vampires (*Living* 146-57). The poem's vampire references are obscure, according to Twitchell, because Coleridge decided to remove the vampire material from the poem to make it more compatible with Christian doctrine. Coleridge also sought to remove the possibility of vampire interpretations from the poem by writing the glosses that point out Christian interpretations, thus explaining why many of the glosses are obscure and incompatible with the poem's content (*Living* 151). Twitchell suggests that Coleridge wanted references to the Ancient Mariner's eyes removed because vampires are noted for their hypnotic eyes. The editor, however, ignored Coleridge's wishes (*Living* 155). It is impossible to know whether Coleridge originally did intend to write a vampire poem in "The Rime of the Ancient Mariner." While Twitchell's interpretation of the poem is intriguing and highly probable, Twitchell may also be overly influenced by early critics who sought, beginning with Arthur Nethercot's *The Road to Tryermaine* (1939), to define Geraldine in Coleridge's "Christabel" as a vampire. Twitchell's case for vampire content in "The Rime of the Ancient Mariner," however, appears more plausible than the likelihood of vampire content in "Christabel."

The most significant influence of a Romantic poet upon the Gothic treatment of the vampire was Lord Byron. Byron's *The Giaour* (1813) is the tale of a giaour, meaning an infidel, in the Middle East who commits transgressions of adultery and murder. For his crimes, the infidel is cursed to be a typical vampire who haunts his own family, but who dislikes his personal need for blood to nourish him: "Yet loathe the banquet which perforce / Must feed thy livid living corse" (761-2). Because of the vampire's remorse, he is more typical of a Gothic wanderer who feels guilt over his crimes than of Byron's usual heroes who celebrate their rebellions. While Byron's poem in itself had little influence upon the Gothic vampire tradition, Byron's authorship of the poem made his contemporaries associate him with the vampire figure. As a result, the first two major treatments of the vampire in fiction were works whose vampire characters were based upon Lord Byron himself. Lady Caroline Lamb's *Glenarvon* and John Polidori's *The Vampyre* were written by people whose personal involvement with Lord Byron resulted in feelings of animosity toward him.

Glenarvon and the Byronic Vampire

Lady Caroline Lamb's *Glenarvon* (1816) is the first novel to make notable use of the vampire figure. The novel contains no actual vampire characters but suggests that its title character has vampiric characteristics. *Glenarvon* is usually passingly referred to as a source for Polidori's *The Vampyre*, considered to be the first vampire tale in English prose fiction, but its own rich use of the vampire metaphor and the novel's overall position within the Gothic wanderer tradition make *Glenarvon* a work that deserves more attention than it has hitherto received. While the work is poorly written and the plot is confusing, Lamb provides a remarkable treatment of the Gothic by blending the supernatural with the realistic. The novel never explicitly creates supernatural events until the final dramatic chapter, but it continually suggests how the supernatural is born of the psychological terror an individual experiences as the result of transgression and guilt. The novel focuses upon two distinctive Gothic wanderers: Glenarvon, who is based on Lord Byron, and the female heroine, Calantha, based upon Caroline Lamb. Glenarvon and Calantha's romantic relationship is consequently Lamb's rewriting of her tumultuous affair with Lord Byron. Lamb wrote the novel to avenge herself against

Lord Byron for abandoning her. She depicts Glenarvon as a type of vampire damned beyond hope while Calantha is redeemed and forgiven her transgressions. Calantha's redemption is surprising in a pre-Victorian novel, making the novel a notable exception in the early Gothic wanderer tradition; Calantha's redemption results from Lamb's identification with the heroine and a desire to vindicate herself from any wrong. Consequently, Lamb creates a remarkable double standard for the Gothic wanderer by allowing the female wanderer to be redeemed while the male wanderer must face damnation. The use of the vampire metaphor for Glenarvon furthers the legitimacy of his damnation while preparing the way for the vampire's popularity throughout nineteenth century Gothic fiction.

From his first appearance in the novel, Glenarvon is considered a dangerous man and is described in terms suggestive of supernatural Gothic wanderers, particularly that of Satan, the Wandering Jew, and the vampire. Calantha first sees Glenarvon in the moonlight, making her feel she is in the presence of a "fallen angel" (121). She is told of Glenarvon's melancholy and depressed state and that "it would surprise you how he howls and barks, whenever the moon shines bright" (122). The howling at the moon is suggestive of a werewolf to modern readers, but more specifically it relates Glenarvon to the vampire who is traditionally restrengthened by moonlight, only implied here in *Glenarvon* but expanded upon in later vampire tales. Calantha also learns that Glenarvon's ancestor, John de Ruthven "drank hot blood from the skull of his enemy" (123), suggestive that Glenarvon's vampiric characteristics are inherited. Lamb bases this anecdote on the actual occurrence of Lord Byron drinking wine from a skull in Newstead Abbey (Wilson, "Notes" 371). Glenarvon's vampirism is also implied in rumors of his death, and in the novel's description of how he keeps nocturnal hours.

> Glenarvon wandered forth every evening by the pale moon, and no one knew whither he went....And when the rain fell heavy and chill, he would bare his forehead to the storm; and faint and weary wander forth, and often he smiled on others and appeared calm, whilst the burning fever of his blood continued to rage within. (178)

Like the vampire, Glenarvon is a nocturnal wanderer, and like Milton's Satan, who feels Hell within, Glenarvon feels the "burning fever of his blood...rage within" (178). Glenarvon's preference for the fiercest of Nature's elements is self-destructive and recalls the Wandering Jew who seeks death but is unable to achieve it. Furthermore, like the Jew, Glenarvon appears to realize that he is cursed so neither man nor Nature can harm him.

> That which was disgusting or terrific to man's nature, had no power over Glenarvon. He had looked upon the dying and

the dead; had seen the tear of agony without emotion; had heard the shriek of despair, and felt the hot blood as it flowed from the heart of a murdered enemy, nor turned from the sickening sight—Even storms of nature could not move Glenarvon. In the dark night, when the tempest raged around and the stormy ocean beat against the high impending cliffs, he would venture forth, would listen to the roaring thunder without fear, and watch the forked lightning as it flashed along the sky. (141-2)

While Glenarvon is not actually supernatural, such descriptions suggest that he, and by extension, Lord Byron, are unnatural in their actions.

The most supernatural aspect of Glenarvon's nature is his metaphorical vampiric ability to drain life from his female victims. While he does not literally drink his victims' blood, he nevertheless drains energy from them, as Byron drained the women he loved and then abandoned them. As Glenarvon and Calantha's relationship progresses, he becomes stronger and more dominant, while she becomes physically and emotionally weak and subservient. Frances Wilson remarks that Glenarvon seems to be draining "the living daylights out of her in order to maintain his own nocturnal existence" (Introduction xx). Glenarvon is not completely monstrous, however, for he warns Calantha of the dangers of loving him, saying "My love is death" (229). He states he is concerned about her fate, while he is "indifferent" (229) regarding his own. Calantha remains constant in her love for Glenarvon, although his warning makes her fear the future. Her friend, Gondimar, warns her to "look to his [Glenarvon's] hand, there is blood on it!" (203), suggesting that, like the Wandering Jew, Glenarvon is marked with a curse. Following this warning, Calantha dreams of a monk, who like an Inquisitor, questions and warns her about Glenarvon. The monk tells her she must ask to see Glenarvon's right hand because "there is a stain of blood on it" but "he [Glenarvon] will not give it you; there is a mark upon it: he dare not give it you" (204). When Calantha relates this dream to Glenarvon, he gives her a "demoniac smile" (204), and holds forth an unblemished hand. Nevertheless, Calantha feels frightened for, "His eyes glared upon her with fierce malignity; his livid cheeks became pale; and over his forehead, an air of deep distress struggled with the violence of passion, till all again was calm, cold, and solemn as before" (204). Glenarvon's metaphorically marked hand and the fierce glare of his eyes are both trademarks of the Wandering Jew, while his paleness again suggests his vampiric nature. Calantha is stunned by his emotional behavior, but she is also irresistibly fascinated by him. In another of Calantha's dreams, Glenarvon appears "pale, deadly, and cold: his hand was ice, and as he placed it upon hers, she shrunk from the grasp of death, and awoke oppressed with terror" (172). Nevertheless, she allows him to manipulate her, feeling sympathy for him when he tells her there is a "horrid secret, which weighed upon his mind" (175). Calantha's concern for Glenarvon makes her think the guilt from this secret has driven him mad.

> He would start at times, and gaze on vacancy; then turn to Calantha, and ask her what she had heard and seen. His gestures, his menaces were terrific. He would talk to the air; then laugh with convulsive horror; and gazing wildly around, enquire of her, if there were not blood upon the earth, and if the ghosts of departed men had not been seen by some. (175-6)

Despite Glenarvon's strange behavior, Calantha continues to love and befriend him even when she feels her love places her on the border of sin. Like Melmoth the Wanderer, Glenarvon seeks a mate to lighten his curse, yet he regrets the afflictions she will receive by sharing his fate. He warns Calantha that he is the Hell she should shun because her association with him will forbid her entering Heaven, but she replies that the hopes and promises of religion and virtue are nothing to her without him (202).

Although Calantha is married, Glenarvon then convinces her to swear an oath of love to him, an oath that will bind their souls together as Christians are bound by their marriage vows. At first, Calantha's inner soul revolts, but then she agrees, feeling one hour with Glenarvon is worth all calamities. She tells Glenarvon she will take the oath because his "words are like the joys of Heaven: Thy presence is the light of life" (218). Calantha has spoken blasphemy, making Glenarvon the light of life, thus comparing him to Lucifer before the fall, and setting him up as a type of Antichrist. She has committed a transgression against God by taking a sacrilegious oath that violates her marriage vow. She has also transgressed against the family by committing adultery. Now she has committed further sin by declaring Glenarvon is "the light of life" as if he were God, thus making her an idolater. Although she feels the impiety of her words, Calantha tells Glenarvon that their souls are now linked and he is her only master (220-1).

The impious marriage ceremony occurs during the moon's half crescent, suggestive of Satan's horns. The moon is also commonly depicted in vampire fiction as providing a source of life for vampires. During the ceremony, the moon casts fearful shadows (219-20), providing an ill omen for the couple's future. Glenarvon gives Calantha a ring, saying that if there is a God, He will be the witness to the marriage vows. Calantha's forehead begins to burn, suggestive of the guilt she feels, as if by the marriage ceremony she has a cursed mark on her forehead like that of the Wandering Jew. This burning suggests her connection now to Glenarvon, because on "his pale forehead....the light of the moonbeam fell" (220), suggesting he is himself cursed.

Once Calantha is damned with Glenarvon, the Narrator explains the moral of the tale, foreshadowing the novel's denouement.

> When man, reposing upon himself, disdains the humility of acknowledging his offences and his weakness before his Creator, on the sudden that angry God sees fit to punish him in his wrath, and he who has appeared invulnerable till that hour, falls prostrate at once before the blow: perhaps then, for the first time, he relents; and, whilst he sinks himself, feels for the sinner whom, in the pride and presumption of his happier day, he had mocked at and despised. There are trials, which human frailty cannot resist—there are passions implanted in the heart's core, which reason cannot subdue; and God himself compassionates, when a fellow-creature refuses to extend to us his mercy or forgiveness. (253)

The moral is that no one is beyond salvation if he or she asks for forgiveness, for God is merciful even when humanity is not. This philosophy, however, Lamb only applies to Calantha while Glenarvon is condemned to damnation because Lamb chooses to depict him as unwilling to repent.

Soon after the sacrilegious marriage ceremony, Glenarvon abandons Calantha, leaving her heartbroken. Similarly, Lamb felt destitute when Byron deserted her, so she depicts Byron metaphorically as a vampire who leaves women feeling lifeless and longing for death after he deserts them (Wilson, Introduction xx). Calantha now repents for her transgressions committed with Glenarvon. She becomes ill and dies, but first she gains her husband's forgiveness, and she feels that God has forgiven her for her sins.

After Calantha's death, Glenarvon has a vision of her as an angel surrounded by celestial light. She tells him to live and be his nation's pride, but when he asks whether she is happy or she still loves him, she becomes pale and ghastly and fades from sight (362-3). Glenarvon's dream occurs on the eve of a battle for Irish freedom, equating it with typical dreams of ill omen that legendary heroes experience before their defeat and death in battle.

Glenarvon distinguishes himself in the following battle, but becomes ill immediately after. He now has a horrendous vision, which provides the climactic and powerful supernatural ending of the novel.

> 'Visions of death and horror persecute me,' cried Glenarvon. 'What now do I behold—a ship astern!....Is it that famed Dutch merchantman, condemned through all eternity to sail before the wind, which seamen view with terror, whose existence until this hour I discredited?' (364-5)

Glenarvon has seen the legendary Flying Dutchman, a ship composed of murderous sailors, who are forced for all eternity to sail the seas, much as the Wandering Jew is continually forced to wander the earth until Judgment Day. The scene is also suggestive of the Ancient Mariner who travels aimlessly about the sea as punishment for his transgression of killing the albatross. Glenarvon sees spectral images on the vessel, including a friar who drowns a woman who loves him. Following this deed,

> ...the monk drew slowly from his bosom the black covering that enshrouded his form. Horrible to behold!—that bosom was gored with deadly wounds, and the black spouting streams of blood, fresh from the heart, uncoloured by the air, gushed into the wave. 'Cursed be the murderer in his last hour!—Hell waits its victim.'....Well was it understood by Glenarvon. (365)

Glenarvon orders his men to follow the phantom ship and they travel from coast to coast after it until Glenarvon, now mad, jumps into the sea. He feels himself sinking into darkness, even when his companions rescue him. Oblivious to those around him, Glenarvon hears a voice condemn him, "you did not bow the knee for mercy whilst time was given you: now mercy shall not be shown" (366) and Glenarvon is condemned to the lowest pits. The novel concludes with the statement, "God is just; and the spirit of evil infatuates before he destroys" (366). This stunning conclusion declares there is no redemption for the Gothic wanderer who shows no mercy to his victims and who does not repent until the last hour. Unlike Calantha, Glenarvon completely fails to gain the reader's sympathy. His failure to repent makes him more typical of the Byronic hero who celebrates his rebellion and transgression than was Byron's own depiction of a vampire in *The Giaour*.

Glenarvon's condemnation is dramatic and stunning even beside the many other Gothic novels of the period. Lamb felt the novel tended to be too intense, so she made several major revisions in the second edition. Despite her obvious disgust with Lord Byron, Lamb toned down the characterization of Glenarvon as satanic (Clubbe 210), and she made Calantha and Glenarvon's relationship intimate, but not suggestively sexual as in the first edition (Clubbe 211). Most strikingly, the second edition is more respectful of religion, all references to "God" being either omitted or replaced by "Father" (Clubbe 212). Lamb also surprisingly predates other Gothic novelists in her use of Catholicism, when its adherents were still politically oppressed and the Gothic continually depicted the Catholic Church as corrupt. In the second edition, Calantha converts to Catholicism before her death, which Lamb felt was explainable by the novel's being set in Catholic Ireland (Wilson, Introduction xxiv). Lamb also adds a paragraph full of pious morality to describe how God forgives Calantha upon her death (Clubbe 212).

Glenarvon's importance in the Gothic tradition and its influence upon the vampire figure cannot be overestimated. While Glenarvon is not a vampire, his vampiric characteristics would influence John Polidori, whose famous story would make the vampire a popular figure in English fiction.

Glenarvon was also the first novel to redeem a transgressive Gothic wanderer figure, two decades before the Victorian period when such redemptions became common. Notably, the redeemed wanderer is a female, thus linking Calantha to the feminine Gothic tradition that seeks to vindicate Eve, and by extension all women, from being transgressors. Lamb's use of Catholicism in the second edition as a means to redemption may have influenced *Dracula*'s use of Catholic religious objects to destroy Dracula, thus vindicating Catholicism from its derogatory image in earlier Gothic novels. Lamb's depiction of a Gothic wanderer as redeemable would allow the vampire to become the most popular Gothic wanderer figure used by novelists to explore the psychological transformation of a person who passes from transgression to redemption as best demonstrated in the later works, *Varney the Vampyre* and *Dracula*.

Glenarvon was largely condemned by the critics, but notably, two Gothic novelists appreciated it. The painter, Northcote, recommended the novel to William Godwin as being a work of great talent. Because Godwin later became good friends with Lamb, he must have agreed (Wilson, "Lamb" 377). Edward Bulwer-Lytton remarked that when he was a schoolboy, *Glenarvon*:

> ...made a deeper impression than any romance I remember, and, had its literary execution equalled the intense imagination which conceived it, I believe it would have ranked among the few fictions which produce a permanent effect upon youth in every period of the world (Wilson, "Caroline" 377).

The novel made such an intense impression upon Bulwer-Lytton because he admired Byron and in youth wished to model his life after him. Later when Bulwer-Lytton met Lamb in 1824, the novel contributed to his infatuation with her, and he hoped he could replace Lord Byron in her affections, although she was clearly not interested in such a relationship (Campbell 5-6). Lord Byron's reaction is perhaps the most interesting though predictable. In a verse he wrote, he stated, "I read Glenarvon, too, by Caro Lamb—/ God damn!" (Maurois 353). He further remarked that if Lamb had written the truth, the book would have been far better, and "As for the likeness, the picture can't be good—I did not sit long enough" (Maurois 353).

While *Glenarvon* was the first novel to redeem the Gothic wanderer, the redemption of Lord Byron and Lady Caroline Lamb is more questionable. The novel ironically foreshadows in Glenarvon's death while fighting for Irish independence, Byron's own death in 1824, during which time he was assisting in the Greek cause for independence, and died in Greece from an illness. Lamb's own dramatic and often immoral life appears to have prevented her soul from achieving rest. Today, Lamb's former home of Brocket Hall is said to be haunted by her ghost, which walks the halls and can be heard playing the piano (Bextor). Perhaps

Lamb's decision to damn Glenarvon/Byron resulted in her own soul's damnation and eternal wandering.

The Vampyre: Establishing Fictional Vampire Elements

Glenarvon first suggested the possibilities for the vampire in fiction, but it was John Polidori's *The Vampyre* (1819) that popularized the vampire as a major figure in Western culture and British literature. Polidori's story was immensely popular upon its publication, largely because Lord Byron was believed to be the author. Critics continue to debate just how much of the story Polidori may have plagiarized from Byron, or at least based upon Byron's intended tale. The story originated during the famous summer of 1816 meeting in Switzerland between the Shelleys, Lord Byron, and Polidori, who was serving as Lord Byron's physician at the time. The group agreed to write ghost stories, as described in the Preface to *Frankenstein*, the result being both that novel and Polidori's *The Vampyre*. Originally, it was Byron who intended to write a tale about a vampire, while Polidori's original story idea resulted in his novel *Ernestus Berchtold*. Byron only wrote a fragment of his intended vampire story and then abandoned it. Polidori borrowed Byron's idea, but a comparison of *The Vampyre* to Byron's fragment shows no significant influence by the fragment upon *The Vampyre*. Twitchell even states that Lord Byron never intended or said he intended to write a vampire story. The fragment of the story contains no evidence that the main character, Darvell, was intended to be a vampire, and he is only described as "a being of no common order" (*Living* 172). Rather, Darvell appears to be a typical Byronic hero who wanders in exile because of some inner demon. Furthermore, when Darvell dies, his flesh rapidly decomposes, while vampires' bodies remain intact. Consequently, Polidori's idea to write a vampire story seems to be original to him (Twitchell, *Living* 114-5). Nevertheless, Polidori himself perpetuated the belief that Byron was the author of his story. He insisted that the work be published anonymously, then informed everyone that Byron had written the tale (Eisler 522). Byron denied authorship of the work, remarking, "If the book is clever it would be base to deprive the real writer—whoever he may be—of his honours;—and if stupid—I desire the responsibility of nobody's dullness but my own" (Grosskurth 343). Ironically, Goethe declared that *The Vampyre* was the best work Byron ever wrote (Twitchell, *Living* 107).

While Byron was neither the author nor literary source of *The Vampyre*, Polidori did base his vampire upon Byron, so Polidori can be accused of slander if not plagiarism (Twitchell, *Living* 108). Polidori's depiction of Lord Byron as a vampire probably resulted from the personal animosity that existed between the two of them, including heated verbal exchanges that eventually resulted in Byron discharging Polidori from his employment. In revenge, Polidori named his vampire Lord Ruthven (and later renamed it Lord Strongmore) so readers would identify the vampire with Lamb's *Glenarvon* whose title character was based on Lord Byron, had vampiric attributes, and was a member of the Ruthven family. Like Glenarvon, Lord Ruthven has the typical traits of a Byronic hero because he is an exile with a mysterious background (Gaull 250). Ruthven's exile is based upon Byron's own position as a social outcast after 1816. The reason for Byron's social ostracism is unclear, but possibly his wife learned of his homosexual and/or incestuous activities. Finding himself being spit upon in the streets, Byron felt it would be more tolerable to travel on the continent than remain in his native land (Twitchell, *Living* 104). He began his restless continental wandering in 1816, hiring Polidori as his physician. Polidori, therefore, witnessed Byron's wanderings which would come to embody both the wanderings of the Byronic hero and the literary vampire.

Mario Praz was the first to claim that the vampire would have never become a famous figure in English literature if it had not been for the Byronic hero or the belief that Byron had written Polidori's story (Twitchell, *Living* 75). While Byron's presumed authorship of *The Vampyre* cannot be underestimated as a cause for the story's popularity, neither can Polidori's creativity be ignored in his treatment of the vampire as a fearsome yet intriguing Gothic wanderer. Macdonald lists four significant innovations Polidori made to the vampire figure to establish the vampire's popularity and future influence upon the Gothic tradition.

1. Polidori makes his vampire not merely a spirit or a reanimated corpse but a being who is able to function in the daily world, whereas earlier folklore had been ambiguous about whether vampires could only be nocturnal.
2. Polidori makes Lord Ruthven an aristocrat. Before Polidori's tale, there were no aristocratic vampires, although aristocrats, in their treatment of the lower classes, were often depicted satirically as vampires.
3. Polidori's vampire is a traveller, which makes him a continual threat because he can travel anywhere.
4. Polidori's vampire is a seducer (thus satirizing Lord Byron). Before, vampires only preyed upon their friends or family members, but now the vampire could attack anyone, making him a greater threat to society. (192-6)

In addition to Macdonald's list, I would include Polidori's use of the vampire as a metaphor for capitalism. As discussed earlier in the chapter on gambling as Gothic transgression, *The Vampyre* uses the gambling motif to comment upon how capitalism can drain one's wealth as a vampire drains a person's blood. Polidori chose to make Lord Ruthven an aristocrat to draw upon the idea of the aristocracy's economic exploitation and political oppression of the lower classes. Lord Ruthven purposely gambles to make the poor lose and the rich win so the status quo will be maintained, which includes Ruthven's own aristocratic position of power.

Consequently, Lord Ruthven's aristocratic role becomes not only a satire of Lord Byron but a symbol of a mythologized upper class. While the aristocracy is interested in ancestral blood lines, Ruthven is interested in blood, and like the declining aristocracy, he needs new blood (and money) to revitalize himself (Punter, *Terror* 119).

Polidori's decision to make his vampire a seducer is partially to satirize Byron's notorious sexual escapades, but it also derives from the conventional sexual fear and anxiety expressed in Gothic novels. The vampire's traditional seduction of his family members is suggestive of incest, but Polidori's decision that his vampire may attack anyone makes the vampire all the more frightening because the disease of vampirism cannot be contained but can spread to anyone like a fatal venereal disease (Macdonald 201). Polidori links Ruthven's aristocratic and gambler roles to his role as seducer because Ruthven chooses only morally superior women to victimize. These women reside upon "the pinnacle of unsullied virtue" from which he seeks to hurl them "down to the lowest abyss of infamy and degradation" (37). Similarly, Ruthven seeks to destroy those who gamble by lowering their social positions. Ruthven's degradation of others is a means to protect his own isolated position of aristocratic power. In addition, Ruthven seeks out those with latent internal weaknesses, bringing these repressed tendencies into action so they are displayed to the world, thus making Ruthven the "catalyst" of others' destructions (Punter, *Terror* 118).

Polidori's innovations of the vampire included not only new attributes but a complex blending of the vampire character with many of the stock motifs of the Gothic wanderer figure. Polidori borrows from the Rosicrucian and Wandering Jew motifs by making Ruthven's eyes have hypnotic powers. In addition, like the Rosicrucian and the Wandering Jew, Ruthven as a vampire has a prolonged lifespan, which he achieves by sucking blood from young women; blood is forbidden for consumption in the Bible, so the vampire's blood drinking is a transgression against the laws of God and Nature (Roberts, *Gothic* 96). Polidori may have also drawn upon Masonic ideas, which were sometimes linked with Rosicrucianism because Masons had to take secret oaths (Macdonald 136). In *The Vampyre*, a secret oath occurs when Aubrey swears to Lord Ruthven that he will not reveal the crimes Ruthven has committed for one year. This oath is similar to those in other Gothic novels, including the vampire works of *Varney the Vampyre* and *Dracula*, which were linked to popular beliefs that secret societies had conspired to cause the French Revolution (Macdonald 192). Polidori, himself, would have been familiar with such oaths because he joined a British sect of the Freemasons, despite his being Catholic and the Catholic Church's excommunication of its members for joining such organizations (Macdonald 193). Although British freemasonry was considered respectable and apolitical in the nineteenth century (Macdonald 193), the secrecy of such groups made them suspect. The use of such oaths in literature, therefore, added to a novel's suspense.

Polidori's tale was so popular that he considered writing a sequel, which he never accomplished (Macdonald 171). Later, the French writer, Cyprien Berard, wrote a sequel *Lord Ruthven ou les vampires*, in which Lord Ruthven dies with a stake driven through his heart and his eyes gouged out (Stuart 47). More significantly, *The Vampyre* inspired all future depictions of vampires by establishing the elements of the vampire character. While Lord Ruthven's lack of remorse notably places him more closely in the Byronic hero tradition than that of the Gothic wanderer, Polidori's successors would adapt the vampire for their own purposes. During the Victorian period, the vampire would become a sympathetic figure in *Varney the Vampyre* and a transgressor capable of redemption in *Dracula*.

Varney the (Sympathetic) Vampyre

The threat Polidori's vampire poses to English society is only a precursor to the more severe threats of Varney the Vampyre and Dracula. Ironically, while Lord Ruthven's vampiric successors are more frightening, their creators are also more sympathetic toward them. The Victorian treatments of the Gothic wanderer, as discussed earlier in the works of Carlyle, Bulwer-Lytton, and Dickens, tend to provide a Christian redemption for the Gothic wanderer, and the Victorian vampire slowly moved toward a similar yet more dramatic redemption. In *Varney the Vampyre or, The Feast of Blood* (1847), the title character is slowly transformed by the author[1] from a monster to an object of sympathy, although he is never allowed full redemption. In *Dracula*, the vampire will be completely redeemed, albeit by force, thus allowing the Gothic wanderer to rest both in body and conscience.

Varney the Vampyre, a penny dreadful novel written in serial installments, is the intermediary novel in the transformation of the vampire from a monster to a redeemable and sympathetic character. Varney slowly makes such a transformation, passing from being a frightful, blood-thirsty beast in the opening chapter to a remorseful and guilt-ridden, almost human character by the novel's end. Varney's first appearance depicts him as severely lacking in humaneness as he attacks Flora Bannerworth.

---

[1] The authorship of *Varney the Vampyre* has never been fully determined. James Malcolm Rymer, a writer of penny dreadfuls, is the most likely candidate, but it's possible Thomas Peckett Prest was the author, or that the two collaborated since there is a notable shift in the writing throughout the time the serial ran, and the two authors collaborated on *The String of Pearls*, which first introduced the character of Sweeney Todd to readers, and ran from 1846-1847, almost the same period as *Varney the Vampyre* from 1845-1847.

> The glassy, horrible eyes of the figure ran over that angelic form with a hideous satisfaction—horrible profanation. He drags her head to the bed's edge. He forces it back by the long hair still entwined in his grasp. With a plunge he seizes her neck in his fang-like teeth—a gush of blood, and a hideous sucking noise follows. The girl has swooned, and the vampyre is at his hideous repast! (4)

Such descriptions are intended to revile and horrify the reader into believing the vampire cannot possibly be human. This passage, however, is the novel's most frightening depiction of the vampire. Had Varney remained only a nocturnal visitor who sucks the blood of innocent maidens, he may have continued to inspire fear in the reader's breast, but despite Varney's engagement in a few more hideous and evil acts, as the novel progresses, Varney is increasingly depicted as a complex and misunderstood being who is obviously trapped by the curse of vampirism, and like the Wandering Jew, wishes for an unobtainable release from his hideously supernatural existence. Even with the author's occasional attempts to make Varney detestable to prolong the suspense and complexity of the narrative, the reader gradually comes to sympathize with the vampire.

The conglomeration of Varney's character as monstrous vampire and sympathetic wanderer is typical in relation to the evolution of the Gothic wanderer in the early Victorian period. Varney himself embodies many of the characteristics of his literary Gothic wanderer predecessors, while he also adds to and enhances the tradition. Varney begins as a villain and monster like Montoni or Lord Ruthven, but he gradually becomes more sympathetic like Milton's Satan or the Wandering Jew. Varney's debt to the Wandering Jew is especially obvious throughout the novel. In the first descriptions of him, the negative attributes of the Jew are used, especially that of the glittering and hypnotic eyes. Within the first few pages, Varney's eyes are described as "those awful, metallic-looking eyes" (3), "his glittering eye" (4) and "the glassy, horrible eyes" (4). More importantly, like the Wandering Jew, Varney is made to wander for an indeterminate amount of time, and he is unable to destroy himself, which ultimately makes him sympathetic. Throughout the novel, Varney unsuccessfully seeks a bride. Eventually, he realizes no woman could ever love him, so weary of his horrid existence, he attempts to kill himself. Varney's misery is so intense that the narrator declares, "We pity thee, Varney!" (771), thus guiding the reader's feelings toward sympathy with a character the reader previously thought a monster. While the Wandering Jew is unable to die because the elements of water and fire refuse to destroy him, Varney is capable of destroying himself, but Nature continually brings him back to life. Whenever Varney dies, moonlight falls upon his corpse and resuscitates him, a type of resurrection that can only happen to a vampire. Varney must find a means of death by which he can be assured that his corpse will not be accidentally restored by the moon's rays. He decides that if he drowns himself, the ocean will pull him into its depths where the moon's rays will not be able to reach him. However, as with the Wandering Jew, the elements refuse to be an accomplice to Varney's death. The sea forces Varney's corpse to float on the waves, and then a storm sweeps a boat out to sea where Varney's body is floating.

The boat's sailors discover the floating body and retrieve it to give it a proper Christian burial. Before the burial can take place, however, the moonlight touches the corpse and Varney is restored to his dreadful existence. The novel clearly states that it is not by chance that Varney was restored, but that Nature or God forbids Varney's death. One of the sailors who rescues Varney's corpse remarks in correlation, "it seems as if we were driven out to sea by some special providence to do this piece of work, and that having done it, the winds and the waves obeyed the hand of their mighty Master, and allowed of our return" (776). Varney now realizes he cannot embrace death as he would wish, declaring, "The dye is cast; my fate has again spoken. Steel shall not slay me, the bullet shall kill me not, fire shall not burn me, and water will not drown while yon bright satellite sails on 'twixt earth and heaven" (782). The same words might have been spoken by the Wandering Jew, and notably, Varney uses the Gothic gambling metaphor to describe his fate.

Varney's character also owes a debt to Milton's Satan. Upon his first appearance in the novel, Varney had been associated with Satan's role as snake because Varney makes a "hissing sound" that protrudes from his throat when he speaks. Toward the novel's close, Varney's words and actions parallel Milton's Satan. Prior to Varney's attempt to drown himself, he had dreamt of walking in a garden, and "All around seemed to speak of the peace and loveliness of an Eden" (772). It was during this dream that he heard a voice tell him to drown himself. Apparently, Varney felt that death would be a way to restore paradise to himself, but suicide is a transgressive short-cut to such an attainment. Varney is now angered that he cannot die or be admitted to paradise, just as in *Paradise Lost*, Satan is angered that he is forbidden Heaven or the glories of Eden. While first regretting that he is about to tempt Adam and Eve, Satan feels unable to seek God's forgiveness, so he declares, "Farewell Remorse: all Good to me is lost; / Evil be thou my Good" (IV, 109-10). Varney's declaration is similar:

> Since death is denied to me, I will henceforward shake off all human sympathies. Since I am compelled to be that which I am, I will not be that and likewise suffer all the pangs of doing deeds at which a better nature that was within me revolted. No, I will from this time be the bane of all that is good and great and beautiful. If I am forced to wander upon the earth, a thing to be abhorred and accursed among men, I will perform my mission to the very letter as well as the spirit, and henceforth

adieu all regrets, adieu all feeling—all memory of goodness—of charity to human nature, for I will be a dread and a desolation! Since blood is to be my only sustenance, and since death is denied to me, I will have abundance of it—I will revel in it, and no spark of human pity shall find a home in this once racked and tortured bosom. Fate, I thee defy! (787)

Varney's determination to scourge the world with evil results in his attacking a beautiful young lady, Clara, whom he first kills, then resuscitates by transforming her into a vampiress, so he may have the mate he has so long desired. The villagers, however, soon realize Clara's corpse is a vampire, so they destroy her with a stake through the heart in a scene that may have later inspired the death scene of Lucy in *Dracula*. Varney now regrets that his evil deeds have resulted in Clara's destruction. Unlike Milton's Satan, who will not give into remorse, Varney's remorse now suggests the possibility of his redemption.

Varney mercifully buries Clara's corpse, and while thus engaged, the Reverend Mr. Bevan finds him. Mr. Bevan, aware that Varney is a vampire, chooses to help him by taking him home so Varney can rest in a safe place. Upon arriving at Mr. Bevan's home, Varney remarks, "I did not fancy that there existed a spot on earth on which I could lie down in peace, and yet it may be here" (846). While earlier Gothic wanderers had been denied rest, for Varney at least the possibility exists. Yet Varney feels that happiness and redemption are impossible for him, so all he can hope for is death. In response, Mr. Bevan tells Varney, "Do not say that. Who knows but that after all your living accomplishes better things?" (846). Varney, however, rejects the possibility that any good comes from his prolonged existence. Mr. Bevan replies that if vampires exist, God must have a purpose for them and humanity should not question the Creator's will (847). Varney, however, remains doubtful and finally, he destroys himself by jumping into a volcano to prevent the "possibility of a reanimation of his remains" (868).

The manner of Varney's death is difficult to interpret. The novel's conclusion seems to suggest that Varney is finally able to achieve rest; however, while Varney feels remorse over Clara's death, the novel shies away from the possibility of Varney's full repentance of his sins and a Christian redemption. Also inexplicable is why the volcano, like the sea earlier, does not reject Varney's body. Varney's death is a deviation from the Wandering Jew legend where the Jew attempts to destroy himself both by drowning and by jumping into a volcano, but he cannot find death by either means. Most likely, the author of *Varney the Vampyre* needed a way to end the serial and the volcano seemed the most believable form of death for an otherwise indestructible character. Apparently, the volcano provides no chance for the moon's rays to reach Varney and revive him. While the ending allows the reader to retain sympathy for Varney, the lack of Varney's redemption leaves the novel devoid of the cathartic ending that a greater novelist would have written, such as Dickens creates for *A Tale of Two Cities*. Nevertheless, the novel suggests the possibility of redemption and emphasizes God's mercy in that Varney is finally able to end his misery. While the novel's ending may not be completely satisfying, its unfulfilled possibilities would be realized in *Dracula*, both the greatest vampire novel and the culmination of the nineteenth century Gothic wanderer tradition.

Dracula's Historical Origins

Despite *Dracula*'s enormous popularity for over a century, to the extent that its title character is a household name and numerous films have been based upon it, the novel has only received significant critical attention since the 1970s. Twitchell suggests that had *Dracula* been published in 1797 rather than 1897, it would be hailed today as an important Romantic or Gothic novel, but because it appeared in the age of Realism and Naturalism, it was dismissed by critics as a "gothic non-sequitur" ("Vampire" 110). While the novel is fairly late for the Gothic tradition that flourished at the beginning of the nineteenth century, much of the novel makes it radically different from its early predecessors. Farson observes that "*Dracula* succeeds partly because it is not Gothic; to the Victorian reader it must have seemed daringly modern" (142). While the sexuality in *Dracula* is surprising in contrast to stereotypical beliefs in Victorians as sexually repressed, as a Gothic novel, *Dracula* is also startlingly different from its predecessors for two reasons: Dracula is never remorseful yet he is still a sympathetic character, and the novel portrays Catholicism as positive and necessary to defeat transgression, as compared to the derogatory depictions of Catholicism in the earlier Gothic novels of Radcliffe, Lewis, and Maturin. Consequently, the novel becomes both the apotheosis of the Gothic tradition while also its nemesis by reversing two of the tradition's most common elements. Finally, *Dracula* manifests that the Gothic's concern with the wanderer figure has itself wandered from its concentration upon the psychological guilt of transgression to how repentance results in redemption because God is merciful.

Stoker is indebted to his Gothic predecessors, but he is also brilliant in his use of historical and literary sources to create *Dracula*. Dracula, the only major Gothic wanderer with a historical basis, has his source in Vlad Tepes, a voivoide or ruler of Wallachia from 1456-1462 (Varnado 103). Vlad Tepes was a fierce warrior whose atrocities caused him to be regarded as a vampire. The Turks termed him Vlad the Impaler because he would impale his prisoners of war, then in a vampiric manner, grotesquely feast among the rows of his victims (Belford 259). For six years, Stoker researched his novel and found himself fascinated with Vlad Tepes. Despite the historical research, however, Stoker kept Dracula's origins ambiguous in the novel to make Dracula mythical in nature rather than a historical and factual portrait. Twitchell observes that the novel's obscure historical background makes the reader unable to predict what will happen or the motivation behind Dracula's behavior (*Living* 133). Such ambiguity enhances the reader's fears because Dracula's existence and the origins of his vampirism are never explained satisfactorily. The novel suggests that Dracula became a vampire because as a warrior he had a love for slaughter, and he was also knowledgeable of alchemy, which allowed him to prolong his life. In the novel, Dr. Van Helsing summarizes Dracula's past:

> ...he is of cunning more than mortal, for his cunning be the growth of ages; he have still the aids of necromancy, which is, as his etymology imply, the divination by the dead, and all the dead that he can come nigh to are for him at his command. (264)

However, this passage is unclear regarding whether by alchemy or necromancy Dracula became a vampire, or if Dracula has the powers of necromancy and control of the dead because he is a vampire. Dracula's family is stated to have long been connected with occultism. Van Helsing remarks of the family:

> The Draculas were, says Arminius, a great and noble race, though now and again were scions who were held by their coevals to have had dealings with the Evil One. They learned his secrets in the Scholomance, amongst the mountains over Lake Hermanstadt, where the devil claims the tenth scholar as his due. In the records are such words as 'stregoica'—witch, 'ordog,' and 'pokol'—Satan and hell; and in one manuscript this very Dracula is spoken of as 'wampyr,' which we all understand too well. (268-9)

Since the family members who had dealings with Satan were scholars, Dracula is typical of Gothic wanderers who quest for forbidden knowledge. Dracula may have sought knowledge of how to prolong his life, which he achieved by transforming himself into a vampire (Perkowski 133), or he may have been cursed with vampirism for his transgression in seeking forbidden knowledge. Dracula's origins in Eastern Europe make him more historical and believable to the reader than he would be if he had Western European ancestry, while also making Dracula's supernatural existence more plausible since Eastern Europe is a place of superstition in comparison to the more "civilized" or "enlightened" West. As Harker remarks in the novel, "every known superstition in the world is gathered into the horseshoe of the Carpathians, as if it were the centre of some sort of imaginative whirlpool" (8). Stoker was also probably influenced to give Eastern origins to Dracula because he was familiar with J.S. LeFanu's *Carmilla* (1872), a vampire story set in Styria. Originally, as testified to by the chapter Stoker deleted from *Dracula* entitled "Dracula's Guest,"

Stoker intended to place Dracula's castle in Styria, before changing its location to Transylvania (Milbank 14). Dracula's Eastern European origins in history and myth make Stoker's tale surpass Polidori's *The Vampyre* and *Varney the Vampyre* because Dracula is more convincingly real as a vampire from a culture that believes in vampires and half remembers them from its ancient past, so Dracula can return in the present as a more plausible threat (Wolf xii).

Dracula: The New Wandering Jew and Anti-Semitism

Stoker's ambiguity about Dracula's origins is part of the novel's strength but a frustration for the literary critic. It is impossible to know how easily Victorian readers accepted the plausibility of Dracula's existence. Readers today cannot recreate such an experience because our culture is saturated with images of vampires that make readers knowledgeable about Dracula from childhood; consequently, those who read *Dracula* today are already willing to suspend their disbelief. Stoker's personal feelings toward his famous character are equally difficult to determine; he appears to have both loathed and sympathized with Dracula, and therefore, placed Dracula in the role of outcast, a role with which Stoker, as an Irishman living in England, may have identified. Dracula's role as racial outsider results from Stoker giving him Jewish attributes and largely basing him on depictions of the Wandering Jew. Although not Jewish, Stoker's first name, Abraham, may have resulted in people believing he was Jewish. His role as Irish outsider may have further allowed Stoker to identify with the Jews as outcasts. Finally, Stoker's homosexual inclinations meant he had to hide his true nature, so Stoker may have felt he was living under a false identity as Dracula must conceal his vampirism to survive (Malchow 155). Dracula's eroticism may have resulted from Stoker's own repressed sexuality. After 1895, Oscar Wilde's famous trial resulted in laws against homosexuality becoming stricter, meaning Stoker would have feared to have his homosexuality discovered. Stoker personally knew Oscar Wilde, so Wilde's situation must have caused Stoker emotional turmoil. Stoker may have even loathed his own sexual inclinations because he feared the discrimination that resulted from Wilde's trial. Consequently, Dracula's roles as outsider, pseudo-Jewish, and sexually deviant may have been an embodiment of those personal qualities that most bothered Stoker. This personal self-loathing may have made Stoker both sympathize with Dracula and simultaneously detest him. Stoker's sympathy toward Dracula resulted in Dracula's redemption, but Stoker's personal self-hatred prevented Dracula's redemption from occurring by any means but violent destruction.

Besides his possible personal identification with the Jews as outcasts, Stoker was very interested in the legend of the Wandering Jew, whose attributes are echoed in Dracula. Stoker may have known the works of Lewis and Maturin, but he was most fascinated by French author Eugene

Sue's *The Wandering Jew* (1845), which depicts the figure as a rebel and Romantic wanderer who achieves the reader's sympathy by his benevolence toward humanity. The Wandering Jew becomes the hero of the work by defeating humanity's real enemies, the Jesuits (Malchow 149, 156). Stoker's fascination with Sue's novel resulted in his heavily researching the Wandering Jew legend in the British Museum, as he did with the vampire legend. Stoker's friend, Hall Caine, later remarked that the Wandering Jew became "one of Bram's pet themes" (Malchow 156), and Stoker would include a section on the Wandering Jew in his book on famous impostors (Malchow 156). As secretary to the famous actor Henry Irving, Stoker even suggested that Irving perform a dramatic version of Sue's novel (Malchow 156). There is good evidence, therefore, that Stoker intentionally used the Wandering Jew as a source for his depiction of Dracula.

Dracula's debt to the Wandering Jew is most obvious in their shared physical characteristics. An 1873 stage version of Eugene Sue's novel, produced by George Lander, describes the Wandering Jew as having "long jet-black hair and jet-black eyebrows, dressed in a long black robe" (Malchow 156-7). Dracula's description is similar and may have been derived from Stoker's memory of the play. Of course, the obvious physical similarity between the Wandering Jew and all vampires is the emphasis upon the eyes. Dracula has the same powerful hypnotic eyes attributed to the Wandering Jew, but Stoker also elaborates upon the eye description by giving Dracula's eyes a red gleam suggestive of the "evil eye." According to Matthew 6:22-3, the eye reflects the state of the soul, and Dracula's eyes suggest this connection early in the novel. When Dracula makes his first appearance, his "eyes gleamed" (26), and later when Dracula sees that Jonathan Harker has cut himself while shaving, his eyes "blazed with a sort of demoniac fury" (34). Such descriptions reveal Dracula's true evil nature (Wolf 10).

Dracula further shares with the Wandering Jew a supernaturally extended life. Both characters converse with great knowledge of the past, which amazes listeners who are ignorant of the speakers' extensive ages. Such is Jonathan Harker's experience upon first hearing Dracula's conversation.

> In his speaking of things and people, and especially of battles, he spoke as if he had been present at them all. This he afterwards explained by saying that to a boyar the pride of his house and name is his own pride, that their glory is his glory, that their fate is his fate. Whenever he spoke of his house he always said "we," and spoke almost in the plural, like a king speaking. I wish I could put down all he said exactly as he said it, for to me it was most fascinating. It seemed to have in it a whole history of the country. (37)

While Dracula and the Wandering Jew share protracted lifespans, they are in opposition in their desires for such long lives. The Wandering Jew is weary of life and longs for death, but Dracula actively seeks to prolong his life by his supernatural activities. William Day observes that for Dracula to become supernatural, he must both be part of the natural world, while correspondingly reversing natural biological processes. In the natural world, the living feed on the dead, but Dracula is the dead who feeds on the living, and by this feeding he prolongs his life (41).

Dracula's active desire to prolong his life is largely achieved by his ability to control Nature. By contrast, the Wandering Jew has no control over Nature, which acts against him as when the water recedes if the Jew attempts to drown himself, or the volcano spits out the Jew if he tries to jump in. Dracula, however, can control Nature, thus prolonging his life by his ability to move about in various forms, granting him numerous advantages and means for seducing potential victims while protecting himself from capture or destruction. In the novel, Dr. Van Helsing explains Dracula's power over Nature:

> ...he can, within limitations, appear at will when, and where, and in any of the forms that are to him; he can, within his range, direct the elements; the storm, the fog, the thunder; he can command all the meaner things: the rat, and the owl, and the bat—the moth, and the fox, and the wolf; he can grow and become small; and he can at times vanish and come unknown. (265)

Dracula's control of the elements suggests his role as Antichrist because he has Christ-like powers. Christ is able to control the elements as in Mark 4:39-41 when he calms a storm at sea to protect his disciples. This idea of a Gothic character controlling the elements is not original to Stoker, who may have borrowed it from Bulwer-Lytton. In Bulwer-Lytton's *The Last Days of Pompeii* (1834), the evil magician, Arbaces, is believed by the other characters to have control over the elements, and in the same author's "The Haunted and the Haunters" (1857), a character remarks that a mesmerist, Richards, has similar powers: "I have seen him affect even the weather, disperse or collect clouds, by means of a glass tube or wand" (322). Dracula's ability to "vanish and come unknown" also links him to the Wandering Jew who inexplicably can appear and disappear from places, especially at moments of historical importance. Stoker borrows the Jew's mysterious movements for Dracula, but provides an explanation for how Dracula achieves such mobility.

Stoker also builds upon the Wandering Jew's connection to the biblical Cain in his depiction of Dracula. The Wandering Jew traditionally bears a mark on his forehead that recalls the mark God gave to Cain for murdering Abel. Beirman states that Stoker was fascinated by the tale of Cain's murder of Abel and planted the biblical story in the novel (Farson

155). Dracula receives a mark like that of Cain when Jonathan Harker strikes him upon the forehead. In revenge, Dracula places a mark upon Mina's forehead, signifying that she belongs to him, so she is now an outcast from heaven like himself (Wolf 270). Dracula is further connected to Cain when his disciple, Renfield, refers to himself as Enoch, the biblical son of Cain (Farson 155).

Stoker made one final connection between Dracula and the Wandering Jew that he later deleted from the final version of *Dracula*. In the original second chapter that was later removed, Jonathan Harker's journey to Dracula's castle includes a stop in Munich, where he sees a performance of Wagner's opera, *The Flying Dutchman*. The story of the Flying Dutchman is similar to that of the Wandering Jew; the Dutch captain must roam the seas forever in a cursed phantom ship until Judgment Day because he defied God by committing murder like the biblical Cain (Belford 217).

While Stoker's interest in the Wandering Jew carried over into aspects of Dracula's character, Stoker's use of Jewish characteristics for Dracula also reflected the growing anti-Semitism of late Victorian England. Anti-Semitism was becoming popular at the end of the nineteenth century because of increased migrations of Eastern European and especially Jewish people into England (Zanger 34). During this period, the press continually discussed the Jewish "problem," largely by attacking the immigration of Jews into England and the financial world, with which they were stereotypically associated (Malchow 130). While Stoker could have had his novel consist of Jonathan Harker's visit to Transylvania, Stoker's decision to have the novel center around Dracula's migration to England is intended to symbolize the migration of Eastern European Jews to England in the late nineteenth century (Malchow 162). Dracula's intent to colonize England with a race of vampires reflects an English fear that the Jews would take over England. The destruction of the "Jewish" Dracula becomes a "socially acceptable" way to express a widespread English desire to rid England of the Jews (Zanger 36). Stoker's self-loathing of himself as an outcast, and his identification with the Jews as outcasts, may have contributed to his depiction of Dracula's murder, thus granting the novel an anti-Semitic layer of meaning.

Besides his literary origins in the Wandering Jew, Dracula has numerous other Jewish attributes, especially his role as a racial outsider. Dracula fears recognition as an outsider while he is in England, so he explains to Jonathan Harker that he wishes to blend in with English society. Dracula's role as "Other," however, largely operates from his being a vampire and his perverse sexual behavior represented by his blood sucking. Dracula as "Other" poses a sexual threat in the novel that flourishes upon myths that Eastern and dark skinned men, including Africans and Jews, have greater sexual prowess than Western European men (Hatten 129, Malchow 149, 151). Such sexual fears of the "Other" resulted in numerous stereotypes of the Jewish people during the Victorian period, including their being rapists, cannibals, and polygamists. Dracula's forced seduction of Lucy and Mina are symbolic of rape. Rape was an activity associated with Jews because of the murders committed by Jack the Ripper. Among the suspects for the identity of Jack the Ripper was a Jewish kosher butcher who had the instruments and the skills required to carry out the mutilations the Ripper inflicted upon his victims (Zanger 42). Of the one hundred thirty people questioned as suspects for being Jack the Ripper, a high proportion of them were Jewish, and ultimately, the police decided Jack the Ripper was probably a lower-class Jew from London's East End (164). The widespread belief that Jack the Ripper was Jewish reflects the racism of Victorian England that sought to blame the Jews for its problems. Stoker capitalized upon this racist stereotyping by depicting Dracula as a sexual predator.

Besides being regarded as rapists, Jewish people were stereotyped with various forms of sexual deviance, including intended corruption of women and the innocent. In George DuMaurier's *Trilby* (1894), Svengali the Jew has hypnotic eyes which he uses to seduce the heroine Trilby to carry out his will. Similarly, Dracula seduces Mina, and then tries to force her to help him in protecting himself from his enemies. Jews were also depicted as corrupting children. In *Oliver Twist* (1838), Fagin preys upon boys, using them as tools for his acquisition of wealth. More severe depictions included Jewish men as cowardly homosexual degenerates who preyed upon innocent boys; such representations easily extended to the metaphor that Jews were like vampires, for vampires seek their victims during nocturnal hours, the same time when homosexuals are most likely to contact one another (Malchow 141, 163). Vampires, Jews, and homosexuals were also all associated with strange smells believed to arise from the bodily emissions of masturbation or the fecund odor of sodomy (Malchow 141). Jewish men were even believed to menstruate; this bleeding provided yet another metaphorical link to vampires (Mulvey-Roberts, "*Dracula*" 830). After Oscar Wilde's trial in 1895, anxieties increased over gender issues, and Stoker, who had his own anxieties over his homosexuality, used such anxieties to make Dracula all the more frightening by suggesting his sexual deviance (Gary Day 82).

More popular as a Jewish stereotype than their perverted sexuality was the belief that Jews were wealthy. Because many Jews were usurers, they were comparable to vampires because they could financially drain their debtors. Blood and money became metaphors for one another because both are necessary to sustain life. Consequently, Jews, and especially usurers, were treated as types of vampires in literature. In Mary Shelley's *Valperga* (1823), usury is associated with vampirism when Castruccio, upon learning that Pepi has engaged in usury, calls Pepi, "Thou vile Jew...A usurer, a bloodsucker!" (216). In Charles Dickens' *Dombey and Son* (1848), during an estate auction "herds of shabby vampires, Jew and Christian, over-run the house" (Pool 98). At least, Dickens admits that

Christians can behave as badly as Jews. In Anthony Trollope's *The Way We Live Now* (1875), the Jewish financier and swindler, Melmotte, is described as swallowing up the property of all whom he does business with, which is likened to his feeding upon the blood of widows and children (Zanger 38). Stoker builds upon such stereotypes by depicting Dracula as extremely wealthy and also miserly in his hiding of his money—he has a hidden treasure in Transylvania which is marked by a blue flame. Dracula's extreme wealth is most dramatically depicted when the male protagonists attempt to capture Dracula at his London house. In the attack, Dracula's clothes are torn, resulting in gold and bank notes falling from his clothing as if he were bleeding money (339). This scene recalls Shylock's famous speech about Jews in *The Merchant of Venice*, "If you prick us, do we not bleed?" (III, i, 56) (Zanger 42).

Stoker also uses typical stereotypes regarding the Jewish religion to enhance Dracula's role as vampire. Jews were falsely believed to drink blood in their religious rituals, although the Old Testament specifically forbid blood consumption (Leviticus 10:14, Deuteronomy 12:23). Furthermore, Jews were frequently depicted as murdering Christians to obtain blood for their Passover feasts (Zanger 37). Dracula's blood consumption, therefore, aligns his activities with the Jewish religion, and makes both appear as the reverse of Christianity. Dracula is likened to the vengeful God of the Old Testament, who demands blood sacrifices; therefore, Dracula's blood consumption reflects the metaphor that the Jewish people's Old Testament religion is a form of vampirism (Malchow 161-2).

These numerous Jewish attributes associated with vampires make Dracula the embodiment of a racist stereotype. His destruction, then, may be read as a form of racist murder and an attempt to preserve racial purity in England. At the same time, his outsider status makes him somewhat sympathetic to a modern reader. Dracula's role as outcast is also based in his Jewish attributes because like the Jews, he is denied the salvation that Christians are promised. Dracula's evil and supernatural nature and his blasphemy of Christianity ultimately cast him in the role of Antichrist.

Dracula as Antichrist: The Gothic Redemption of Catholicism

When comparing Lord Ruthven and Varney to Dracula, the first two characters appear almost laughable beside the horror of Dracula's character. Dracula entices and fascinates readers because of the extremity of his evil. Not only has Dracula committed multiple transgressions of life-extension, sexual promiscuity, and religious blasphemy, but as an embodiment of Satan, he becomes God's rival, a type of Antichrist, who seeks to convert the world to vampirism. Consequently, *Dracula* transcends its Gothic genre to become a religious novel about the mysteries of religion and the salvation of humanity. Most remarkable about the novel's religious aspects is that it not only redeems its evil Gothic wanderer, but it does so by embracing Catholicism, which had previously been depicted in the Gothic tradition as a more horrendous and depraved religion than even Judaism.

The early Gothic novels of Radcliffe, Lewis, and Maturin were full of corrupt Catholic priests and nuns who commit hideous crimes. Exceptions to these negative depictions of Catholicism, such as Polidori's *Ernestus Berchtold*, Fanny Burney's *The Wanderer*, and the second edition of Lamb's *Glenarvon* depicted Catholicism positively but did little to defend it against its detractors. By the Victorian period, however, Gothic novels had discontinued their abuse of the Catholic Church. One probable reason for this shift was the passage of the Catholic Emancipation Act in 1829, which gave Catholics the same legal rights as Protestants, so further literary attacks against Catholicism would have been tasteless and pointless (Ellis, *Castle* 207). Furthermore, the Oxford Movement of the 1830s resulted in several Anglican clergyman converting to Catholicism and achieving high positions in that Church, including John Henry Newman who was admitted to the Roman Catholic Church in 1845 and later became a cardinal. Stoker's choice to reintroduce Catholicism to a major role in the Gothic novel was innovative in itself, but to depict Catholicism positively was remarkably daring. Catholicism may even be described as the true hero of *Dracula* because it is the tool by which Dracula is finally destroyed. While early Gothic novels had depicted Catholicism as a religion of superstition, in *Dracula*, the superstitions are treated as orthodox religious beliefs that can defeat a vampire. Stoker's novel theorizes that to destroy vampires, one needs sacred Catholic objects such as crucifixes and the Eucharistic host, which symbolize and embody God's power.

It is unclear why Stoker chose to give Catholicism such an important emphasis in *Dracula*. While Stoker was an Anglican, his Irish background must have made him familiar with the Catholic religion. Jules Zanger observes that prior to *Dracula*, literary vampires could be destroyed without religious methods, as were Oneiza in *Thalaba the Destroyer*, Lord Ruthven, and Varney. Zanger also remarks that while the crucifix, rosary, and host were all traditionally associated with the vampire, Stoker was the first writer to give them such emphasis (39-40). Perhaps Stoker felt that for a Gothic wanderer to be adequately redeemed, a Christian redemption was necessary, as Bulwer-Lytton or Dickens had already suggested. The Gothic wanderers of these novelists, however, were not evil supernatural beings; therefore, Dracula would need a more powerful and dramatic method of redemption. Since Stoker's audience would be predominantly English Protestants, they may have resented or found laughable any depiction of vampire hunting by their own clergy. Stoker may have also realized that the majority of his readers would be largely ignorant about Catholicism so the religious methods by which Dracula is destroyed would be less questionable to readers. Ironically then, Catholicism's redemption in the Gothic may have been due to the same religious ignorance as were its earlier derogatory depictions.

To enhance Dracula's role as transgressor and Antichrist figure, Stoker has Dracula commit blasphemy against not only Christianity, but specifically, against Catholicism. Dracula's blood-consumption is portrayed as a blasphemous inversion of the Catholic doctrine of transubstantiation in which the Eucharist's bread and wine literally transform into Christ's body and blood. Hatten observes that Dracula is a "Christian literalist" who believes that the blood is the life, but who rejects the blood of Christ, by which he can achieve eternal spiritual life, in preference for the blood of his victims, which will prolong his physical life (126). Dracula both perverts Christian theology and transgresses against the Bible's prohibition against drinking blood (Deuteronomy 12:16, Leviticus 17:10-2, and Genesis 9:4). Leviticus 17:10-12 explicitly prohibits consumption of blood because blood is to be given to God as sacrifice for atonement. Anyone who drinks blood will be rejected by God.

> And if anyone, whether of the house of Israel or of the aliens residing among them, partakes of any blood, I will set myself against that one who partakes of blood and will cut him off from among his people. Since the life of a living body is in its blood, I have made you put it on the altar, so that atonement may thereby be made for your own lives, because it is the blood, as the seat of life, that makes atonement. That is why I have told the Israelites: No one among you, not even a resident alien, may partake of blood. (New American Bible)

Dracula's consumption of blood makes him an outcast from God. The blood, however, provides Dracula with strengthened life and supernatural abilities, thus granting Dracula a form of "at/one/ment" with the source of all Being, so that he is godlike (Hatten 126).

Dracula's role as Antichrist is further emphasized in his follower Renfield, who accepts Dracula's teaching that the blood is the life. Renfield compares himself to the biblical Enoch, not only Cain's son but also the other Enoch who was the great-grandfather of Noah, saying he is "somewhat in the position which Enoch occupied spiritually," then explains, "Because he [Enoch] walked with God" (299). While Dr. Seward does not at once understand Renfield's analogy, Renfield can compare himself to Enoch walking with God (Genesis 5:24) because Renfield is the servant of Dracula, who as Antichrist places himself on God's level. Renfield also refers to Dracula as "Master," a parody of how Christ is commonly addressed in the gospels (William Day 144). The strongest comparison between Dracula and Christ is Dracula's immortality and his power to resurrect the dead. Dracula's power is limited, however, because he can only resurrect the physical body whereas Christ can also resurrect the soul (Varnado 97). Dracula believes, nevertheless, that by resurrecting people as vampires, he can be God's equal as Creator of a new race (Farson 157).

Dracula's role as Antichrist primarily functions around his inversion of the Catholic sacraments. Besides his blood-consumption being an inversion of the sacrament of the Eucharist, Dracula's activities make allusions to the sacraments of baptism and marriage. All three sacraments are defiled during the dramatic scene in which Dracula seduces Mina. Dracula breaks into the bedchamber of Mina and Jonathan, and while Jonathan remains asleep, Dracula symbolically rapes Mina. First Dracula sucks Mina's blood; then he forces her to consume his own. The scene is symbolically a primal one in which Dracula is the strong and potent father while Jonathan lies asleep, but nevertheless a witness to the parents' sexual activity (Roth, "Suddenly" 64). The primal significance is intensified when the other male characters enter the room and witness this scene. The Gothic emphasis upon patriarchy and its faults are here evident both because Dracula takes on a paternal role of power and his aristocratic position as a count gives him the "droit du seigneur," right of the lord, to violate any woman he chooses (Bentley 32). By sucking Mina's blood, Dracula is consummating his relationship with her, a symbolic type of marriage. Dracula then tells Mina, in words resembling those of the Catholic marriage ceremony, that she is now "flesh of my flesh; blood of my blood; kin of my kin; my bountiful wine-press for a while; and shall be later on my companion and my helper" (319). Dracula's speech is biblical in tone for Eve was flesh of Adam's flesh, having been formed from Adam's rib (Wolf 255). Like Milton's Satan, Dracula has chosen the weaker of the two sexes to prey upon as the easiest way to bring about the fall of humanity. Following Mina's seduction by Dracula, Jonathan remarks that he would rather become a vampire with Mina than have her be alone. Similarly, in *Paradise Lost,* Adam eats the apple so he will not be separated from Eve. According to Catholic doctrine, if Jonathan became a vampire, even if out of love for Mina, he would be guilty of sin and suicide because he would lose his soul. While Dracula interprets his seduction of Mina as a marriage, Van Helsing regards it as a defilement of the sacrament of baptism, referring to it as "the Vampire's baptism of blood" (357). Mina has been baptized or initiated into the knowledge of the vampire, making her Dracula's follower, just as a Catholic is baptized to demonstrate that he or she is a follower of Christ.

Dracula's sacrilegious inversion of the sacraments conveys how closely interlinked are good and evil in Stoker's novel (Wolf 264). This connection is all the more apparent when the protagonists fight Dracula with the very sacraments he profanes. When the men discover Dracula with Mina, they drive him away by holding up the sacred Eucharistic host (313). They also use the Eucharistic host to sanctify the soil upon which Dracula sleeps so he is unable to rest. Wolf points out that the use of the host by Van Helsing is a profanation against Catholic doctrine's prohibition against the body of Christ touching the earth. Theoretically, a host that touches the earth should immediately decay, but Van Helsing places hosts upon the soil of Dracula's coffins without their being destroyed (Wolf 188, 264). That the hosts do not decay may reflect Stoker's ignorance about Catholic beliefs, or Stoker's belief that because the soil in Dracula's coffins is holy ground, the host would not decay upon it. Stoker is himself responsible for the idea that vampires can only sleep upon holy ground, another means by which Stoker sought to demonstrate the close alignment between good and evil (Wolf 264). While Dracula's need to sleep on holy ground is another sign of his profanation of the sacred, Wolf argues that it may also be a sign or foreshadowing of hope for Dracula's redemption (215).

The Redemption of Dracula

Dracula's redemption is more complex and difficult than the redemption of other Gothic wanderers because he feels no remorse for his transgressive actions, and he does not seek release from his vampiric nature. Nevertheless, without sentimentalizing him, Stoker presents Dracula as sympathetic because his vampirism possesses him so that his soul is unable to repent. Van Helsing even observes that some good has resulted from Dracula's existence:

> There have been from the loins of this very one great men and good women, and their graves make sacred the earth where alone this foulness can dwell. For it is not the least of its terrors that this evil thing is rooted deep in all good; in soil barren of holy memories it cannot rest. (269)

Dracula's existence has brought about good by his descendants, and ironically, he can only rest on the soil where their holy bodies have been buried. Stoker may have derived the idea that Dracula has brought about some good from *Varney the Vampyre* when Mr. Bevan told Varney not to wish for death, "Do not say that. Who knows but that after all your living accomplishes better things?" (846). Stoker is again depicting how closely aligned are good and evil, and that despite Dracula's vampirism, his soul retains a desire for salvation (Wolf 215). Van Helsing believes Dracula should be pitied because he is unable to redeem himself although he subconsciously desires it. This belief inspires the characters to take it upon themselves as a sacred duty to destroy Dracula's body so his soul may be freed.

Phyllis Roth observes that Dracula attains the reader's sympathy in several passages where he is raised above merely a hated monster to a position where he is both "dignified" and "pitiable" (*Bram* 95-6). The two key scenes where Dracula achieves sympathy are based in the novel's moral and theological belief in redemption and the ultimate power of good over evil. The passages grant Dracula a psychological complexity far beyond that of a mere stereotypical villain. The first scene occurs at Dracula's castle when Jonathan feels fascination for the Count despite his recent realization that he is a prisoner in Dracula's castle. Jonathan finds Dracula's conversation about Transylvanian history to be "most fascinating" (37). The significant role of the Count's family in his nation's history grants him an air of dignity and importance. Dracula's words suggest that he embodies a noble tradition that has been forgotten by the modern world, and Jonathan feels that Dracula's words have nearly transported him back in time, just as his journey by train to Eastern Europe has been like a journey from the modern world of Western logic and science to the medieval past. Dracula represents a forgotten knowledge which Jonathan is now made aware of and can carry back with him to the West. Consequently, Dracula's speech reveals his importance as one who has a contribution to make to the West in terms of his knowledge and even his embodiment of older and more mythical ways of life. Dracula acquires further sympathy in this scene because he is the last of his race who seeks to preserve a diminishing way of life, although Jonathan does not realize this race is one of vampires. While Dracula will ultimately be destroyed, Jonathan records this information into his journal to preserve it, and later when the history of the crusade against Dracula is written, Dracula's knowledge is imparted to the world.

Dracula acquires even greater sympathy when Mina tells the men that they should pity Dracula because he suffers from his vampirism. Dracula's victimization of Mina has allowed her to understand the anguish he suffers as a vampire; she reminds the men that she and Lucy have become like vampires, yet the men still love them, and Dracula deserves the same understanding.

> Jonathan dear, and you all my true, true friends, I want you to bear something in mind through all this dreadful time. I know that you must fight—that you must destroy even as you destroyed the false Lucy so that the true Lucy might live hereafter; but it is not a work of hate. That poor soul who has wrought all this misery is the saddest case of all. Just think what will be his joy when he, too, is destroyed in his worser part that his better part may have spiritual immortality. You must be pitiful to him, too, though it may not hold your hands from his destruction. (341-2)

Jonathan is less willing to act with Christian understanding toward Dracula because the cursed mark on Mina's brow has made her an "outcast from God" (341). In his desire for revenge, Jonathan exclaims, "May God give him into my hand just for long enough to destroy that earthly life of him which we are aiming at. If beyond it I could send his soul for ever and ever to burning hell I would do it!" (342). Mina counters his argument by again comparing herself to Dracula, "Just think, my dear....I, too, may need such pity; and that some other like you—and with equal cause for anger—may deny it to me!" (342). Mina preaches the Christian practice, "Do unto others as you would have them do unto you," and she takes on a role like the Virgin Mary because she intercedes for Dracula as the Virgin Mary intercedes with God to save souls (Weissman 74).

While the quest to destroy Dracula is necessary to extinguish his threat to humanity, the quest becomes a religious crusade comparable to those of the Middle Ages. The protagonists become crusaders intent to destroy an infidel, Dracula the vampire, but also to free the holy land, which is Dracula's soul (Zanger 39). The crusade's religious connotation is apparent when the protagonists make a compact around a crucifix, yet another example of Catholicism's role in the novel.

> The Professor stood up and, after laying his golden crucifix on the table, held out his hand on either side. I [Mina] took his right hand, and Lord Godalming his left; Jonathan held my right with his left and stretched across to Mr. Morris. So as we all took hands our solemn compact was made. (265-6)

Van Helsing then remarks, "We go out as the old knights of the Cross to redeem...we are pledged to set the world free" (355). Van Helsing sees their quest as a Christ-like sacrifice to redeem humanity because they "are willing to peril even our own souls for the safety of one we love—for the good of mankind, and for the honour and glory of God" (356). Dracula has become both the obstacle and the goal of the quest, for he is to be both destroyed and redeemed.

While the protagonists can interpret their need to destroy Dracula as an act of Christian mercy and kindness, the narrative is one-sided by being solely written from the protagonists' point of view. Because Dracula is depicted as having Eastern and Jewish attributes, his destruction can be interpreted as a form of racist genocide that leaves a deeply disturbing portrait of the writer and his culture. The novel persuades the reader to identify with the protagonists and to believe their mission is just. Roth argues that the novel's protagonists use Christianity as an excuse to validate their destruction of Dracula. Surprisingly for such a modern novel, Dracula is never allowed to speak for himself. When Dracula does speak, his words are filtered through the writing of his enemies. Carol Senf observes that the novel presents only one side of the story in the form of a biased and never objective narrative ("*Dracula*" 95). Furthermore, the redemption of Dracula's soul when he is destroyed is questionable since only Mina Harker describes it, although her sympathy for Dracula makes her the most reliable narrator despite her having been his victim. That Dracula is redeemed and is pleased with this redemption is suggested by the sign of peace that appears on his face after he is killed. Nevertheless, only Mina's word testifies to this redemption. She describes Dracula's death after he is stabbed in the heart as:

> It was like a miracle; but before our very eyes, and almost in the drawing of a breath, the whole body crumbled into dust and passed from our sight.
>
> I shall be glad as long as I live that even in that moment of the final dissolution, there was in the face a look of peace, such as I never could have imagined might have rested there. (414-5)

This miraculous look of peace upon Dracula's face validates the protagonists' Christian crusade against Dracula. The protagonists can feel honorable about the murder, not only because they have eliminated Dracula's threat, but as Roth remarks, they can read the peaceful expression as a "thank you note" from Dracula for freeing his soul by physically destroying him (*Bram* 116). How to interpret Dracula's death, therefore, is rather simple for the protagonists. The men have killed Dracula out of love for Mina. Quincey Morris even acquires Christ-like status by himself being killed in the sacrificial battle (Kilgour 57). Terry Heller argues that because Dracula's murder is an act of love on the protagonists' part, it is less a killing than a "transformation" (82). His death illustrates Christ's teaching that we can only gain our lives by losing them (Raible 107). The transformation occurs for Mina as well, for the moment Dracula dies, the mark on Mina's forehead is washed clean as snow (416).

The protagonists' interpretation of Dracula's death, however, is not necessarily shared by the reader. Modern readers may feel that Dracula has become merely the scapegoat for the characters, and his destruction somehow relieves all their sexual and racist anxieties. His death, therefore, occurs primarily because of the characters' self-interested motives. Is it fair to force redemption upon Dracula, who never felt the need or desire to be redeemed? Furthermore, if Dracula is representative of the Jewish people, how is his death to be interpreted? Does the novel suggest that like Dracula, the Jewish people are ignorant of their need for redemption because they refuse to accept Christ as the Messiah, and consequently, they must either be destroyed or converted for their own good and that of humanity? Ultimately, perhaps the only resolution to be made about the Jewish issue in the novel is that Stoker had contradictory or unresolved feelings, which makes the novel too complex to read with either a completely pro or anti-Jewish interpretation. Maggie Kilgour remarks that the real hero of *Dracula* is writing because only when the characters assemble together all the various texts can they understand Dracula well enough to destroy him (53, 56). Writing is equally the hero for the protagonists because they can interpret Dracula's death from their own point of view, thus vindicating themselves from any wrongdoing or questionable motives. Interpretation of Dracula's death remains more difficult for the reader.

Dracula's destruction symbolizes a revolutionary overthrow of the tyrannical aristocratic and patriarchal power he represented to allow for a new order, a new future, and even a new century. Waller comments "From the dust of the King-Vampire and the blood of the primal tyrant comes the restoration or the creation of a new patriarchy based on the family and on God the Father" (qtd. in Williams 122). With Dracula's death, Paradise has been restored. The novel's conclusion, therefore, is the perfect ending for the entire nineteenth century Gothic tradition that sought to restore paradise and make the Gothic wanderer's desire for its restoration possible by his own redemption. Dracula's soul has been redeemed, while for the protagonists, a domestic form of paradise upon earth has been established. The Gothic's repeated concern with the sanctity of the family has been fulfilled by the establishment of a new family, whose members are all intertwined by links of blood and friendship. The "Note" at the novel's end states: "Seven years ago we all went through the flames; and the happiness of some of us since then is, we think, well worth the pain we endured" (416). This final entry is fittingly written by Jonathan Harker who also made the novel's first entry, so the work acquires a circular pattern that returns the characters to the innocence they knew before Dracula's threat, yet it is wise innocence because they have gained knowledge from Dracula. The passing of seven years since Dracula's death is a symbolic amount of time that suggests the idyllic life the protagonists now have. That their present happiness was "well worth the pain we endured" recalls the biblical promise of good arising from evil as Adam and Eve's transgression ultimately resulted in Christ's sacrifice.

The paradise restored in the novel is a domestic one centered upon the announcement at the novel's end that Mina and Jonathan have a child. The child has a bundle of names for all the protagonists who fought against Dracula, but he is commonly called Quincey in memory of the man who died in the struggle and was the one who ultimately killed Dracula. Quincey Morris died a sacrificial death, and so like Sidney Carton, he is remembered by his friends' naming their child after him. Jonathan also informs the reader, "It is an added joy to Mina and to me that our boy's birthday is the same day as that on which Quincey Morris died. His mother holds, I know, the secret belief that some of our brave friend's spirit has passed into him" (416). While such sentimentality expresses a wish to believe Quincey died as a martyr, and therefore, he will always be remembered, Mark Hennelly observes that the child is also born on the anniversary of Dracula's death (90). This date may then be symbolic of a subversive statement beneath the text that Dracula has not been forgotten but metaphorically lives on. Furthermore, Dracula has significantly contributed to the domestic circle and the child around which it centers. Hennelly wisely points out that because Mina drank Dracula's blood, it has entered into her veins and she may have passed it on to her son (89). Van Helsing had said earlier that "great men and good women" (269) have sprung from Dracula's loins, and Mina's son may now be regarded as one of them, making the young Quincey the physical manifestation of the good that Dracula had to contribute. Hennelly states that the child is symbolic of the forbidden knowledge Dracula possessed and which, as Harker wished earlier, has now been preserved, although unexpectedly in Harker's own child (90). The protagonists' knowledge of Dracula will also be passed on to the young Quincey as Van Helsing declares, "This boy will some day know what a brave and gallant woman his mother is. Already he knows her sweetness and loving care; later on he will understand how some men so loved her, that they did dare much for her sake" (416). Quincey will learn of Dracula, but he will also learn how love has defeated evil.

The young Quincey ultimately becomes a symbol of the future and the approaching twentieth century, in which he will achieve adulthood. Furthermore, if Quincey has Dracula's blood in his veins, he is representative of the entire group of protagonists, not only because he shares their names, but because he may share all of their blood. Leatherdale observes:

> He [Quincey] is linked to the band of Dracula's adversaries in more than just their names: he also has their blood. Worse, he has that of Dracula flowing through his veins. His mother has sucked the blood of Dracula, who had previously sucked that of Lucy, who had already received transfusions from Seward, Van Helsing, and Holmwood. The only blood not in the boy is that of Quincey Morris, his nominal 'father,' for Lucy died before she could transmit his blood to Dracula. (qtd. in Senf, *Vampire* 70)

Stoker must have intended such a symbolic blood transfusion into Quincey Harker. Hennelly observes that all the child's shared names suggest he is representative of all the branches of society and both the East and West for he is American, British, Dutch, Transylvanian, upper and middle class combined (90). Quincey's shared blood further supports such a reading. Furthermore, because Dracula had lived for centuries, he provides the young Quincey with a link to the ancient past, making him an Everyman figure who carries on the traditions of the past into the twentieth century for the future of the entire human race. All of the good blood in the young Quincey is sure to predominate over any evil taints in Dracula's blood, and Van Helsing's earlier statement that from Dracula's loins sprung "great men and good women" (269) suggests that the young Quincey is a symbol of hope. While Dracula is never allowed to speak for himself in the novel, he may have had the last word by his blood being passed on to Quincey. Ultimately, Dracula's redemption includes his role as the vessel through which all the blood, and consequently the bravery and goodness of his adversaries, is passed on to Quincey; therefore, while Dracula may represent the past, he indirectly helps to create hope for the future.

With this final scene from *Dracula*, the tradition of the nineteenth century Gothic wanderer comes to an end. *Dracula* is the culmination of the tradition with the main character's roots in Milton's depiction of Satan as evil yet sympathetic, but Dracula goes beyond Satan to be redeemed, and by his redemption, a domestic paradise is restored. The conservatism of the early Gothic wanderer tradition had condemned transgression and offered little hope for redemption, but by the Victorian period, writers like Carlyle, Bulwer-Lytton, and Dickens had suggested that redemption was possible. *Dracula*, though a product of the late Victorian period, is daringly modern in its suggestion that redemption is possible for the worst transgressors, even if they do not seek forgiveness. At the same time, *Dracula* is Stoker's attempt to safeguard embattled Victorian values from modernism and to preserve the romance of the family (Belford xii). Consequently, *Dracula* is the ultimate revision of the century old Gothic wanderer figure because it displays that transgression can have positive results, including the preservation of the sacred family.

Chapter XI - Modern Interpretations: from Wanderer to Superhero

The End of Fear:
The Gothic Wanderer's Evolution to Superhero

With Dracula redeemed and at rest, one would have thought the Gothic would rest as well and die out as a literary form, but the exact opposite has happened. The Gothic has continued throughout the twentieth, and now well into the twenty-first century, to transform and reinvent itself and in a manner its nineteenth century authors never would have dreamt, but I believe in many ways that would have pleased them a great deal.

In this short epilogue, it is impossible to treat over a century of Gothic literature in detail, so I will simply make some broad statements about how the Gothic wanderer figure has been depicted and transformed since the 1897 publication of *Dracula*.

Evolution and the Gothic

One significant event of the Victorian era I have not yet discussed would end up to be as terrifying for many of the Victorians as the French Revolution had been for their grandparents. This new "horror" would ultimately reshape, transform, and rebirth the Gothic in a new form the early nineteenth century authors never could have imagined.

While ghosts, transgressions, forbidden knowledge, and vampires were frightening enough, nothing was more frightening than to have the religious structure upon which all of the Gothic was based suddenly revealed to be false or at least misleading. The theory of evolution was a true Gothic horror that shook the very foundations of religion and everything mankind thought it understood about itself; man was plummeted into a new type of horror—the possibility that God was not completely in charge, and that life was meaningless—an existential type of vision that perhaps only Mary Shelley would have foreseen.

While such a statement regarding the theory of evolution's importance upon the Gothic form might seem a bit of a stretch—after all, the works I have already discussed that were published after Darwin's monumental *The Origin of Species* (1859), including *Carmilla*, *Trilby*, and *Dracula*, make no direct references to evolution—the increasing popularity of the adventure/quest novel is couched in this sudden search for the truth about human origins, and the theme of imperialism would be deeply at the core of these books and influence *Dracula* and other works set in England.

Before the British novelists made any real strides in discussing evolution in their novels, the adventure novel set in a strange land was being born in France in the works of Jules Verne, whose *A Journey to the Center of the Earth* (1864) was an early fictional exploration of the horror that arose from evolution's implications. In the novel, the main characters explore the interior of the earth, discovering a prehistoric world filled with dinosaurs and other creatures—these monsters provide enough terror for any Gothic novel—and Gothic words (in an English translation) are frequently used throughout the book, including "monstrous," "horrible," "hideous nightmare," and "fearful monster." Amid these horrors is the discovery of human bones and a skull that prove man existed in the "Quarternary period" (228). After these discoveries, the narrator remarks:

> Up to the present moment, marine monsters, fish, and such like animals had alone been seen alive!
>
> The question which rendered us rather uneasy, was a pertinent one. Were any of these men of the abyss wandering about the deserted shores of this wondrous sea of the center of the earth?
>
> This was a question which rendered me very uneasy and uncomfortable. How, should they really be in existence, would they receive us men from above? (230-31)

This fear of being confronted by prehistoric man—the very kind of man whom they would number among their ancestors—is a frightening one, and while the main characters never have a face-to-face confrontation with prehistoric humans, they do catch a glimpse of such creatures in what is, in my opinion, the most Gothic and terrifying moment in the novel. The beings the main characters witness are like giants—humans twelve feet tall—whom at first they can't even conceive may be early forms of humans. The first prehistoric man they see is driving a group of cattle, and Henry, the narrator, says to his uncle that they must hurry away because "No human creature can with impunity brave the ferocious anger of these monsters" (234) to which his uncle replies that he is wrong because they are actually looking at humans, "I behold a human being—a being like ourselves—a man!" (234). For a moment, the humans from the surface "remained profoundly still, speechless with surprise" (234) before the nephew drags his uncle away in fear. Later, when they are away from that "terrible monster" the nephew still finds himself unable to believe he has seen a prehistoric man:

> No, it is utterly impossible! Our ears must have deceived us, and our eyes have cheated us! We have not seen what we

believed we had seen. No human being could by any possibility have existed in that subterranean world! No generation of men could inhabit the lower caverns of the globe without taking note of those who peopled the surface, without communication with them. It was folly, folly, folly! nothing else!

I am rather inclined to admit the existence of some animal resembling in structure the human race—of some monkey of the first geological epochs, like that discovered by M. Lartet in the ossiferous deposit of Sansan.

But this animal, or being, whichsoever it was, surpassed in height all things known to modern science. Never mind. However unlikely it may be, it might have been a monkey—but a man, a living man, and with him a whole generation of gigantic animals, buried in the entrails of the earth—it was too monstrous to be believed! (234-35)

In short, for the narrator, the possibility that man has evolved—mankind's very origins—becomes the true Gothic horror!

And yet, as time went by, the theory of evolution became the Gothic's new redeemer, and while plenty of vampires and werewolves would exist in not only the books but the films of the twentieth century until the genre became tiresome with its sameness as sequel after sequel of horror films had Dracula, Frankenstein, and the Wolfman all in the same movie, the Gothic also took upon itself a new transition, away from the horror and toward the glory of man.

For if man had evolved, if natural selection had made him the superior being, did that not make man ultimately autonomous from God? Had he not succeeded by virtue of his own greatness? Was there then anything truly Gothic at all about mankind or his existence that could be viewed as negative? The fear, the horror, those religious "mind-forged manacles" that the Romantic Age had railed against were no longer needed. And so, what then was left for the Gothic but to turn fear on its head? Man's wisdom and strength, because of evolution, were now to be celebrated in a character with typical Gothic origins, an obscure birth and past, family secrets to be revealed in a mysterious manuscript, and yet to be not the child of transgression, fear, and guilt, but to be a very hero, and a superhero at that! It would be another fifty years following the publication of *A Journey to the Center of the Earth* before this character was created, but the building blocks to bring about the Gothic wanderer's evolution had been laid.

The Imperial Gothic

Jules Verne may have been one of the great inventors of the adventure novel, but his successors were less interested in the prehistoric world than ancient civilizations, exploring Africa and seeking cities of gold. And so from *A Journey to the Center of the Earth*, the adventure novel became a quest for mankind's forgotten origins in lost civilizations and mysterious ancient lands. Foremost of the novelists who sent his characters out seeking for lost civilizations was H. Rider Haggard. In *She* (1887), one of the world's all time bestselling novels that has never been out of print, Haggard would introduce an immortal Gothic figure in a forgotten land, the first of the "lost world" subgenre of adventure novel. The title character, more properly called, "She-who-must-be-obeyed," is a witch of great powers, a white woman ruling over a native tribe, who has predicted to her people the coming of the white adventurers, Horace Holly, his nephew Leo Vincey, and their servant Job. When Holly is granted audience with She, he is overcome by her beauty, falling to his knees before her. She reveals that she has lived for two thousand years and is awaiting the reincarnation of her lover whom she has slain in a fit of rage.

She becomes attracted to Leo, who has been wounded, and she determines to make him immortal so they can be together forever. She takes the men to a great cavern and an eternal flame, the Spirit of Life. Vincey is afraid to enter the flame so She does so to calm his fears. However, the flame causes her to return to her true age so she quickly withers away. Before her death, she states, "I shall come again, and shall once more be beautiful, I swear it—it is true!" (340). Haggard made certain She kept her promise by bringing her back first in *Ayesha, or The Return of She* (1906), and then in *Allan and She* (1921), in which he brought together his other great creation Allan Quatermain, first introduced in *King Solomon's Mines* (1885).

Haggard's works were not only adventure novels filled with Gothic elements, but they expressed the growing theme of the "Imperial Gothic" frequent in works of the period, along with a fear of "reverse colonialism." Works such as Joseph Conrad's *Heart of Darkness* (1903) depicted what could happen to someone who became overly influenced by the natives and the jungles, but what would be worse was if the natives came to England and destroyed it. This "reverse colonialism" is expressed in *She* when the title character considers visiting England; Holly expresses his fear over this possibility by saying:

> The terrible *She* had evidently made up her mind to go to England, and it made me absolutely shudder to think what would be the result of her arrival there....In the end she would, I had little doubt, assume absolute rule over the British dominions, and probably over the whole earth, and, though I was sure that she would speedily make ours the most glorious and prosperous empire that the world had ever seen, it would be at the cost of a terrible sacrifice of life. (318)

Judith Wilt cites this threat in *She* as a type of "counter-attack" upon Britain for its invasion of Africa and as an archetypal example of the "reverse colonialism" that would be common in British works of this time and until World War I (622-24).

Similarly, Dracula seeks to conquer England; Stoker does not allow Dracula to succeed, but later novelists were less restrained with their imaginations. Kim Newman in his *Anno Dracula* (1992) and its sequels, envisions a world where Dracula has succeeded and even married Queen Victoria, while the British people largely choose to become vampires.

The adventure novel and its focus on lost civilizations became popular as the empire also allowed for archaeologists to discover true lost civilizations. The mummy as a Gothic wanderer would become a popular figure beginning in this time; Stoker would depict a mummy in his novel *The Jewel of the Seven Stars* (1903)—another case where a powerful immortal comes to England and threatens it—in this case through an archeologist's efforts to revive Queen Tera, an ancient Egyptian mummy. The themes of mummies and foreign threats to England and the United States would become all too frequent in the twentieth century, especially in films—even giant spiders from South American jungles and no end of scientific experiments gone wrong would make their way into the United States to threaten its people. But first, the British Empire would inspire the creation of literature's first true superhero who was strong enough to pick up the Gothic and turn it on its head.

Tarzan: The Gothic Wanderer Turned Superhero

Surprisingly, it would be an American author, Edgar Rice Burroughs, who would combine theories of evolution, the Imperial Gothic, and the Gothic wanderer figure to create a superhero Gothic wanderer free of guilt.

I realize some readers will think my discussion of *Tarzan of the Apes* (1914) is a stretch in terms of my defining it as being within the Gothic novel tradition, but it definitely has Gothic elements. The novel is also a celebration of Darwin's theory of evolution in many ways. No longer does evolution distance man from God—it makes him like a god—Burroughs is especially fond of calling Tarzan the "forest god" throughout the twenty-four novels in the Tarzan series.

The opening pages of the first book, *Tarzan of the Apes*, are very Gothic. Lord Greystoke and his wife are aboard a ship taken over by a mutinous crew; the Greystokes see the captain and his loyal men slaughtered, but rather than kill the Greystokes, the mutineers decide to set the husband and wife ashore on the coast of Africa where they are forced to fend for themselves amid the jungle's horrors. Eventually, the terrifying apes kill the Greystokes, but not before Alice Greystoke gives birth to a son, Tarzan, who survives because Kala, a she-ape, has recently had her own child die, so she adopts Tarzan as her son. Tarzan grows up among the apes, quite the Gothic wanderer in his outcast role among the tribe for how he is different. He is weaker than the apes, although he soon realizes he is smarter.

Gothic elements come into play when the boy discovers his parents' cabin. Like a ruined castle full of secrets, here Tarzan learns the truth about his origins—that he is human. He also learns to read—discovering his father's journal—one of those Gothic manuscripts that reveal family secrets. Evolution theory is used in the novel to show that while Tarzan is not physically as strong as the jungle's beasts, he is able to use his father's knife to kill them, and over time, he uses his intelligence to create weapons and set traps and prove his superiority, not only over the apes, gorillas, and other beasts, but ultimately, over the black natives of Africa as well—the text is very racist in this respect, but the product of Burroughs' time. It is no accident that Tarzan is descended from English nobility—had his parents been French peasants or blacks, he doubtless would not have been so successful since evolutionary theories also resulted in racist distinctions. Ultimately, Tarzan's superiority allows him to kill the apes' leader, Kerchak, so Tarzan can take his own place as "king" of the apes.

Later, when Professor Porter and his party are marooned in Africa, Tarzan encounters not only Jane but also his cousin, William Cecil Clayton, who has inherited Tarzan's ancestral estate in England because it is assumed Tarzan's parents died and no one knows of Tarzan's birth or existence. Tarzan eventually befriends the party, saving Jane from numerous dangers in the jungle—which provides plenty of moments of Gothic horror for everyone except Tarzan who is himself a Gothic horror to the Americans and English in the party, and later, to anyone in the series who crosses Tarzan and feels his wrath.

Eventually, Tarzan, with the help of a friend, is able to prove his identity as Lord Greystoke. At first, he conceals and renounces his heritage because Jane is in love with his cousin, Clayton, but everything is worked out for him in the first sequel *The Return of Tarzan* (1915). Tarzan's inheritance goes back to the Gothic emphasis upon primogeniture and concerns over who has the right to inherit property and titles. Tarzan's desire to keep his identity secret is also Gothic in the sense that he possesses a forbidden secret, one he fears will upset the social order, and especially Jane's happiness. Tarzan is himself not all that keen on revealing his identity and going to live in civilization, which is full of hypocrisy, thieves, and liars—truly a more evil and Gothic place than the jungle where animals are incapable of lying.

In the sequels, Tarzan and Jane spend their time between England and their large property in Africa. Tarzan frequently goes off on adventures in the jungle, including visiting the lost city of Opar (in keeping with the Lost City genre that H. Rider Haggard first invented) and rescuing the occasional white person lost in the jungle.

Burroughs, admittedly, focuses on evolution far more than the Gothic in the novels. The most horrible creatures in the novels are actually mutants. For example, the ape men of Opar are evolutionary freaks of nature—not at all supernatural. In other Tarzan novels, Burroughs makes it clear that the natives are superstitious and their religions fake. There is not space in this work to go into detail about all the references to religion and evolution in the Tarzan novels, much less in Burroughs' other works—notably the Caspak series where characters evolve within their own lifetimes.

Burroughs turns on their head, or even rejects, Gothic themes by the way he treats religion and superstition. He also was clearly aware of many of his contemporaries and predecessors in terms of Gothic and adventure/lost city works. To this day, perhaps the best book on Burroughs' works is Richard A. Lupoff's *Edgar Rice Burroughs: Master of Adventure* (1965), which includes a thorough discussion of Tarzan's literary ancestors and his descendants. Most notable among his literary ancestors is H. Rider Haggard's *Nada and the Lily* (1892), in which the main character Galazi slays a wolf, wears its skin, and finds he can command the wolves (Lupoff 225-6). Lupoff notes that we do not know Burroughs' sources or inspiration but he analyzes the most likely sources.

Despite Burroughs' usual rejection of the supernatural, he made one significant exception that confirms for me Tarzan's role as a Gothic wanderer figure transformed into a superhero. Tarzan already had the typical hero and Gothic wanderer origins, but he was lacking the trait of having an extended life until late in the series. As decades passed and the novels remained set in the present day, Tarzan obviously had to be aging so Burroughs may have felt he needed a way to keep Tarzan young since obviously a fifty year old man would be less likely to perform incredible feats of strength, including wrestling with crocodiles. Consequently, Burroughs gifted Tarzan with immortal life—and he did it twice.

In *Tarzan's Quest* (1936), Burroughs tells the story of two whites who seek the secret to longevity. The secret is held by a bloodthirsty African tribe that creates longevity pills composed of various ingredients, including parts of young girls; consequently, to gain eternal life by swallowing the pills, one must perform an act of cannibalism—reminiscent of Catholic theology where the consumption of the bread and wine are the literal Body and Blood of Christ and by accepting them, one accepts Christ, thereby guaranteeing one's eternal life. By the end of *Tarzan's Quest*, Tarzan has stopped the tribe from performing its rituals, but he is left with several of the pills that he, Jane, and a couple of other characters, including Nkima, Tarzan's monkey friend, swallow; Tarzan, thereby, becomes immortal. This form of immortality might be dismissed as a scientific concoction, but curiously, Burroughs did not settle for it.

Later in *Tarzan and the Foreign Legion* (1947), Burroughs has Tarzan explain that he has perpetual life because of a witch doctor he helped while in his youth and who had lived since the eighteenth century. The witch doctor bestowed extended life upon Tarzan in a lengthy ceremony.

As a result, Tarzan looks like he's still in his twenties (he would have been almost sixty by the time of the novel's publication since he was born in 1888 in the novels. Tarzan states that he might still die by a bullet or from being killed by a wild animal, but he will not die of old age. This time, Tarzan's immortality is the result of magic or the supernatural—what Burroughs commonly mocked as superstition in his novels, but here as Burroughs himself was aging—he would have been seventy-one when this twenty-second novel in the series was published, and he lived to complete only two more Tarzan books—he finally decided to let a little of the superstitious supernatural creep into the story to keep his character forever young.

Tarzan has now gone from having a typical Gothic origin to achieving Gothic immortality, but without the Gothic preconditions of committing a transgression that would make him cursed to wander and live forever. Instead, Tarzan chooses to extend his own life—just as he has always chosen to live life on his own terms.

I need not go into great detail about Tarzan being a type of superhero. He is really the first superhero character, the first one in the popular imagination, who would quickly become a staple of film and comic books and influence the creation of other superheroes. Not only does Tarzan have incredible strength and amazing athletic abilities, but he is highly intelligent (the literary Tarzan is a far cry from the grunting Johnny Weissmuller film version), and he creates his own form of justice in the jungle. He is the fulfillment of Nietzsche's Superman, living by his own moral code and rejecting religious paradigms, long before the comic book Superman existed, and although Burroughs prefers terms like "forest god" for Tarzan—and the books are filled with hero worship type terms for him—in *Tarzan and the Forbidden City* (1938) he is even referred to as "this super-man" (115). Perhaps because *Superman* debuted as a comic strip in 1938, Burroughs felt he could not use that term but he liked it nevertheless and realized it could be applied to Tarzan so he hyphenated it. In fact, I would argue that Tarzan, because he is human unlike Superman with super powers and from another planet, is a superior creation as far as superheroes go.

In summary, Tarzan has little of the Gothic about him, yet he has Gothic origins in his lost family history, the manuscript he discovers, and his extended life. He has no guilt, and although he has nothing to transgress against, he would not live with guilt if he did commit a transgression. He is autonomous—what the nineteenth century Gothic wanderer had originally wished for but failed to achieve. He is man free of guilt and religion and able to live on his own terms.

Tarzan's Superhero Literary Descendants

Comic book superheroes may seem like a stretch as well for the Gothic, but I believe they have captured the popular imagination and influenced many of our more Gothic characters today. A character like Tarzan, with his superhuman strength and abilities, doubtless paved the way for characters like Superman and Batman. Like Gothic characters, Superman has mysterious origins (actually coming from another planet) and like many Gothic characters, he must hide his true identity. Yet he is a benefactor of mankind, much like Zanoni would have been. Surprisingly, Siegel, one of Superman's creators, did not cite Tarzan as an influence, but he did cite John Carter, the hero of Burroughs' Mars series, stating, "Carter was able to leap great distances because the planet Mars was smaller that [sic] the planet Earth; and he had great strength. I visualized the planet Krypton as a huge planet, much larger than Earth."[2] I don't believe the Mars novels have as Gothic a connection, but the influence is comparable—Siegel probably knew Tarzan if he knew John Carter. Another Gothic aspect to Superman is his cape. The few hero types Superman was based upon, such as Hercules and Samson, did not sport capes. In *Superman at Fifty: The Persistence of a Legend*, Gary Engle described the cape as being without "precedent in popular culture."[3] However, the cape was actually part of the Gothic tradition, worn by Dracula and more recently by The Phantom of the Opera—another sign that the Gothic darkness had been adapted for the forces of good.

Superman's immediate popularity led to a craving for more superheroes, so the next year, 1939, Batman appeared. Batman is perhaps the most Gothic of the early superheroes and many literary critics have mentioned him in discussing vampire fiction because of his bat costume. Batman may lack Superman's powers, but he has a horrific past—he sees his parents gunned down before him by a criminal—inspiring him to fight evil. Another Gothic connection is that he lives in Gotham City, a dark city filled with crime and bearing an appropriate name. Batman himself is typically a much darker character and also more of a detective than Superman. His creators give credit to Sherlock Holmes among the characters who influenced his creation.[4]

Batman's darker nature is more in line with his literary Gothic grandparents, and that darkness would become more and more common in superhero figures as the twentieth century continued. While the supernatural had little influence any longer, horror still created fear in the human heart—only ghosts had been replaced with man's own self-created horrors, largely as the result of science. Mary Shelley's *Frankenstein* began the science fiction genre by showing what happened when humans messed with Nature and sought forbidden knowledge. Science fiction would continue to have numerous examples of how humans destroyed the world and created horror. H.G. Wells' novels are notable examples, especially in *The Island of Dr. Moreau* (1896) where scientific experiments on animals

---

[2] http://en.wikipedia.org/wiki/Superman Accessed October 29, 2011.
[3] http://en.wikipedia.org/wiki/Superman Accessed October 29, 2011.
[4] http://en.wikipedia.org/wiki/Batman Accessed October 29, 2011.

are extreme and disastrous because they interfere with nature. Superhero mutants were not far behind, taking this fear to new levels to create superior human beings. While the fear of science creating problems for humanity continues, even scientific mutations could now become superheroes.

In the X-Men comic book series (created in 1963), a group of mutants is trained to become superheroes, despite their being social outcasts; the series has several themes typical of Gothic wanderer figures, including anti-Semitism[5]—it's as if the Wandering Jew has finally become the superhero.

I am admittedly no expert on comic book superheroes, but I think this quick summary provides enough comparison for others to research Gothic literature's influence on our superhero characters. What makes one a superhero in these stories is the very thing that made him an outcast, even a transgressor, cursed to wander the earth in nineteenth century Gothic literature.

The Modern Heroic Vampire

Gothic literature has come a long way over the course of two centuries. Today, the average theatre-goer, comic book enthusiast, or horror novel reader doubtless knows little if anything about Ancient Mariners, Wandering Jews, or Rosicrucians—they are the grandparents of modern horror literature, perhaps those ghosts that haunt the Gothic family still, but they have been replaced with Mummies, Zombies, and Werewolves. Yet the nineteenth century vampire is still highly recognizable to today's audience of readers and film-goers. More vampire novels seem to be published every year; we have been inundated with vampire television series in recent years, including *Buffy the Vampire Slayer* (film 1992, television series 1997-2003) and *The Vampire Diaries* (television 2009—present), and films, including those based on popular novels such as *Interview with a Vampire* (1994) and *Twilight* (2008). If anything speaks to the Gothic's survival, it is how we love our vampires today.

Dracula has never ceased to be popular, and numerous film versions have been made of the book, even a Broadway musical, but it was Anne Rice's debut novel *Interview with the Vampire* (1976) that really started a new trend in vampire fiction. Rice did her homework in writing her first vampire novel and it shows in the character of Louie who is very much the product of his nineteenth century literary ancestors. Although Louie is the novel's main character, he is contrasted with a character in many ways his antagonist—Lestat—one of the most iconic figures of literature in recent years.

The novel is told from Louie's point of view, beginning with how he was changed into a vampire by Lestat in late eighteenth century New

---

[5] http://en.wikipedia.org/wiki/Xmen Accessed October 29, 2011.

Orleans. The two become companions, but Louie is largely horrified by his new role as a vampire, refusing to feed off humans, and sucking blood only from animals. Louie also demands answers regarding vampires' origins. Lestat does not know much, other than that he was himself changed by an older vampire. As Louie finds himself more disgusted with Lestat, he considers leaving him, only to have Lestat turn a young child, Claudia, into a vampire to make Louie feel responsible for caring for her. The plan works for a while, but as Claudia grows older, she becomes angry that she will age mentally but always have a child's body. Eventually, she tries to kill Lestat, but when she is unsuccessful, a fight ensues between the three vampires and Louie and Claudia burn Lestat—or so they believe.

Wishing to know if others of their kind exist, Louie and Claudia then travel to Europe to try to find other vampires. Their search begins in Eastern Europe, home of the famed Dracula; Rice interestingly avoids building on the Dracula myth by having Louie disappointed in the vampires he finds there—little more than animated corpses and degenerates. Eventually, Louie and Claudia go to Paris where they meet vampires like them; however, Lestat shows up and informs the other vampires that Louie and Claudia tried to kill him. Louie is spared, but the vampires destroy Claudia.

The novel is told by Louie to a man who has come to interview him, and in the end, Louie confesses he is tired of being a vampire after nearly two centuries. Louie is a reluctant vampire, turned against his will, not a transgressor at all, yet feeling guilt over his situation, so very much in the tradition of nineteenth century Gothic. But Rice, who clearly knows the Gothic tradition from references she makes in her books, moved the tradition into a new direction by making Lestat attractive, and not guilty or unhappy about being a vampire. In the sequels, Lestat becomes the primary character.

Besides glamorizing a vampire in Lestat, Rice removes her characters from the Christian world that controlled the vampires of earlier works. Rice's fascination with Catholicism, her leaving the religion, returning, and then leaving again, has received much attention in the press, but her conflict with Christianity also made her shy away from stories of her vampires being cursed by God. Instead, in the third book *Queen of the Damned* (1986), she creates an elaborate tale of the vampires' origins based in ancient Egypt. The Judeo-Christian tradition has no place in this story.

Later, however, in the fifth novel *Memnoch the Devil* (1995), Lestat meets the Devil, who calls himself Memnoch. The Devil takes Lestat on a journey through Heaven and Hell and he retells history from his point of view, seeking to turn Lestat to his side—Lestat takes on a role here not unlike Milton's Eve to Satan. Memnoch claims he is not evil but actually working for God. Lestat is left confused by his experience, having witnessed Christ's crucifixion and received St. Veronica's veil. Later, Memnoch admits he may have been manipulating Lestat for his own purposes. The book is confusing and intentionally hard to pin down in terms of its meaning, and it fails to make any statements about Rice's vampiric world's existence within a Christian universe.

While the rest of Rice's vampire novels may be entertaining, they become repetitive and add little to the vampire legend. Rice quit writing vampire novels after converting to Christianity, but in 2008, following her return to Christianity, Rice admitted that she was thinking about writing one last vampire novel:

> Yes, I am contemplating one last novel involving the Vampire Lestat, and the Talamasca, the fictional organization I created years ago in the Vampire novels....The novel, if ever written, would be entirely Christian in framework and would involve Redemption. It would affirm my dedication to Christ and my belief in Him and my commitment to write only for Him.[6]

One wonders whether Rice ever will write such a novel considering the many non-Christian elements in the previous novels.

Perhaps Rice's original intentions, before her return to Christianity, can best be summed up in an interview Rice gave, published in 1996 after she finished *Memnoch the Devil*, in which she stated:

> In the West we grow up with the concept of original sin, which means in all creeds, it seems, that we are flawed, we have fallen, we are bad and must be redeemed. That's the basis of Catholicism as well as Protestantism, and I venture to say the basis of Judaism too. Now I'm looking for a new way to see us. I'm looking for a new neutrality or secularism from which to start to make a moral world, a good world. In other words, forget an inherited sin or flaw. Say we are simply here and we are not inherently bad or inherently innocent either. We are simply human. But the obligation to be good remains. In fact, it becomes even more pressing because in a secular world we are both child and parent. (Riley 293)

Later, in 2005, after her return to Christianity, Rice stated, "The vampire was sort of a metaphor for being beyond the reach of God. Well, not beyond the reach, because I don't believe anybody is really beyond the reach of God. But being an outsider" (Associated Press 18).

In the end, Rice succeeded in glamorizing the vampire figure and making it less-guilt ridden. Rice's vampires are very human in their

---

[6] http://current.com/community/88854124_anne-rice-and-jesus-save-lestat-but-can-vampires-accept-christ-into-their-undead-lives.htm Accessed October 30, 2011.

psychological make-up and attractive to readers. Her distancing the novels from the Christian framework creates both relief and tension in the storyline; however, I feel Rice failed in completely creating a non-Christian universe for her characters. Her own conversion back to Christianity caused her to abandon her work, which was becoming tiresome and repetitive anyway. Nevertheless, she paved the way for a new, attractive, even sexy vampire figure to appear.

Finally, I will end my discussion with Stephenie Meyer's phenomenally successful *Twilight* series. In the novels, a human woman, Bella, chooses to be with a vampire, Edward Cullen, and in the last book of the series *Breaking Dawn* (2008), Bella decides to marry the vampire and have his baby.

Meyer has stated that she knew nothing of the vampire tradition when she wrote her novels, and the books are without references or even many of the trappings of traditional Gothic fiction. In numerous interviews Meyer has admitted her lack of knowledge about the horror and vampire traditions. In one interview, she stated:

> I'm not a vampire person. Before I started writing about them, I'd never seen a vampire movie. I'd seen pieces of them, but I'd never been to a vampire movie. I've never read a book about vampires. I'm really not into horror, so I don't know the genre.[7]

The vampire, however, had become such a part of popular culture that one would be able to know all about the basic characteristics of vampires without ever reading a vampire novel or watching a full-length film. Despite Meyer's lack of knowledge of the Gothic tradition, interestingly, she begins the first book *Twilight* with a significant biblical quote: "But of the tree of the knowledge of good and evil, thou shalt not eat of it: For in the day that thou eatest thereof thou shalt surely die" (Genesis 2:17). Here is the very concern that begins the Gothic wanderer's journey—man chooses to search for forbidden knowledge, and he is cursed to wander the earth as a result.

But Bella makes the choice to be with Edward, even to have his child. Bella's marriage to Edward would be a crime, a terrible transgression two centuries earlier, but on the very day I am writing this, I visited my local library where I saw an announcement, just three weeks before the release of the film of *Breaking Dawn: Part I*, that the library will host a pre-wedding party for Bella and Edward. In other words, readers are celebrating Edward and Bella's marriage, and it's not a marriage of good and evil because the Christian viewpoint that controlled the Gothic for so long has been broken.

---

[7] http://www.reelz.com/article/686/interview-with-twilight-author-stephenie-meyer/ Accessed October 31, 2011.

Conclusion

What is left now for the Gothic to do? The Gothic wanderer has been redeemed, become a hero, and even become marriage material! But more importantly, forbidden knowledge is no longer viewed as forbidden. Man is allowed to seek to better himself rather than to live in guilt. He can become a true man, a superman. Or, he can mock vampires and other Gothic characters in campy, cheesy, horror films that lack sincerity—their storylines no longer driven by guilt, transgression, or even romance, but simply cheap laughs.

But what do these changes say about the twenty-first century audience and its view of the Gothic? I believe it represents that readers and filmgoers today no longer live under the confines of religious guilt and transgression, or the need for redemption.

Mankind is no longer concerned with guilt or living in fear in the same way—or at least not to such an extent—as our ancestors were at the time of the French Revolution. As I write these words in 2011, just days after Muammar Gaddafi has been killed, freeing Libya from forty-two years of his tyranny, just months after Egypt declared itself liberated, and as President Barack Obama has announced that U.S. troops will finally be leaving Iraq where another dictator has been overthrown, and long after France and the rest of the Western World have become democratic, I cannot help but believe that man has finally begun to realize that he can think for himself and be free rather than enslaved by his fears. We are now able to stand up for ourselves, to think for ourselves, not to need a king or a church to speak for us. We are able to talk to God ourselves rather than having an intercessor or someone who tries to control us by pretending to know what God says and leading us into the superstition that caused the horrors in Gothic novels.

We have shaken fear from us, or at least we are shaking it away, because, as Carlyle's Teufelsdrockh realized, the universe is our Father's. It is the twenty-first century, we are in a new millennium and the millennialism that Percy Shelley dreamt of may finally become our reality. Do we still have fears—yes, we fear plagues, we fear wars—we are human and fear is part of the human condition—but do we need to be Gothic wanderers? No, we have learned we do not need to be victims, transgressors, slaves to our fear or to other men who want us to live in fear. Instead, we may choose to be free.

Our ancestors had much to fear at the time of the French Revolution, and so did they have plenty to fear over the last two centuries, with the discovery of Evolution, and the age of Industrialism, not to mention the World Wars, terrorism and economic woes, and all else that followed in the wake of the twentieth and twenty-first centuries, yet the human race has persevered through it all. There are always naysayers among us, but most of us would not trade places with our ancestors. We are better off, as a human race, than we have ever been. We have far to go, but we are learning to conquer fear, to shake from us the mind-forged manacles that have controlled us.

The Gothic began as a dialogue, a place to explore human fear, a place to decide what was justified behavior, and what was transgression against God and the moral order. Somehow, I hope the Gothic novelists are aware that the dialogue they began is slowly being rendered unnecessary. That mankind has evolved and is learning, perhaps slowly, but still learning, not to be controlled by its fears. There is a long way to go, and the popularity of the Gothic is not going to diminish anytime soon, but the sun is rising and illuminating even the darkest, most haunted parts of the castle, and the human mind.

Bibliography

Primary Works

Austen, Jane. *Emma*. 1816. Oxford, Gr. Brit.: Oxford UP, 1990.

Austen, Jane. *Pride and Prejudice*. 1813. New York: Washington Square, 1964.

Balzac, Honore. *Melmoth Reconciled*. 1835. Trans. Ellen Marriage. *The Quest for the Absolute and Other Stories*. Philadelphia: Gebbie, 1898. 276-330.

Balzac, Honore. *The Quest for the Absolute*. 1834. Trans. Ellen Marriage. *The Quest for the Absolute and Other Stories*. Philadelphia: Gebbie, 1898. 1-222.

Blake, William. *The Marriage of Heaven and Hell*. 1790-3. *English Romantic Writers*. Ed. David Perkins. New York: Harcourt Brace Jovanovich, 1967. 68-75.

Brontë, Charlotte. *Jane Eyre*. 1847. New York: Bantam, 1986.

Brontë, Emily. *Wuthering Heights*. 1847. Bantam, 1983.

Burke, Edmund. *Reflections on the Revolution in France*. 1790. *Burke, Paine, Godwin, and the Revolution Controversy*. Ed. Marilyn Butler. Cambridge, Gr. Brit.: Cambridge UP, 1994. 33-49.

Burney, Fanny. *Camilla or A Picture of Youth*. 1796. Oxford, Gr. Brit.: Oxford UP, 1983.

Burney, Fanny. *Cecilia, or Memoirs of an Heiress*. 1782. Oxford, Gr. Brit.: Oxford UP, 1992.

Burney, Fanny. *Evelina or the History of a Young Lady's Entrance Into the World*. 1778. Oxford, Gr. Brit.: Oxford UP, 1988.

Burney, Fanny. *The Wanderer; or, Female Difficulties*. 1814. Oxford, Gr. Brit.: Oxford UP, 1991.

Burroughs, Edgar Rice. *Tarzan and the Forbidden City*. 1938. New York: Ballantine Books, 1977.

Burroughs, Edgar Rice. *Tarzan and the Foreign Legion*. 1947. New York: Ballantine Books, 1981.

Burroughs, Edgar Rice. *Tarzan of the Apes* and *The Return of Tarzan*. 1914 & 1915. New York: Quality Paperback Book Club, 1995.

Burroughs, Edgar Rice. *Tarzan's Quest*. 1936. New York: Ballantine Books, 1980.

Byron, George Gordon. *Cain: A Mystery*. 1821. *Byron: Poetical Works*. Ed. Frederick Page. London: Oxford UP, 1974. 520-45.

Byron, George Gordon. "Darkness." 1816. *English Romantic Writers*. Ed. David Perkins. New York: Harcourt Brace Jovanovich, 1967. 795-6.

Byron, George Gordon. "A Fragment." 1816. The Vampyre *and* Ernestus Berchtold: or, The Modern Oedipus*: Collected Fiction of John William Polidori*. Ed. D.L. Macdonald and Kathleen Scherf. Toronto, Can.: U of Toronto P, 1994. 173-6.

Byron, George Gordon. *The Giaour*. 1813. *The Works of Lord Byron*. Ed. Ernest Hartley Coleridge. Vol. 3. New York: Charles Scribner's Sons, 1904. 75-146. 13 Vols.

Byron, George Gordon. *Manfred: A Dramatic Poem*. 1817. *English Romantic Writers*. Ed. David Perkins. New York: Harcourt Brace Jovanovich, 1967. 810-28.

Carlyle, Thomas. *Sartor Resartus: The Life and Opinions of Herr Teufelsdrockh*. 1838. New York: Odyssey, 1937.

Coleridge, Samuel Taylor. "The Rime of the Ancient Mariner." *The Norton Anthology of English Literature*. Ed. M.H. Abrams et al. Vol. 2. 5th ed. New York: W.W. Norton, 1986. 2 Vols. 335-52.

Conrad, Joseph. *Heart of Darkness*. 1903. New York: Penguin, 1995.

Darwin, Charles. *The Origin of Species*. 1859. New York: Signet Classics, 2003.

Dickens, Charles. *Bleak House*. 1853. New York: Bantam, 1992.

Dickens, Charles. *The Old Curiosity Shop*. 1841. New York: Peebles, n.d.

Dickens, Charles. *A Tale of Two Cities*. 1859. New York: Bantam, 1983.

Eliot, George. *Adam Bede*. 1859. New York: Penguin, 1980.

Eliot, George. *Daniel Deronda*. 1876. New York: Harper & Brothers, 1961.

Gaskell, Elizabeth. *Mary Barton: A Tale of Manchester Life*. 1848. New York: Penguin, 1996.

Godwin, William. *The Adventures of Caleb Williams, or Things As They Are*. 1794. New York: Rinehart, 1960.

Godwin, William. "Enquiry Concerning Political Justice, and its Influence on Morals and Happiness." 1793. *Burke, Paine, Godwin, and the Revolution Controversy*. Ed. Marilyn Butler. Cambridge, Gr. Brit.: Cambridge UP, 1994. 149-169.

Godwin, William. *St. Leon*. 1799. New York: Oxford UP, 1994.

Goethe, Johann. *The Sorrows of Young Werther.* 1774. Ed. David E. Welbery. Princeton, NJ: Princeton UP, 1995. Vol. 11 of *Goethe: The Collected Works.* 12 Vols.

Haggard, H. Rider. *Ayesha: The Return of She.* 1906. In *Ayesha: The Return of She* and *Benita: An African Romance.* New York: New Orchard Editions, 1986. 1-198.

Haggard, H. Rider. *Benita, An African Romance.* 1906. In *Ayesha: The Return of She* and *Benita: An African Romance.* New York: New Orchard Editions, 1986. 199-335.

Haggard, H. Rider. *King Solomon's Mines.* 1885. *The Works of H. Rider Haggard.* Roslyn, NY: Black's Readers Service Company. 1928. 355-493.

Haggard, H. Rider. *She.* 1887. *The Works of H. Rider Haggard.* Roslyn, NY: Black's Readers Service Company. 1928. 173-354.

Haggard, H. Rider. *She and Allan.* 1921. New York: Ballantine, 1978.

Johnson, Samuel. *The History of Rasselas, Prince of Abyssinia.* 1759. *The Norton Anthology of English Literature.* Ed. M.H. Abrams et al. Vol. 1. 6th ed. New York: W.W. Norton, 1994. 2 Vols. 2314-78.

Lamb, Lady Caroline. *Glenarvon.* 1816. London, Gr. Brit.: J.M. Dent, 1995.

LeFanu, J.S. "Carmilla." *In a Glass Darkly.* Vol. 3. London, Gr. Brit.: R. Bentley & Son, 1872. 3 Vols. 49-270.

Lewis, Matthew. *The Monk.* 1795. New York: Oxford UP, 1980.

Lytton, Edward Bulwer. "The Haunted and the Haunters." 1857. *Classic Ghost Stories* by Charles Dickens and Others. New York: Dover, 1975. 293-330.

Lytton, Edward Bulwer. *The Last Days of Pompeii.* 1834. New York: Thomas Y. Crowell, n.d.

Lytton, Edward Bulwer. *Zanoni.* 1842. Boston: Estes and Lauriat, 1892. Vol. 18 of *Bulwer's Novels Edition Deluxe.* 32 Vols.

Marlowe, Christopher. *The Tragical History of Doctor Faustus.* 1604. *The Norton Anthology of English Literature.* Ed. M.H. Abrams et al. Vol. 1. 6th ed. New York: W.W. Norton, 1994. 2 Vols. 768-801.

Maturin, Charles. *Melmoth the Wanderer.* 1820. New York: Oxford UP, 1989.

Meyer, Stephenie. *Breaking Dawn.* New York: Little, Brown, 2008.

Meyer, Stephenie. *Twilight.* New York: Little Brown, 2005.

Milton, John. *Paradise Lost.* 1667. *John Milton: Complete Poems and Prose.* Ed. Merrit Y. Hughes. New York: Macmillan, 1957. 207-469.

Newman, Kim. *Anno Dracula.* 1992. London, Gr. Brit.: Titan, 2011.

Poe, Edgar Allan. "The Fall of the House of Usher." *The Heath Anthology of American Literature*. Ed. Paul Lauter. Vol. 1. 2nd ed. Lexington, MA: D.C. Heath, 1994. 1382-95.

Polidori, John. *Ernestus Berchtold or, The Modern Oedipus*. The Vampyre *and* Ernestus Berchtold: or, The Modern Oedipus: *Collected Fiction of John William Polidori*. Toronto, Can.: U of Toronto P, 1994. 51-143.

Polidori, John. *The Vampyre*. 1819. The Vampyre *and* Ernestus Berchtold: or, The Modern Oedipus: *Collected Fiction of John William Polidori*. Toronto, Can.: U of Toronto P, 1994. 33-49.

Power Records. *A Story of Dracula, the Wolfman and Dracula*. Newark, NJ: Peter Pan Records, 1975.

Radcliffe, Ann. *The Mysteries of Udolpho*. 1794. New York: Oxford UP, 1988.

Rice, Anne. *Interview with the Vampire*. 1976. New York: Alfred A. Knopf, 2007.

Rice, Anne. *Memnoch the Devil*. New York: Alfred A. Knopf, 1995.

Rice, Anne. *Queen of the Damned*. New York: Alfred A. Knopf, 1988.

Rice, Anne. *The Tale of the Body Thief*. New York: Alfred A. Knopf, 1992.

Rice, Anne. *The Vampire Lestat*. New York: Alfred A. Knopf, 1985.

Rice, Anne. *The Witching Hour*. New York: Alfred A. Knopf, 1990.

Rymer, James Malcolm or Thomas Peckett Prest. *Varney the Vampyre or, The Feast of Blood*. 1847. New York: Dover, 1972. 2 Vols.

Shelley, Mary Wollstonecraft. *Frankenstein*. 1818. New York: Scholastic, 1969.

Shelley, Mary Wollstonecraft. *The Last Man*. 1826. Lincoln: U of Nebraska P, 1993.

Shelley, Mary Wollstonecraft. *Valperga or, The Life and Adventures of Castruccio, Prince of Lucca*. 1823. Oxford, Gr. Brit.: Oxford UP, 1997.

Shelley, Percy. "Alastor; or, the Spirit of Solitude." 1816. *Shelley: Poetical Works*. Ed. Thomas Hutchinson. London, Gr. Brit.: Oxford UP, 1973. 14-30.

Shelley, Percy. "Ghasta; or, the Avenging Demon." 1810. *Shelley: Poetical Works*. Ed. Thomas Hutchinson. London, Gr. Brit.: Oxford UP, 1973. 853-6.

Shelley, Percy. "Hellas: A Lyrical Drama." 1822. *Shelley: Poetical Works*. Ed. Thomas Hutchinson. London, Gr. Brit.: Oxford UP, 1973. 446-82.

Shelley, Percy. *Prometheus Unbound: A Lyrical Drama*. 1820. *English Romantic Writers*. Ed. David Perkins. New York: Harcourt Brace Jovanovich, 1967. 980-1019.

Shelley, Percy. "Queen Mab: A Philosophical Poem." 1813. *Shelley: Poetical Works*. Ed. Thomas Hutchinson. London: Oxford UP, 1973. 762-838.

Shelley, Percy. "Sadak the Wanderer." 1829. *Gothic Immortals: The Fiction of the Brotherhood of the Rosy Cross* by Marie Roberts. London, Gr. Brit.: Routledge, 1990. 215-6.

Shelley, Percy. *St. Irvyne or, The Rosicrucian: A Romance*. 1811. Eds. Roger Ingpen and Walter E. Peck. New York: Gordian, 1965. 107-99. Vol. 5 of *The Complete Works of Percy Bysshe Shelley*. 10 Vols.

Shelley, Percy. "The Wandering Jew." 1810. *The Complete Poetical Works of Percy Bysshe Shelley*. Boston: Houghton Mifflin, 1901. 573-89.

Shelley, Percy. "The Wandering Jew's Soliloquy." 1887. *The Complete Poetical Works of Percy Bysshe Shelley*. Boston: Houghton Mifflin, 1901. 573.

Southey, Robert. *The Curse of Kehama*. 1810. Boston: Houghton, Mifflin, n.d. 1-334. Vol. 4 of *The Poetical Works of Robert Southey with a Memoir*. 5 Vols.

Southey, Robert. *Thalaba the Destroyer*. 1801. *The Poems of Robert Southey*. Ed. Maurice H. Fitzgerald. London, Gr. Brit.: Oxford UP, 1909. 23-116.

Stoker, Bram. *Dracula*. 1897. New York: Dell, 1971.

Stoker, Bram. "Dracula's Guest." 1914. *Classic Ghost Stories* by Charles Dickens and Others. New York: Dover, 1975. 64-75.

Stoker, Bram. *The Jewel of Seven Stars*. 1903. New York: Tor, 1999.

Verne, Jules. *A Journey to the Center of the Earth*. 1864. New York: Penguin, 1986.

Wallace, Lew. *The Prince of India*. New York: Harper and Brothers, 1893. 2 Vols.

Walpole, Horace. *The Castle of Otranto*. 1764. *The English Novel Before the Nineteenth Century*. Eds. Annette Brown Hopkins and Helen Sard Hughes. Boston: Ginn, 1915. 483-577.

Wells, H.G. *The Island of Dr. Moreau*. New York: Tor, 1996.

Wordsworth, William. *The Borderers: A Tragedy*. 1842. *Wordsworth: Poetical Works*. Ed. Thomas Hutchinson. New Ed. revised by Ernest De Selincourt. Oxford, Gr. Brit: Oxford UP, 1989. 29-62.

Wordsworth, William. "Ode: Intimations of Immortality from Recollections of Early Childhood." 1807. *Wordsworth: Poetical*

Works. Ed. Thomas Hutchinson. New Ed. revised by Ernest De Selincourt. Oxford, Gr. Brit: Oxford UP, 1989. 460-2.

Wordsworth, William. *The Prelude 1799, 1805, 1850.* New York: W.W. Norton, 1979.

Films

A Nightmare on Elm Street. Dir. Wes Craven. Perf. Heather Langenkamp, Johnny Depp, and Robert Englund. New Line Cinema, 1984.

Bram Stoker's Dracula. Dir. Francis Ford Coppola. Perf. Gary Oldman, Keanu Reeves, and Anthony Hopkins. Columbia, 1992.

Breaking Dawn: Part I. Dir. Bill Condon. Perf. Kristen Stewart, Robert Pattison, and Taylor Lautner. Summit Entertainment, 2011.

Bud Abbott and Lou Costello Meet Frankenstein. Dir. Charles Barton. Perf. Bud Abbott, Lou Costello, Lon Chaney Jr., and Bela Lugosi. Universal, 1948.

Crown and Country with Edward Windsor. Dir. Robin Bextor. Carlton Television, 1998.

Dracula 2000. Dir. Patrick Lussier. Perf. Gerard Butler, Justine Waddell, and Jonny Lee Miller. Dimension Films, 2000.

Friday the 13th. Dir. Sean S. Cunningham. Perf. Betsy Palmer, Adrienne King, and Jeannine Taylor. Paramount, 1980.

Interview with the Vampire. Dir. Neil Jordan. Perf. Tom Cruise, Brad Pitt, and Antonio Banderas. Geffen Pictures, 1994.

Love at First Bite. Dir. Stan Dragoti. Perf. George Hamilton, Susan Saint James, and Richard Benjamin. Melvin Simon Productions, 1979.

Twilight. Dir. Catherine Hardwicke. Perf. Kristen Stewart, Robert Pattison, and Taylor Lautner. Summit Entertainment, 2008.

Secondary Works

Abrams, M.H. *Natural Supernaturalism: Tradition and Revolution in Romantic Literature.* 1971. New York: W.W. Norton, 1973.

Abrams, M.H. et al, eds. *The Norton Anthology of English Literature.* Vol. 1. 6th ed. New York: W.W. Norton, 1993. 2 Vols.

Adelstein, Michael E. "A Wandering Author." *Fanny Burney.* New York: Twayne, 1968. 117-29.

Anderson, George K. *The Legend of the Wandering Jew.* Providence, RI: Brown UP, 1965.

Anderson, Howard. "Introduction." *The Monk* by Matthew Lewis. New York: Oxford UP, 1980. v-xxiv.

Andrews, S.G. "Shelley, Medwin, and The Wandering Jew." *Keats-Shelley Journal.* 20 (1971): 78-86.

Arnstein, Walter L. *Britain Yesterday and Today: 1830 to the Present*. 7th ed. Lexington, MA: D.C. Heath, 1996.

Associated Press. "Queen of New Orleans takes up new life in California. *The Mining Journal*, Marquette, Michigan. (Dec 26, 2005): 14, 18.

Baldick, Chris. "Introduction." *The Oxford Book of Gothic Tales*. New York: Oxford UP, 1992. xi-xxiii.

Baldick, Chris. "Introduction." *Melmoth the Wanderer* by Charles Maturin. New York: Oxford UP, vii-xix.

Begnal, Michael H. *Joseph Sheridan LeFanu*. Cranbury, NJ: Bucknell UP, 1971.

Belford, Barbara. *Bram Stoker: A Biography of the Author of* Dracula. New York: Alfred A. Knopf, 1996.

Bentley, Christopher. "The Monster in the Bedroom: Sexual Symbolism in Bram Stoker's *Dracula*. *Dracula: The Vampire and the Critics*. Ed. Margaret L. Carter. Ann Arbor, MI: UMI Research P, 1988. 25-34.

Birkhead, Edith. *The Tale of Terror: A Study of the Gothic Romance*. 1921. New York: Russell and Russell, 1963.

Bleiler, E.F. "Introduction to the Dover Edition." Rymer, James Malcolm or Thomas Peckett Prest. *Varney the Vampyre or, The Feast of Blood* by James Malcolm Rymer or Thomas Peckett Prest. Vol. 1. New York: Dover, 1972. 2 Vols. v-xv.

Blind, Karl. "Wodan, the Wild Huntsman, and the Wandering Jew." *The Wandering Jew: Essays in the Interpretation of a Christian Legend*. Eds. Galit Hasan-Rokem and Alan Dundes. Bloomington: Indiana UP, 1986. 169-89.

Bloom, Edward A. and Lillian D. Bloom. "Introduction." *Camilla or A Picture of Youth*. 1796. By Fanny Burney. Oxford, Gr. Brit.: Oxford UP, 1983.

Bloom, Harold. "Frankenstein, or the New Prometheus." *Partisan Review* 32 (1965): 611-8.

Blumberg, Jane. *Mary Shelley's Early Novels*. Iowa City: U of Iowa P, 1993.

Botting, Fred. "*Frankenstein* and the Language of Monstrosity." *Reviewing Romanticism*. Ed. Philip W. Martin. New York: St. Martin's, 1992. 51-9.

Briggs, Asa. *Victorian Cities*. New York: Harper and Row, 1963.

Brookes, Gerry H. *The Rhetorical Form of Carlyle's* Sartor Resartus. Berkeley: U of California P, 1972.

Brown, Dan. *The Da Vinci Code*. New York: Doubleday, 2003.

Burgan, William M. "Masonic Symbolism in *The Moonstone* and *The Mystery of Edwin Drood.*" *Dickens Studies Annual: Essays on Victorian Fiction* 16 (1987): 257-303.

Burwick, Roswitha. "Goethe's *Werther* and Mary Shelley's *Frankenstein.*" *The Wordsworth Circle.* 24.1 (1993): 47-52.

Byers, Thomas B. "Good Men and Monsters: The Defense of Dracula." *Dracula: The Vampire and the Critics.* Ed. Margaret L. Carter. Ann Arbor, MI: UMI Research P, 1988. 149-57.

Campbell, James L. *Edward Bulwer-Lytton.* Boston: Twayne, 1986.

Carter, Margaret L. *Specter or Delusion?: The Supernatural in Gothic Fiction.* Ann Arbor, MI: UMI Research Press, 1987.

Cavaliero, Glen. *The Supernatural and Gothic Fiction.* Oxford, Gr. Brit.: Oxford UP, 1995.

Cheadle, Brian. "Mystification and the Mystery of Origins in *Bleak House.*" *Dickens Studies Annual: Essays on Victorian Fiction* 25 (1996): 29-47.

Christensen, Allan Conrad. *Edward Bulwer-Lytton: The Fiction of New Regions.* Athens: U of Georgia P, 1976.

Clemit, Pamela. "Introduction." *St. Leon* by William Godwin. New York: Oxford UP, 1994. vii-xxvi.

Clery, E.J. "The Politics of the Gothic Heroine in the 1790s." "*Frankenstein* and the Language of Monstrosity." *Reviewing Romanticism.* Ed. Philip W. Martin. New York: St. Martin's, 1992. 69-85.

Coates, John. "*Zanoni* by Bulwer-Lytton: A Discussion of its "philosophy" and its possible influences." *Durham University Journal (DUJ)* 76.2 (1984): 223-33.

Coolidge, Archibald C. "Charles Dickens and Mrs. Radcliffe: A Farewell to Wilkie Collins." *The Dickensian* 58.2 (1962): 112-6.

Cordery, G. "The Gambling Grandfather in *The Old Curiosity Shop.*" *Literature and Psychology* 33.1 (1987): 43-61.

Craft, Christopher. "'Kiss me with Those Red Lips': Gender and Inversion in Bram Stoker's *Dracula.*" *Dracula: The Vampire and the Critics.* Ed. Margaret L. Carter. Ann Arbor, MI: UMI Research P, 1988. 167-94.

Cutting, Rose Marie. "Defiant Women: the Growth of Feminism in Fanny Burney's Novels." *Studies in English Literature* 17 (1977): 519-30.

Cutting, Rose Marie. "A Wreath for Fanny Burney's Last Novel: *The Wanderer*'s Contribution to Women's Studies." *College Language Association Journal* 20 (1976): 57-67.

Cutting-Gray, Joanne. *Woman as 'Nobody' and the Novels of Fanny Burney.* Gainesville: UP of Florida, 1992.

Day, Gary. "The State of Dracula: Bureaucracy and the Vampire."
    Rereading Victorian Fiction. Eds. Alice Jenkins and Juliet John.
    New York: St. Martin's, 2000. 81-95.
Day, William Patrick. *In the Circles of Fear and Desire: A Study of Gothic
    Fantasy*. Chicago: U of Chicago P, 1985.
DeLamotte, Eugenia C. *Perils of the Night: A Feminist Study of Nineteenth-
    Century Gothic*. New York: Oxford UP, 1990.
Doody, Margaret Anne. "Deserts, Ruins and Troubled Waters: Female
    Dreams in Fiction and the Development of the Gothic Novel."
    Genre 10 (1977): 529-72.
Doody, Margaret Anne. *Frances Burney: The Life in the Works*. New
    Brunswick, N.J.: Rutgers UP, 1988.
Doody, Margaret Anne. "Heliodorus Rewritten: Samuel Richardson's
    Clarissa and Frances Burney's *Wanderer*." *The Search for the
    Ancient Novel*. Ed. James Tatum. Baltimore, MD: John Hopkins
    UP, 1994. 117-31.
Doody, Margaret Anne. "Introduction." *The Wanderer; or, Female
    Difficulties*. 1814. By Fanny Burney. Oxford, Gr. Brit.: Oxford UP,
    1991.
Doody, Margaret Anne, Robert L. Mack, and Peter Sabor. "Burney and
    Race Relations: Appendix II." *The Wanderer; or, Female
    Difficulties*. 1814. By Fanny Burney. Oxford, Gr. Brit.: Oxford UP,
    1991. 884-7.
Doody, Margaret Anne, Robert L. Mack, and Peter Sabor. "The French
    Revolution in *The Wanderer; or, Female Difficulties*: Appendix I."
    The Wanderer; or, Female Difficulties. 1814. By Fanny Burney.
    Oxford, Gr. Brit.: Oxford UP, 1991. 875-883.
Doody, Margaret Anne, Robert L. Mack, and Peter Sabor. "Geography."
    The Wanderer; or, Female Difficulties. 1814. By Fanny Burney.
    Oxford, Gr. Brit.: Oxford UP, 1991. 888-92.
Dussinger, John A. "Kinship and Guilt in Mary Shelley's *Frankenstein*."
    Studies in the Novel 8 (1976): 38-55.
Eigner, Edwin M. "Charles Darnay and Revolutionary Identity." *Dickens
    Studies Annual: Essays on Victorian Fiction*. 12 (1983): 147-59.
Eisler, Benita. *Byron: Child of Passion, Fool of Fame*. New York: Alfred A.
    Knopf, 1999.
Ellis, Kate Ferguson. *The Contested Castle: Gothic Novels and the
    Subversion of Domestic Ideology*. Urbana: U of Illinois P, 1989.
Ellis, Kate. "Monsters in the Garden: Mary Shelley and the Bourgeois
    Family." *The Endurance of* Frankenstein: *Essays on Mary Shelley's
    Novel*. Eds. George Levine and U.C. Knoepflmacher. Berkeley: U of
    California P, 1974. 123-42.

Ellis, Kate Ferguson. "Subversive Surfaces: The Limits of Domestic Affection in Mary Shelley's Later Fiction." *The Other Mary Shelley: Beyond Frankenstein*. Eds. Audrey A. Fisch et al. New York: Oxford UP, 1993. 220-34.

Epstein, Julia. *The Iron Pen: Frances Burney and the Politics of Women's Writing*. Madison: U of Wisconsin P, 1989.

Escott, T.H.S. *Edward Bulwer: First Baron Lytton of Knebworth*. Port Washington, N.Y.: 1970.

Farson, Daniel. *The Man Who Wrote* Dracula*: A Biography of Bram Stoker*. New York: St. Martin's, 1975.

Findlay, Ian. "Edward Bulwer-Lytton and the Rosicrucians." *Literature and the Occult: Essays in Comparative Literature*. Ed. Luanne Frank. Arlington, TX: U of Texas at Arlington, 1977. 137-46.

Fitzgerald, Maurice H. "Editor's Preface." *The Poems of Robert Southey*. Ed. Maurice H. Fitzgerald. London, Gr. Brit.: Oxford UP, 1909. iii-xii.

Flanders, Wallace Austin. "Godwin and Gothicism: *St. Leon*." *Texas Studies in Literature and Language*. 8 (1966): 533-45.

Franklin, J. Jeffrey. "The Victorian Discourse of Gambling: Speculations on *Middlemarch* and *The Duke's Children*." ELH 61.4 (1994): 899-921.

Franklin, Stephen L. "The Editor as Reconstructor: Carlyle's Historical View As a Shaping Force in the Fiction of *Sartor Resartus*." *Ball State University Forum* 18.3 (1977): 32-9.

Gallagher, Catherine. "Duplicity of Doubling in Dickens's *A Tale of Two Cities*." *Dickens Studies Annual: Essays on Victorian Fiction*. 12 (1983): 125-45.

Gallagher, Catherine. *Nobody's Story: The Vanishing Acts of Women Writers in the Marketplace 1670-1820*. Berkeley: U of California P, 1994.

Gamer, Michael. "'The Most Interesting Novel in the English Language': An Unidentified Addendum to Coleridge's Review of *Udolpho*." *The Wordsworth Circle*. 24.1 (1993): 53-4.

Gamer, Michael. "Genres for the Prosecution: Pornography and the Gothic." *PMLA* 114.5 (1999): 1043-54.

Gaull, Marilyn. *English Romanticism: The Human Context*. New York: W.W. Norton, 1988.

Georgas, Marilyn. "Dickens, Defoe, the Devil and the Dedlocks: The "Faust Motif" in *Bleak House*." *Dickens Studies Annual: Essays on Victorian Fiction*. 10 (1982): 23-44.

Gilbert, Sandra M. and Susan Gubar. *The Madwoman in the Attic*. New Haven, CT: Yale UP, 1984.

Goldberg, Michael. *Carlyle and Dickens*. Athens: U of Georgia P, 1972.

Goldsmith, Steven. "Apocalypse and Gender: Mary Shelley's *Last Man*." *Unbuilding Jerusalem: Apocalypse and Romantic Representation*. Ithaca, NY: Cornell UP, 1993. 261-313.

Gordon, Jon B. "Narrative Enclosure as Textual Ruin: An Archaelogy of Gothic Consciousness." *Dickens Studies Annual: Essays on Victorian Fiction* 11 (1983): 209-38.

Graham, Kenneth W. "Emily's 'Demon-Lover': The Gothic Revolution and *The Mysteries of Udolpho*." *Gothic Fictions: Prohibition / Transgression*. Ed. Kenneth Graham. New York: AMS, 1989. 163-71.

Graham, Kenneth. "Preface." *Gothic Fictions: Prohibition/Transgression*. Ed. Kenneth Graham. New York: AMS, 1989. xiii-vii.

Griffin, Gail B. "'Your Girls That You All Love Are Mine': Dracula and the Victorian Male Sexual Imagination." *Dracula: The Vampire and the Critics*. Ed. Margaret L. Carter. Ann Arbor, MI: UMI Research P, 1988. 137-48.

Grosskurth, Phyllis. *Byron: The Flawed Angel*. Boston: Houghton Mifflin, 1997.

Haggerty, George E. *Gothic Fiction / Gothic Form*. London, PA: Pennsylvania State UP, 1987.

Halperin, John. *Egoism and Self-Discovery in the Victorian Novel: Studies in the Ordeal of Knowledge in the Nineteenth Century*. New York: Burt Franklin, 1974.

Harrold, Charles Frederick. "Introduction." In *Sartor Resartus: The Life and Opinions of Herr Teufelsdrockh* by Thomas Carlyle. New York: Odyssey, 1937. xiii-lxxvi.

Hasan-Rokem, Galit and Alan Dundes, eds. *The Wandering Jew: Essays in the Interpretation of a Christian Legend*. Bloomington: Indiana UP, 1986.

Hatten, Burton. "The Return of the Repressed/Oppressed in Bram Stoker's *Dracula*. *Dracula: The Vampire and the Critics*. Ed. Margaret L. Carter. Ann Arbor, MI: UMI Research P, 1988. 117-35.

Heller, Tamar. *Dead Secrets: Wilkie Collins and the Female Gothic*. New Haven, CT: Yale UP, 1992.

Heller, Terry. "The Aesthetics of the Horror Thriller: Stoker's *Dracula*. *The Delights of Terror: An Aesthetics of the Tale of Terror*. Urbana, IL: U of Illinois P, 1987. 72-86.

Hennelly, Mark M. "*Dracula*: The Gnostic Quest and Victorian Wasteland." *Dracula: The Vampire and the Critics*. Ed. Margaret L. Carter. Ann Arbor, MI: UMI Research P, 1988. 79-92.

Hirsch, Gordon D. "The Mysteries in *Bleak House*: A Psychoanalytic Study." *Dickens Studies Annual: Essays on Victorian Fiction* 4 (1975): 132-52.

Homans, Margaret. "Bearing Demons: Frankenstein's Circumvention of the Material." *Bearing the Word: Language and Female Experience in Nineteenth-Century Women's Writing*. Chicago: U of Chicago P, 1986. 100-19.

Hornback, Bert G. *"Noah's Arkitecture": A Study of Dickens's Mythology*. Athens: Ohio UP, 1972.

Hughes, Merritt, ed. *John Milton: Complete Poems and Prose*. New York: Macmillan, 1957.

Hume, Robert D. "Exuberant Gloom, Existential Agony, and Heroic Despair: Three Varieties of Negative Romanticism." *The Gothic Imagination: Essays in Dark Romanticism*. Ed. G.R. Thompson. n.p.: Washington State UP, 1974. 109-27.

Hunt, Lynn. *The Family Romance of the French Revolution*. Berkeley: U of California P, 1992.

Hurwitz, S. "Ahasver, the Eternal Wanderer: Psychological Aspects." *The Wandering Jew: Essays in the Interpretation of a Christian Legend*. Eds. Galit Hasan-Rokem and Alan Dundes. Bloomington: Indiana UP, 1986. 210-26.

Isaac-Edersheim, E. "Ahasver: A Mythic Image of the Jew." *The Wandering Jew: Essays in the Interpretation of a Christian Legend*. Eds. Galit Hasan-Rokem and Alan Dundes. Bloomington: Indiana UP, 1986. 195-210.

Jacobus, Mary. "Is There a Woman in This Text?" *New Literary History* 14 (1982): 117-41.

James, Elizabeth and Helen R. Smith. *Penny Dreadfuls and Boys' Adventures: The Barry Ono Collection of Victorian Popular Literature in The British Library*. Bury St. Edmunds, Gr. Brit.: The British Library, 1998.

Johnson, Barbara. "The Last Man." *The Other Mary Shelley: Beyond Frankenstein*. Eds. Audrey A. Fisch et al. New York: Oxford UP, 1993. 258-66.

Johnson, Edgar. *Charles Dickens: His Tragedy and Triumph*. New York: Simon and Schuster, 1952. 2 Vols.

Jones, Ernest. *On the Nightmare*. New York: Loveright, 1951.

Kahane, Claire. "The Gothic Mirror." *The (M)other Tongue: Essays in Feminist Psychoanalytic Interpretation*. Eds. Shirley Nelson Garner et al. Ithaca, NY: Cornell UP, 1985. 334-51.

Kaplan, Fred. *Dickens and Mesmerism: The Hidden Springs of Fiction*. Princeton, NJ: Princeton UP, 1975.

Kelly, Gary. "History and Fiction: Bethlem Gabor in Godwin's *St. Leon.*" *English Language Notes* 14 (1976-7): 117-20.

Kermode, Frank. *The Sense of an Ending: Studies in the Theory of Fiction.* New York: Oxford UP, 1966. reprint 1977.

Kilgour, Maggie. "Vampiric Arts: Bram Stoker's Defence of Poetry." *Bram Stoker: History, Psychoanalysis and the Gothic.* Eds. William Hughes and Andrew Smith. New York: St. Martin's, 1998. 47-61.

Kramer, Dale. *Charles Robert Maturin.* New York: Twayne, 1973.

Lamb, John B. "Domesticating History: Revolution and Moral Management in *A Tale of Two Cities.*" *Dickens Studies Annual: Essays on Victorian Fiction* 25 (1996): 227-43.

Lamb, John B. "Mary Shelley's *Frankenstein* and Milton's Monstrous Myth." *Nineteenth Century Literature.* 47.3 (1992): 303-19.

Lindsay, Jack. *Charles Dickens.* New York: Philosophical Library, 1950.

Loregy, Robert E. *Charles Robert Maturin.* Cranbury, NJ: Associated UP, 1975.

Lowe-Evans, Mary. Frankenstein: *Mary Shelley's Wedding Guest.* New York: Twayne, 1993.

Luke, Hugh J. "*The Last Man*: Mary Shelley's Myth of the Solitary." *Prairie Schooner* 39 (1966): 316-27.

Lupoff, Richard A. *Edgar Rice Burroughs: Master of Adventure.* 1965. New York: Ace Books, 1968.

Lyons, Shawn R. "Fact and Fiction: The French Revolution in the Works of Charles Dickens and Frances Burney." Thesis. U of Alaska at Anchorage, 1995.

Lytton, Earl of. *Bulwer-Lytton.* Denver: Alan-Swallow, 1948.

Lytton, Earl of. *The Life of Edward Bulwer First Lord Lytton.* London: MacMillan, 1913. 2 Vols.

Macainsh, Noel. "Queensland, Rosicrucians, and A Strange Story—Aspects of Literary Occultism." *LINQ* 11.3 (1983): 1-17.

MacCaffrey, Isabel Gamble. Paradise Lost *as "Myth."* Cambridge, MA: Harvard UP, 1959.

Macdonald, D.L. *Poor Polidori: A Critical Biography of the Author of* The Vampyre. Toronto, Can.: U of Toronto P, 1991.

Macdonald, D.L. and Kathleen Scherf. "Introduction." The Vampyre *and* Ernestus Berchtold: or, The Modern Oedipus: *Collected Fiction of John William Polidori.* Toronto, Can.: U of Toronto P, 1994. 1-29.

Madoff, Mark S. "Inside, Outside, and the Gothic Locked-Room Mystery." *Gothic Fictions: Prohibition/Transgression.* Ed. Kenneth Graham. New York: AMS, 1989. 49-62.

Malchow, H.L. *Gothic Images of Race in Nineteenth-Century Britain*. Stanford, CA: Stanford UP, 1996.

Marcus, David D. "The Carlylean Vision of *A Tale of Two Cities*." *Studies in the Novel* 8 (1976): 56-68.

Maurois, Andre. *Byron*. 1930. New York: Frederick Ungar, 1964.

Mays, Milton A. "*Frankenstein*: Mary Shelley's Black Theodicy." *Southern Humanities Review* 3 (1969): 146-53.

McInerney, Peter. "*Frankenstein* and the Godlike Science of Letters." *Genre* 13.4 (1980): 455-75.

McMaster, Juliet. "The Silent Angel: Impediments to Female Expression in Frances Burney's Novels." *Studies in the Novel* 21 (1989): 235-52.

McSweeney, Kerry and Peter Sabor. "Introduction." *Sartor Resartus* by Thomas Carlyle. New York: Oxford UP, 1987. vii-xxxiii.

McWhir, Ann. "The Gothic Transgression of Disbelief: Walpole, Radcliffe and Lewis." *Gothic Fictions: Prohibition/Transgression*. Ed. Kenneth Graham. New York: AMS, 1989. 29-47.

Meige, Henry. "The Wandering Jew in the Clinic: A Study in Neurotic Pathology." *The Wandering Jew: Essays in the Interpretation of a Christian Legend*. Eds. Galit Hasan-Rokem and Alan Dundes. Bloomington: Indiana UP, 1986. 190-4.

Mellor, Anne K. "Introduction." *The Last Man* by Mary Shelley. Lincoln: U of Nebraska P, 1993. vii-xxxvi.

Mellor, Anne K. *Mary Shelley: Her Life, Her Fiction, Her Monsters*. New York: Methuen, 1988.

Mellor, Anne K. "Possessing Nature: The Female in *Frankenstein*." *Romanticism and Feminism*. Ed. Anne K. Mellor. Bloomington: Indiana UP, 1988. 220-32.

Meyers, Jeffrey. *Homosexuality and Literature 1890-1930*. London, Gr. Brit.: Athlone, 1977.

Mighall, Robert. "Sex, History and the Vampire." *Bram Stoker: History, Psychoanalysis and the Gothic*. Eds. William Hughes and Andrew Smith. New York: St. Martin's, 1998. 62-77.

Milbank, Alison. "'Powers Old and New': Stoker's Alliances with Anglo-Irish Gothic." *Bram Stoker: History, Psychoanalysis and the Gothic*. Eds. William Hughes and Andrew Smith. New York: St. Martin's, 1998. 12-28.

Miles, Robert. *Ann Radcliffe: The Great Enchantress*. Manchester, Oxford, Gr. Brit.: Manchester UP, 1995.

Mishra, Vijay. *The Gothic Sublime*. New York: State U of New York P, 1994.

Moers, Ellen. "*Bleak House*: The Agitating Women." *The Dickensian* 69 (1973): 13-24.

Moers, Ellen. "Female Gothic." *The Endurance of* Frankenstein: *Essays on Mary Shelley's Novel*. Eds. George Levine and U.C. Knoepflmacher. Berkeley: U of California P, 1974. 77-87.

Moers, Ellen. *Literary Women*. Garden City, NY: Doubleday, 1976.

Morrow, Bradford and Patrick McGrath. "Introduction." *The New Gothic: A Collection of Contemporary Gothic Fiction*. Eds. Bradford Morrow and Patrick McGrath. New York: Vintage, 1992. xi-iv.

Mulvey-Roberts, Marie. "Dracula and the Doctors: Bad Blood, Menstrual Taboo and the New Woman." *Bram Stoker: History, Psychoanalysis and the Gothic*. Eds. William Hughes and Andrew Smith. New York: St. Martin's, 1998. 78-95.

Murray, E.B. *Ann Radcliffe*. New York: Twayne, 1972.

Nabokov, Vladimir. "Nabokov on *Bleak House*: Excerpts from *Lectures on Literature*." *Bleak House*. 1853. By Charles Dickens. New York: Bantam, 1992. ix-xxiii.

The New American Bible. New York: Thomas Nelson, 1971.

Oates, Joyce Carol. "Frankenstein's Fallen Angel." *Critical Inquiry* 10.3 (1984): 543-54.

Oddie, William. *Dickens and Carlyle: The Question of Influence*. London, Gr. Brit.: Centenary, 1972.

Paley, Morton D. "*The Last Man*: Apocalypse without Millenium." *The Other Mary Shelley: Beyond* Frankenstein. Eds. Audrey A. Fisch et al. New York: Oxford UP, 1993. 107-23.

Paulson, Robert. "Gothic Fiction and the French Revolution." *ELH* 48 (1981): 532-54.

Paulson, Ronald. *Representations of Revolution (1789-1820)*. New Haven, CT: Yale UP, 1983.

Perkins, Pam. "Private Men and Public Women: Social Criticism in Fanny Burney's *The Wanderer*." *Essays in Literature* 23 (1996): 69-83.

Perkowski, Jan L. *The Darkling: A Treatise on Slavic Vampirism*. Columbus, OH: Slavica, 1989.

Ping, Tang Soo. "*Frankenstein, Paradise Lost*, and "The Majesty of Goodness." *College Literature* 16 (1989): 255-60.

Pollin, Burton R. "Philosophical and Literary Sources of *Frankenstein*." *Comparative Literature* 17 (1965): 97-108.

Pool, Daniel. *What Jane Austen Ate and Charles Dickens Knew: From Fox Hunting to Whist—The Facts of Daily Life in Nineteenth-Century England*. New York: Simon & Schuster, 1993.

Pratt, Branwen Bailey. "Carlyle and Dickens: Heroes and Hero-Worshippers." *Dickens Studies Annual: Essays on Victorian Fiction*. 12 (1983): 233-46.

Praz, Mario. *The Romantic Agony*. 1933. Trans. Angus Davidson. London: Oxford UP, 1952.

Pritchard, Allan. "The Urban Gothic of *Bleak House*." *Nineteenth-Century Literature* 45.4 (1991): 432-52.

Punter, David. *The Literature of Terror: A History of Gothic Fictions from 1765 to the present day*. New York: Longman, 1980.

Punter, David. "Narrative and Psychology in Gothic Fiction." *Gothic Fictions: Prohibition/Transgression*. Ed. Kenneth Graham. New York: AMS, 1989. 1-27.

Raible, Christopher Gist. "Dracula: Christian Heretic." *Dracula: The Vampire and the Critics*. Ed. Margaret L. Carter. Ann Arbor, MI: UMI Research P, 1988. 105-7.

Rauch, Alan. "The Monstrous Body of Knowledge in Mary Shelley's *Frankenstein*." *Studies in Romanticism*. 34.2 (1995): 227-53.

Read, Walter L. "The Pattern of Conversion in *Sartor Resartus*." *ELH*. 38.3 (1971): 411-31.

Riley, Michael. *Conversations with Anne Rice*. New York: Ballantine, 1996.

Roberts, Bette B. "The Horrid Novels: *The Mysteries of Udolpho* and *Northanger Abbey*." *Gothic Fictions: Prohibition/Transgression*. Ed. Kenneth Graham. New York: AMS, 1989. 89-111.

Roberts, Marie. *Gothic Immortals: The Fiction of the Brotherhood of the Rosy Cross*. London, Gr. Brit.: Routledge, 1990.

Roberts, Marie. "Mary Shelley: Immortality, Gender, and the Rosy Cross." *Reviewing Romanticism*. Ed. Philip W. Martin. New York: St. Martin's, 1992. 60-8.

Ronald, Ann. "Dickens' Gloomiest Gothic Castle." *Dickens Studies Newsletter* 6.3 (1975): 71-5.

Roth, Phyllis A. *Bram Stoker*. Boston: Twayne, 1982.

Roth, Phyllis A. "Suddenly Sexual Woman in Bram Stoker's *Dracula*." *Dracula: The Vampire and the Critics*. Ed. Margaret L. Carter. Ann Arbor, MI: UMI Research P, 1988. 57-65.

Sanders, Charles Richard. "The Byron Closed in *Sartor Resartus*." *Studies in Romanticism*. 3.2 (1964): 77-108.

Sedgwick, Eve Kosofsky. *Between Men: English Literature and Male Homosocial Desire*. New York: Columbia UP, 1985.

Sedgwick, Eve Kosofsky. *The Coherence of Gothic Conventions*. 1980. New York: Methuen, 1986.

Senf, Carol A. "*Dracula*: The Unseen Face in the Mirror." *Dracula: The Vampire and the Critics*. Ed. Margaret L. Carter. Ann Arbor, MI: UMI Research P, 1988. 93-103.

Senf, Carol. *The Vampire in Nineteenth Century English Literature.* Bowling Green, OH: Bowling Green State U Popular P, 1988.

Sherwin, Paul. "*Frankenstein*: Creation as Catastrophe." *PMLA* 96 (1981): 883-903.

Sigman, Joseph. "Adam-Kadmon, Nifl, Muspel, and the Biblical Symbolism of *Sartor Resartus*." *ELH* 41 (1974): 233-56.

Simmons, Clare A. "Fables of Continuity: Bram Stoker and Medievalism." *Bram Stoker: History, Psychoanalysis and the Gothic.* Eds. William Hughes and Andrew Smith. New York: St. Martin's, 1998. 29-46.

Simmons, James R. "'Every Discernible Thing in It was Covered with Dust and Mould': Radcliffe's Chateau-le-Blanc and Dickens's Satis House." *The Dickensian* 93.1 (1997): 11-3.

Smith, Johanna M. *Mary Shelley.* New York: Twayne, 1996. Soyka, David. "Frankenstein and the Miltonic Creation of Evil." *Extrapolation* 33.2 (1992): 166-77.

Stonehouse, J.H., ed. *Reprints of the Catalogues of the Libraries of Charles Dickens and W.M. Thackeray.* London, Gr. Brit.: Piccadilly Fountain, 1935.

Stuart, Roxana. *Stage Blood: Vampires of the 19th-Century Stage.* Bowling Green, OH: Bowling Green State U Popular P, 1984.

Svendsen, Kester. *Milton and Science.* Cambridge, MA: Harvard UP, 1956.

Svilpis, J.E. "The Mad Scientist and Domestic Affections in Gothic Fiction." *Gothic Fictions: Prohibition/Transgression.* Ed. Kenneth Graham. New York: AMS, 1989. 63-87.

Swingle, L.J. "Frankenstein's Monster and Its Romantic Relatives: Problems of Knowledge in English Romanticism." *Texas Studies in Literature and Language.* 15 (1973): 51-65.

Tannenbaum, Leslie. "From Filthy Type to Truth: Miltonic Myth in Frankenstein." *Keats-Shelley Journal.* 26 (1977): 101-13.

Tennyson, G.B. *Sartor Called Resartus: The Genesis, Structure, and Style of Thomas Carlyle's First Major Work.* Princeton, NJ: Princeton UP, 1966.

Tichelaar, Tyler R. "'Christabel': Coleridge's Conflict Between Christianity and Celtic Pantheism." *Michigan Academician* 27 (1995): 493-501.

Timko, Michael. "Splendid Impressions and Picturesque Means: Dickens, Carlyle, and the French Revolution." *Dickens Studies Annual: Essays on Victorian Fiction.* 12 (1983): 177-95.

Twitchell, James B. *The Living Dead: A Study of the Vampire in Romantic Literature.* Durham, NC: Duke UP, 1981.

Twitchell, James. "The Vampire Myth." *Dracula: The Vampire and the Critics.* Ed. Margaret L. Carter. Ann Arbor, MI: UMI Research P, 1988. 109-16.

Tysdahl, B.J. "St. Leon: Recalcitrant Gothicism." *William Godwin as Novelist*. London, Gr. Brit.: Athlone, 1981. 77-96.

Vanden Bossche, Chris R. "Desire and Deferral of Closure in Carlyle's *Sartor Resartus* and *The French Revolution*. *The Journal of Narrative Technique* 16 (1986): 72-8.

Varnado, S.L. *Haunted Presence: The Numinous in Gothic Fiction*. Tuscaloosa: U of Alabama P, 1987.

Veeder, William. *Mary Shelley and* Frankenstein: *the Fate of Androgyny*. Chicago: U of Chicago P, 1986.

Waring, Walter. "Sartor Resartus." *Thomas Carlyle*. Boston: Twayne, 1978. 47-57.

Wasson, Richard. "The Politics of Dracula." *Dracula: The Vampire and the Critics*. Ed. Margaret L. Carter. Ann Arbor, MI: UMI Research P, 1988. 19-23.

Waxman, Barbara Frey. "Victor Frankenstein's Romantic Fate: The Tragedy of the Promethean Overreacher as Woman." *Papers on Language and Literature* 23 (1987): 14-26.

Weissman, Judith. "Women and Vampires: *Dracula* as a Victorian Novel." *Dracula: The Vampire and the Critics*. Ed. Margaret L. Carter. Ann Arbor, MI: UMI Research P, 1988. 69-77.

Wiesenfurth, Joseph. "*Adam Bede* and Myth." *Papers on Language and Literature* 8 (1972): 39-52.

Williams, Anne. *Art of Darkness*. Chicago: U of Chicago P, 1995.

Wilson, A.N. *God's Funeral*. New York: W.W. Norton, 1999.

Wilson, Angus. *The World of Charles Dickens*. New York: Viking, 1970.

Wilson, Frances. "Caroline Lamb and Her Critics." *Glenarvon*. 1816. By Lady Caroline Lamb. London, Gr. Brit.: J.M. Dent, 1995. 375-96.

Wilson, Frances. "Introduction." *Glenarvon*. 1816. By Lady Caroline Lamb. London, Gr. Brit.: J.M. Dent, 1995. xvii-xxxvi.

Wilson, Frances. "Notes." *Glenarvon*. 1816. By Lady Caroline Lamb. London, Gr. Brit.: J.M. Dent, 1995. 367-74.

Wilson, John R. "*Sartor Resartus*: A Study in the Paradox of Despair." *Christianity and Literature* 23.2 (1974): 9-27.

Wilt, Judith. "Imperial Mouth: Imperialism, the Gothic and Science Fiction." *Journal of Popular Culture* 14 (1981): 618-28.

Wolf, Leonard, ed. *The Annotated Dracula: Dracula by Bram Stoker*. New York: Clarkson N. Potter, 1975.

Wolff, Robert Lee. *Strange Stories and Other Explorations in Victorian Fiction*. Boston: Gambit, 1971.

Wolstenholme, Susan. *Gothic (Re)visions: Writing Women as Readers*. Albany: State U of New York P, 1993.

Zanger, Jules. "A Sympathetic Vibration: Dracula and the Jews." *English Literature in Transition (1880-1920)*. 34.1 (1991): 33-44.

Zatlin, Linda Gertner. *The Nineteenth Century Anglo-Jewish Novel*. Boston: Twayne, 1981.

Zemka, Sue. "From the Punchmen to Pugin's Gothics: the Broad Road to a Sentimental Death in *The Old Curiosity Shop*." *Nineteenth Century Literature* 48.3 (1993): 291-309.

Zimansky, Curt R. "Shelley's 'Wandering Jew': Some Borrowings from Lewis and Radcliffe." *Studies in English Literature (1500-1900)*. 18.4 (1978): 597-609.

Index

Africa, 247, 249–51
Africans, 232
Ahasuerus. *See* Wandering Jew
Alexander, William
   History of Women, 107
angelic sin, 37, 53, 77
anti-Semitism, 43–44, 52, 53, 56, 229, 232
Arnold, Matthew, 49
atheism, 75
atonement, 236
Austen, Jane
   Emma, 106
   Pride and Prejudice, 105
autonomy
   Gothic Wanderer's quest for, 62, 66, 71, 82, 116, 122, 169, 174, 184
   in *Frankenstein*, 132, 136
   in *Melmoth the Wanderer*, 78
   in *Paradise Lost*, xvi, 15, 16
   in *The Monk*, 36
Balzac, Honore de
   Melmoth Reconciled, 53, 81
baptism, 237
Bastille, 8, 32, 184, 198, 199, 203
Batman, 252–53
Beckford, William, xi, 130
Berard, Cyprien
   Lord Ruthven ou les vampires, 223
Bible
   Deuteronomy, 234, 236
   Genesis, 46, 197, 236, 257
   Leviticus, 234, 236
Blake, William, 1, 171

Bloom, Harold, 130, 135, 136, 139
Bronte, Charlotte
   Jane Eyre, xi, 19
Bronte, Emily
   Wuthering Heights, xi, 19
Brown, Dan
   The Da Vinci Code, xiv
Buffy the Vampire Slayer, 254
Bulwer-Lytton, Edward, 49, 75, 79, 184, 194, 207, 209, 219, 223, 231, 235, 244
   "The Haunted and the Haunters", 49, 231
   as Carlyle's disciple, 183
   friendship with Dickens, 203
   The Last Days of Pompeii, 231
   Zanoni, 75, 79, 184–92, 194, 195, 202, 203, 207, 253
   Zanoni as revision of *Melmoth the Wanderer*, 183
   Zanoni compared to *A Tale of Two Cities*, 184–92
Burke, Edmund, 5–7, 64, 144
Burney, Fanny
   Camilla, 109, 110, 111
   Cecilia, 109, 110, 111
   Evelina, 102–5, 109, 110, 111
   The Wanderer, 11, 99–128, 165, 184, 235
Burroughs, Edgar Rice
   Caspak series, 251
   John Carter character, 253
   Tarzan novels, 249–53
Byron, George Gordon, Lord, 93, 105, 149, 154, 158, 170, 171, 175, 183

as depicted in *Glenarvon*, 213–20
Childe Harold, 170
influence on Polidori's *The Vampyre*, 220–23
The Giaour, 213
Byronic hero, 169, 170, 218, 220
Cain and Abel, 19, 46, 171, 201, 202, 231, 232, 236
Caleb Williams. *See* Godwin, William
Calvinism
predestination, 81
Campbell, John
Hermippus Redivivus, 65
Campbell, Thomas, 154
Carlyle, Thomas, 165–83
French Revolution, 195, 198, 199
Sartor Resartus, 165–83
Carmilla. *See* LeFanu, J.S.
Castle of Otranto, The. *See* Walpole, Horace
Catholic Church
Catholicism, xiv, 19, 34, 50, 52, 54, 210, 222, 251
Catholicism in *Dracula*, 219, 235–38
Catholicism in *Glenarvon*, 218, 219
Chaucer, Geoffrey, 45
Christ-figure, 175, 181, 205
Christianity, 8, 39, 60, 63, 117, 170, 176, 177, 185
affirmed in *Zanoni*, 184
Anne Rice's conversion to, 255–57
as symbol, 168
Carlyle's desire to revise, 167
Dickens' use of, 205
forced conversion to, 52
in *Dracula*, 234, 236, 240
Mary Shelley's rejection of, 143, 148
modern move away from, xv
prohibition against usury, 44

reconfirmed in *Sartor Resartus*, 177
Rosicrucian attempts to revitalize, 60
Rosicrucians depicted as anti-Christian, 60
salvation through Christ, 48
secularized by Romantics, 143
secularized in *St. Leon*, 66, 68
Wandering Jew's rejection of, 46
Christmas, 210
Coleridge, Samuel Taylor, 1, 53, 171
Christabel, 213
The Rime of the Ancient Mariner, 48–50, 53, 56, 160, 161, 212–13, 217
Conrad, Joseph
Heart of Darkness, 248
Croly, George
Salathiel, 56
curse
in *A Tale of Two Cities*, 201
in *Glenarvon*, 215
curse of prolonged life
and the Wandering Jew, 44
in *Melmoth the Wanderer*, 78
in *St. Irvyne*, 77
curse of vampirism, 224
Danton, 4
Darwin, Charles
The Origin of Species, 245, 249
Dickens, Charles, xi, xii, xv, 20, 79, 183, 192, 209, 223, 227, 233, 235, 244
A Tale of Two Cities, 79, 183, 193, 194, 195–208, 227
A Tale of Two Cities as revision of *Zanoni*, 183–84
Bleak House, 20, 193
Carlyle's influence upon, 192–95
Dombey and Son, 233
Gothic elements in novels, 192–95
Oliver Twist, 194, 233

The Mystery of Edwin Drood, 202
The Old Curiosity Shop, 193–94
Dippel, Johann Konrad, 131
Dracula. See Stoker, Bram
dreams, xii, 31, 245, 258
  Adam's dream in *Paradise Lost*, 139
  in *A Tale of Two Cities*, 200
  in *Dracula*, 31
  in *Frankenstein*, 134, 136, 144, 146
  in *Glenarvon*, 215, 217
  in *St. Irvyne*, 76
  in *Varney the Vampyre*, 225
  of deceased/vampires, 211
DuMaurier, George, 233
  Trilby, 49, 57, 233, 245
Eliot, George, 183
  Adam Bede, 108
elixir of life, 65, 131, 185
  and Rosicrucians, 9, 50, 59
  in *Frankenstein*, 132
  in *St. Leon*, 51, 67, 73, 171
  in *Zanoni*, 188
  metaphorical use in *The Wanderer*, 116
Enoch, son of biblical Cain, 232, 236
Ernestus Berchtold. See Polidori, John
Eucharist, 236, 237
Everyman
  figure in literature, 124, 165, 166, 181, 201, 243
  in *Sartor Resartus*, 174–76, 177–80
evil eye, 44, 230
evolution, xv, 249, 250
  and life-extension, 66, 67, 159
  Darwin's theory of, 245–47
  Dickens' theories of historical evolution, 197, 206
  social evolution, 133
excommunication, 210, 222

Existentialism, 129, 134, 135, 147, 153
  in *Frankenstein*, 134–44, 147–49
  in *The Last Man*, 153–56
Faust
  Christopher Marlowe's *Dr. Faustus*, 37, 53
Feminine Gothic, 10–17, 21, 29–34, 129, 147, 148
  as revision of *Paradise Lost*, 21–23
  as revision of *Paradise Lost*, 40
  as revision of *Paradise Lost*, 133
  compared to *Frankenstein*, 135, 146
  Glenarvon as, 219
  The Mysteries of Udolpho as, 87
  The Wanderer as, 107, 126
Fielding, Henry, 103
Flying Dutchman, 217, 232
forbidden knowledge, xi, 14, 15, 26, 34, 40, 55, 59, 63, 79, 84, 245, 253, 257, 258
  and gambling in *St. Leon*, 90
  and Rosicrucianism, 61
  in *A Tale of Two Cities*, 200
  in *Dracula*, 228, 243
  in *Frankenstein*, 131, 135, 137, 147
  in *Melmoth the Wanderer*, 37, 53, 77
  in *The Monk*, 34
  in *The Mysteries of Udolpho*, 24, 37
  in *The Wanderer*, 107, 116, 125
  in *Zanoni*, 187
Foster, Hannah Webster
  The Coquette, 107
Frankenstein. See Shelley, Mary
Franklin, Benjamin, 131
Freemasons, 9, 202, 222
French monarchy, 5, 13, 67, 131
French Revolution, xii, xiv, 1–12, 17, 41, 62, 63, 64, 131, 144,

154, 170, 184, 194, 222, 245, 258
  in *A Tale of Two Cities*, 195–208
  in *The Wanderer*, 101, 108, 121, 122
  in *Zanoni*, 190–91
Gaddafi, Muammar, 258
gambling, xiv, 79–98
  in *Ernestus Berchtold*, 94–97
  in *St. Leon*, 51, 65, 70, 88–92
  in *The Last Man*, 151, 156–58
  in *The Mysteries of Udolpho*, 29, 85–88
  in *The Vampyre*, 92–94, 221
  in *Varney the Vampyre*, 225
Gaskell, Elizabeth
  Mary Barton, 108
genocide, 240
ghosts, 34, 48, 176, 200, 219, 220
Glenarvon. See Lamb, Caroline, Lady
Godwin, William, 8, 50, 115, 129, 133, 144, 159, 184, 219
  Caleb Williams, 16, 50, 63, 115
  opinion on French Revolution, 5–7
  St. Leon, 5, 8, 33, 50–52, 54, 63–75, 81, 88–92, 92, 93, 96, 129, 133, 151, 159, 171, 175, 184, 192
  St. Leon's influence on *St. Irvyne*, 75–77
  St. Leon's influence on *The Last Man*, 81
  St. Leon's influence on *Zanoni*, 79, 185
Goethe
  The Sorrows of Young Werther, 45, 170
Gospel of Work
  in *Sartor Resartus*, 175
Greek Orthodox Church, 210
guillotine, 9, 190, 191, 203, 205, 207
Haggard, H. Rider, 49, 248, 250, 251
  Benita, 49
  King Solomon's Mines, 248
  Nada and the Lily, 251
  She, 248–49
heretics, 210
homosexuality, 221, 229, 233
Hood, Thomas, 154
hypnotism. See mesmerism
Illuminati, 9, 131
imagination, 25, 27, 28, 96, 127, 131, 159, 162, 180, 219, 252
Imlay, Fanny, 142
immortality
  achievable through science, 66
  and over-population, 66
  and Rosicrucianism, 63
  as blasphemy, 61
  elixir of, 67
  in *A Tale of Two Cities*, 195–208
  in *Dracula*, 236
  in *She*, 248
  in Tarzan novels, 251
  in *The Jewel of the Seven Stars*, 249
  in *The Last Man*, 150–51
  in *The Wanderer*, 113–16, 124
  in Wordsworth's "Intimations of Immortality", 174
  in *Zanoni*, 184–91
  on earth, 79
  through freedom from disease, 61
Imperial Gothic, 247–49
incest, 4, 20, 94, 96, 97, 211, 222
Industrial Revolution, xv
Inquisition
  in *Melmoth the Wanderer*, 38, 54, 78
  in *St. Leon*, 50, 52, 67
Irving, Henry, 230
Jack the Ripper, 233
Jesuits, 230
Jewish. See Judaism and Wandering Jew
Johnson, Samuel, 24, 176, 177
  Rasselas, 24

Judaism, 43, 48, 210, 256
  in *Caleb Williams*, 50
  in *Dracula*, 229, 232, 240, 241
  in *Sartor Resartus*, 177
  in *Trilby*, 56
  Jewish characters in *Melmoth the Wanderer*, 52
  Jewish people blamed for Christ's death, 46, *108*
  Wandering Jew as metaphor for Jewish people, xiv, 43, *210*
Judgment Day, 44, 202, 217, 232
Keats, John, 149, 171
  Lamia, 212
Kermode, Frank
  The Sense of an Ending, 168, 169
King, Stephen, xii, 40
Knights Templar, 65
Lamb, Caroline, Lady
  Glenarvon, 209, 213–20, 220, 221, 235
Lander, George, 230
LeFanu, J.S., 228
  Carmilla, 228, 245
Lewis, Matthew
  The Monk, 8, 19, 30, 33, 34–37, 37, 39, 43, 45, 46–48, 48, 49, 50, 76, 78, 227, 229, 235
Libya, 258
loss of faith
  in *Sartor Resartus*, 181
lost civilizations
  lost cities, 248, 249
Louis XVI, 198, 199
Love at First Bite, x
Malthus, Thomas, 66
manuscripts
  as Gothic device, 200
  in *A Tale of Two Cities*, 203
  in *Dracula*, 228
  in *Ernestus Berchtold*, 97
  in *Melmoth the Wanderer*, 56
  in *Sartor Resartus*, 165, 172, 178
  in *Tarzan of the Apes*, 250

  in *The Last Man*, 150, 158
  in *Zanoni*, 186
Martineau, Harriet, 183, 192
Masculine Gothic, 10–17, 21, 33, 40, 148
  and domestic tragedies, 88
  and first person point of view, 147
  and forbidden knowledge, 40
  and *Melmoth the Wanderer*, 37
  and *The Monk*, 36
  and vampire novels, 212
  as response to Feminine Gothic, 23, 33
  as revision of *Paradise Lost*, 29–36
  as social criticism, 40
  as tragedy, 62
  relation to *Frankenstein*, 129
masturbation, 233
Maturin, Charles
  Melmoth the Wanderer, 9, 33, 34, 37–40, 49, 50, 52, 53–57, 75, 77–79, 79, 81, 183, 184, 190, 191, 216, 227, 229, 235
Melchizedek, 51, 171
Melmoth the Wanderer. See Maturin, Charles
mesmerism, 49–50, 57, 212, 222, 224, 230, 233
Messiah, 241
Meyer, Stephenie
  Twilight series, 257
millenarianism, 133
Milton, John
  Paradise Lost, xvi, 1, 10, 11, 12–41, 43, 53, 59, 63, 77, 79, 90, 107, 111, 123, 126, 131, 134, 146, 147, 156, 161, 162, 167, 170, 189, 194, 197, 200, 214, 224, 225, 226, 237, 244, 255
  Paradise Lost's influence on Feminine Gothic, 21–23
  Paradise Lost's influence on *Frankenstein*, 134–44

Paradise Lost's influence on Masculine Gothic, 29–34
Paradise Lost's influence on *The Mysteries of Udolpho*, 23–29
money, xv, 24, 44, 69, 70, 81, 83, 84, 85, 87, 88, 89, 91, 92, 93, 94, 95, 106, 112, 120, 152, 193, 222, 233
Monk, The. See Lewis, Matthew
mummy, 124, 249
Muslims, 69
Mysteries of Udolpho, The. See Radcliffe, Ann
Napoleon
Napoleonic Wars, 171
Natural Supernaturalism, 165, 176–77, 176, 193
Nature
and Romanticism in *The Last Man*, 149, 160
and Romanticism in *The Wanderer*, 116–23
and science, 77, 253
and Wandering Jew and vampires, 214, 222, 224, 231
Book of Nature by Rosencreutz, 60
in *Frankenstein*, 132, 136, 138
in *Paradise Lost*, 140
in *St. Irvyne*, 76
in *St. Leon*, 71
in *Zanoni*, 185
laws of, 79
man's reconciliation with, 61
The Book of Nature by Rosencreutz, 60
transgression against, 17
Negative Romanticism, 134
New Testament, 177
Newman, John Henry, Cardinal, 235
Newman, Kim
Anno Dracula, 249
North Pole, 146, 172
Obama, Barack, 258

Oedipal conflict, 141, 146
Old Testament, 177, 234
original sin, 206, 211, 256
orphans, 4, 51, 150, 191
Oxford Movement, 235
Paradise Lost. See Milton, John
parricide, 6, 203
Passover, 234
Peacock, Thomas Love
Nightmare Abbey, 77
penny dreadful novels, 223
philosopher's stone
and Rosicrucians, 9, 59, 60
in *Frankenstein*, 132
in *St. Leon*, 50, 67, 72, 91
relation to gambling, 81
similarities to in *Ernestus Berchtold*, 96
Poe, Edgar Allan
"The Fall of the House of Usher", 20
comments on *Melmoth the Wanderer*, 78
Polidori, John
Ernestus Berchtold, 11, 81, 92, 94–97, 220, 235
The Vampyre, 9, 81, 96, 97, 213, 218, 220–23, 223, 229, 235
The Vampyre, gambling theme, 92–94
Prest, Thomas Peckett, 223
primogeniture, 17–21, 28, 35, 39, 250
prolonged life
as a curse, 43
Purgatory, 210
Queen Victoria, 249
racial purity, 234
Radcliffe, Ann
The Mysteries of Udolpho, xi, 9, 20, 23, 29, 30, 34, 37, 81, 103, 105, 153, 227, 235
The Mysteries of Udolpho, as revision of *Paradise Lost*, 23–29

The Mysteries of Udolpho,
  gambling theme, 85–88
Reign of Terror, 2, 62, 109, 190, 206
Reincarnation, xv, 248
religion
  influence on Gothic. *See*
    Judaism and Catholicism
Rice, Anne, 254–57
  Interview with the Vampire, 254
  Memnoch the Devil, 255, 256
  Queen of the Damned, 255
Richardson, Samuel
  Sir Charles Grandison, 31
Robespierre, 4, 190, 192
Robinson, Henry Crabb, 130
Roger of Wendover, 45
Romantic Wanderer figure, 1, 11–14
Romanticism, 105
  and *Dracula*, 227
  and myth of consciousness, 149, 157
  and myth of consciousness in *Zanoni*, 189
  and the Satanic School of poetry, 170
  and the Wandering Jew, 46, 49
  Anti-Romanticism in *The Wanderer*, 101, 105, 115, 116–23
  in *Frankenstein*, 130–31
  in *Sartor Resartus*, 169, 180
  influenced by *The Monk*, 43
  Negative Romanticism, 134
  Paradise Lost's influence upon, 10
  rejection of in *The Last Man*, 149–50, 159–61
  view of French Revolution, 1–3
Rosicrucianism, xiv, 9, 43, 57, 59–79, 88, 116, 131, 183, 201, 222, 254
  in *A Tale of Two Cities*, 195–208
  in *Frankenstein*, 130–31

  in *Melmoth the Wanderer*, 77–79
  in *St. Irvyne*, 75–77
  in *St. Leon*, 50–52, 63–75
  in *Zanoni*, 184–92
  origins of, 59–63
  Rosicrucian novel as rewrite of *Paradise Lost*, 59
Rowson, Susannah
  Charlotte Temple, 107
Rymer, James Malcolm, 223
sacrifice
  Dr. Manette's in *A Tale of Two Cities*, 201
Sade, Marquis de, 8
Sartor Resartus. *See* Carlyle, Thomas
Schubart, Christian
  Der Ewige Jude, 45, 46
Second Coming, The, 202, 206
self-sacrifice
  Adam's in *Paradise Lost*, 22
  and Gothic Wanderer's redemption, 209
  Carton's in *A Tale of Two Cities*, 196, 202
  Christ's for human salvation, 143, 200, 240, 242
  in *Frankenstein*, 143
  in *Zanoni*, 191
  theme in *Sartor Resartus*, 181
sexual deviance, 108, 233
Shakespeare, William
  The Merchant of Venice, 234
Shelley, Mary
  Frankenstein, xi, xv, 9–12, 33, 75, 77, 133, 149, 150, 162, 179, 220, 247, 253
  Frankenstein and existentialism, 147–49
  Frankenstein as existential revision of *Paradise Lost*, 134–44
  Frankenstein, critical history, 129–31
  Frankenstein, theme of family and illegitimacy, 144–47

The Last Man, xv, 81, 92, 129, 131, 135, 154, 178
The Last Man as rejection of Romanticism, 149–50
The Last Man, deconstruction theories, 158–62
The Last Man, existential plague, 153–56
The Last Man, gambling with Fate, 156–58
The Last Man, Lionel Verney as Gothic Wanderer, 151–53
The Last Man, the Sibyl's prophecy, 150–51
Valperga, 233
Shelley, Percy, ix, xi, xvi, 2, 131, 133, 150, 159
Alastor, 170
Prometheus Unbound, 76
St. Irvyne, 75–77, 77, 81, 131, 133
Smollett, Tobias, 103
sodomy, 233
Southey, Robert, 1, 2
Thalaba the Destroyer, 212, 235
Spenser, Edmund
The Faerie Queene, 14
St. Irvyne. See Shelley, Percy
St. Leon. See Godwin, William
Stoker, Bram
Dracula, xi, 9, 11, 31, 32, 49, 129, 209, 210, 219, 222, 223, 226, 227, 229, 245, 246, 247, 249, 253, 254, 255
Dracula, Catholicism in, 234–38
Dracula, historical origins, 227–29
Dracula, redemption theme, 238–44
Dracula, use of Wandering Jew, 229–34
The Jewel of the Seven Stars, 249
Stonehenge, 104, 123, 125
Sue, Eugene

The Wandering Jew, 230
suicide
  and vampires, 211, 225, 237
  gambling as form of, 84
  in *Sartor Resartus*, 170, 176
  in *The Last Man*, 154, 157, 158
  in *The Sorrows of Young Werther*, 170
  Polidori's, 92
  Wandering Jew's attempts, 45
Superhero
  Gothic influence on, 252–54
Superman, 252–53
Sweeney Todd, 223
Tale of Two Cities, A. See Dickens, Charles
Tarzan. See Burroughs, Edgar Rice
transubstantiation, 236
Transylvania, 229, 232
Tree of Knowledge, 15, 38
Trilby. See DuMaurier, George
Trollope, Anthony
  The Duke's Children, 83
  The Way We Live Now, 234
usury
  moneylending, 44, 233
vampire, 208–44
Vampire Diaries, The, 254
Vampyre, The. See Polidori, John
Varney the Vampyre, 9, 209, 212, 219, 222, 223–27, 229, 234, 235, 238
Verne, Jules
  A Journey to the Center of the Earth, 246–48
Virgin Mary, 210, 240
Vlad Tepes
  Vlad the Impaler, 227
Wallace, Lew
  The Prince of India, 56
Walpole, Horace
  The Castle of Otranto, xi, 8
Wanderer, The. See Burney, Fanny
Wandering Jew, xiv, 43, 52, 59, 63, 65, 96, 165, 171, 202, 210, 222, 224, 226, 254

as metaphor for Jewish people, 43–44
in pre-Gothic texts, 45
in *The Monk*, 46–48
influence on *A Tale of Two Cities*, 198, 201, 202
influence on *Ancient Mariner*, 48–50
influence on *Dracula*, 229–34
influence on *Glenarvon*, 214
influence on *Melmoth the Wanderer*, 53–57
influence on *Sartor Resartus*, 171–77
influence on *St. Leon*, 50–52
influence on *The Wanderer*, 105–16
Weishaupt, Ada, 131
Weissmuller, Johnny, 252
werewolves, x, 210, 214, 247, 254
West, Jane
  Letters to a Young Lady, 107
Wilde, Oscar, 229, 233
Wollstonecraft, Mary, 144
  opinion on French Revolution, 5–7
Wordsworth, William, 2, 105, 150, 160, 171, 174
  "Intimations Ode", 160
X-Men, 254
Zanoni. *See* Bulwer-Lytton, Edward
zombies, 254

About the Author

Tyler R. Tichelaar holds a Ph.D. in Literature from Western Michigan University, and Bachelor and Master's Degrees in English from Northern Michigan University. He has lectured on writing and literature at Clemson University, the University of Wisconsin, and the University of London. Tyler is the regular guest host of Authors Access Internet Radio and the current President of the Upper Peninsula Publishers and Authors Association. He is the owner of his own publishing company Marquette Fiction (www.MarquetteFiction.com) and Superior Book Promotions (www.SuperiorBookPromotions.com), a professional book review, editing, and proofreading service.

Tichelaar is the author of numerous historical novels, including *The Marquette Trilogy* (composed of *Iron Pioneers*, *The Queen City*, and *Superior Heritage*) the award-winning *Narrow Lives*, and *Spirit of the North: a paranormal romance*. His other scholarly works include *King Arthur's Children: a Study in Fiction and Tradition*. He is currently working on an Arthurian historical fantasy series, beginning with *King Arthur's Legacy*, in which he intends to weave many Gothic elements. For updates on Tyler R. Tichelaar's Arthurian novels, visit www.ChildrenofArthur.com.

Please visit **www.GothicWanderer.com** for blog updates on current trends in gothic literature and criticism.

Did you know King Arthur had many other children besides Mordred?

Depending on which version of the legend you read, he had both sons and daughters, some of whom even survived him. From the ancient tale of Gwydre, the son who was gored to death by a boar, to Scottish traditions of Mordred as a beloved king, Tyler R. Tichelaar has studied all the references to King Arthur's children to show how they shed light upon a legend that has intrigued us for fifteen centuries.

King Arthur's Children: A Study in Fiction and Tradition is the first full-length analysis of every known treatment of King Arthur's children, from Welsh legends and French romances, to Scottish genealogies and modern novels by such authors as Parke Godwin, Stephen Lawhead, Debra Kemp, and Elizabeth Wein. King Arthur's Children explores an often overlooked theme in Arthurian literature and reveals King Arthur's bloodline may still exist today.

Arthurian Authors Praise *King Arthur's Children*

"Author Tyler R. Tichelaar has performed impeccable research into the Arthurian legend, finding neglected details in early sources and reigniting their significance. Great brainstorming fun! I am proud to add this to my personal collection of Arthurian non-fiction."

—Debra Kemp, author of *The House of Pendragon* series

"Tyler R. Tichelaar's in-depth analysis of the plausibility of King Arthur's children reaffirms the importance the King Arthur legacy continues to have for society and the need of people all over the world to be able to connect to and believe in King Arthur and Camelot."

—Cheryl Carpinello, author of *Guinevere: On the Eve of Legend*

Learn more at www.ChildrenOfArthur.com

COMING IN 2013!

KING ARTHUR'S LEGACY:
BOOK I IN THE CHILDREN OF ARTHUR SERIES

He felt suddenly as if a siren's song were calling to him from across the sea, from an enchanted land, an island kingdom named England. He had always pictured England as a magical fairy tale realm, ever since his childhood when he had first read the legends of King Arthur and the Knights of the Round Table.

Magic existed in the thought of England's green hills, in the names of Windsor Castle, Stonehenge, and the Tower of London. It was one of the few lands still ruled by a monarch, perhaps a land where fairy tales might still come true. Maybe even a place where he might at last find a father.

All his life, Adam Morgan has sought his true identity and the father he never knew. When multiple coincidences lead him to England, he will not only find his father, but mutual love with a woman he can never have, and a family legacy he never imagined possible. Among England's green hills and crumbling castles, Adam's intuition awakens, and when a mysterious stranger appears with a tale of Britain's past, Adam discovers forces are at work to bring about the return of a king.

For updates on Tyler R. Tichelaar's Arthurian novels, visit:
www.ChildrenofArthur.com

Tyler R. Tichelaar Embarks Into Gothic Fiction

SPIRIT OF THE NORTH
A Paranormal Romance

In 1873, orphaned sisters Barbara and Adele Traugott travel to Upper Michigan to live with their uncle, only to find he is deceased. Penniless, they are forced to spend the long, fierce winter alone in their uncle's remote wilderness cabin. Frightened yet determined, the sisters face blizzards and near starvation to survive. Amid their difficulties, they find love and heartache—and then, a ghostly encounter and the coming of spring lead them to discovering the true miracle of their being.

Influenced by the Gothic tradition, Tichelaar weaves stories within stories, including ghost stories and a tale of Paul Bunyan, all containing supernatural elements. And among them is the tale of Annabella Stonegate, a minor character in some of Tichelaar's previous novels, whose story is told in full here. "Annabella was a ghost in a story I wrote in middle school," says Tichelaar, "she has haunted me for more than a quarter of a century, insisting I tell her full story. I think I have finally satisfied her insistence."

For more information, visit www.MarquetteFiction.com

CPSIA information can be obtained
at www.ICGtesting.com
Printed in the USA
LVHW082352010519
616362LV00008B/297/P